I0868709

Mediterranean Wooden Shipbuilding

Brill's Studies in Maritime History

Series Editor

Gelina Harlaftis (*Ionian University, Greece*)

Editorial Board

Maria Fusaro (*University of Exeter, U.K.*)
Michael Miller (*University of Florida, U.S.A.*)
Amelia Polonia (*University of Porto, Portugal*)
David Starkey (*University of Hull, U.K.*)
Malcom Tull (*Murdoch University, Australia*)

VOLUME 2

The titles published in this series are listed at *brill.com/bsmh*

Mediterranean Wooden Shipbuilding

Economy, Technology and Institutions in Syros in the Nineteenth Century

By

Apostolos Delis

BRILL

LEIDEN | BOSTON

Cover Illustrations: *Syra*, three photographs put together to create a panoramic view of Syros Island, Greece. Created between 1850 and 1880. Photographic print: albumen. Courtesy of the Library of Congress (call Number: LOT 7738).

Library of Congress Cataloging-in-Publication Data

Delis, Apostolos, author.

Mediterranean wooden shipbuilding : economy, technology and institutions in Syros in the nineteenth century / by Apostolos Delis.

pages cm. — (Brill's studies in maritime history ; volume 2)

Includes bibliographical references and index.

ISBN 978-90-04-30614-1 (hardback : alk. paper) — ISBN 978-90-04-30615-8 (e-book) 1. Shipbuilding industry—Greece—Syros—History—19th century. 2. Ships, Wooden—Greece—Syros—Design and construction. 3. Ships, Wooden—Greece—Syros—History—19th century 4. Sailing ships—Greece—Syros—History—19th century. 5. Shipyards—Greece—Syros—History—19th century. 6. Hermoupolis (Greece)—Economic conditions—19th century. 7. Syros Island (Greece)—History, Naval—19th century. I. Title II. Title: Shipbuilding economy, technology and institutions in Syros in the nineteenth century.

VM299.7.G8D44 2015
623.82'07--dc23

2015032380

This publication has been typeset in the multilingual "Brill" typeface. With over 5,100 characters covering Latin, IPA, Greek, and Cyrillic, this typeface is especially suitable for use in the humanities. For more information, please see www.brill.com/brill-typeface.

ISSN 2405-4917
ISBN 978-90-04-30614-1 (hardback)
ISBN 978-90-04-30615-8 (e-book)

Copyright 2016 by Koninklijke Brill NV, Leiden, The Netherlands.
Koninklijke Brill NV incorporates the imprints Brill, Brill Hes & De Graaf, Brill Nijhoff, Brill Rodopi and Hotei Publishing.
All rights reserved. No part of this publication may be reproduced, translated, stored in a retrieval system, or transmitted in any form or by any means, electronic, mechanical, photocopying, recording or otherwise, without prior written permission from the publisher.
Authorization to photocopy items for internal or personal use is granted by Koninklijke Brill NV provided that the appropriate fees are paid directly to The Copyright Clearance Center, 222 Rosewood Drive, Suite 910, Danvers, MA 01923, USA. Fees are subject to change.

This book is printed on acid-free paper.

To My Mother

Contents

Acknowledgements

This book is based on a PhD thesis defended in 2010 at the Ionian University. It was funded by the research project PENED 2003 which is financed by the European Union (75%) and the Greek Ministry of Development (25%) and was further processed in the IMS/FORTH in the framework of ELISTOKAINO project within GSRT's KRIPIS action, funded by Greece and the European Regional Development Fund of the European Union under the O.P. Competitiveness and Entrepreneurship, NSRF 2007–2013.

List of Illustrations

Illustrations

Maps

Figures

Tables

Schemes

Maps

MAP 1 *Seafaring ports and areas of shipbuilding timber provenance* (created by Aris Kydonakis).

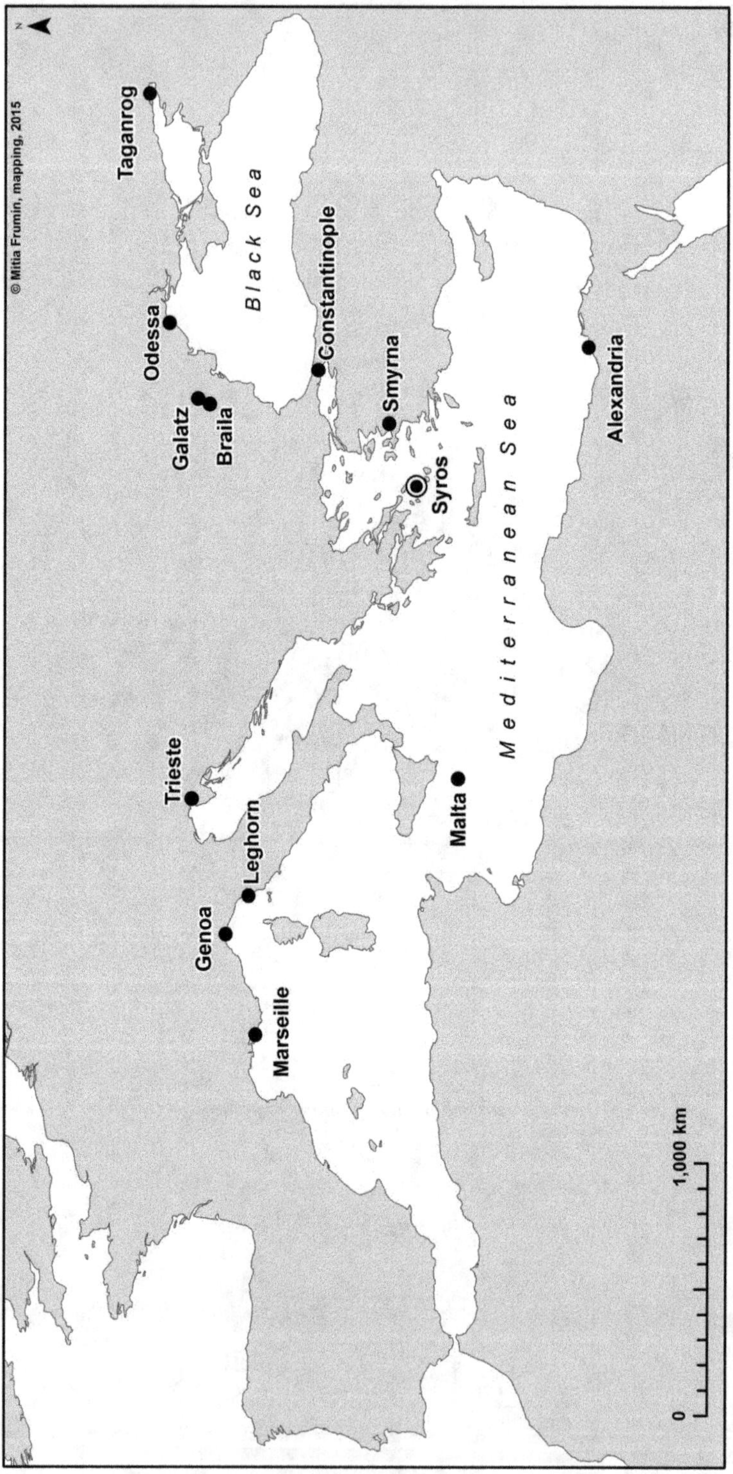

MAP 2 *Syros and its commercial partners* (created by Mitia Frumin).

MAP 3 *Syros Harbor and its working areas* (processed by Aris Kydonakis and based on a map by L. Zavos (around 1840), published in Ioannis Travlos and Aggeliki Kokkou, *Ερμούπολη. Η δημιουργία μίας νέας πόλης στη Σύρο στις αρχές του 19ου αιώνα* [*Hermoupolis. The creation of a new town in Syros in the beginning of the 19th century*]. Athens: Commercial Bank of Greece, 1980).

Introduction

Hermoupolis, the capital of the island of Syros, has been extensively studied by Greek historians over the past three decades. The rich archival material preserved in the General State Archives of Cyclades in Hermoupolis and the singular birth and evolution of this insular city has become a very attractive subject for modern historians. This city of refugees, which grew out of the maelstrom of war events during the Greek War of Independence (1821–1829), very soon became the biggest port in the Aegean, and one of the most important in the eastern Mediterranean. It was also a centre of the transit trade attracting human and material capital, and a nodal point for transactions between the Greek Kingdom, the Ottoman Empire, the Black Sea, and Western Europe. Its main advantage, aside from its position as a navigation crossroad at the heart of the Aegean and its safe natural harbour, was the know-how of its merchant class, who had networks with the great commercial ports of the Mediterranean, the Black Sea, and Western Europe.

The singularity of Hermoupolis applies on several different levels. It was the very first urban area of the Greek Kingdom, due not only to the inflow of a large population to a single area, bur mainly due to the development of its urban institutions and the mentality of its inhabitants, who came mainly from Chios, Smyrna, and Aivali, all of which were commercial crossroads with a long cosmopolitan tradition. It is also a singular case, developing within an insular space with no history of administrative or economic eminence, let alone an urban tradition. Besides this, Cyclades had never before experienced any comparable phenomenon of population agglomeration, and there were remarkably diverse cultural characteristics and a great potential for economic growth, given that this was such a restricted geographical area. Hermoupolis lacked a hinterland from which its population could support their livelihood. Therefore, relying only upon their own labour, this largely proletarian people had to focus on commercial exchanges, trading services and crafts. As a result, the rapid and unexpected influx of a numerous and diverse population with a tradition of urban life, who were forced to develop economic activities in the secondary and the tertiary sectors, created an unprecedented and singular phenomenon in the predominantly rural landscape of the Greek Kngdom.

In this context, shipbuilding became a fundamental economic activity for Hermoupolis, and has remained the spearhead of its secondary sector from its founding until the present day. Today, the *Neorion Shipyards* of Syros is the only industry that remains active, and the only secondary sector activity with the potential for further development, despite the serious problems it

© KONINKLIJKE BRILL NV, LEIDEN, 2016 | DOI 10.1163/9789004306158_002

faces on a daily basis. In the nineteenth century, the position of Hermoupolis as the great transit and maritime centre made shipbuilding a necessity, a complementary but vital activity in the chain of services offered by the port of Syros. A key contribution to this was offered by the Chiots, who were numerous in the new city and, long before the Greek War of Independence, had acquired the know-how and the experience in trade, shipping and shipbuilding, thanks to the eminent position of Chios on the trade routes of the Levant from the period of the Genoese occupation (1346–1566) onwards. Shortly after the end of the War of Independence and the formation of the Greek Kingdom in the mid-1830s, the recomposition of the Greek-owned fleet began. This fleet sailed predominantly along the routes between the Black Sea and the Mediterranean ports.

During this period and for most of the nineteenth century, the shipbuilding and ship repair zones of Hermoupolis were a fundamental structural component in the Greek-owned sailing fleet's mechanism of growth. The rapid and economical construction and repair of sailing ships played a large part in the reproduction, maintenance, and growth of the fleet in the maritime centre, which provided every type of service for commercial ships and their navigational necessities. Therefore, the shipbuilding centre developed alongside the maritime centre, which differed from a shipbuilding area in its capacity to cover all that was required for the construction or the repair of sailing ships. Prime materials like timber, pitch, and tar, and components and equipment like nails, pulleys, ropes, chains, and anchors were available in the warehouses of the port of Syros. And, last but not least, they supplied capital and credit for craftsmen, captains, and shipowners, which made the shipyards of Hermoupolis a convenient place for transactions and transformed them into a veritable shipbuilding centre for the Greek-owned and foreign merchant ships that worked the Eastern Mediterranean and the Black Sea.

The analysis of the shipbuilding activity of Hermoupolis presented in this book is based upon three axes: economic, technological and institutional. These are the three basics aspects of productive activity, and capture the main characteristics, the framework, and the historical dynamics of that activity. The analysis will also focus on the macro- and micro-historical levels, with particular emphasis upon the protagonists who contributed to the creation and the growth of the shipbuilding industry in Syros.

The first chapter is divided into three parts. The first part examines the historical conditions of the foundation of the city of Hermoupolis, the capital of Syros after 1822, and the role and character of the port and the city in a national and an international context, according to theoretical models of urban history. The second part focuses on fundamental aspects of everyday life in a restricted insular urban area, including housing and architecture, food habits, sanitary conditions, crime, and other social pathogenies and forms of leisure and socializing within the population. The third part illustrates each of the shipping sectors that developed in Hermoupolis and made its port an international maritime centre. Those sectors are the following: port registry, marine insurance, shipping finance, the second-hand vessels market, the maritime intelligence centre, the nodal point of steamship navigation, the maritime stores and materials market, and the shipbuilding and ship repair centre.

The second chapter discusses the nature and characteristics of shipbuilding as an economic activity and its social and cultural implications. Furthermore, it examines the position of the Syros shipbuilding industry in the Greek economy and the level of know-how at both a national and an international level. It also explores such factors as the foundation, growth and decline of the Syros shipbuilding industry, using interdisciplinary hermeneutical tools mainly adopted from mainstream economics and economic geography. These include the necessary neo-classical factors of production of land, labour, and capital in the formation of the industry, the search for the competitive advance that led to its growth, and the factors that led to its decline, such as the advent of steam, the role of markets, and the reallocation of resources. Finally, the chapter analyses the contribution of wooden shipbuilders to the transition from sail to steam.

The third chapter is divided into three parts: the first part attempts to integrate shipbuilding production within the market framework, examining the output of the period 1830–80 according to the long and short shipping and shipbuilding cycles, and compares the output of Syros with other shipyards in Mediterranean, Northern European and North Atlantic countries. The second part analyzes the economics of the shipbuilding industry, including the individual and total costs, the price comparison with other Greek and foreign shipyards, and the estimation of the contribution of Syros's wooden shipbuilding to the GDP of the Greek economy in the nineteenth century. The last part measures productivity through the average tonnage of ships built (and provides an international comparison), delivery times, and the maximum capacity of Syros's shipyards. Finally, an overall estimation of the economic performance of the industry is given.

The fourth chapter is also divided into three main parts: the first concerns the institutional procedure for the construction of a ship in Syros in the examined period. A detailed analysis is presented of the formal and informal practices, norms, and institutions between owners and shipbuilders, by examining of the documents (agreements, property documents) that were stipulated as notarial acts. This analysis of terms and conditions serves to assess the level of transaction costs in the Syros market and the behavioral practices and mentalities of the protagonists. The second part concerns the technical procedures of ship construction. Shipbuilding agreements offer rich and detailed information about the methods of assembling the hull, and enable us to follow the construction phases and the types of material used in a nineteenth century Mediterranean shipyard. The final part deals with the types of ship built in the shipyards of Syros. Sailing vessels are classified according to the number of masts, their hull or rigging denomination, and the shipbuilding tradition to which they belonged (either Mediterranean or Northern European): these are compared with the ship types built in other Mediterranean shipyards. Finally, an analysis is presented of the brig, the ship type that dominated the shipyards of Syros and the Greek-owned fleet in the nineteenth century, and which was one of the most widespread commercial types of sailing vessels worldwide.

The protagonists of the fifth chapter are the shipowners/investors. The analysis of demand presented is based on three main aspects: a) *the groups of origin* (Chios, Psara, Hydra), b) *the occupational groups*, and c) *the distribution of ownership of the ships* (single-owned ships, two or three owners, and so on). Each of these three aspects is analysed according to three criteria: a) *the number of people* (e.g. how many from Hydra, how many merchants, how many single owners), b) *the total tonnage*, and c) *the monetary value of the ships built*. This analysis illustrates in detail the percentage of each geographical and occupational group in the Syros shipbuilding market, the geographical range of its clientele, the background of their maritime know-how, the patterns of ownership, and the rate of dependency from the shipbuilidng centre of the Aegean. Finally, the last categorization concerns the most important individual shipowners/investors according to the value of ships built and their socio-economic profile.

The last chapter is divided in two broad parts: a) The shipbuilding enterprises, and b) The factors of production (labour, capital, land and raw materials). The shipbuilders are classified according to the productivity and volume of their business. It examines the formation of an elite group of shipbuilders, the structure of their business, and their strategies, following the theoretical framework of Entrepreneurial and Business History and Economic Sociology. Regarding labour, the chapter describes the specialization, the division of labour, and the hierarchy formed among the shipyard workers, and provides information about remuneration. Regarding capital, the sources of financing and lending practices to shipbuilders are explored. The land is examined both as a cost factor and as an issue of increasing antagonism in the use of the workspace (between traditional and factory industries) after 1860. Finally, an analysis is presented of the mechanism of ancillary activities, in connection with the operation of the shipbuilding industry: namely, the making and supply of shipbuilding raw materials and maritime stores and equipment.

The aim of this study is to chart the emergence of shipbuilding activity in Hermoupolis in the age of sail as one of the most important aspects of the city's economy. This emergence has hitherto not been studied as thoroughly as it deserves to be. This was an activity which in the nineteenth century gave the port of Syros an added value, thanks to the ship construction and repair services it provided, and which made it a necessary stop for all Greek and foreign ships sailing through the Aegean. This was also an activity that connected Hermoupolis with the entire geographic range of expanding sailing shipping, from the Black Sea to the Western Mediterranean, even reaching up to Britain and the North Sea. It also marked an irrevocable period of prosperity and international importance for the city, in which shipbuilding played a major part. Finally, this was an activity which continues into the present, with the evidence of this heritage being tangible for all of us today. Despite the problems of increasing shrinkage and the lack of any future prospects for the sector, in the southwestern part of Syros harbour next to the modern establishment of *Neorion Shipyards*, the ship repair and the shipbuilding zones, both specializing in wooden hulls, are still active today.

CHAPTER 1

The City and the Maritime Centre

From a Refugee Settlement to a Port-City

Charles Sigisbert Sonnini was delegated by the King of France, Louis XVI, to survey the "Greek archipelago" in the last quarter of the eighteenth century, and he can be characterized as the person who predicted the creation of Hermoupolis. In his work *Voyage en Grèce et en Turquie fait par ordre de Louis XVI*, published in 1801, he suggested the creation of a redistribution centre for the wholesale and retail trade in the Aegean, which would be able to ensure the availability of basic foodstuffs such as cereals and wine for the insular populations and for the victualling of ships. These foodstuffs would be available at a lower price than those offered by the great commercial centers of the Levant, Smyrna and Thessaloniki. Furthermore, it would have the infrastructures and warehouses needed to become a commercial and maritime centre which could serve the needs of domestic and international shipping. All the above services would be managed by a large urbanized population, familiar with the practices and the trends of trade, who would be able to foresee, satisfy and shape the needs of the market.[1] After a generation, political and economic events led to the outbreak of the Greek War of Independence and military events led to the creation of the centre which Sonnini predicted would boost the insular economy: Hermoupolis, in the island of Syros. The French delegate had been doubly successful, as he had also suggested that the centre should be located on the island of Chios. The urbanized character of its inhabitants and their long tradition in trade and proto-industry were ideal preconditions for success. History did justice to Sonnini, as the Chiots were the most dynamic and successful part of the population of the new town built on the coast of Syros harbor after 1822.

One of the most dramatic consequences of the Greek War of Independence was the masses of refugees who escaped from massacres or fled as the Ottoman military forces advanced and occupied rebel areas. These refugees created new settlements and new areas in existing towns like Pronoia in Nafplio, or

1 Eleftheria Zei, 'La proposition du voyageur Ch. Sonnini sur l'organisation du commerce français dans l'Archipel grec (Voyage en Grèce et en Turquie, Paris, 1801): une première théorie d'insularité économique', *Proceedings of 4th International Congress of Maritime History*, Corfu, 2004. (In CD-Rom).

© KONINKLIJKE BRILL NV, LEIDEN, 2016 | DOI 10.1163/9789004306158_003

entirely new towns like Hermoupolis on the Island of Syros, the largest refugee town and, later, one of the most important towns in the Greek Kingdom.[2] The massacres of Kydonies (1821), Chios (1822), Psara and Kasos (1824) were the main causes that led thousands of civilians to settle on the coast of Syros's harbour, as well as on many of the Aegean islands left untouched by the Ottoman troops, a phenomena to which the local populations did not react in a very positive manner.[3] The wanderings of the Chiot Loukis Laras (the romance was based on a manuscript which referred to the life of the Chiot merchant Loukas Zifos) and his family between Mykonos and Tinos, until they eventually settled in Syros, give an eloquent description of the conditions under which the refugees lived in these circumstances.[4] Harsh ways of living, precarity and insecurity dominated the settlement created on the semi-deserted coast of Syros by Greek people from every part of the rebel areas of the Ottoman Empire. However, the majority were mainly from the Asia Minor coast and the islands of the eastern Aegean, from Kydonies, Moschonisia, Chios, Smyrna and Psara.[5] The socio-economic and cultural background of these people was to be decisive, as we shall see, in the shaping of the character of the newly emerging town, and would mark its place in the Eastern Mediterranean in decades to come.

Until the arrival of the refugees, the Island of Syros was inhabited by a small catholic community—and, among them, a tiny orthodox minority—on the upper part of the western hill, which is known today as Ano Syros.[6] This community, whose presence on the island dates back to the Middle Ages, enjoyed the protection of the Holy See and the great catholic powers of France and the Hapsburg Monarchy. France, in particular, was among the first western nations that managed to place the entire catholic population of the Ottoman Empire under its protection, as a result of the capitulations regime signed with the

2 Kostas Komis, «Μετακινήσεις πληθυσμών. Πολεμικές καταστροφές και νέες εγκαταστάσεις.», ["Population transportation. War disasters and new settlements."], in *Ιστορία του Νέου Ελληνισμού, 1770–2000* [*History of Modern Hellenism, 1770–2000*], ed. Vassilis Panayotopoulos, vol. 2, (Athens: Ellinika Grammata, 2003), 235–44.

3 Komis, «Μετακινήσεις πληθυσμών», 236–37.

4 Dimitrios Vikelas, *Λουκής Λάρας*, [*Loukis Laras*], (Athens: Estia Publishers, 2000), κγ΄.

5 Timoleon Ambelas, *Ιστορία της νήσου Σύρου από των αρχαιοτάτων χρόνων μέχρι των καθ'ημάς.* [*History of the island of Syros from Ancient Times to the present day*], (Hermoupolis, 1874), 499–511; Andreas Drakakis, *Ιστορία του οικισμού της Ερμουπόλεως Σύρας, 1821–1825.* [*History of the settlement of Hermoupolis* (*Syros*), *1821–1825*], vol. A΄, (Athens, 1979), 30–31, 50, 110–21.

6 Drakakis, *Ιστορία του οικισμού*, vol. A, 3.

Sublime Porte in 1535.[7] However, with the arrival of the refugees, this status quo was set to change, along with the entire historical trajectory of the island. The local inhabitants' decision to remain faithful to the Ottoman Empire during the Greek War of Independence had a beneficial effect upon the island's commercial and maritime traffic, as the Porte gave the exclusive right to the port of Syros to visa the documents of ships coming from Constantinople or other ports of the empire.[8] Therefore, the neutrality of Syros in the Greek-Turkish conflict, the French protection of the catholic population, the acknowledgement of the Porte for the devotion of the local community and the safe and naturally well-endowed harbour were decisive factors as regards the influx of masses of refugees.[9] The locals, on the other hand, didn't appreciate the arrival and settlement of the newcomers, especially after 1822, when their numbers increased rapidly.[10] Frangiskos Salachas, a member of one of the most influential and wealthy families of Syros and a shipowner and landowner in the largest part of Syros' coastal area demonstrated hostile behavior towards the refugees and a pro-Ottoman attitude.[11] Paradoxically, this enmity between the Catholic and Orthodox communities was the key to the survival of both communities during the Greek War of Independence, and gave the refugees the opportunity to develop their activity undisturbed, and also to enjoy the positive effects of the protection which the Catholic powers offered to the local catholic community.

Initially, the settlement of the refugees had a temporary character, due to the insecurity caused by wartime developments, the complete lack of infrastructure supporting basic living, and their hope of returning to their homelands. Therefore, the settlement had the appearance of an irregular mass of wooden and tin huts, barely meeting even the most minimal housing needs.[12] This sense of temporariness and the difficulties facing the refugees in these early years meant that for a long time, the settlement retained an ugly aspect;

---

7 Drakakis, *Ιστορία του οικισμού*, vol. A, 14–17; Christina Agriantoni – Aggeliki Fenerli, *Hermoupolis-Syros. A historical tour*, (Athens: Olkos Publishers, 2000), 16.

8 Drakakis, *Ιστορία του οικισμού*, vol. A, 16–17.

9 Drakakis, *Ιστορία του οικισμού*, vol. A, 15–17; Vikelas, *Λουκής Λάρας*, ιβ.

10 Ambelas, *Ιστορία της νήσου Σύρου*, 510.

11 Aggeliki Fenerli, "Τα πρώτα βήματα οικοδόμησης της Ερμούπολης". ["The first steps in the building of Hermoupolis"], (Paper presented in the 22th *Hermoupolis Seminars*, Hermoupolis, July 5–15, 2006), 3.

12 Drakakis, *Ιστορία του οικισμού*, vol. A, 30, 50, 163; Of the same author "Πρωτότυποι νομικοί θεσμοί εις την οικιζόμενην Ερμούπολιν (1821–1830)" ["Original legal institutions in Hermoupolis (1821–1830)"], *Επετηρίς του Κέντρου Ιστορίας του Ελληνικού Δικαίου της Ακαδημίας Αθηνών* [*Yearbook of the Center for the History of Greek Law in the Academy of Athens*], 18, (1971), 171–72.

even by 1829, stone buildings were the exception, with most still being made of timber.[13]

The population concentrated in the coastal area of Syros harbour during the war period (1821–1828) was estimated to surpass 20,000, although the first census of 1828 revealed that Hermoupolis had 13,805 inhabitants, and the rest of the island, including the town of Ano Syros, had 6,392 inhabitants.[14] Part of the population living in the upper part of the town were refugees (some sources mention 1,134 souls), like the merchant from Smyrna Manolis Geroussis, who until 1828 preferred to live there and work in the harbor, because living conditions were far better than in the coastal zone, with its unregulated and rough buildings, lack of water supply and an unhealthy climate. In April 1833, an article in an Athenian newspaper that encouraged the inhabitants of Hermoupolis to accept it as their new homeland described the town as follows: '*all the buildings and streets are as irregular and ugly as they are due to the previous temporariness and insecurity of the general situation, which is now over. Everyone who resides and lives here intends to reside and live somewhere else*'.[15]

However, the war, the neutrality of the locals and the professional background of the refugees quickly turned the coast of Syros into a flourishing commercial port. During the war, all the previous commercial and maritime places in the Aegean (such as Chios, Psara and Kasos) were either destroyed by the Ottoman and Egyptian fleets, or (like Hydra and Spetses) were participating in the war on the Greek side. This left Syros as the only remaining free trading zone, and the only safe harbour for ships moving to and from the ports of the Ottoman Empire.[16] Important documentation from the Provisional Greek Government provides us with the earliest known registry of the arrival of ships into the newly founded Port Authority of Syros, during the period 4.8.1823

13 Aggeliki Fenerli, 'Σχέδια της Ερμούπολης και η έναρξη του σχεδίου πόλης' ['Plans of Hermoupolis and the beginning of the final city's plan'], (Paper presented in the 21st *Hermoupolis Seminars*, Hermoupolis, June 28–July 10, 2005), 6.

14 Emile Kolodny, "Ερμούπολις-Σύρος. Γέννησις και εξέλιξις μιάς ελληνικής νησιωτικής πόλεως" ["Hermoupolis-Syros. Birth and evolution of a Greek insular town"] *Επετηρίδα Εταιρείας Κυκλαδικών Μελετών* [*Yearbook of the Society of Cycladic Studies*], (1969), 255.

15 Maria-Christina Chatziioannou, *Οικογενειακή στρατηγική και εμπορικός ανταγωνισμός. Ο οίκος Γερούση τον 19ο αιώνα.* [*Family Strategy and Commercial Competition. The Firm of Gerousis in the 19th Century*], (Athens: Cultural Foundation of National Bank, 2003), 88; Andreas Frangidis, *Ιστορία της νήσου Σύρου.* [*History of the island of Syros*], (Athens: Association of the Syriots of Athens and Piraeus, 1975), 46–56, 75, 384–389; Andreas Drakakis, *Ιστορία του οικισμού της Ερμουπόλεως (Σύρας), 1827–28* [*History of the settlement of Hermoupolis (Syros), 1827–1828*] vol. B', (Athens: 1983), 106–111; Ioannis Vlahogiannis, *Χιακό Αρχείο* [*Archive of Chios*], vol. E, (Athens: 1910), 20–21.

16 Kolodny, "Ερμούπολις-Σύρος", 253.

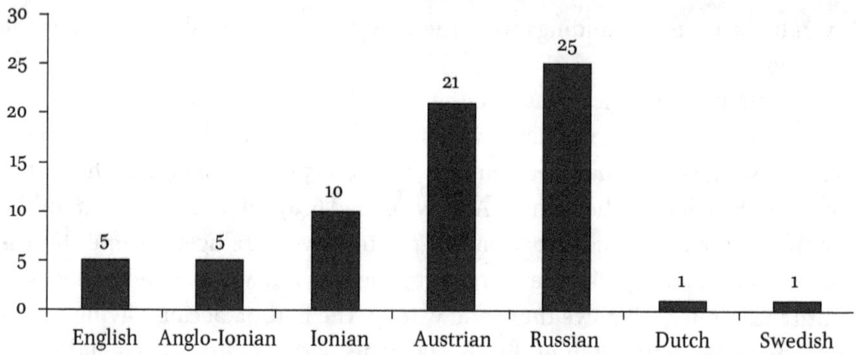

FIGURE 1.1 *Ships arrivals at Syros harbor (4.8.1823–8.10.1823).*
SOURCE: PROCESSED DATA FROM GENERAL STATE ARCHIVES, ATHENS, VLAHOGIANNIS COLL. REGISTERS OF WAR OF INDEPENDENCE/KAPODISTRIA, FILE N. 16.

and 8.10.1823. During this short period the arrival of 77 ships was registered, of a total 11,428 tons and 150.36 tons in average. As Figure 1.1 shows, the majority of ships carried Austrian, Russian and Ionian flags, although these ships belonged to three ethnic groups: the Dalmatians and the Italians (subjects of the Hapsburg Monarchy) and the Ionians, especially from Cephalonia, who carried Ionian, British-Ionian and Russian flags.

Under the circumstances described above, the port of Syros provided the opportunity for all sorts of transactions, including the smuggling of cereals and other commodities, the sale of booties and piratical vessels, currency counterfeiting, and slave trading (mainly captives of war). In this type of neutral trade zone, everyone could buy and sell anything, and the merchants and shipowners of Syros, who were involved in all those affairs during the conjuncture, managed to create their own initial accumulation of capital, which was to be essential to the development of their future business in the port.[17]

The Character of the New Port-City

From its outset, the character of the new developed town was mainly commercial and maritime. Modern historiography has described its basic function as

17 Drakakis, *Ιστορία του οικισμού*, vol. A, 227–31, 256–72; idem "Πρωτότυποι νομικοί θεσμοί", 177–92.

serving as a centre of transit trade in the eastern Mediterranean.[18] This role and function was perfectly in tune with the needs of international trade, as most of the Mediterranean port-cities in the nineteenth century (Livorno, Marseille, Trieste etc.) were basically transit trade stations.[19] Hermoupolis, up to a certain point, belongs to each of the three following categories of city, according to the theory of urban history: (a) industrial and mining cities (b) port and railway cities, and (c) commercial and administrative cities. Hermoupolis was a port with a developed secondary sector (shipyards, tanneries), a tertiary sector (trade and shipping), and was also the capital of the Prefecture of Cyclades after the creation of the Greek Kingdom.[20] However, the key function that decided its fortune, its initial growth, its heyday and its progressive decline in the nineteenth century was the role of its port as centre of transit trade and the redistribution of commodities in the eastern Mediterranean.

The definition of the role and place of Hermoupolis in the system of cities in the nineteenth century will be approached through two theoretical models: the *central place system* and the *network system*. According to the first model, the city has a central role as an administrative, economic or cultural centre for other cities or areas. Therefore, according to this hierarchical system, the city has a leading position and, to a certain degree, a historical connection with the centralized and assimilative character of some urban areas or cities in the service of the national state. According to the second model, the city complements the role to other cities based on its specific functions, and constitutes a necessary link in the chain of functions within the system as a whole. Historically, this system has been identified with capitalism,

---

18 Vassilis Kardasis, *Σύρος. Σταυροδρόμι της ανατολικής Μεσογείου (1832–1857)*. [*Syros. A crossroad of the Eastern Mediterranean (1832–1857)*], (Athens: Cultural Foundation of National Bank, 1987); Christina Agriantoni, *Οι Απαρχές της Εκβιομηχάνισης στην Ελλάδα τον 19° αιώνα*, [*The Beginnings of Industrialization in Greece in the 19th century*], (Athens: Historical Archive of the Commercial Bank of Greece, 1986), 84–97.

19 McCulloch J.R., *Dictionary, practical, theoretical and historical of Commerce & Commercial Navigation*, (London: 1859), 801, 848, 1358–59; Foreign Office, Annual Series, *Report by Consul Inglis on the trade and commerce of Leghorn for the year 1883*, 664; Fulvio Babudieri, «Maritime Commerce of the Habsburgh Empire: The Port of Trieste, 1789–1913», in *Southeast European maritime commerce and naval policies from the mid-eighteenth century to 1914*, ed. Apostolos E. Vacalopoulos, Constantinos D. Svolopoulos, Béla K. Király, (Thessaloniki: Institut for Balkan Studies, 1988), 228–29.

20 Jean-Luc Pinol, *Ο κόσμος των πόλεων τον 19ο αιώνα* [*The world of the cities in the 19th century*], (Athens: Plethron Publishers, 2000), 50; Paul M. Hohenberg – Lynn Hollen Lees, *The making of urban Europe, 1000–1994*, (Cambridge, Massachusetts & London: Harvard University Press, 1995), 232.

characterized by transnationalism and expansion beyond frontiers. In such a system, the interdependency and influence of the cities is not related to spatial proximity, as in the *central place system*, but is instead related to the dynamics and the special contribution of the city to the functioning of the system itself. Thus, the main feature of this system is its fluidity, which is distinct from the transnational and cosmopolitan character of the cities, and which depends upon the evolution of the main economic functions of the city and determines its importance within the system.[21]

Hermoupolis can be placed in both models, with a quite different role in each, and a different account of the evolution in its historical role. In the *central place system*, the city is an economic, administrative and cultural centre relative to the rest of the islands of Cyclades and other nearby areas. In the nineteenth century, its market is not only a centre of redistribution and for the supply of commodities, but also a meeting place facilitating transactions between many of the inhabitants of the Aegean and beyond. As the headquarters of the Prefecture of Cyclades, Hermoupolis exercises a princely role relative to the rest of the islands, which depend upon its mediation to the central government for funding, works of public utility and other necessities. Other important services, such as the court of justice and the hospital, reinforce its prestige and power and make it a necessary destination and a point of attraction for the people of Cyclades. Furthermore, in symbolic and cultural terms, Hermoupolis was (and still is) a capital, albeit a regional one, able to reproduce and convey standards and archetypes to regularly or periodically visiting islanders through the diffusion of ideas in oral or printed forms, and through the representations/images of the large urban centre and its habits and lifestyle, as compared with the rural microcosm of the Cycladic villages.

However, especially over the first half century of its life, Hermoupolis also belonged to the *network system* of the port-cities of the Mediterranean, Black Sea and Western Europe. Its special functions, in terms of the transit trade and as a shipping and shipbuilding centre, made it an indispensable partner in the long chain of port-cities, all of which served the capitalist economy of the nineteenth century, the growing demand for goods for the increasing urban population of Western Europe, and the provision of raw materials for its developing industries. The prosperity of Hermoupolis depended in large part upon the harvests and the export of cereals from the Black Sea, and the commensurate demand from the markets of Western Europe for raw materials, cereals and other agricultural products. Equally important, in terms of the uninterrupted flow of trade affairs and sea transport, was the geopolitical balance

21 Hohenberg – Lees, *The making*, 4–6, 238–44, 281–82.

TABLE 1.1 *The population of Hermoupolis in the nineteenth century.*

Year	Population	Rate of growth %
1828	13,805	–
1832	15,469	12.05
1842	11,170	−27.79
1848	19,410	73.77
1853	19,981	2.94
1861	18,511	−7.36
1870	20,996	13.42
1879	21,540	2.59
1889	22,104	2.62
1896	18,760	−15.13

Source: For the years 1832, 1842, 1853 Kostas Komis, *Ιστορική δημογραφία του νεοελληνικού χώρου. Πηγές (19ος αιώνας)* [*Historic demography of the Neohellenic area. Sources* (*19th cent.*)], (Ioannina: 2002), 95; For the rest Kolodny, "Ερμούπολις-Σύρος", 255.

between the Greek Kingdom, the Ottoman Empire and the Great Powers of Russia, England and France. Its main direct partners were the ports of Odessa, Taganrog, Constantinople, Alexandria, Trieste, Livorno and Marseille, and the network of Greek enterprises which had been established in these ports since the late eighteenth century was a key element. Even today, as the capital of Cyclades, Hermoupolis is a dominant place in the region according the *central place system*. However, its heyday and its cosmopolitan character depended on its position in the *network system*. From the third quarter of the nineteenth century, its port gradually became less important due to structural changes in the organization of international trade and technological advances in the communications and transports; as a result it declined, as new ports such as Piraeus emerged and took up a more central position in the *network system*.

The population of Hermoupolis (see table 1.1) had risen up to 1896, when a significant decrease begun, which continued until the arrival of Greek refugees from Asia Minor, as a consequence of the defeat of the Greek Army and the Great Fire of Smyrna in the summer of 1922.[22]

There were significant exceptions to this upward trend in 1842 and, to a lesser degree, in the period 1853–56, due to the diplomatic crisis between

22 Kolodny, "Ερμούπολις-Σύρος", 256.

TABLE 1.2 *Population figures of Hermoupolis and other port-cities in Mediterranean and Black Sea in the middle of the nineteenth century.*

Town	Year	Population
Hermoupolis	1853	19,981
Taganrog	1856	18,000
Odessa	1852	71,392
Trieste	1850–51	82,596
Livorno	1858	114,081
Genoa	1858	119,610
Smyrna	1852	150,000
Marseille	1851	195,257

Source: Table 1.1 and McCulloch, *Dictionary, practical*, 629–630, 801, 848, 928–929, 1212, 1266, 1358–59.

Greece and Turkey over the Eastern Question issue, the hostile measures taken against Greek trade and shipping, and complications caused by the Crimean War.[23] However, there was an upward trend in population size (6.35%) during the examined period, which indicates that the labour market in Hermoupolis offered possibilities of employment as a maritime centre over the whole period, initially as a transit trade centre, and after the 1860s as the result of the development of its industries.[24]

In its heyday in the middle of the nineteenth century, Hermoupolis was a town of 20,000 inhabitants, and despite its importance as a commercial and maritime centre in the network of Mediterranean and Black Sea port-cities, it had a much smaller population than Marseille, Smyrna, Genoa or Livorno (see table 1.2). However, in the 1850s Hermoupolis was only twenty-five years old, and very new in comparison with old established ports such as those mentioned above; furthermore, it had been developed within a very restricted area

23 Theodoros Sakelaropoulos, *Οι κρίσεις στην Ελλάδα. Οικονομικές, πολιτικές και κοινωνικές όψεις. (1830–1857)* [*The crises in Greece, Financial, social and political aspects, (1830–1857)*], vol. A, (Athens: Kritiki Publishers, 1994), 109–31 and vol. B, 111; Archive du Ministère des Affaires Étrangères, Correspondence Consulaire et Commerciale Syra (from now on AMAE, CCC, Syra), vol. 2, 18.10. 1842, 332, the French consul at Syros reports that due to the diplomatic problems between Greece and Turkey, many Greek shipwoners adopted the Russian flag.

24 Agriantoni, *Οι Απαρχές της Εκβιομηχάνισης*, 97–98, 197, 210; Newspaper *Ήλιος* [*Helios*], n. 882, 16.9.1903, n. 907, 28.5.1904, n. 908, 8.6.1904 and n. 910, 28.6.1904.

of the harbour of a small island of just 84 square kilometres in total, which led to a very densely populated agglomeration.

Its insular geographical position was considered a particularity—and indeed an anachronism—in relation to the rest of the Mediterranean port-cities; according to Kolodny, this was *"the last phase of transition from insular ports-entrepôt to continental ports."*[25] Moreover, despite the fact that the development of the Greek-owned merchant marine occurred in small insular communities on the Aegean and the Ionian seas (such as Hydra, Spetses or Cephalonia), the perspectives for the long-term maintenance of the leadership of such an insular economy seemed meagre if not unattainable; this was due to the rapidly changing international economy of the nineteenth century and the centralized policies of national states such as the Greek Kingdom.[26] Furthermore, the development of the great Mediterranean and Black Sea ports such as Trieste, Livorno, Marseille and Odessa was the result of systematic governmental policy implemented by the states to which they belonged, and free-port status was conceded to most of them. On the other hand, the existence of Hermoupolis was a "legacy" of the events of the War of Independence, and not the result of the Greek government's choice, as Piraeus was later to be. That is why Greek governments persistently refused to confer the status of free-port upon Hermoupolis, despite the continuous and tenacious efforts of the latter's entrepreneurial class throughout the nineteenth (and up to the beginning of the twentieth) century.[27]

Indeed, Hermoupolis's insular position was a native weakness, and limited the possibilities for further spatial and demographic expansion, as well as limiting the possibility for readjustment to the new conditions brought about by the second industrial revolution; the development of the railways, steam navigation and the telegraph rendered worthless mediation services in trade. In his 1883 report concerning the changes taking place the port states, the British

25 Kolodny, "Ερμούπολις-Σύρος", 255–56, 286.

26 Christos Loukos, "Ερμούπολη. Μία ελληνική πόλη σε παρακμή στο β'μισό του 19ου αιώνα", ["Hermoupolis, a city in decline in the second half of the nineteenth century"], *Νεοελληνική πόλη. Οθωμανικές κληρονομιές και ελληνικό κράτος*, [*Neohellenic polis. Ottoman legacies and Greek State*], Πρακτικά του Διεθνούς Συμποσίου Ιστορίας, Β', [Proceedings of International Symposium of History], vol. B, (Athens: EMNE, 1985), 597.

27 AMAE, CCC, Syra, vol. 1, 3.3.1837, pp. 233–234, 25.4.1838, p. 310, vol. 2, 19.12.1839, pp. 71–75, 9.11.1840, pp. 168–169, 18.10.1842, p. 332, vol. 4, 28.6.1853, p. 65; Newspaper *Αίολος* [*Eolos*], n. 26, 10.2.1845, n. 31, 17.3.1845, n. 38, 5.6.1845, n. 510, 24.6.1854; Newspaper *Ερμούπολις* [*Hermoupolis*], n. 49, 29.12.1864, n. 20, 1.1.1865, n. 21, 9.1.1865; Foreign Office, Annual Series, Syra, (from now on F.O. Syra) *Report by Consul Binney on the Trade and Commerce of the Cyclades during the Year 1874*, 21.8.1875, 1552–1555. (Translation of a pamphlet of the Syros Chamber of Commerce in 1874); Newspaper *Ήλιος*, n. 801, 18.12.1903.

consul at Livorno wrote: "*In 1834 this place was one of the main centres of transit trade in Mediterranean… But it was impossible to maintain this position after the rapid developments in land and sea transports… today these advantages* [the cereals warehouses for transit] *are no longer useful, for the cargoes of cereals are transported directly from the Black Sea to London in British steamers*". Someone had only to replace Livorno for Hermoupolis to be presented with precisely the same picture.[28] However, Hermoupolis showed considerable resistance and adaptability to the changes, thanks to new forms of investments by its entrepreneurial class, for instance in steam powered factories (flour mills, tanneries, textiles). At the same time, it also remained an important centre of steam navigation and a headquarters for local shipowners (such as Rethimnis and Kouloukountis, originally from Kasos), who sustained the declined shipping industry in Hermoupolis during the first half of the twentieth century.[29]

The Urban Area and Its Society

In terms of its size, Hermoupolis is a typical town of the first half of the nineteenth century. Like many European towns of the period, it was possible to cross the town on foot in a short time (which remains true today, as the town hasn't grown much larger).[30] Because the town was built within a strictly limited area, the use of space was not very differentiated. There were, of course, some economic activities like shipbuilding and tanneries located on the west coast of the harbour at the limits of the residential areas, but there were also many other commercial and manufacturing activities within the urban area, which caused serious problems and provoked reactions and protests against the town authorities. Butchers and other shopkeepers selling raw hides and vegetables, and who blocked and polluted the town's streets with their merchandise, were permanent targets of the local newspapers.[31] In general, it was a town

28 Foreign Office, Annual Series, *Report by Consul Inglis on the Trade and Commerce of Leghorn*, 1883.

29 Christina Agriantoni, "Προσαρμογές του επιχειρηματικού κόσμου της Ερμούπολης" ["Adaptations of the entrepreneurs of Hermoupolis"], *Σύρος και Ερμούπολη. Συμβολές στην ιστορία του νησιού, 15ος–20ος αι.* [*Syros and Hermoupolis. Contributions to the history of the island, 15th–20th cent.*], ed. Christina Agriantoni and Dimitris Dimitropoulos, (Athens: INE/EIE, 2008), 143–53; K. Gerasimidis – E. Monoyios, *Το πανόραμα της Σύρου* [*The panorama of Syros*], (Syros: 1933), 121–22, 171–72.

30 Pinol, *Ο κόσμος των πόλεων*, 101.

31 Newspapers *Αίολος*, n. 308–309–310, 16.7.1850; *Αστήρ των Κυκλάδων* [*Astir ton Kykladon*], n. 214, 21.5.1861, n. 244, 16.12.1861, n. 579, 11.5.1868; *Ερμούπολις*, n. 25, 6.2.1865.

"of limited free space, made up of makeshift materials tightly squashed around the port area, where tanneries, shipyards, smitheries, horse-drawn flour mills, dyer's shops and cemeteries are next to warehouses, shops and houses"[32] A similar picture of the same period can be drawn of European and North-American cities, due to the lack of developed urban transportation and the need for greater proximity between residential areas and worksites.[33]

The undifferentiated usage of urban space and the lack of paving, lighting and cleanliness in the streets made it difficult to circulate within the town, and offered a grim picture to visitors as well as to its inhabitants.[34] In 1830, the elderly public notary Skarlatos Maximos complained that at his age, he was unable to move in the rough and muddy streets of Hermoupolis during the night, and was therefore forced to send his assistant to redact the will of a moribund man.[35] Local newspapers protested on constant basis about health and safety in the town, and about the image it presented civilized western European visitors: '*The foreign visitors in the town sneer at us because of the filthiness of the public spaces, and everyone who has seen European towns is getting saddened by this situation. Some of the streets look like the alleys of the Jewish quarters in the Turkish towns, not like the streets of the second city of Greece.*'[36] Even in 1872, the British consul of Syros reports that the streets in the town were irregular and ill-paved.[37] The model to follow was, of course, the towns and cities of Western Europe, and the model to avoid was that of the Ottoman towns.

The municipal authorities exerted serious efforts to solve the above problems by building enclosed specialized markets for the public, such as the Butchery market, the Fish market and the Grocery market, which concentrated small shopkeepers into one delimited space and thus made them

32 Aggeliki Fenerli, "Ο καλλωπισμός της πόλης. Ένας πρωτότυπος συμμετοχικός τρόπος χρηματοδότησης δημοσίων κτιρίων στην Ερμούπολη (19ος αι.)" ['The embellishment of the town. An original participatory method to finance public buildings in Hermoupolis (19th cent.)"], *Η πόλη στους νεότερους χρόνους. Μεσογειακές και Βαλκανικές όψεις (19ος–20ος αι.)* [*The city in modern times. Mediterranean and Balkan aspects (19th–20th cent.)*], Proceedings of the second international congress, (Athens: EMNE, 2000), 174.

33 Pinol, *Ο κόσμος των πόλεων*, 103–05.

34 Newspaper *Ερμής*, n. 227, 24.7.1843.

35 Γενικά Αρχεία του Κράτους, Αρχείο Νομού Κυκλάδων, [General State Archives, Archive of District of Cyclades, Syros] (from now on GSA, Syros), Archive of Notary Maximos Talaslis, Corpus of Books of the Public Notary of Syros Skarlatos Maximos: Γ', Dowries and Wills of the Public Notary of Syros, vol. A, 1827, n. 5772, 1.12.1830.

36 Newspaper *Ερμούπολις*, n. 25, 6.2.1865.

37 F.O. Syra, *Report by Consul Ruby*, 14.12.1872, 123.

easier to control.[38] In general, local authorities showed considerable and systematic care for the urban infrastructures. From the beginning, along with the enclosed markets, they built customs and transit houses, schools, a hospital, the quarantine, a municipal coffee house, the "Apollo" theatre and the Gentlemen's Club.[39] In any case, Hermoupolis was not much worse than other cities of the Levant during this period, if we are to believe the testimony about Smyrna left by the Chiot Andreas Syngros (a banker, and one of the Greek great magnates of the nineteenth century). During his maiden voyage from Syros to Constantinople in 1845, he writes: '*the town of Smyrna was not beautiful then; filthy and ill-paved streets and big public stores which are ungraceful and wooden, and which look like ruins*'.[40]

The fact that a large population had settled in a very restricted area without many resources and (at least at first) without any an adequate infrastructure for basic living, had negative effects on the quality of life. Hermoupolis suffered all the problems of many nineteenth century European urban areas: among the most important were the lack of a water supply, disease and high infant mortality.[41] Fresh water was very scarce, and was an expensive good for the people of Hermoupolis.[42] Plague struck the town in 1840, but no further details are known about its scale and effects.[43] In the summer of 1854, cholera was transmitted by French troops bound to the Crimean War front to Hermoupolis, as well as to Piraeus and Athens. In Hermoupolis alone, 365 people died, and the popular classes suffered greater losses due to poor hygiene, bad housing conditions and malnutrition.[44] Local archival sources are very eloquent concerning

---

38 Fenerli, "Ο καλλωπισμός της πόλης", 175.

39 Ioannis Travlos – Aggeliki Kokkou, *Ερμούπολη. Η δημιουργία μίας νέας πόλης στη Σύρο στις αρχές του 19ου αιώνα* [*Hermoupolis. The creation of a new town in Syros in the beginning of the 19th century*], (Athens: Commercial Bank of Greece, 1980), 102–42.

40 Andreas Syngros, *Απομνημονεύματα*, [Memoirs], (Athens: Estia, [1908], 1998) vol. A', 93.

41 Eric Hobsbawm, *The age of revolutions* (*1789–1848*), (New York; Vintage Books, 1996), 203–04; Hohenberg – Lees, *The making*, 258. Pinol, *Ο κόσμος των πόλεων*, 193–96.

42 Aggeliki Fenerli, "Το πρόβλημα του νερού στην Ερμούπολη (1823–1923)" ["The problem of water supply in Hermoupolis (1823–1923)"], (Paper presented in the 24th *Hermoupolis Seminars*, Hermoupolis, July 3–15, 2008).

43 Newspaper *Ερμής*, n. 95, 27.7.1840.

44 Newspaper *Αίολος*, n. 516, 7.8.1854 and n. 524, 30.9.1854; Christos Loukos, "Επιδημία και κοινωνία. Η χολέρα στην Ερμούπολη (1854)" ["Disease and Society. The Cholera in Hermoupolis (1854)"], *Μνήμων* [*Mnimon*], 14, (1992), 49–61.

the high rates of infant mortality in the middle of the nineteenth century, and big Western European cities experienced similarly unfortunate trends.[45]

Harsh living conditions in the town were the cause of social "diseases", related to the poverty experiences by the lower classes, while criminality was also strengthened by the mass of new arrivals to the heavily trafficked port of Hermoupolis, particular from the Ottoman provinces. According to the local press, petty theft and burglary was commonplace, and robbery from commercial houses or offices was systematic, and carried out by well organized "professionals" such as those who, in May 1868, broke the strong box belonging to the merchant and shipowner Panagiotis Geralopoulos, after having entered his office using a passkey in the same building hosting the court of first instance.[46] In general, criminality in Hermoupolis was more focused on petty crime and property crimes, which reflects the socio-economic inequalities in the town.[47]

In the busy port of Hermoupolis, prostitution was another widespread phenomenon. Since its very beginning, prostitution was concentrated in the southwestern outskirts of the urban area, after the Psariana quarter and behind the shipbuilding zone. The neighborhood was called "small huts" (kalyvakia) or "lodgings" (katalymata), and its existence provoked a range of reactions related to the moral implications of the phenomenon, as well as to the spread of venereal diseases.[48] Abandoned infants presented the city with another very serious social issue, a phenomenon which was due to frequent relations between unmarried couples and to the inability of many poor women to raise their children.[49]

Hermoupolis was clearly stratified, and the hierarchichal nature of its society was reflected in many ways, such as the spatial division of the rich and poor's neighborhoods, in various aspects of material life, and in the lifestyle

45 GSA, Syros, Historical Archive of Municipality of Hemoupolis, D/Registry Office (E) Deaths. Handy book of deceases, n. 1, 1848–1852; Pinol, *Ο κόσμος των πόλεων*, 192.

46 Newspaper *Αίολος*, n. 294, 1.4.1850, n. 511, 1.7.1854; *Ερμής* n. 230, 14.8.1843; *Αστήρ των Κυκλάδων*, n. 235, 15.10.1861, n. 579, 11.5.1868; *Ερμούπολις*, n. 10, 24.10.1864.

47 Hohenberg – Lees, *The making*, 264.

48 Newspaper *Ερμής*, n. 232, 28.8.1843; Thomas Drikos, *Η πορνεία στην Ερμούπολη το 19ο αιώνα (1820–1900)*, [*The prostitution in Hermoupolis in the 19th century (1820–1900)*], (Athens: Ellinika Grammata, 2002), 17–27, 83–87.

49 Christos Loukos, "Τα έκθετα βρέφη της Ερμούπολης. Τα πρώτα θύματα της παθολογίας μίας κοινωνίας;" ["The abandoned infants of Hermoupolis. Were they the first victims of a social pathology?"], *Αφιέρωμα στον πανεπιστημιακό δάσκαλο Βασ. Βλ. Σφυρόερα από τους μαθητές του*, [*A tribute to the University teacher Vassilis Sfiroeras from his students*], (Athens: Lyhnos Publishers, 1992), 247–64.

and mentality of each social group. The elite of Hermoupolis was based upon wealth, as was to be expected in a new town where the most developed activities were those of trade and shipping in the "*age of capital*". Merchants, bankers or industrialists—in the second half of the century—and some shipowners constituted the town's elite, along with the bourgeoisie of knowledge, which included doctors, lawyers, professors and high-ranking officials.[50] The middle class had a more heterogeneous composition, and included many less wealthy merchants, shopkeepers, clerks, captains, shipowners and craftsmen, who were mainly the owners of the means of production.[51] The lower class or the poor of the town also included representatives of all sorts of occupations and professions, who were largely depended on wages. These were sailors, gardeners, craftsmen, porters, boatmen, servants, nurses, prostitutes and, later, industrial workers.[52]

In the early years of Hermoupolis, each group of refugees from a specific place of origin was not only characterized by a dominant professional tradition (the Ipsariotes were sailors and the Chiots were merchants or shipbuilders), but they also settled in specified area, thus creating quarters named after their place of origin, such as Idreika (from Hydra), Kardamilitika (from Kardamyla in the northeast of Chios) or Psariana (from Psara); some of them are still preserved today like Psariana or Vrontado (from a small town a few kilometers north of Chios).[53] The wealthy mostly resided in the quarter of Agios Nikolaos, and the adjacent Vaporia, which was the most expensive area in the northeastern part of the town. Important members of the elite lived there at least until the 1870s, including Nikolaos Prassakakis, a Chiot merchant and Mayor of Hermoupolis in 1837–40 and 1848–50, and also the Chiots Ioannis L. Rallis (who was Mayor in the period 1843–46), Theodoros I. Rodokanakis, Mikes. S. Galatis, Zorzis Negrepontes, Amvrosios Damalas (Mayor in the period 1853–62), and other merchants such as Konstantinos Pangalos from Argos, Grigorios Paikos from Thessaloniki and Ilias Kehagias from Amfissa, whose houses are still preserved and registered for the purpose of historical research.[54] Alongside

50 Kostas Raptis, "Αστικές τάξεις και αστικότητα στην Ευρώπη, 1789–1914" ["Bourgeois class and bourgeoisie in Europe 1789–1914"], *Μνήμων* [*Mnimon*], 20, (1998), 214–16.

51 Geoffrey Crossick – Heinz-Gerhard Haupt, *The petit bourgeoisie in Europe, 1780–1914. Enterprise, family and independence*, (London-New York: Routledge, 1995), 1–10; Pinol, *Ο κόσμος των πόλεων*, 248–49.

52 Processed data from Database *Hermoupolis Censuses 1860*, Institute for Mediterranean Studies, (http://cities.ims.forth.gr/search_census.php?l=1&townid=4).

53 Frangidis, *Ιστορία της νήσου Σύρου*, 51; Agriantoni-Fenerli, *Hermoupolis-Syros*, 10.

54 Agriantoni-Fenerli, *Hermoupolis-Syros*, 99–108.

merchants, the bourgeois of knowledge also lived in this area, such as the doctor Iossif Votaros, the lawyer Iossif Issaias, and the professor and owner of an American modeled school Christos Evangelidis.[55] However, according to the 1861 census, others lived in the area including some craftsmen, shopkeepers and people from the lower social strata; this mix of people was also a characteristic of other port-cities of the mid-nineteenth century, such as Marseille.[56]

The quarter around Metamorphosis, the oldest church in the town (1825), was situated between the elite quarter of Agios Nikolaos and the popular quarter of Psariana. A large proportion of the middle classes lived in this area, but also some members of the upper classes, such as the Chiot magnate Stamatios I. Proios, the Chiot merchant Mikes. K. Salvagos, the industrialist George Veltsos, and doctors, lawyers and some teachers. Most of the inhabitants in this area were members of the *petit bourgeoisie*: clerks, shopkeepers, craftsmen, shipbuilders and some fishermen.[57] The quarter of Psariana or Kimisis on the south-western side of the bay (named after the church of Kimisis in Theotokou, the second oldest church in the town) and the adjacent area west of it, the neighbourhood of Agios Georgios around the cemetery, were the areas dominated by the popular classes. The majority of sailors lived in Psariana (the majority were indeed from Psara) but residents of this area included many others associated with maritime professions, such as fishermen, shipyard workers, caulkers as well as many tanners, shopkeepers, mainly butchers and greengrocers; this was due to the proximity of the area to their worksites, as the shipyards, tanneries, and the Public Butchery and Vegetables Market were all nearby. In Agios Georgios, very few residents were involved in trade professions, with the exception of a few greengrocers, bakers and dairy men, and the neighbourhood was overwhelmed by shipyard workers, tanners, blacksmiths, dyers, sailors, fishermen, boatmen, servants, porters, etc.[58]

Many of the upper class houses around Agios Nikolaos and Metamorphosis were characterised by splendour and comfort, reflecting the wealth and the aesthetic of the local elite. In terms of style, there was a gradual evolution away from the first houses, which preserved features of Ottoman architecture and the palaces and mansions of neoclassical style after 1840.[59] Mainly these were two storey houses which varied in size, architectural style,

---

55 Database *Hermoupolis Censuses 1861*, op. cit.

56 Pinol, *Ο κόσμος των πόλεων*, 236.

57 Agriantoni-Fenerli, *Hermoupolis-Syros*, 86–92; Database *Hermoupolis Censuses 1861*, op. cit.

58 Database *Hermoupolis Censuses 1861*, op. cit.

59 Travlos-Kokkou, *Ερμούπολη*, 154–56.

layout and decoration. Konstantinos Pangalo's house, built in 1838 in the Ottoman style (which today is 20, Apollo Street) had three bedrooms, two parlours and a courtyard, while between 1834–36 in the same street, the mansion of the Chiot Nikolaos Prassakakis was built, designed by the German architect Erlaher.[60] A decade later, the house of Argyrios Tarpohtsis from Serres (a merchant and Mayor in the period 1846–48) at the corner of Chariton and Apollo streets, was built at a cost of 62,000 drachmas, and included nine bedrooms, two parlours, two kitchens, hajat (a sort of Ottoman style balcony), storerooms, servant's rooms, latrines, cisterns and other auxiliary spaces. Subsequent to the bankruptcy of Tarpochtsis and the loss of its mayoral office, in the summer of 1848, the house passed to the Chiot merchant Amvrosios Damalas, according to the property contract.[61]

The middle and lower classes houses, mainly in Metamorphosis and Psariana, varied from one to two storey houses, bearing different elements and influences of the insular, folk and neoclassical styles.[62] The house bought by the Ipsariot captain Dimitrios Kalimeris from Argyrios Tarpohtsis in 1839 in the Psariana quarter cost 1,450 drachmas, and included a parlour, a small hall, two bedrooms and a kitchen, and was probably a one storey house.[63] The two adjacent houses, which the Ipsariot shipbuilder Georgios Dramitzas built for his six-members family in 1839–40, where also one storey houses: the first included a parlour, two bedrooms, kitchen and a courtyard; the second included a parlour and a bedroom.[64] As for the two-storey houses in Psariana, from 1841 the Chiot shipbuilder Frangoulis Sehas owned a house with a parlour, a dining room, two bedrooms, a kitchen, a cistern, a well, a latrine and courtyards on both sides of the building on the ground floor, and a parlor, a dining room, three bedrooms, a kitchen and a latrine on the upper floor. However, most of the poorer peoples' houses were one storey houses made up of a single space, sometimes with a courtyard, where human beings and domestic animals often were living together.[65]

---

60 GSA, Syros, Notary Andreas David, n. 7183, 3.6.1838; I. Travlos-Kokkou, *Ερμούπολη*, 156, illustration 62 and 159–61; Agriantoni – Fenerli, *Hermoupolis-Syros*, 101–03.

61 GSA, Syros, Notary Andreas David, n. 20941, 10.5.1848; Newspaper *Αίολος* n. 209, 14.8.1848; *Ερμής* n. 375, 2.12.1848; Agriantoni – Fenerli, *Hermoupolis-Syros*, 97, 99–100.

62 Agriantoni-Fenerli, *Hermoupolis-Syros*, 116–117.

63 GSA, Syros, Notary Andreas David, n. 9797, 6.12.1839.

64 Op. cit. n. 12.987, 2.3.1842.

65 Op. cit. n. 30.856, 5.5.1859; Despina Nikolaou, "Αναζητώντας τους εργάτες στη Σύρο του 19ου αιώνα" ["Searching the workers at Syros in 19th century"], (MA diss., University of Crete, 2004), 102–03.

Alimentation was a significant factor, due to the great divide between the social classes in Hermoupolis. The first generation of upper and middle classes in the town had adopted the civil virtues of austerity, frugality and continence in their eating habits, according to Andreas Syngros. He reported that: '*the wealthiest were nourished as destitutes. Meat was a luxury and was served only at lunchtime. An oka* (equivalent of 1,282 kg) *of meat was considered enough for a family of between four and seven people and intended only for one type of recipe... As for fish, the biggest, like mullets, snappers and saddled breams were rarely seen at the tables of the wealthiest, and only in small quantities. For example, for six people 100 dramia* (one fourth of oka, equivalent of 320 gr) *of mullet was considered enough*'.[66] This mentality seems to have changed in the second half of the nineteenth century. In the early 1890s, the moneylender Stefanos Rigas, originally from Zagora of Mount Pelion, consumed more meat, mainly beef, eggs and dairy products on a daily basis than starchy food like pasta, potatoes and rice. Also the rentier "husband from Syros", described in Emmanuel Roidis novel of the same period, hired the Milanese cook of Ano Syro's bishop '*who was known to all of Cyclades for her ravioli, shrimp soup and lenten gurnard*'. Both were a long way from the bourgeois spirit of austerity in the first half of the century, as described by Syngros.[67]

On the other hand, the diet of the popular classes was much poorer and based mainly on cereals. Therefore, famine and the rising cost of cereals threatened social cohesion, and could have been a cause for rioting by the poor. Besides, the first known strike in the history of Greece, which was organized by workers of the shipyards and tanneries of Hermoupolis in 1879, was provoked by the speculative devaluation of marketable currencies from local merchants and industrialists, which substantially affected the purchasing power of the local working class for bread, their basic foodstuff.[68]

The forms and means of socialization, and of social life more generally, was another factor in the demarcation between social classes in Hermoupolis. The main meeting place for the bourgeois was the gentlemen's club. This institution, imported from England, spread very rapidly in Hermoupolis, and became

66 Syngros, *Απομνημονεύματα*, vol. A', 60–61.

67 Christos Loukos – Demetra Samiou, "Οικονομική συμπεριφορά, ψυχολογία και βιοτικό επίπεδο ενός συριανού τοκιστή: Στέφανος Δ. Ρήγας" ["Economic behaviour, psychology and standards of living of a money lender from Syros: Stefanos D. Rigas"], *Θεωρία και μελέτες ιστορίας* [*Theory and historical studies*], n. 11, (Athens: EMNE-Mnimon, 1991), 57, 78; Emmanuel Roidis, *Ψυχολογία Συριανού Συζύγου* [*Psychology of a husband from Syros*], (Thessaloniki: Ianos Publishers, 2005), (written in 1894), 48–49.

68 Newspaper *Αίολος*, n. 297, 14.1.1854; Nikolaou, 'Αναζητώντας τους εργάτες', 71–73, 119–25.

the only daily meeting place for men (and occasionally women) when a ball was organized. The first gentlemen's club was "Hermes", which was founded in 1836 and belonged to the Chiot party, while two years later saw the founding of the "Club of the Hermoupolitans", which belonged to the anti-Chiot party. These were the two political coalitions in the city during the first generation of settlers. From as early as 1844, there were three clubs, the 'Club of the Hermoupolitans", the "Hellas" and the "Commercial Club" (which might have been the former "Hermes" of the Chiots) hosted in a beautiful 1822 island-venetian style mansion, which is still very well preserved in the centre of Hermoupolis today. This must have been the house that Syngros recalled seeing on his first visit to the Chiot club as an adolescent in 1842. In 1864, all these Gentlemen's clubs were unified to form one club, the "Hellas", in its then new splendid building (still today one of the town's jewels) in the central square (which today is Miaoulis Square, formerly King Otho and Leotsakos), as a proof of social pacification between the town's factions, based on the various groups of origin.[69] The main daily activities in the club were billiards card-playing, along with reading the newspapers which the club offered to its members. However, the most important events for the local bourgeoisie were the balls at Christmas and Carnival time, as well as on other occasions. These balls offered the opportunity for the women of the bourgeoisie to violate the sacrosanct of men's fellowship and relaxation, and were their chance to socialize and show off their fashion achievements. '*There dominated the luxury of ladies' dresses and the elegance of the youth; there showed the fashion; there love affairs begun*'.[70]

The promenades in Central Square or in Vaporia (after Agios Nikolaos Square, also known as Terpsithea due to its panoramic view) were another public area for social intercourse and demonstration between the bourgeois. Unfortunately for the bourgeois, people from the popular classes also circulated in these same public spaces, as was to be expected in a town where rich and poor neighborhoods were very close together, and open spaces for socializing were very limited. Moreover, the public behavior of some of the poorer people constituted a challenge and an insult to the morals of the bourgeoisie: '*King Otho Square is the only public space where our good society spends some time for promenade in public and entertains itself; unfortunately, this central area, especially during festivities, is becoming inaccessible in the evenings, for malignant people with no respect for authorities' orders nor morality sing*

69 GSA, Syros, Notary Andreas David, n. 15.922, 3.1.1844; Newspaper *Ερμούπολις*, n. 11, 31.10.1864; Agriantoni-Fenerli, *Hermoupolis-Syros*, 56, 69; Syngros, *Απομνημονεύματα*, vol. A', 65.

70 Syngros, *Απομνημονεύματα*, vol. A', 65–66; Roidis, *Ψυχολογία Συριανού Συζύγου*, 9.

shameful songs and they do all sorts of nasty things, and they force the honest citizens to leave the area', as nobody, of course, wants his family to be exposed to such kinds of harassment.'[71]

On the other hand, the coffee houses and taverns were places where the popular classes socialized. These places had a very bad reputation among the bourgeois, who thought that the coffee houses were frequented by idlers and malefactors.[72] Besides, the bourgeois considered the poor—whether workers or not—to be a danger and threat to the social order.[73] The repeated ordinances throughout the nineteenth century to ban the use of musical instruments without police permission, and the violation of working hours, confirmed the failure of enforcement measures in the places where the impoverished proletariat would relax and let off steam.[74] However, worst of all from the point of view of the bourgeoisie, was that the entertainments of the common stock would continue until very late at night in the streets of the town, where: '*it is with regret to hear people after midnight or at dawn, drunk or not, wandering in the streets of the town in groups, singing obscene songs and disturbing the peace of the residents, who need to rest in order to go to work the next day*'.[75] Therefore, for the bourgeois, it was necessary for prohibitive measures to concentrate on '*wherever there is major necessity, that is, on the streets and not only in the taverns and the hotels which are irrelevant for the peace of the families*'.[76]

The Maritime Centre

Hermoupolis as a port-city was a centre of the transit trade between the eastern Mediterranean, the Black Sea and Western Europe. Alongside this, in its earliest stages Hermoupolis had developed many sectors of the shipping industry, which made its port the most important maritime centre in the Aegean and the eastern Mediterranean. These sectors included: (a) the port registry (b) a charter and intelligence centre (c) a marine insurance centre (d) a maritime loan market (e) a second hand vessels market (f) a steam navigation nodal

71 Newspaper *Αστήρ των Κυκλάδων*, n. 233, 30.9.1861; Nikolaou, "Αναζητώντας τους εργάτες", 56.

72 Nikolaou, "Αναζητώντας τους εργάτες", 108–09.

73 Nikolaou, "Αναζητώντας τους εργάτες", 58–67; Eric Hobsbawm, *The Age of Capital, 1848–1875.*, (Greek transl. Athens: Cultural Foundation of the National Bank, 2003), 327–30.

74 Drikos, *Η πορνεία στην Ερμούπολη*, 59–60; Nikolaou, "Αναζητώντας τους εργάτες", 109.

75 Newspaper *Ερμούπολις*, n. 3, 5.9.1864; Nikolaou, "Αναζητώντας τους εργάτες", 110.

76 Newspaper. *Αστήρ των Κυκλάδων*, n. 244, 16.12.1861.

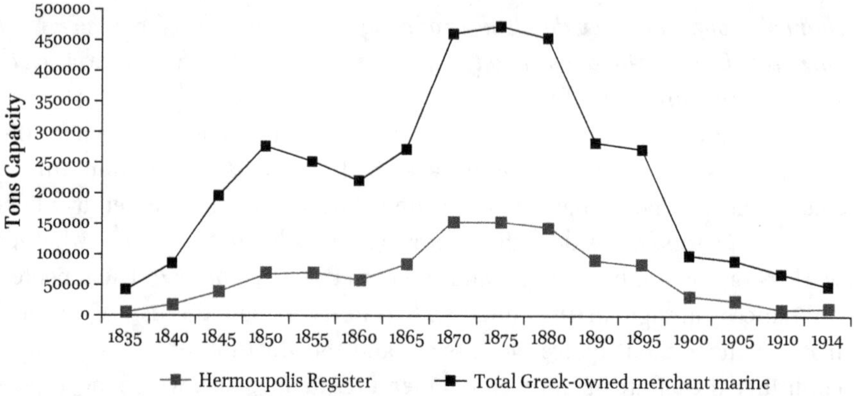

FIGURE 1.2 *Syros port registry/Total Greek-owned merchant marine, 1835–1914.*
SOURCE: PROCESSED DATA FROM G. HARLAFTIS & N. VLASSOPOULOS, *HISTORICAL REGISTER 'PONTOPOREIA'. SAILING SHIPS AND STEAMSHIPS, 1830–1939*, (ATHENS: ELIA PUBLISHERS, 2002).

point (g) a maritime stores depot and supplies market, and (h) a shipbuilding and ship repair centre.

Syros became a port registry in 1834, and belonged to the second department of a total of four among the 22 national ports, along with Andros, Mykonos, Santorini and Milos.[77] In 1835, Syros was the largest port in the Greek Kingdom in terms of fleet size (29.129 tons); Spetses followed (14.958 tons), and then Hydra (11.547 tons). On January 1 1853 the fleet of Syros increased by 186,65%, to reach a total of 83.501 tons, followed by Spetses (38.699 tons) and Galaxidi (28.950 tons).[78]

As shown in Figure 1.2, according to the data covering the period 1835–1914, between a third and a fifth of the total registered capacity of sailing vessels of the Greek-owned merchant marine was concentrated in the port of Syros. The parallel course of the two curves further demonstrates the importance of Syros shipping to the total sailing merchant Greek-owned fleet, and also the common fortunes of both sailing merchant fleets. For the greater part of the

77 Konstantinos Papathanassopoulos, *Ελληνική εμπορική ναυτιλία (1833–1856). Εξέλιξη και αναπροσαρμογή*. [*Greek Merchant Marine, (1833–1856). Development and Readjustment*], (Athens: Cultural Foundation of National Bank, 1983), 71–84.

78 General State Archives, Athens, King Otho Archive, Ministry of Marine, [ΓΑΚ/ΚΥ, Αρχείο Περιόδου Όθωνος, Υπουργείο Ναυτικών] (from now on GSA, Athens, KOA, Marine) file, 41 and 43.

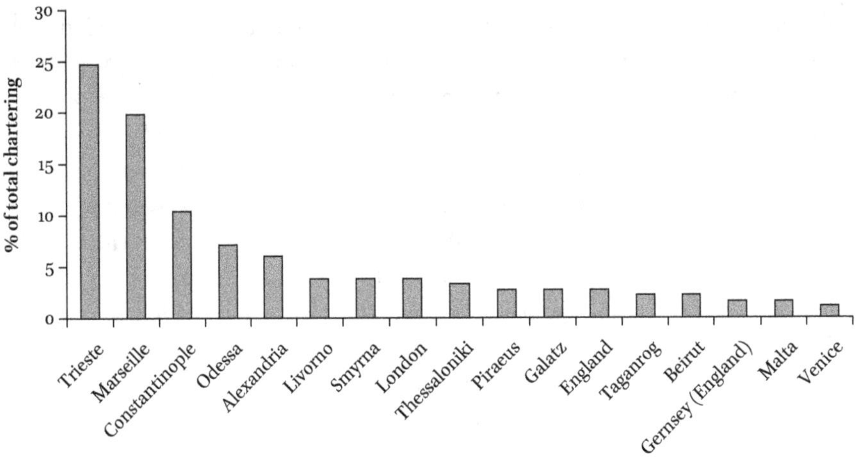

FIGURE 1.3 *Ships destinations according to charter parties stipulated at Syros in the years 1835–1845, 1852–1858.*
SOURCE: GSA, SYROS, NOTARY ANDREAS DAVID, 1835–1845; AMAE, CCC, SYRA, VOL. 3, 1852–1858.

nineteenth century, the port of Syros was a kind of "barometer" for the situation of the Greek-owned merchant marine as a whole.

The port of Syros was a centre of chartering and information about the freights market. The main destinations (see Figure 1.3) were Trieste in the Adriatic, Marseille in the western Mediterranean, Constantinople and Alexandria in the eastern Mediterranean, and Odessa in the Black Sea. Research into freight and knowledge about the current state of affairs in shipping and trade were linked to commercial information circulated through formal and informal channels. Formal channels included the local newspapers which published news regarding trade and shipping, as well as commodity prices, currency prices, and ship entrances and clearances. Informal channels were the many meeting and working places in the port, as well as the coffee houses. Two of these, well known from available sources, were those of the merchant and shipowner Panagiotis Geralopoulos (originally from Smyrna) and Andreas Kosmas (originally from Hydra), which were situated on the eastern side of the port. Outside these coffee houses, many auctions of indebted ships and cargoes also took place.[79]

79 Apostolos Delis, "Ερμούπολη (Σύρος): το ναυπηγικό κέντρο της ιστιοφόρου ναυτιλίας, 1830–1880" ["Hermoupolis (Island of Syros): the shipbuilding centre of the sailing merchant marine, 1830–1880"], (PhD diss., Ionian University), 2010, 299–300.

The marine insurance sector was already developed in the early 1830s. Five insurance companies are mentioned in a source from 1832.[80] Ten years later, the number had increased to seven, but and then reduced to six,[81] and the crisis of 1848 led to the bankruptcy of all except one, the '*Hellas*' insurance company.[82] As far as Hermoupolis was concerned, the crisis of 1848 was related to the grain trade, which seriously affected the Greek-owned merchant marine. Over the years 1845–47, Western Europe experienced catastrophic harvests and economic crises that led to the massive importation of cereals, especially from the Black Sea.[83] The Greek-owned vessels, which were among the main carriers of cereals from the Black Sea, enjoyed very high freight rates during these years, and this led to massive investments in shipping and shipbuilding.[84] But the return of good harvests in Western Europe, and a decrease in the demand for cereals in the year 1848, led to a fall of freight rates. This had serious consequences in the context of the Greek-owned merchant marine, as the massive investments of previous years had indebted the shipowners, and they could not achieve profitable employment for their vessels. This restraint gave rise to a domino effect, as the captains of the vessels committed a series of barratries, often supported by the Greek consuls established in foreign ports, in order to sell the cargo for thermselves and collect the insurance premium.[85] The last stage of this 'drama' was the bankruptcy of all (except one, as previously mentioned) of of the insurance companies of Hermoupolis.[86] This had seriously negative effects for the reputation of the Greek merchant marine, as insurance companies avoided insuring Greek ships (the only surviving insurance company in Hermoupolis, '*Hellas*', restricted its operations). The bad reputation of Greek captains, as well as problems and

---

80 Vlahoiannis, *Χιακό Αρχείο*, vol. 4, 400. The insurance companies of Hermoupolis with a letter published in the newspaper *Αθηνά* [*Athina*] n. 73, 3.12.1832, are expressing their gratification to a Greek Royal Marine officer for having arrested a pirate vessel.

81 Newspaper *Ερμής*, n. 173, 11.7.1842, a letter was published from the insurance companies of Hermoupolis expressing their gratification to Theodoros Xenos, Greek consul of Smyrna, for having chased cases of barratry. Also see Kardasis, *Σύρος*, 206, table 29, where the number of insurance companies was reduced to 6 in the year 1844 and 1846, but some of them are no more appear (due to bankruptcy) and new ones are listing in his table.

82 AMAE, CCC, Syra, vol. 3, 3.6.1851.

83 Harry Hearder, *Europe in the 19th century, 1830–1880*, (London: Longman, 1988), 111; Sakellaropoulos, *Οι κρίσεις*, vol. B, 14–23; Kardasis, *Σύρος*, 75–76.

84 Delis, "Ερμούπολη (Σύρος)", figure 3.2 and page 95; Kardasis, *Σύρος*, Table 18, 122; newspaper *Αίολος*, n. 312, 3.5.1851.

85 *Ερμής*, n. 416, 20.9.1850; *Αίολος*, n. 347, 31.3.1851; AMAE, CCC, Syra, vol. 3, 20.4.1849, 264.

86 AMAE, CCC, Syra, vol. 3, 3.6.1851.

crises in the grain trade, (on which Greek shipping largely depended) brought about a serious crisis for Greek merchant marine, which lasted until at least until 1851[87] when the Greek Government took measures to safeguard its more important industry, with positive effects.[88] In 1857, there were three insurance companies in Hermoupolis, and between 1861 and 1876 six more were founded.[89] Generally, the conjunctures and the problems facing the Greek-owned sailing merchant marine had a strong influence on the fortunes of the insurance companies of Hermoupolis.

An equally important financial facilities sector, closely related to the insurance sector, was that of maritime loans. Hermoupolis was the most important capital market in the Greek Kingdom, and among the most important in the eastern Mediterranean. Generally, maritime loans were the basic source of shipping finance over the whole examined period, and were a profitable alternative ground for capital investments by the merchant and shipping entrepreneurial class of Hermoupolis. The documentation from the notary archives provides thousands of cases of maritime loans stipulated in the first three decades of the port-city's life. The lenders were usually private individuals, merchants, seamen, or shipwrights, but were sometimes people from other professions who were also involved in speculative business. Hermoupolis lacked banking institutions that would finance shipping. The foundation of an agency of the National Bank of Greece in 1842 had no impact on shipping finance, and in general, the local market was firmly controlled by the usurers, who were mostly Chiot merchants, and were among the main sources of shipping finance and credit facilities.[90]

87 AMAE, CCC, Syra, vol. 3, 24.7.1852, 433–434, and, vol. 3, 4.10.1852, 447; *Ερμής*, n. 416, 20.9.1850; *Αίολος*, n. 321, 21.4.1851 and n. 322, 3.5.1851.

88 This was the introduction of '*Libretto*', with legislative act (codified as ΡΗΔ) of 13.11.1851, basically a book, on which the shipowners and captains were obliged to register all their maritime loans by chronological order, except of the latest which was made for immediate voyage necessities. For the positive effects of the introduction of *Libretto* see AMAE, CCC, Syra, vol. 3, 29.7.1851, 390–392, vol. 3, 6.4.1853, vol. 4, 28.6.1853; Newspaper *Αίολος*, n. 339, 23.6.1851. Also, Kardasis, *Σύρος*, 203 and Christos Hadjiiossif, «Crise conjoncturelle et problèmes structurels dans la marine marchande grecque au XIXe siècle: Les réactions de l'état et des intérêts privés», in *Actes du IIe Colloque International d'Histoire. Economies Méditerranéennes. Equilibres et Intercommunications. XIIIe–XIXe siècles*, ed. M.C. Chatziioannou and A. Tabaki, (Athens: INR/NHRF, 1986), 379–81.

89 Delis, "Ερμούπολη (Σύρος)", 39–40.

90 About the conflict between the usurers of Hermoupolis and the National Bank of Greece, see Kardasis, *Syros*, 190–282.

TABLE 1.3 *Geographical distribution of maritime loans in Hermoupolis market, 1841–65.*

Place of origin of the borrower captain	Number of maritime loans
Hermoupolis	75
Kasos	55
Spetses	35
Hydra	13
Dalmatian Coasts	10
England	9
Italian Peninsula	8
Cephalonia	8
Mykonos	8
Lemnos	6
Andros	6

Source: General State Archives, Prefecture of Cyclades, Notary Andreas David, 1841–1865.

Two types of maritime loan can be distinguished: (1) those made before the departure of a ship, raised exactly for the necessary initial expenditures of the voyage, such as the wages of seamen, food supplies and rigging equipment;[91] (2) those made during the voyage (usually the homeward route), which were more urgent, such as for necessary repairs to sailing ships, supplies and other provisions. The first type of loan had an almost fixed monthly interest, which slightly varied between 2–2.75%; the ship was mortgaged to the lender until the loan was repayed. In fact, local newspapers were full of auctions of mortgaged ships, in cases when ship owners were unable to repay these loans. As regards the second type of loan, the borrowers were mostly foreigners, and therefore the risk was greater. The interest was much higher, between 5–15% and was paid once, when the ship arrived at its destination. However, as the risk was very high, they mortgaged the ship as well as her cargo.

The geographical range of captains seeking finance for their voyages in the port of Syros was very wide. Among the Greeks, the most frequent clientele for the local financiers was from the island of Kasos, in the south eastern Aegean (then part of the Ottoman Empire), from the leading pre-1821 maritime insular

91 The always present phrase in a maritime loan contracts is "*…received from him for the equipment, rigging, wages and food supplies of the seamen, without these (money) would have been impossible to set sail this ship.*"

communities of Hydra and Spetses, and from Hermoupolis itself. Furthermore, captains from nearby Santorini, Mykonos and Andros, from Cephalonia in Ionian Islands, from the northwestern Aegean island of Skopelos and the western Greece mainland port of Galaxidi sought out loans in the market of Hermoupolis. Also, foreign captains from Adriatic ports such as Venice, Fiume, Trieste, Ravenna, Bocche di Cattaro, Porto Re, as well as from north European ports, such as Mary Port, Bristol and Hull in Britain, Nyborg and Aarhus in Denmark, Hannover and Hamburg in Germany, all raised loans for repairs and supplies in order to continue their voyages.[92] For Greek and foreign captains, Hermoupolis was a necessary stop, where they could satisfy their demands for shipping finance and other services.

Hermoupolis was also a great market for second hand vessels. The available documentation provides a lot of evidence about the buying and selling of vessels and the people involved in such affairs, from a very wide geographical context. People from Hermoupolis, especially those who had origins in Chios (mostly merchants but also many captains) and from Psara (mostly seamen), had an important share of this business, but so did many from other maritime communities in the Aegean and Ionian Seas, such as Kasos, Hydra, Spetses and Cephalonia, as well as Greek merchants from southern Russia and western Mediterranean ports. Through their representatives, they all knew that Hermoupolis was a great market offering opportunities for second-hand vessels.

The basic factors that determined the prices of second-hand vessels were the freight rates, the age of the vessel, the condition of the vessel and the expectations of the shipowners of changes in the shipping market.[93]

One of the main problems relating to the age of sold vessels is that we do not always know when they were built. Only the documents relating to previous ownership are mentioned, which do not always reveal the age of the vessel. The condition of the vessels is rarely mentioned, but in the last part of the contract, the buyer always had to declare that he was satisfied after an inspection of his future property. In the cases of ships whose age is known, we noticed that ships or shares were sold when the ship was relatively new. Many of them occurred in the same year, or at most three or four years later. As shown in Table 1.4, in 1852 (which was a recession year), depreciation fluctuated between 25.5 and 69%. That same year, the trend in the average price of second-hand vessels was

92 Delis, "Ερμούπολη (Σύρος)", 41–42.

93 Martin Stopford, *Maritime Economics*, (London-New York: Routledge, 1997), 101–03. Stopford mention also the inflation as a factor of influence on ship prices, but we are unable to account it in the context of the 19th century sailing fleet economics.

TABLE 1.4 *Sample of sales of second-hand sailing vessels, 1844–56.*

Age of vessel*	Year of sale	Ship type	Capacity	Price of construction	Sale price	% Depreciation
0(4)	1852	Brig	350	90,000	67,000	−25.56
1(5)	1851	Goleta	50	6,250	6,000	−4.00
1(9)	1846	Bombarda	32	4,860	4,050	−16.67
2(0)	1854	Brig	176	20,000	18,750	−6.25
2(3)	1852	Brig	211	42,000	25,000	−40.48
2(6)	1844	Goleta	63	10,000	8,100	−19.00
2(6)	1854	Brig	162	24,000	17,000	−29.17
2(9)	1856	Bombarda	73	14,000	11,300	−19.29
3(6)	1847	Bombarda	40	6,000	8,000	33.33
3(8)	1852	Brig	195	48,000	15,000	−68.75
4(0)	1856	Goleta	53	9,000	5,680	−36.89
4(0)	1854	Brig	219	38,000	40,000	5.26
4(0)	1853	Brig	210	42,000	20,000	−52.38
4(0)	1854	Bombarda	70	12,500	7,000	−44.00
5(0)	1854	Goleta	80	15,500	10,000	−35.48
5(0)	1850	Brig	248	36,000	36,000	0.00
5(2)	1854	Brig	106	8,000	8,000	0.00
5(8)	1852	Brig	224	43,000	20,000	−53.49
7(0)	1846	Brig	147	19,980	12,000	−39.94
8(0)	1847	Brig	253	42,271	39,500	−6.56
10(4)	1850	Brig	163	36,000	12,700	−64.72

Source: Delis, "Ερμούπολη (Σύρος)", 108. * The first figure is referring to years and the second in () is referring to months.

downward, and freight rates had just recovered after the 1849–52 recession. The four-month-old brig *Loukas* (350 tons) was sold at one fourth of her initial value. In contrast, in 1847 (a peak year) the eight-year- old brig *Kantinto* (253 tons) was sold at 6.5% below her initial price, and the bombarda *Evangelismos* (40 tons) which was three and a half years old, was sold at a profit of 33%. However, it seems that in certain cases, low freight rates did not affect the price of second-hand vessels. In 1850, in the middle of the shipping depression, the five years old brig *Ipsosis tou Timiou Stavrou* (248 tons) was sold at her initial price, but the sale value of the ten years and four months old brig *Adamantios*

Korais (163 tons) had depreciated by 64.72%. In another difficult year, 1854, the four-year-old brig *Georgios* (219 tons) was sold at a profit of 5.26%, whereas the two and a half year old brig *Zorzis* (162 tons) depreciated by 29.17%.

Hermoupolis had, at a very early stage, become a nodal point of Steamship Navigation. Until the establishment of the headquarters of the first Greek Steamship Navigation Company in 1857, the '*Hellenic Steamship Navigation Company*', different foreign companies had established themselves there, as an important station in the eastern Mediterranean, a link which connected the major ports and routes between east and west. Already, two steamship companies, one belonging to the French government and the Austrian 'Lloyd' had included Hermoupolis in both of their two lines established in the Mediterranean.[94] From the very beginning, Hermoupolis became a contested ground for the commercial interest of both Austrians and French in the area, as a controlling point for the Levant trade, and strongly connected with the commercial houses of Constantinople, Smyrna and Alexandria. Steamship companies in that period had a complementary role in sea transport, as they mainly provided mail and passenger services, and important money packages between the merchants, and were much safer and quicker than sailing ships.[95] Trieste and Marseille were among the busiest Mediterranean ports and, furthermore, Greek trade and shipping had established the most prosperous trading communities in the western Mediterranean there. Therefore, safe, quick and effective communication and money transfer between them and the merchants of Hermoupolis was of vital importance for the business in the Levant, and steamship connections were an essential means of providing for this, promoting both (a) the national and commercial interests of these powers in Levant and (b) the merely commercial interests of the merchant houses (Greek in large part) which had been established in these national contexts (Austria and France). Of course, this competition benefited Hermoupolis.[96] Overall,

94 The first of the French lines followed the route: Marseille-Livorno-Civitavecchia-Naples-Malta-Syros-Smyrna-Constantinople and vice versa. The second was limited in the eastern Mediterranean and followed the route: Piraeus-Syros-Alexandria and vice versa. Similar policy followed by the Austrians as they had a long route from Trieste-Ancona-Corfu-Patras-Piraeus-Syros-Smyrna-Constantinople and vice versa and a shorter one from Syros-Crete-Alexandria and vice versa. Papathanasopoulos, *Ελληνική εμπορική ναυτιλία*, 100, 261–62.

95 AMAE, CCC, Syra, vol. 1, 3.3.1837, 232, the French consul mention the gratitude of the local merchant society for the steamships service, especially concerned for the safety of the money packages, as there was little confidence to Greek captains of sailing ships, caused to cases of barratry.

96 The worry of the French Consul for the effectiveness of the Austrian Lloyd and the preference shown by the merchant of Hermoupolis to them as well as his suggestions for the

the French were less effective than the Austrian Lloyd, which had a stable presence in the eastern Mediterranean for 20 years, until the foundation of the '*Hellenic Steamship Navigation Company*' and beyond. French lines ceased their voyages in 1845, and the following year a new French company, '*Rostand*', established its presence in Hermoupolis.[97] However, they also ended their services in the 6th August 1851, to be replaced by another French company called the '*Messageries Nationales*', on 5th November of the same year.[98] The decision of the Austrian Lloyd to transfer its headquarters to Piraeus in 1853 provoked a serious reaction in local press, reflecting the worries of the merchant community about the loss of their economic pre-eminence, and the future of their business on the island.[99]

The British presence of steamship navigation on Hermoupolis was sporadic, and unlike the Austrian and French presence, did not have a significant influence on local economic interests. However, there was a short-lived British presence in the period 1842–45 and another company of Liverpool & Glasgow appeared in 1851.[100] Five years later, the '*Cunard*' of Liverpool also occasionally used the port of Hermoupolis on its route to and from Liverpool and Constantinople.[101]

The foundation of the '*Hellenic Steamship Navigation Company*', which established its headquarters in Hermoupolis in 1857, was a crucial event in terms of the economic prospects of the port-city. The final decision was made after a long period of contention between the financiers of Hermoupolis and those of Patras (the main export centre of raisin in Greece), regarding the location of the company's headquarters. This affair also involved the National Bank of Greece and the Greek Government, which were among the main financiers, as well as promoters and guarantors for the raising of the necessary

---

amelioration of the services of the French lines are expressed in AMAE, CCC, Syra, vol. 3, 27.5.1844, 35, ibid., vol. 3, 25.11.1848, 177 and vol. 3, 24.12.1849.

97 For the announcement of the transfer of the station of the French steamship from Hermoupolis to Piraeus see *Αίολος*, n. 61, 3.11.1845. For '*Rostand*' company see AMAE, CCC, Syra, vol. 3, 25.11.1848, and vol. 3, 24.12.1849; Kardasis, *Σύρος*, 131.

98 AMAE, CCC, Syra, vol. 3, 26.7.1852, 436–38; Kardasis, *Σύρος*, 131.

99 *Αίολος*, 7.2.1853; *Ερμής*, 7.1.1853. In contrast *Ένωσις* [*Enosis*], 11.2.1853, disagrees to the rest of the press and present a different, more optimistic thesis about the effects of the transfer of the company's headquarters to Piraeus.

100 AMAE, CCC, Syra, vol., 3, 25.11.1848, 176; Kardasis, *Σύρος*, 130; For the presence of the Company of Liverpool & Glasgow, AMAE, CCC, Syra, vol. 4, 26.8.1853, 60–63; Kardasis, *Σύρος*, 131.

101 This line was following the route Liverpool-Gibraltar-Malta-Constantinople. In the return voyage some times was touch in Thessaloniki and Smyrna, AMAE, CCC, Syra, vol. 5, 22.8.1856, 9–11.

capital.[102] The establishment of the headquarters, and especially the foundation of the Arsenal in 1861, the first industrial establishment of the city, inaugurated the entrance of mechanized industry to Hermoupolis, and opened up economic perspectives and opportunities whose results have lasted until the present day.[103]

---

102 The long and full of interesting episodes account of about the conflict of interests for the foundation of the steamship company presents Papathanassopoulos, *Ελληνική εμπορική ναυτιλία*, especially chapters 6 & 7. Also Kardasis, *Σύρος*, 130–38. About the argumentation of the local press defending Hermoupolis, as the right choice for the establishment of the headquarters of the *'Hellenic Steamship Navigation Company'* see the newspaper *Τηλέγραφος των Κυκλάδων* [*Tilegrafos ton Kikladon*], n. 59, 16.6.1856.

103 The British council mentioned that in 1871 the Arsenal of the company employed 130 people. F.O. Syra, *Report by Consul Ruby on the Trade and Commerce of the Cyclades during the Year 1871*, 14.12.1872, 123 and in the year 1874, F.O. Syra, *Report by Consul Binney on the Trade and Commerce of the Cyclades during the Year 1874*, 16.12.1874, 125 mentioned that the Arsenal employed 120 people, which enjoyed the best average wages and less working hours, among the rest of the local industries.

CHAPTER 2

Syros Shipbuilding: An Industry before Industrialization

The Shipbuilding Activity: Definition Issues

According to the conventional division of economic activities, shipbuilding as a productive activity theoretically belongs in the secondary sector. However, matters are more complicated as regards wooden shipbuilding, which is not usually included in discussions about the industry and industrialization of shipbuilding, but is instead treated as a complementary sector of shipping. In the last quarter of the nineteenth century, shipbuilding assimilated many features of the second industrial revolution and acquired a factory character, with an extensive use of machinery and a high cost fixed capital investment.[1] Even nineteenth century wooden shipbuilding is difficult to categorize as a pre-industrial, proto-industrial, or industrial activity. The reason for this is that wooden shipbuilding does not consist of a single manufacturing process from raw material to a specific finished product. Instead, it requires different parallel or sequential production processes, and the use of different raw materials (wood, metals, canvas and hemp) from craftsmen of different kinds with specific skills and specializations, in order to complete a very complex final product: the ship.

Furthermore, in the case of shipbuilding, the conventional scheme of urbanization as a precondition of industrialization and the concentration of labour in factories through the intermediary phase of proto-industrialization and the putting out system, does not apply. Shipbuilding followed an independent course connected to commerce and shipping, which preceded the industrial

1 Cees de Voogd, "Shipbuilding, Commercial", in *The Oxford Encyclopaedia of Maritime History*, ed. John B. Hattenford, (Oxford-New York: Oxford University Press, 2007), 3, 572–75; Sjoerd Hengst & Alan A. Lemmers, "Shipyards", in *The Oxford Encyclopaedia*, 3, op. cit., 703–06; Eric W. Sager – Gerald E. Panting, *Maritime Capital, The shipping industry in Atlantic Canada, 1820–1914*, (Montreal and Kingston: McGill-Queen's University Press, 1990), 70–71, 77; Simon Ville, "The Transition to Iron and Steel Construction", in *Sail's Last Century. The Merchant Sailing Ship, 1830–1930. Conway's History of the Ship*, ed. Robert Gardiner, (London: Conway Maritime Press, 1995), 69, 73.

© KONINKLIJKE BRILL NV, LEIDEN, 2016 | DOI 10.1163/9789004306158_004

revolution.[2] In every society in contact with water, shipbuilding was the most advanced and complex technological activity and is still today considered to be an *avant guard* technology.[3] The sailing ship was and remains an extremely complex and sophisticated mechanism, requiring specialized knowledge for its construction, its operation, and its participation in a common culture with a specific system of informal rules and values: the maritime culture.[4] The necessity of this specific know-how and participation in the culture of maritime societies, as a precondition for the construction and operation of the ship, led to a much earlier division of labour in shipping and shipbuilding than the advent of the Industrial Revolution.[5] In the hull of a sea vessel, every timber has its own name and performs a specific structural role, and the same applies to the rigging. Moreover, every wooden or metallic element in the hull and the rigging is made by a specialized craftsman (including carpenters, joiners, caulkers, pulley makers and ironsmiths), and in the operation of the ship, every man on board was assigned a different specialized task, subject to a very strict hierarchy and division of labour.

Shipbuilding developed certain "industrial" characteristics long before Industrial Revolution, and escaped the workshop dimension. From early modern times, there was in the Arsenal of Venice a large and concentrated workforce, a clear division of labour and wages, a hierarchically structured administration, and the systematic management of human and material resources by directors, the *armirai*, who were not shipbuilders but state officials and bureaucrats. From the sixteenth century, its method of organized production and high cost fixed capital was, according to Carlo Cipolla "*more*

2 Franklin F. Mendels, "Proto-Industrialization: The First Phase of the Industrialization Process", *The Journal of Economic History*, vol. 32, n. 1, The Tasks of Economic History (March, 1972), 241–61; Ogilvie C. Sheilagh & Cerman Markus "The Theories of Proto-Industrialization", in *European proto-industrialization*, ed. Ogilvie C. Sheilagh and Cerman Markus (Cambridge: Cambridge University Press, 1996), 1–11; Kriedte Peter, Schlumbohm Jurgen and Medick Hans, *Industrialization before Industrialization. Rural Industry in the Genesis of Capitalism*, (Cambridge: Cambridge University Press, 1981); Deane Phyllis, "The Industrial Revolution in Great Britain", in *The Fontana Economic History of Europe*, ed. Carlo Cipolla, vol. 1, (London: Collins/Fontana Books, 1976), 191–92.

3 William H. Thiesen, *Industrializing American Shipbuilding. The transformation of ship design and construction, 1820–1920*, (Gainesville: University Press of Florida, 2006), 1–2; Cees de Voogd, "Shipbuilding, Commercial", 566.

4 Basil Greenhill, "Introduction" in *Sail's Last Century*, op. cit., 17–19.

5 Eric Sager, *Seafaring Labour: The Merchant Marine of Atlantic Canada, 1820–1914*, (Kingston, Montreal, London: McGill-Queen's University Press, 1989), 14.

the prototype of a modern factory than the appendix of the old artisan yards."[6] There are similar cases in the Modern European Period in the Royal shipyards in Deptford, Chatham, Woolwich and Sheerness, also with high cost fixed capital. In addition, large private establishments such as those of the Dutch East India Company (VOC) and other private shipyards that began operating in the seventeenth century had features of factory organization, constant personnel, verticalization in raw materials and significant fixed capital (such as docks and cranes), and a company business organization that lasted longer than a single generation.[7]

From a technological point of view, the construction of a ship was and still is considered an achievement that demands careful planning, application, and monitoring at every phase of production, as well as needing investment in the most advanced available technical know-how, bearing in mind that a ship is a very complex mechanism designed to be exposed to the dangers of the seas. Therefore, every launch of a sea vessel is a feasting occasion not only for the owners and builders, but for the entire community that lives and flourishes from activities related to the sea. The symbolic dimension of the technological achievement is reflected in the reputation of shipbuilders both within and outside the communities in which they live and work. In the nineteenth century, master shipbuilders such as Isaac Webb, his son William Webb, Donald McKay in New York, and Alexander Stephen in Dundee and Glasgow, were considered living legends: they enjoyed a level of social recognition that no other artisan could hope to achieve in their own lifetime.[8] The recognition of shipbuilders and their ascent in the social hierarchy was due not only to their creative and technological achievement, but also because they were holders of the means of production, like the merchants and factory owners. Similarly, during the

---

6 Carlo Cipolla, *Before the Industrial Revolution. European Society and Economy, 1000–1700*, (London: Routledge, 1993), 74. For the organization of production in the Arsenal of Venice see also Frederick Lane, *Venice: a maritime republic*, (Baltimore: The John Hopkins University Press, 1973), 163–64; Robert C. Davis, *Shipbuilders of the Venetian Arsenal. Workers and Workplace in the Pre-industrial City*, (Baltimore: The John Hopkins University Press, 1991), 47–82.

7 Cipolla, *Before the Industrial Revolution*, 67; Cees de Voogd, "Shipbuilding, Commercial", 3, 580; Richard W. Unger, "Technology & industrial organization: Dutch Shipbuilding to 1800", *Business History*, XVII, 1, (1975), 56–72.

8 William Armstrong Fairburn, *Merchant Sail*, v, (Main: 1945–55), 2783–2806; Unknown, *A Shipbuilding History, 1750–1932. Alexander Stephen & Sons Ltd*, (London-Cheltenham: 1932); David Mc Gregor, *Merchant Sailing Ship, 1850–1875. The Heyday of Sail*, (London: Conway Maritime Press, 1984), 20–23.

second and third quarter of the nineteenth century, master shipwrights in Syros such as Pantelis Maskas, Nikolaos Pagidas, Mikes Potous, and Christofis Krystallis enjoyed the recognition of both local society and the entrepreneurial class (as we shall see in Chapter Six).

Aside from the technological and symbolic dimensions, from an economic point of view the ship was mainly a capital good, a high cost investment, and an economic unit capable of producing high added value.[9] Therefore, as well as specialized know-how, its construction demanded a significant amount of capital. During the period of merchant capitalism, this capital was concentrated in the hands of a few, such as merchants, bankers, shipowners or wealthy shipbuilders. Partnership and borrowing were necessary in order to raise funds, and a high capital return was expected on such a significant investment.[10]

Prior to the Industrial Revolution, shipbuilding in Europe was one of the very few "*heavy industries able to produce a big product to distribute large quantities of raw materials and to amass a long list of finished or semi-finished materials to assemble*."[11] While the organization and the scale of production of shipbuilding involves elements preexisting the later factory organization, its classification as an economic activity remains problematic. The scale, organization, and relations of production varied from the smallest to the largest shipyards, while the mechanization of production and the general level of technology make it difficult to classify the industry among the conventional activities of the factory type. Therefore, the use of the term 'industry' in its classical sense is not appropriate in describing wooden shipbuilding, although structural characteristics such as the scale, the wage dependence of a skilled labour force, the division of labour, and the mobilization of important capital and material resources may correspond to an industrial type of growth. What we can be sure of is that wooden shipbuilding and sailing ships, even though they had begun to develop earlier, co-existed with the achievements and progress of the first and second industrial revolution, and were basic tools of the capitalist economy on its course towards industrialization and the unification of the world economy in the Modern Period.[12]

---

9 Sager – Panting, *Maritime Capital*, 18–19.

10 Greenhill, "Introduction", 9.

11 Unger, "Technology & industrial organization", 56.

12 Sager, *Seafaring Labour*, 14; Gerald S. Graham, "The ascendancy of the sailing ship, 1850–85", *The Economic History Review*, New Series, vol. 9, n. 1, (1956), 74–88.

The Syros Shipbuilding Industry at the Domestic and International Levels

Shipbuilding in the Ionian and Aegean Seas has distant roots, but the industry grew considerably in the second half of the eighteenth century and experienced a boom during the French and Napoleonic Wars. This was a period characterized by the long and continuous rise of freight rates, during which Greeks assumed the role of neutral seafaring Ottoman subjects and carried most of the Mediterranean trade, replacing the devastated merchant fleets of the belligerent nations.[13] Thus, during this period, shipbuilding developed in many coastal and insular areas of both the Ionian and the Aegean. Some were very active, such as Messolonghi, Chios, Hydra and Spetses, and there were many others operating on a smaller scale. After Greek Independence and the founding of the National State (1830), shipbuilding continued in many areas where it had previously developed, as well as beginning for the first time in many places. Spetses, Hydra, Galaxidi, Skopelos and Skiathos were among the biggest, in terms of pre-Independence activity, whereas Piraeus and Syros where newly engaged in shipbuilding. As concerns technology, shipbuilding represented a continuation of established pre-Independence practices. The brig first adopted by the seafarers of Hydra from the mid-1790s, and by the rest of the Greeks on a massive scale after 1815, became the main ship type of the Greek fleet, and continued as such until 1880. At the production level, only Galaxidi (after Syros) produced vessels for the seagoing trade of over 100 tons on average.[14]

In Syros, shipbuilding became an almost industrial phenomenon, as described in the newspaper *Enosis* (*Ένωσις*) in 1856: "*With no doubt, Syros's shipyards are the most developed, and the number of ships built is by far higher than any other in the country. All the necessary* [materials] *for the construction of the ship are available in the town, and hundreds of workers and ironsmiths work on this every day and enjoy satisfactory wages that afford them a comfortable*

13 Vassilis Kremmydas, "Quelques aspects de la navigation et des liaisons commerciales en Mediterranee, au XVIII[e] au debut du XIX[e] siecle", in *Actes du IIe Colloque International d'Histoire*, Tome I, op. cit., 143, 150, 161; Douglass North, "Ocean Freight Rates and Economic Development 1750–1913", *The Journal of Economic History*, vol. 18, n. 4. (December 1958), 541–42; Gelina Harlaftis – Sofia Laiou, "Ottoman state policy in Mediterranean Trade and Shipping, c. 1780–c. 1820: The Rise of the Greek-Owned Ottoman Merchant Fleet", in *Networks of Power in Modern Greece*, ed. Mark Mazower (New York: Columbia University Press, 2008), 1–34.

14 Kostas Damianidis, *Ελληνική Παραδοσιακή Ναυπηγική* [*Greek Vernacular Boatbuilding*], (Athens: Hellenic Bank of Industrial Development, 1998) 28–30.

life."[15] At the same time, a comment in the journal *Pandora* (*Πανδώρα*) confirmed that Syros was "*the most important and at the same time the best of all of our shipyards*" whereas the French consul of Syros in 1853 states that: "*A Hydra, à Spezzia, à Galaxidi, à Cranidi, à Poros, à Egina, à Miconi, à Andros, à Santorin, au Pirée, on construit des Navires, mais il y a que Syra qui possède véritablement un Chantier de Constructions Navales constamment en activité. Plusieurs entrepreneurs y ont chacun leurs cales, où ils construisent soit à forfait, soit pour leur compte, soit à la journée, navires de toutes dimensions, depuis le plus petit caïque, jusqu'au plus grand trois-mâts*."[16] The differences between Syros and the rest of the Greek shipyards did not lie in the technology employed in ship construction, but in the large workforce, the scale of production, the year round (as opposed to seasonal) activity, and the intense rhythms of vessel delivery.

The concentration of such a large amount of entirely wage-dependent labour in an urban environment with clear social stratification was a novel phenomenon in the context of the newly founded Greek National State, and was certainly one of the basic preconditions for the later development of factories in Syros.[17] The journeyman/worker as a distinguished social and professional category in Syros is largely identified with shipyards and tanneries, and this is reinforced by the first strike in the history of Modern Greece in 1879, which started principally within these two sectors.[18] The workforce of the shipyards fluctuated, according to periods of production growth and decline, and data about this are few and sparse. The smallest reported number is 962 workers in 1852, and the maximum is 1500 workers in 1845. However, these figures are likely to include not only those who worked on ship construction in particular, but also craftsman of all categories employed in auxiliary trades.[19] Until 1858, shipbuilding was the most important activity of the secondary sector in the Greek economy, according to estimations of GDP.[20] If Syros had the largest share of shipbuilding production in the entire country and was the only

15 Newspaper *Ένωσις*, n. 217, 3.8.1856.

16 Journal *Πανδώρα*, 7, 1856–57, 165; AMAE, CCC Syra, vol. 4, 28.6.1853, 77.

17 Christina Agriantoni, « Η θέση της Ερμούπολης στην Ελληνική Οικονομία τον 19ο αιώνα. Οι παγίδες των πηγών» ["The position of Hermoupolis in Greek Economy in the nineteenth century. The deception of sources."], *Τα Ιστορικά-Historica*, 1, (1983), 194.

18 Nikolaou «Αναζητώντας τους εργάτες».

19 Kardasis, *Σύρος*, 171.

20 George Kostelenos, Sokratis Petmezas et al. *Πηγές οικονομικής ιστορίας της Νεότερης Ελλάδας. Ποσοτικά στοιχεία και στατιστικές σειρές. Ακαθάριστο Εγχώριο Προϊόν, 1830–1939*, [*Sources of economic history of Modern Greece. Quantitative data and statistical series. Gross Domestic Product*, 1830–1939], (Athens: Historical Archive of National Bank of Greece—Center of Programming and Economic Research, 2007), 94.

shipbuilding centre in Greece at the time, then perhaps shipbuilding deserves to be characterized as the first industry of Syros.[21] The Syros shipyards also created very important linkages within the local, regional, and interregional economy. Backward linkages reveal connections to the growth of the timber trade, metallurgy, rope manufacture and maritime stores, and forward linkages such as the timber and maritime stores trade fueled the shipping economy of many smaller Aegean maritime communities, which engaged as transporters in the supply of shipbuilding materials to Syros. This will be examined in detail in Chapter Six.

The Level of Shipbuilding Technology in the International Context

The construction of wooden sailing ships in Syros and other Greek shipyards was no different to the methods applied in the pre-Independence period. The mechanization of production is nonexistent, and the construction of iron or composite hulls for sailing ships never took place in Greece. However, until 1880 the wooden sailing ship remained the dominant sea vessel in the Mediterranean, and perhaps worldwide. The steamship needed more than a half century of continuous technical improvements to become competitive and eventually to surpass the sailing ship as a cargo carrier. Its use was initially limited to passenger and mail transportation. The crucial moment came with the introduction of the compound engine in the 1860s, which reduced coal consumption, but this innovation was also related to a large extent with the opening of the Suez Canal in 1869.[22] Despite the technical evolution of the steamship, which was completed with the introduction of the triple expansion engine in 1887, it is interesting to note that the total tonnage of sailing ships in Britain was not surpassed by steamships until the 1890s, while the sailing ship remained competitive in the coastal trade and on certain ocean trade routes until at least 1914.[23]

As concerns the sailing ship, the construction of iron, composite, or steel hulls was almost exclusive to Britain. In other countries, the development of metal hulls was related mostly to the construction of steamships. But even in

---

21 Agriantoni, *Οι Απαρχές της Εκβιομηχάνισης*, 89.

22 Graham, "The ascendancy", 227–47; Knick C. Harley, "Aspects of the Economics of Shipping, 1850–1913", in *Change and Adaptation in Maritime History. The North Atlantic Fleets in the 19th century* ed. Lewis R. Fischer – Gerald E. Panting, (St John's: Memorial University of Newfoundland, 1985), 175–77.

23 Sarah Palmer, "The British Shipping Industry, 1850–1914", *in Change and Adaptation in Maritime History*, op. cit., 101; Harley, "Aspects of the Economics of Shipping", 175; Yrjö Kaukiainen, *A History of Finnish Shipping*, (New York-London: Routledge, 1993), 107–08.

this case, the construction of metal sailing ships in Britain did not surpass the tonnage of wooden ones until the end of the 1860s. The main reasons for the construction of iron sailing ships in Britain were the shortage of homegrown timber, which was regularly imported from the Baltic and Canada, and the abundance of iron deposits, which facilitated the development of the heavy metallurgic industry. Aside from the technical advantages of iron over wood as a material, because it was more resistant, more flexible, lighter, and allowed for the possibility of building larger hulls, the most crucial factor proved to be the reduction in iron prices from 1856, which resulted in a downward trend in the production cost of iron hulls at the expense of wooden ships.[24] The development in construction of iron sailing ships was not widespread across Britain as a whole, but flourished in areas which had previously developed a heavy iron and steel industry, such as Clyde, Belfast, and the Northeast of England. Before 1866, it seems that these three areas, along with Liverpool, had made the transition to iron construction. Countries with important shipbuilding industries such as the USA, Canada, France, Norway, and Italy had not invested heavily in iron and steel sailing ships, and could perhaps not compete with British industry, which enjoyed a first mover advantage in a sector that had already created the preconditions for the spread of an improved industrial product.[25] Iron and steel sailing ships and steamships were products of the second industrial revolution and the technical innovations in metallurgy, which had since 1860s changed the character of the industry, and which had as a consequence seen the intensification of capital investment in shipbuilding and ship operations.[26] However, during the period 1830–70, steamships and metal hull-built sailing ships had a very limited presence and, with some exceptions, the dominant technology in Continental Europe, North America and Britain was the wooden sailing ship: most shipyards were labour intensive industries with a minimal level of mechanization.[27] The ship types built in the nineteenth century were common, at least as regards the medium and large tonnage vessels in Mediterranean, northern Europe, and on the other side of the Atlantic.

24 Ville, "The Transition to Iron and Steel", 53, 60, 62, 68; Harley, "Aspects of the Economics of Shipping", 174.

25 Ville, "The Transition to Iron and Steel", 69, 72; Jeffrey J. Safford, "The Decline of the American Merchant Marine 1850–1914: an Historiographical Appraisal" in *Change and Adaptation in Maritime* History, op. cit., 51–86; Alfred D. Chandler, Jr., *Scale and Scope: The Dynamics of Industrial Capitalism*, (London: Harvard University Press, 1990), 34.

26 Alan Lougheed, "Industry and technical change", in *The European Economy 1750–1914: A Thematic Approach*, ed. Derek H. Aldcroft and Simon P. Ville, (Manchester: Manchester University Press, 1994), 158–63.

27 David Mc Gregor, "The Wooden Sailing Ship over 300 Tons", in *Sail's Last Century*, op. cit., 29.

Full rigged ships, barques, barquentines, brigs and schooners were all achievements of northern European and north Atlantic maritime technology, and were imposed gradually in the Mediterranean and the rest of the world as the dominant technology that standardized shipbuilding production in the field of trump shipping.[28]

Therefore, wooden shipbuilding in Syros during the period under examination was not a backward reality in a much-modernized international environment. The actual differences related more to the size of vessels built, and to the technical design of the hull and rigging, rather than the level of technology used in the shipyards. There are more similarities between Syros and the shipyards of other countries in the organization of production, in relations of production, in the level of technology and construction methods. This is due to the fact that they all occupied a different place in the supply chain and transport services of the most internationalized sector of modern times: the seaborne trade.

Factors of Rise of Syros Wooden Shipbuilding in the Nineteenth Century

A basic precondition for the creation and evolution of an economic activity is the existence of a level of demand that is able to mobilize the supply forces to organize the production process. In Syros, demand comes from the merchant and shipowning class of the town itself and, more broadly, from the shipowners of the Aegean and Ionian maritime communities, such as Hydra, Andros, Santorini, and Cephalonia, as well as from Greek diaspora merchants from Black Sea and Mediterranean ports. All the above seafarers and merchants formed the shipowning class of the Greek-owned fleet, who from the eighteenth century were already specialized in the grain trade between eastern Mediterranean and the Black Sea to western ports. Greek commercial firms established in Mediterranean and Black Sea ports, and even in Northern Europe (England, the Netherlands) had already created networks of cooperation before the formation of the Greek national state in 1830, in order to control the production, the price and the trade in cereals and other bulk

28 Tommaso Fanfani, "Lo scenario generale", in *La penisola italiana e il mare. Costruzioni navali trasporti e commerci tra XV e XX secolo*, ed., Tommaso Fanfani, (Naples: Edizione Scientifica Italiana, 1993), 4–6.

commodities.[29] Greek shipowners, who sometimes coincided with the above merchants, were the main carriers serving these Greek commercial networks, and they financed the construction of new sailing vessels to meet the demand for grain trade transport services and for trump shipping in general.

A second precondition for the growth of a productive activity such as shipbuilding is labour, which was available in great numbers in Syros. A considerable segment of this large workforce had previously worked extensively in the shipyards of Ottoman Greece, and had acquired important skills, experience, and know-how in ship construction. Furthermore, this labour force owned no property and had settled in an urban environment with no alternative source of income from agriculture or stockraising. They thus ideally fulfilled a basic requirement of industrial growth.

Syros was a small and arid island without productive resources or raw materials, and this could have been a stimulus for the development of productive activity, insofar as all the necessary shipbuilding materials, such as timber, iron, canvas, pitch, tar, and hemp were imported, contrary to other Greek areas like Galaxidi, Skiathos, and Skopelos, which at least had important timber resources available nearby. Nevertheless, in this period Syros was the most important maritime centre in the Eastern Mediterranean, and shipbuilding materials, maritime stores and other commodities flocked to its warehouses in great quantities, making access to essential inputs an easier and perhaps less expensive task. According to the externalities theory proposed by Alfred Marshall, one advantage of the agglomeration of small scale enterprises in industrial districts (a result of localization economies) was the easier and less costly access to basic inputs, due to the proximity of the agglomerating enterprises to the market.[30]

The cost of land for shipbuilding enterprises in Syros was extremely low. This was no different from other areas worldwide, as the infrastructure of a private pre-industrial shipbuilding yard was rudimentary and low cost, and could easily be transferred to many beaches, bays and havens if necessary, making land a low cost factor.[31] The land in Syros, a sandy beach on the western coast

29 Gelina Harlaftis, *A History of Greek-Owned Shipping: The Making of an International Tramp Fleet, 1830 to the Present Day*, (London and New York: Routledge, 1996), 8–51.

30 Masahisa Fujita & Jaques-Francois Thisse, *Economics of Agglomeration, Cities, Industrial Location and Regional Growth*, (Cambridge: Cambridge University Press, 2002), 7–8; Ash Amin, "Industrial Districts", in *A Companion to Economic Geography*, ed. Eric Sheppard & Trevor J. Barnes, (Malden-Oxford, Victoria: Blackwell Publishing, 2003), 152–53.

31 Ville, "Shipbuilding in the Northeast", in *Shipbuilding in the United Kingdom in the 19th Century: a Regional Approach*, Research in Maritime History, 4, ed., Simon Ville, (St John's,

of its harbour, belonged to the municipality and the state: shipbuilders paid between 15 and 20 drachmas per ship, and over time, some of the wealthiest shipbuilders managed to appropriate the plots where they had established their yards.[32] In Syros, at the end of 1820s, it seems that all the necessary conditions were in place for the creation of the shipbuilding industry. Its integration in a market economy of international scale and the evolution of the port into one of the most important maritime centres mobilized the productive forces, who exploited the advantages and the business opportunities offered by this great port of the newly founded Greek Kingdom.

The Search for the Competitive Advantage

During the first decades that followed the foundation of the Greek Kingdom, Hermoupolis was one of the three "*poles of urban development*" along with Patras and Piraeus, and was the second largest city of Greece until 1870. Patras was an export centre, mainly of currants from Peloponnese, the staple of the Greek economy throughout the nineteenth century, and Piraeus developed at a steady but very slow pace until 1860. Thus, Hermoupolis was the only sizeable urbanized centre of developed economic life and capital flows integrated into the international economy. At the time, Greece was a thinly populated and geographically fragmented country, without a unified internal market.[33] At a regional level, the important port-cities in the eastern Mediterranean, such as Thessaloniki, Smyrna, Constantinople and Alexandria all faced serious infrastructural port inadequacies for the growing movement of ships, and all lacked the necessary levels of market organization. Along with other institutional problems and issues of internal order, this made Hermoupolis the only integrated and specialized maritime market in the heart of the Aegean, on the route between western ports and Constantinople and the Black Sea ports.[34]

It appears that the concepts of the market and the city are complementary: it is hard to imagine the existence of one in the absence of the other. Although the identification of a market with a specific physical space is not the only way

---

Newfoundland: International Economic History Association, 1993), 33–34; in the same volume see also: Starkey, "The Shipbuilding Industry of Southwest England, 1790–1913," 92.

32 Kardasis, *Σύρος*, 176.

33 Agriantoni, *Οι Απαρχές*, 77–105; Idem, «Η ελληνική οικονομία», *Ιστορία του Νέου Ελληνισμού, 1770–2000*, ['Greek Economy', *History of Modern Hellenism*, 1770–2000], vol. 5, (Athens: Ellinika Grammata, 2003), 59.

34 Donald Quataert, "The Age of Reforms, 1812–1914", in *An Economic and Social History of the Ottoman Empire, 1300–1914*, ed. Halil Inacik and Donald Quataert, (Cambridge: Cambridge University Press, 1994), 802; Newspaper *Ἑρμῆς*, n. 239, 16.10.1843, n. 244, 20.11.1843 and n. 247, 11.12.1843.

to conceive it, this is its primordial form, and is an essential structural element in an urban environment.[35] The theory of urbanization economies offers a plausible explanation for the development of markets in urban environments and of the fundamental reasons for the creation of urban areas. According to economic geography theory, these reasons include the reduction of transport costs, handling, distribution, and the supply of goods and the exchange of ideas.[36] Cities are institutional and physical spaces of contact and transaction, facilitated by existent infrastructures and access to goods, services, and markets, which reduce transaction costs considerably.[37] Parallel phenomena or consequences of urbanization include the localization of economies, which often develop in urban environments, and firms or industrial units of the same or similar field concentrated in a specific area, which reduces costs due to the easier and cheaper access to inputs, services, institutions, and innovations.[38]

The two types of economies described are the basic forms of agglomeration economies. Agglomeration economies have been used as a basic analytical and explanatory tool in the study of urban and regional growth. It has been suggested that the concentration of many firms in a specific area is a key factor in success, especially as far as regards the issues of increasing returns and the competitiveness between cities or regions. Increasing returns are obtained through pecuniary externalities, productivity externality, and innovation externality. In competitive situations, agglomeration contributes to the reduction of transaction costs between firms, thanks to spatial proximity, personal contact, and vertical disintegration, which push firms to concentrate on their basic activity, served by other suppliers of goods and services in the local market.[39] Agglomeration economies theory was refined by Porter, who developed the theory of clusters, emphasizing the importance of geographic position as a key element in the competitive advantage of firms.[40] According to

35 Richard Swedberg, "Markets in Society", in *The Handbook of Economic Sociology*, ed. Neil J. Smelser and Richard Swedberg (Princeton and Oxford: Princeton University Press, 2005), 238.

36 Edward L. Glaeser, "Urban and Regional Growth", in *The Oxford Handbook of Economic Geography*, ed. Gordon Clark, Maryann Feldman and Meric Gerlter (Oxford: Oxford University Press, 2003), 84.

37 Neil M. Coe, Philip F. Kelly & Henry W.C. Yeung, *Economic Geography. A Contemporary Introduction*, (Malden-Oxford-Victoria: Blackwell Publishing, 2007), 137.

38 Coe et al., *Economic Geography*, 137; Peter Sunley, "Urban and Regional Growth", in *A Companion to Economic Geography*, op. cit., 192–93.

39 Sunley, "Urban and Regional Growth", 188–94; Coe et al. *Economic Geography*, 137.

40 Michael E. Porter, "Locations, Clusters, and Company Strategy", in *The Oxford Handbook of Economic Geography*, op. cit., 253–73.

localization economies theory, similar advantages are enjoyed by industrial districts. Alfred Marshall groups these under three basic categories: (a) advantages due to the formation of a local pool of labour; (b) advantages due to the proximity of suppliers and auxiliary firms in the same or relative sector; (c) advantages due to the circulation of knowledge, information, and innovation through the local network.[41] Moreover, the non verticalized structure of small and medium production units leads to a further division of labour and to specialization in a specific product or phase of production, thus developing a kind of complementarity and interdependence. The above conditions create broader impacts on the urban environment and its social fabric. This is what Marshall named the "*industrial atmosphere*", a culture according to which a city's specialized industrial activity becomes part of an urban identity, incorporated into local consciousness as an integral part. It creates a system of moral values between local firms, and generally reinforces firms through the mutual and informal flow of knowledge, ideas, and techniques, as well as through brand awareness in the region and identification of firms as producers of a given product.[42]

Elements of both forms of agglomeration economy (urbanization and localization economies) can be seen in the port of Syros. All kinds of shipping and trade businesses were concentrated in the urban area of the harbour and town, and these were able to take advantage of their access to the most internationalized market in the Aegean. The eastern and central parts of the harbour specialized in the commercial activities of the port. The custom house, the transit trade warehouses, coffee houses, stores, etc. were located there. The western part saw a concentration of the 'industrial' activities of shipping and trade, the ship repairing zone and the shipbuilding yards. In Syros, the access to inputs was easier than elsewhere in the Aegean, as long as the port was the main depot for various commodities, including the necessary raw materials and the maritime stores for ships and shipbuilding. Furthermore, the presence of numerous specialized craftsmen in various industries related to shipbuilding did not lead shipbuilding enterprises to verticalize, but instead to focus upon their main activity. Another important effect of the proximity of businesses in Syros was information spillover, as ideas, innovations and techniques

---

41 Sunley, "Urban and Regional Growth", 188; Philip McCann, "Regional Development: Clusters and Districts", in *The Oxford Handbook of Entrepreneurship*, ed. Mark Casson, Bernard Yeung, Anuradha Basu and Nigel Wadeson, (New York: Oxford University Press, 2006), 655–56.

42 Amin, "Industrial Districts", 152–53; Bjorn T. Asheim, "Industrial Districts", in *The Oxford Handbook of Economic Geography*, op. cit., 415–16; Coe et al. *Economic Geography*, 139.

were transmitted from craftsman to craftsman: working next to one other, they developed relations of cooperation, trust, competition, and interdependence. Generally, the concentration of related businesses and industries in the port of Syros had a significant effect on transaction costs saving. Its market provided the possibility of building or repairing a ship or of purchasing a second-hand one; as documentation shows, in the same area and in a very short time, it was possible to hire a captain and crew or to raise a maritime loan and charter a ship, which was a particular cost advantage for local and non-local shipowners and captains. Therefore, the competitive advantage of Syros's shipbuilding industry lies in the port-city itself, as a geographic location as well as an economic entity, an expanded market with diversified activities.

In Syros, shipbuilding seems to have occupied a central position in the symbolic representation of the achievements of the city, as reported in newspapers and local history texts. The existence and the prosperity of Syros were identified with trade, shipping, and industry, and shipbuilding had a primary position in this scheme: furthermore, rise or recession in production was used as an indicator of the city's general economic course. Indeed, it seems that the "*industrial atmosphere*" was part of everyday life, and that Syros was considered the shipbuilding centre *par excellence*, at both the national and inter-regional level, with a particular reputation for the quality of its ship construction.

The official institutions of the port-city, such as the chamber of commerce, the custom house and the transit trade administration, along with the informal institutions such as the business networks among the actors within the port and more widely along Mediterranean, western European and Black Sea ports, were integrated into economic life, defining the character and the dominant mentality of the city. The phenomenon of embeddedness, as it has been defined, refers to the integration of institutions, traditions and cultures, and is an important dimension in any search for a complete evaluation of the competitive advantage of cities.[43] Similar importance has been accorded to the historical and geographical trajectory of each city, connected to the uniqueness of its historical role, as determined by conjuncture and the broader political and economic context, which is dynamic and in a constant state of change.[44] Syros formed its own path dependence in the given historical conjuncture, determined by its geographical position, its insular particularity, the dominant

43 Eric Sheppard, "Competition in Space and Between Places", in *A Companion to Economic Geography*, op. cit., 180; Mark Granovetter, "Economic action and social structure: The problem of Embeddedness", in *The sociology of economic life*, ed. Mark Granovetter and Richard Swedberg, (Colorado-Oxford: Westview Press, 2001), 51–76.

44 Sheppard, "Competition in Space and Between Places", 180–81.

mentality and accumulated expertise of its population (elites and non-elites) in commercial, maritime and industrial activities. Syros defined its historical evolution and created its own competitive advantage, which also established the position and evolution of its shipbuilding industry.[45]

Factors of Decline in the Syros Shipbuilding during the Nineteenth Century

The decline of wooden shipbuilding in Syros, which became evident in 1870, is a complex phenomenon. Its first symptoms, due to structural causes in the shipping and shipbuilding sector, first appeared during the 1850s. The factors which decisively contributed to the decline of demand for new sailing ships and the loss of eminence of wooden shipbuilding in Syros and in the Greek economy can be grouped under three categories: (a) the increasing penetration of steam at the expenses of sail in maritime transports in the last quarter of the nineteenth century; (b) the role of maritime markets and the new economic context in shipping during the same period; (c) the shift of capital to other more profitable forms of investments, like factories.

The Role of Steam

According to contemporary perceptions of the problems faced by Greek-owned shipping, a basic cause was the rapid penetration of the steamer in the last quarter of the nineteenth century into markets and routes that had traditionally been dominated by sailing ships. The identification of a Greek-owned merchant marine with the sailing ship was due to the strong dependencies of the maritime communities with economic, social, and cultural causes. The new technology of steam required structural changes in the organization and operation of the shipping enterprise. It required high initial capital investment, high operating costs of the ship, and different specialized capabilities and skills on the part of seamen, which had a profound effect on the knowledge, values, and attitudes of maritime communities, and undermined the income, survival, prosperity and social norms and institutions that had developed over the years around the economy of sailing shipping.[46] Despite the fact

45 Douglass North, *Institutions, Institutional Change and Economic Performance*, (Cambridge: Cambridge University Press, 1990), 112–17.

46 *Έκθεσις περὶ τῆς καταστάσεως τῆς Ἑλληνικῆς Ναυτιλίας καὶ περὶ τῶν ληπτέων κυβερνητικῶν μέτρων πρὸς ἐμψύχωσιν καὶ προαγωγίν αυτῆς.* [*Report on the situation of the Greek merchant marine and the Government measures for its encouragement and promotion*] Συνταχθεῖσα

that the supplanting of sail by steam was widely accepted and was a reality that people engaged in shipping experienced in the last two decades of the nineteenth century, it is especially interesting that this was accompanied by the strongly ingrained belief that the sailing ship would not disappear, despite the advances of steam, and that it would remain a constant and advantageous alternative form of maritime transport.[47] Different proposals based upon this belief were advanced during the period, proposing support of the sailing merchant marine by the government through subsidies for new built ships, tax exemption for imported shipbuilding material, nautical and technical education, organization of the legal framework, and with reference to relevant projects carried out in other countries in the period, such as France and Italy.[48]

Sailing ships remained competitive at least until 1914 in certain markets and on certain routes, such as the coastal trade and on some oceanic routes that steamships had not yet penetrated.[49] However, this was not enough to support the growth of productive activity and a range of auxiliary trades, which had lost their roles as the basic suppliers for sailing ships in trump shipping. A consequence of the reduction of demand for sailing ships was the gradual marginalization of Syros wooden shipbuilding from 1870s, which addressed an increasingly shrinking market and was considered technologically obsolete. It is perhaps indicative that the average tonnage of the ships built in the years 1872–74 and 1879–81 amounted to less than one hundred tons.[50]

ὑπὸ Ἐπιτροπῆς διορισθείσης ὑπὸ τοῦ Ὑπουργείου τῶν Ναυτικῶν [By a committee of the Ministry of Marine], Syros, 1899, 9.

47 Πρακτικά Επιτροπής Εμποροπλοιάρχων Σύρου, «Περὶ ἐμψυχώσεως τῆς ἑλληνικῆς ἐμπορικῆς ναυτιλίας», [Proceedings of the Committee of Syros captains, "For the encouragement of the Greek Merchant Marine"], Syros, 1881, 5–15; A contrary view to this belief expressed by the Ithaki shipowner I. Theofilatos, who questioned the long term survival of sailing ship to the progresses of steam navigation technology in a paper published in A.N. Vernardakis, *Περὶ τοῦ ἐν Ἑλλάδι ἐμπορίου.*[*About the commerce in Greece*], (Athens: 1885), 245.

48 Πρακτικά Επιτροπής Εμποροπλοιάρχων Σύρου, 16–31; *Ἔκθεσις περὶ τῆς καταστάσεως…*, 9–13, 35–39.

49 Vernardakis, *Περὶ τοῦ ἐν Ἑλλάδι ἐμπορίου*, 193; *Ἔκθεσις περὶ τῆς καταστάσεως…*, 10; Marco Doria, "La marina mercantile a vela in Liguria dalla metà dell'Ottocento alla prima guerra mondiale", in *A Vela e a Vapore. Economie, culure e istituzioni del mare nell' Italia dell' Ottocento*, ed. Paolo Frascani, (Rome: Donzelli Editore, 2001), 105–07.

50 F.O. Syra, *Diplomatic & Consular Reports on Trade & Finance, Greece, Syros*, 1871–1881.

The Role of the Markets

At the international level, in the period 1860–90 the price of a sailing ship fell by a third due to technical improvements and the fall of the price of iron, which favoured metal hull construction.[51] Along with this, freight rates also decreased in the three last decades of the nineteenth century, and remained at a lower level than in the pre-1870 period, forcing shipowners to seek ways to reduce their operating costs. Furthermore, in the 1850s the world tonnage capacity increased by 50% and by a third in the next decade. Given that the average life of a sailing ship is fifteen to twenty years, the return to increased demand for new tonnage took several years.[52] Thus, in the last thirty years of the nineteenth century, there was an oversupply of sailing ships in the markets, especially from Britain, at the expense of orders for new ships. Most second hand sailing vessels were bought by countries with a sailing shipping tradition that had not yet completed the transition to steam, such as Norway, Finland, and Greece.[53]

Foreign purchases of second-hand sailing ships from Greek shipowners in the 1870s and 1880s had a clear impact on the new building market and the Syros shipyards, which were a major supplier of the Greek-owned fleet.

According to Table 2.1, the ratio of new ships was higher than Syros port registry in the 1840s, which meant that the Syros shipyards were theoretically able to cover the demand of Syros ship registry, which in turn held 21.9% of the entire Greek-owned fleet in 1840s and 27.33% over the examined period (1845–75). In 1850, the percentage of shipbuilding output in relation to port registry reduced by 40%, compared to the previous period (1846–50), but real recession is documented in 1860s, which culminated in 1871–75 when the sailing ships built covered only 23.79% of the Syros port registry. In this period, the latter (along with the total of Greek-owned fleet) reached its highest levels in

51 Harley, "Aspects of the Economics", 173–74.

52 Lewis R. Fischer – Helge W. Nordvik, «Θαλάσσιες μεταφορές και ενοποίηση της οικονομίας του βόρειου Ατλαντικού, 1850–1914», ["Maritime transports and integration of the North Atlantic economies, 1850–1914"], in *Ιστορία και Ναυτιλία*, [*History and Shipping*], ed. Gelina Harlaftis, (Athens: Stachi Publishers, 2001), 277–78, 290–94; Harley, "Aspects of the Economics", 170, 181–82.

53 Yrjö Kaukiainen, "Aspects of competition between steam and sail", in *Sail and Steam: selected maritime writings of Yrjö Kaukiainen*. Research in Maritime History, 27, ed. Lars U. Scholl & Merja-Liisa Hinkkanen, (St John's, Newfoundland: International Economic History Association, 2004), 120; Marco Doria, "La marina mercantile", 104; Simon Ville, "Transport and Communications", in *The European Economy. A thematic approach, 1750–1914*, op. cit., 184–215; Harlaftis, *A History of Greek-owned shipping*, 140; Kaukiainen, *A History of Finnish*, 104, 108, 123.

TABLE 2.1 *Ratio of shipbuilding output/registered ships in Syros, 1841–75.*

Period	Capacity of new ships built	Capacity of registered ships	Percentage of ships built on ship registry %
1841–1845	39,570.73	37,726	104.88
1846–1850	75,807.74	67,206	112.80
1851–1855	40,250.18	66,972	60.10
1856–1860	41,274.47	54,741	75.40
1861–1865	22,245.46	83,198	26.74
1866–1870	85,356.35	151,239	56.44
1871–1875	35,741.00	150,226	23.79

Source: Delis 'Ερμούπολη (Σύρος)', 68.

terms of tonnage capacity. The oversupply of sailing ships of the Greek-owned fleet, a fact that was also due to the purchases of many foreign second-hand sailing vessels, was to cause a deep recession and decline in Syros shipbuilding, from which it would never recover. Greek-owned sailing ships would continue to operate as long as they proved to be a viable and profitable option for their owners; nevertheless, their numerical superiority shrunk significantly from 1875 to 1902, when the total capacity of steamships surpassed that of sailing ships, and the transition from sail to steam took place.[54]

The Reallocation of Resources

A third factor, perhaps related to the decline of wooden shipbuilding, was the capital shift to industries from the 1860s onwards. Looking first at the international level, we must mention the shift of capital from sailing shipping to the factories and towards landlubber investments in general, from various countries with previously extensive deep sea sailing fleets and developed shipbuilding industries. In the USA, from the second half of the 1850s, the ocean sailing fleet was already collapsing, due to the increased construction costs in relation to its main competitor (Great Britain). Its protective maritime policy after the Civil War, which led to the loss of external markets, discouraged investments in shipping, and shifted capital to other sectors such as the manufacturing

54 Harley, "Aspects of the Economics", 173; Harlaftis, *A History of Greek-owned shipping*, 133.

industry.[55] In Atlantic Canada, a similar shift to industrial type investments was started in the 1870s by former shipowners, who played an important role in the industrialization of the country. Finland also experienced this shift towards industrialization in the two last decades of the nineteenth century, through investments in the processing of wood products, when this material was no longer an advantage for the country's shipbuilding industry after the fall in demand for wooden sailing ships.[56]

In Hermoupolis, the first developed mechanized sectors were related to manufacturing activities (milling and tannery) with an established history in the local economy.[57] According to Christina Agriantoni, the first appearance of mechanized production in these two sectors therefore seemed to be a normal evolution of previous developed activities within a new technological and organizational context. From the beginning of the 1860s, the appearance of steam powered mills and investments in the milling industry were related to rearrangements in the international grain trade after the Crimean War. As a result, there were related efforts to preserve the international character of the port of Syros as an export port, after it lost its importance as a centre of the transit trade, and to support the sailing merchant marine, which was strictly connected to and dependent upon the grain trade. Despite initial intentions, the shift of investments eventually resulted in "*the first massive reallocation of resources and labor to industry, thus inaugurating the changes in the local economy that would be completed two decades later.*"[58] In 1872, there were eleven factories in Hermoupolis, most of these steam powered mills and tanneries. Two years later the number had fallen to six, due to the 1870s recession in industrial activity in Greece, after the boom of the previous decade.[59] Unfortunately, our

55 Safford, "The Decline of the American Merchant", 81; John G.B. Hutchins "The Declining American Maritime Industries: An Unsolved Problem, 1860–1940", *The Journal of Economic History*, vol. 6, Supplement: The Tasks of Economic History, (May 1946), 111; Albert Faucher, "The Decline of Shipbuilding at Quebec in the Nineteenth Century", *The Canadian Journal of Economics and Political Science / Revue canadienne d'Economique et de Science politique*, vol. 23, n. 2, (May, 1957), 206–08; Daniel Vickers with Vince Walsh, *Young Men and the Sea. Yankee Seafarers in the Age of Sail*, (New Haven-London: Yale University Press, 2005), 211–13.

56 Sager-Panting, "Staple Economies and the Rise and Decline of the Shipping Industry in Atlantic Canada, 1820–1914", in *Change and Adaptation in Maritime History*, op. cit., 28–29; Kaukiainen, *A History of Finnish Shipping*, 123–25.

57 Kardasis, *Σύρος*, 148–58.

58 Agriantoni, "Προσαρμογές του επιχειρηματικού κόσμου", 145–48.

59 F.O. Syra, *Diplomatic & Consular Reports on Trade & Finance, Greece, Syros*, 14.12.1872 and 16.12.1874.

data are very scarce, and do not give a clear picture of the source of funds in industry or their reallocation from shipbuilding to factories. There were clear connections between the industrialists and the merchant class in Hermoupolis, and the shift of some local capitalists from trade and shipping to factories has been proven: still, we cannot state with any certainty the facts concerning the reallocation of capital from one sector to another. Similar problems face the reallocation of human labour; there were two hundred workers in the tanneries in 1853, and the number had increased to six hundred in 1872, including those who working in the town's three steam powered tanneries and in non-steam powered enterprises.[60] According to the Municipality Rolls, the occupational category of worker/journeyman in the 1860s and 1870s increased considerably, whereas tanners were almost identified as factory workers. At the same time, the number of occupational categories (shipbuilding, carpenters, joiners and sawyers) also increased, which does not facilitate the formulation of hypotheses about the reallocation of human resources from shipyards to tanneries or to other factories more generally. Furthermore, it is hard to believe that factories would have hired specialized craftsmen that had been trained and worked their art in a semi-independent state (such as shipbuilding workers), and then turned them into disciplined factory workers engaged in a totally different kind of work.

The Transition to Steam: Continuities and Discontinuities

Despite the founding of the factory of the *Hellenic Steam Navigation Company* in Syros in 1861, it remained a repairing unit, and did not contribute to the training of shipbuilders for work in the new steam technology. Generally, Greek wooden shipbuilders had very little if any involvement in the construction or repair of steamships. The new technology of steam engines and metal processing was an achievement of the class of engineers, who mostly came from the 'workshop of the world.' Their lack of this specific knowledge, along with the issues of necessary capital (and perhaps mentality) kept traditional shipbuilders apart from any engagement in modern shipbuilding, with the exception of the construction of a wooden dock, built by the Syros shipbuilder Nikolaos Pagidas for the *Hellenic Steam Navigation Company* in 1857. The phenomenon of the transition from wooden to modern shipbuilding by engineers

60 Kardasis, *Σύρος*, 153; F.O. Syra, *Diplomatic & Consular Reports on Trade & Finance, Greece, Syros*, 14.12.1872.

(not traditional shipbuilders) was not a Greek particularity, but also occurred in other countries, such as the USA and Britain.[61]

Although the Syros shipbuilders were not involved in steamship construction and had no impact in the modernization of the Greek-owned trump fleet, the fact remains that Syros was the shipping and shipbuilding centre of the eastern Mediterranean, and its accumulated funds and expertise were instrumental in the establishment of the steamship company, the dissemination of steam, and the transition of some Greek shipowners to steam navigation. During the period of the massive shift of Greek shipowners to steamships between 1880 and 1910, Syros merchants and bankers held the largest share of any investing groups in the Greek-owned steamship fleet, as compared to other capitalists from Constantinople, the Black Sea and the Bank of Athens. Very wealthy capitalists from the Syros shipping market like the Chiot merchants, Negrepontes, Mavrocordatos and Vafiadakis, along with factory owners like Tsiropinas, Ladopoulos and Karellas, financed Greek shipowners like the Chiots (established in Chios) Andreadis, Pithis and Los, Kouloukountis from Kasos, and Leonardos Vatis, who was originally from Andros but had long-since settled in Syros.[62]

Overall, during all this period up to now, both modern and wooden traditional shipbuilding have co-existed in Syros. The former, known as *Neorion Shipyards*, was and still is mainly a repairing unit but with significant improvements and upgrades in infrastructure, mainly since 1970, remains today the only industrial establishment of the city despite it struggles to survive. On the other hand wooden shipbuilding and ship repairing zones from the turn to the twentieth century and due to the decline of the sailing seagoing ship, were more and more specialized in the construction and repairing of small coasters, fishing boats and caiques as long as these types of vessels provide employment and income in Greece.

61 Thiesen, *Industrializing American Shipbuilding*, 17–23.

62 Harlaftis, *A History of Greek-owned shipping*, 136–39.

CHAPTER 3

Production, Productivity, and Performance of the Shipbuilding Industry

Shipbuilding Cycles, Historical Conjuncture, and Productive Performance

This analysis will focus predominantly on new ships, since historical data for ship repairs are insufficient and do not allow one to construct a systematic series of costs and prices. Nonetheless, it is still possible to offer a general picture about procedures and costs based on select examples. The main corpus of data is available from notarial sources from the General State Archive of Syros and concern the years 1828–1866. From 1870–1880 documentation is based on aggregate figures from the British Consul of Syros and from 1867–1870 on the Historical Register of Shipping '*Pontoporeia*.'[1]

A first step in any evaluation of the shipbuilding production of Syros is to estimate its total share of the entire Greek-owned fleet.

According to Figure 3.1, the share of Syros' shipbuilding production as a percentage of the Greek-owned fleet is higher in the 1840s and the 1850s, but it declines markedly in the following two decades. Even if a share of 19.44% and 13% in the 1860s and 1870s is far from negligible, especially if one considers that this total comprises a very wide geographical market of new and second-hand ships, it is clearly below the total market share during the previous decades, when the island of Syros was the focal centre of the Greek-owned merchant marine. The data identifies a gradual loss in the island's eminence as a centre for the merchant marine. A similar trend is noticeable in the shipbuilding production's share to the port registry of Syros (see Table 2.1), where a gradual, yet steady decline is noted beginning in the 1860s.

Shipbuilding Industry and the Markets

Trends in shipbuilding output are related to the markets in which the production is addressed and integrated. These markets are subdivided into: a) the wider world market and the regional dependent markets of various commodities (e.g. raw materials, processed, semi-processed, or industrial products), which according to their size and type influenced the volume of

1 Harlaftis – Vlassopoulos, *Historical Register 'Pontoporeia'*.

© KONINKLIJKE BRILL NV, LEIDEN, 2016 | DOI 10.1163/9789004306158_005

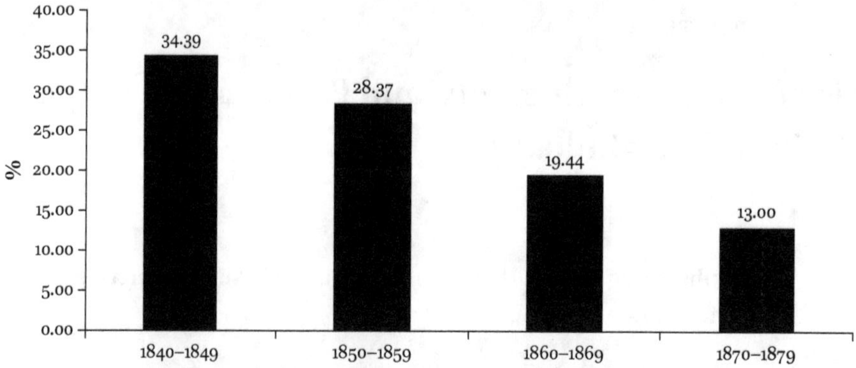

FIGURE 3.1 *Percentage of Syros' shipbuilding output in tonnage compared to the total Greek-owned fleet, 1840–1879.*
SOURCE: PROCESSED DATA FROM APPENDIX 3.2.1.

SCHEME 3.1 *Articulation of markets in the maritime transport business.*

trade and the entire business of maritime transport; and b) the shipping market itself, of which shipbuilding along with the freight market and the market for second-hand vessels were integrated parts.[2] As is natural, the shipping market was dependent on trends in the world and regional markets. It was predominantly the supply factor which responds to the demand for transport services.[3] Therefore, the growth or the shrinking of a fleet, and the

2 Stopford, *Maritime Economics*, 77–80, 114–17.

3 Stopford, *Maritime economics*, Table 4.1, 115; Basil Metaxas, *The Economics of Tramp Shipping*, (London: Athlone Press, 1971), 43–44.

current state of affairs in the shipping market, tended to align with the course of international and regional trade, and it was certainly influenced by the same factors which affected trade.[4]

The factors that affected demand are distinguished to exogenous and endogenous. The exogenous factors were multiple and included events such as wars, political changes, and governmental decisions, but also phenomena like bad harvests, natural disasters, and climatic changes.[5] The endogenous factors were related to the structure and the dynamics of the international and regional economy and the mechanisms of responsiveness and adjustment to contemporary economic situations and their eventual changes.[6] Freight rates are especially good indicators of market trends, as they reflect a balance between the supply and demand of shipping services. When there was an abundance of ships, freight rates fell, yet when there was a scarcity they tended to rise, ultimately influencing the decisions of shipowners for new investments.[7]

Generally, freight rates were subjected to great fluctuations due to the elasticity of demand and the difficulties of supply to make timely adjustments, especially in the short term when supply levels remain inelastic.[8] Fluctuations in freight rates also led to the phenomenon of shipping cycles in the markets. These cycles were constantly repetitive, if not predictable for its evolution and duration, and became endemic phenomena in the function of the shipping industry. Ultimately, they sought to equilibrate between supply and demand. The duration, as it is said, was never a given, but it was distinguished in two types of cycles: a) the short-term, which could last a few years, and b) the long-term, which could last for decades.[9] Shipping cycles were distinguished in four consecutive phases, which according to Stopford are (1) trough, (2) recovery, (3) peak, and (4) collapse, and according to Metaxas (1) recovery, (2) peak, (3) fall, and (4) recession.[10]

Shipbuilding as an industry was a depended activity from shipping and transport demand, and it was subjected to the same freight rate fluctuations of

4 Yrjö Kaukiainen, "Growth, diversification and globalization: Main trends in International Shipping since 1850", in *International Merchant Shipping in the 19th and 20th centuries. The comparative dimension*, Research in Maritime History, n. 37, ed. Lewis R. Fischer – Even Lange, (St John, Newfoundland: International Economic History Association, 2008), 2–9; Or as Metaxas states, *The Economics*, 184 "Fluctuations in freight rates tend to synchronize with those of international trade."

5 Metaxas, *The Economics*, 37–40.

6 Stopford, *Maritime economics*, 118–22.

7 Op. cit., 115–17.

8 Metaxas, *The Economics*, 101, 199.

9 Stopford, *Maritime economics*, 38–48.

10 Stopford, *Maritime economics*, Figure 2.1, 43; Metaxas, *The Economics*, 200.

shipping cycles that affected both production and prices. On the demand side, with the exception of freight rates, other important factors were the prices of second-hand vessels, general financial liquidity in the market, the availability of credit, and the expectations of investors.[11]

Shipbuilding Industry of Syros and the Grain Trade: A Case of a Dependent Demand

The shipbuilding production of Syros and the Greek-owned merchant marine were directly interdependent from 1830–1880. Both were integrated into the Mediterranean and Black Sea markets and indirectly in the northern regions of Western Europe and Great Britain.[12] The Greek-owned fleet was specialized already by the second-half of the eighteenth century in the transport of trump cargoes, in particular cereals from the eastern Mediterranean and the Black Sea to ports in the western Mediterranean.[13] Greek specialization in the transport of cereals and other trump cargoes continued after the foundation of the Greek National State in 1830 and became a basic feature of the Greek-owned merchant marine for the entire nineteenth century even up to the present day.[14]

To a large degree, the interconnection of the Greek-owned merchant marine and the transport of cereals were due to the consolidation of entrepreneurial networks of Greek merchants in the port cities of the eastern Mediterranean, e.g. Black Sea, Danube, and Western Europe. Greek business networks were based mainly on trust relationships due to kinship and common origin ties,

---

11 Stopford, *Maritime economics*, 110, 472–74; Siri Pettersen Strandenes, "Economics of the market for ships", in *The handbook of maritime economics and business*, ed. Costas Th. Grammenos (London-Hong Kong: LLP, 2002), 199–200.

12 Gelina Harlaftis, *Ιστορία της Ελληνόκτητης Ναυτιλίας* [*History of the Greek-owned shipping*], (Athens: Nefeli, 2001), 91–108, Table 2.1 and schemes 2.4, 2.5, 2.6 and 2.7.

13 Gelina Harlaftis, "The Fleet 'dei Greci': Ottoman and Venetian Greeks in the Mediterranean Sea-trade, Eighteenth Century", in *Making Waves in the Mediterranean*, ed. M. d'Angelo, G. Harlaftis and C. Vassallo, (Messina: Istituto di Studi Storici Gaetano Salvemini, 2010), 383–416.

14 Harlaftis, *A History of Greek-owned shipping*, 11, 20–21. It is worth to mention a passage of I.N. Theofilatos about the specialization of Greek shipowners to trump cargoes and cereals in the nineteenth century: «*Up to now our merchant marine, except few recent exceptions, was limited to sailing ships, which mainly transported cereals from the ports of Black Sea, the Sea of Azov, the Danube area and the rest of the Eastern Mediterranean, to the ports of Adriatic Sea, Italy, Austria, France, England and Greece, from where they returned most of the times in ballast, except for those who returned from England with coal or other commodities.*» *Οἰκονομική Ἐπιθεώρησις* [*Economic Review*], year 10, n. 118, December 1882, 424–30, republished in Papathanassopoulos, *Ελληνική εμπορική ναυτιλία*, 319.

as well as to a common culture. The most characteristic of this circumstance was Gelina Harlaftis' study into the "*Chiot Network*."[15] From 1833–1860, Greeks controlled 43% of the foreign trade in Odessa, while during the same period specific entrepreneurs such as Rallis, Rodocanachis, Mavros, Papudoff, and Zarifis controlled 62% of the foreign trade in all Greek commercial houses and 26% of the total grain export businesses in the city.[16] The city of Odessa during this period was the main port of export for Black Sea cereals. The main destination ports were Marseille and Livorno, which acted as redistribution centres for cereals to Western Europe, and those destinations where branches of Greek businesses were already well-established.[17] Syros in this context acted as one of the intermediary depots of transit trade, as well as a great maritime and shipbuilding centre in the eastern Mediterranean and, of course, the Greek-owned merchant marine.

Based on the above analysis, there was an obvious connection between the grain trade, the Greek-owned merchant marine, and shipbuilding production. The state of affairs in grain trade was a true barometer for Greek ship owning business, and the freight rates of cereals represented the gauge of demand for transport services. In this context, shipping income became a coefficient that captured the economic performance of shipping entrepreneurship of the period; it was itself influenced by the course of freight rates. Shipbuilding production, in turn, was the second coefficient of response to the changes of demand. This was expressed through changes in freight rates, while the fluctuation of output was considered to be a consequence of the rising or the falling trend of the two variables (shipping income and demand).[18] The response of supply to demand was therefore powered by the flow of capital invested in new ships and originated from the profitability of shipping income.

Any evaluation of Syros' shipbuilding production from 1835–1880 must take place within the context of the shipping market's relation to the freight rate of cereals and shipping income figures. The aim here is to pinpoint the influences of the two related variables on the output and emphasize the main trends of the shipbuilding activity on Syros in the context of the shipping industry. One must take note that shipping was not the only source of capital on the island during the nineteenth century. There were also profits from the

15 Harlaftis, *A History of Greek-owned shipping*, 39–68.

16 Vassilis Kardasis, *Έλληνες ομογενείς στη ΝότιαΡωσία, 1775–1861*. [*Greeks in Southern Russia, 1775–1861*] (Athens: Alexandria, 1998), 196, Table 7.1 and 206 Table 7.4.

17 Harlaftis, *A History of Greek-owned shipping*, 4–8; Kardasis, *Έλληνες ομογενείς*, 124, 181–83, Table 6.8.

18 Metaxas, *The Economics*, 43.

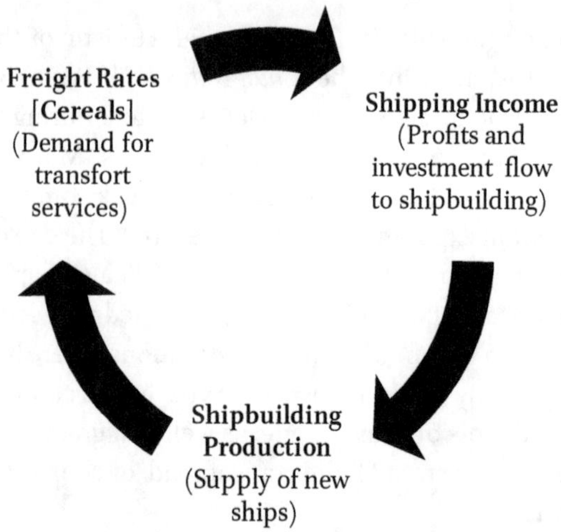

SCHEME 3.2 *Interdepended factors in shipping and shipbuilding industry.*

business activities of merchants, which regrettably is incomplete due to the lack of tangible data.

The prices of freight rates outlined here concern the route between Odessa and Marseille.[19] This route was chosen over Odessa and Livorno or Odessa and Northern Europe since it was more frequent and long lasting. Besides, Livorno lost its competitive advantage as the main centre of redistribution of cereals for Britain and Western Europe, first in 1847 with the repeal of the Corn Laws in Britain and later in 1860 with the city's integration into the Italian National State.[20]

Shipping income, as mentioned above, measures the profitability and growth of shipping. The share of shipping income during the first decades of the Greek Kingdom was one of the basic sources of cash flow for the young economy. The percentage to the total GDP reached as high as 36% from 1835–1845 and 1845–1855, while in the following two decades it fell to 16% and 19% respectively.[21] This demonstrates the special position the sailing merchant

---

19 Gelina Harlaftis and George Kostelenos, "International shipping and national economic growth: shipping earnings and the Greek economy in the nineteenth century", *Economic History Review*, 65, 4, (2012), 1413–14.

20 Despina Vlami, *Το φιορίνι, το σιτάρι και η οδός του Κήπου. Έλληνες έμποροι στο Λιβόρνο 1750–1868.* [*The Florin, the Grain and the Garden Street. Greek Merchant in Livorno, 1750–1868*], (Athens: Themelio, 2000), 170–73.

21 G. Harlaftis and G. Kostelenos, 'Services and economic growth: estimating shipping income in the 19th century Greek economy', Greek Economic History Society working paper (available at http://hdoisto.gr/gr/library/seminar-proceedings), Table 7, 37–38.

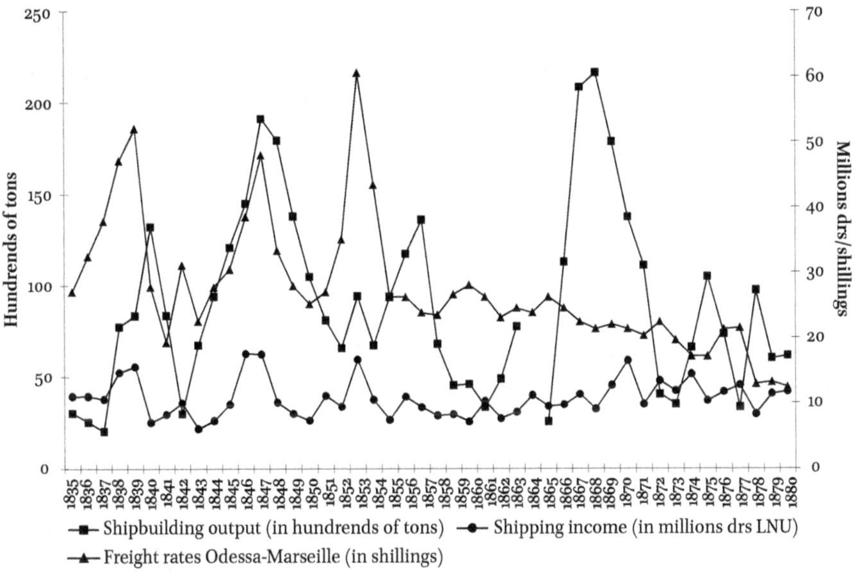

FIGURE 3.2 *Shipbuilding output/Shipping income/Freight rates Odessa – Marseille.*
SOURCE: APPENDIX 3.2.2.

marine held in the Greek economy from 1835–1875. Therefore, shipping income should be viewed as a basic factor, which along with freight rates, influenced the decisions of shipowners for new investments and the general supply of capital to related sectors of the shipping industry.[22] The prices of shipping income taken into consideration here concern all Greek shipping enterprises, not only those belonged in the National State. The shipbuilding yards of Syros served the demands of shipowners active within a much wider geographical framework than just Greece. The state of affairs depended mostly on developments on a regional and international scale.

Long Shipbuilding Cycles

According to Figure 3.2, two long shipbuilding cycles are distinguishable. In the first, comprising the years from 1835–1855, shipbuilding production was harmonious with freight rates and shipping income. If anything this confirms the interconnection between the three and the dependence of the orders for new ships from the other two factors. The second long shipbuilding cycle

22 Ibid., 37. See also the flow of capital from the shipping earnings to the markets of new and second hand ships in Stopford, *Maritime economics*, 80, Figure 3.1.

comprised the years from 1855–1880, when freight rates ceased fluctuating and remained fairly stable at lower prices. The recession of freight rates in the second long cycle were related to the increasing market share gained by steamships transporting cereals from Odessa to England and Western Europe, and a general decline in freight rates during the last quarter of the nineteenth century.[23]

Perhaps the most important factor was that the shipbuilding trends were no longer aligned with the freight rates from Odessa. This is not necessarily an indication that cereals ceased to be a major business enterprise for Greek ships, but, rather, a reminder that the Danube and the Sea of Azov developed into important outlets of the grain trade for Greek ships than they had been before.[24] The loss of the primary importance of Odessa for Greek commercial interests was due in large part to structural changes in the grain trade after the Crimean War (1853–1856), whose conclusion eventually led to the abolishment of serfdom in Russia by 1861. The expanded use of steamships and communication via telegraph also impacted the stability of the transport industry, especially with the sizable penetration of Jewish enterprises in the grain trade that seriously reduced Greek profit margins.[25] Inevitably, these changes affected the market orientation of ships. From 1855 onwards, all consular reports or Syros newspapers regarding Syriot ships mention the arrival of cargoes of cereals from Azov and the Danube, and no longer from Odessa.[26] This shift is further confirmed from the cargoes of cereals from Greek ships that were

23 AMAE, CCC Syra, vol. 5, 17.12.1857, 221; Patricia Herlihy, *Odessa: a history, 1794–1914*, (Cambridge Mass.: Harvard Ukrainian Research Institute, 1986), 107–08; C. Knick Harley, 'Ocean Freight Rates and Productivity, 1740–1913: The Primacy of Mechanical Invention Reaffirmed', *The Journal of Economic History*, 48, 4, (Dec., 1988), 860–61, 863.

24 For the rise of exports of cereals in the Azov area and the preference of the English market for the quality *Ghirka* especially after the Crimean War see, Kardasis, *Έλληνες ομογενείς*, 159, 173, 190.

25 Evridiki Sifneou, 'Οι αλλαγές στο ρωσικό σιτεμπόριο και η προσαρμοστικότητα των ελληνικών εμπορικών οίκων' [The changes in Russian grain trade and the adaptability of the Greek merchant houses], *Τα Ιστορικά-Istorica*, vol. 40, (June 2004), 77–87; Kardasis, *Έλληνες ομογενείς*, 235–36.

26 AMAE, CCC Syra, from vol. 4, 8.8.1855 and every three months up to vol. 5, 21.5.1858; Newspaper *Τηλέγραφος τῶν Κυκλάδων* [*Cyclades Telegraph*], n.59, 16.6.1856, n.87, 31.12.1856, n. 88, 12.1.1857, n. 113, 9.7.1857, n. 118, 13.8.1857; For the Syros ships seeking freight in Constantinople for the Azov and Danube ports see AMAE, CCC, Syra, vol. 4, 5.4.1855, 5.8.1855, 9.9.1855, 24.6.1855, 2.3.1856, vol. 5, 10.9.1856, 4.6.1857, 17.12.1857.

arriving in Marseille in 1860, 1870, and 1880, a period dominated by Galatz, Braila and Taganrog.[27]

Short Shipbuilding Cycles I (1838–61)

The two long shipbuilding cycles are subdivided into shorter cycles, which lasted from a few years up to a decade at the most. An analysis of these patterns helps one understand the deeper causes of fluctuation in production and connects them to historical considerations. Three short cycles are distinguishable within the first: a) 1838–1842, b) 1843–1852, c) 1853–1861.

From 1828–1837, output in production reached a low level. An exception to this trend was in 1833, when output reached 6,355 tons. In the same year, grain prices in Odessa reached their highest figures from 1818–1847.[28] In 1836–1837, Ermoupolis experienced its first deep crisis due to local opposition against the economic policies of the government, the competition of other ports on a regional and international level, and the low demand for cereals from western European countries. The latter was due to good harvests in Europe and instigated the bankruptcy of Greek merchants and barratries of Greek captains.[29] It is characteristic that in 1836–1837 the shipyards on Syros saw their lowest level of production with 2,532 and 2,033 tons respectively.

The year 1838 is considered to be a 'take-off' point for Syriot shipyards.[30] Production was increased by 280% (see Figure 3.2) compared to the previous year and reached 7,746 tons. A similar spike occurred in the same year for the freight rates of grain, shipping income, and grain prices in London and Odessa.[31] This noticeable upward trend in production levels peaked in 1840, when for the first time it surpassed 13,000 tons). Substantial growth was interrupted in 1842, when, due to a second commercial crisis, production fell to 2,989 tons. The current crisis was due to: a) problems of the Eastern Question which affected the bilateral relations of the Ottoman Empire and Greece, and

27 Harlaftis, *A History of Greek-owned shipping*, 307–11.

28 Kardasis, *Έλληνες ομογενείς*, Table 6.7, 178–79.

29 For an extensive analysis of the causes and effects of the crisis in 1836–37 see, Sakelaropoulos, *Οι κρίσεις στην Ελλάδα*, A', 109–31. Crises gave the opportunity to the merchant community of Syros to ask for a free-port status, an issue that was repeated in the entire nineteenth century and became a cause of friction with the Greek government; See AMAE, CCC, Syra, vol. 1, 3.3.1837, 233–234 and 25.4.1838, 310; Also, Kardasis, *Σύρος*, 56.

30 For the use of the term 'take off' in the economic history see W.W. Rostow, "The Beginnings of Modern Growth in Europe: An Essay in Synthesis", *The Journal of Economic History*, 33, 3, (Sept., 1973), 547–80.

31 Kardasis, *Έλληνες ομογενείς*, Table 6.7, 178–79.

the hostile measures of the former against Greek trade and shipping,[32] and b) new legislative and sanitary measures of the Greek government against the liberal ideas of the merchant class of Syros that had negative effects on shipping and trade.[33] One consequence of the crisis was that 600 inhabitants from the quarter of 'Psariana' left Syros and moved to the Ottoman Empire, as the Ottoman government offered economic incentives to those who returned to their homeland.[34] Characteristic of the exogenous factors that affected the shipbuilding production in 1842 is that grain freight rates and shipping income increased considerably compared to the previous two years.

The second short cycle (1843–1852) lasted almost a decade and is often characterised as the 'golden period' of Syriot shipyards and the entire Greek-owned fleet. From this period onward, cereals determined the course of shipping and the shipbuilding business. Its peak occurred in 1847, when shipyards on the island produced a record 19,112 tons. At the same time, other factors of trade and shipping reached similar figures. Grain export from Odessa had a record of 2,016,692 quarters,[35] while shipping income surpassed 62 million drachmae from 1846–1847 compared to 35 million in 1845.[36] As the contemporary McCulloch explained, the peak was due to "*a consequence partly of the abundant harvest of the previous year, and partly and, perhaps principally of the scarcity and high prices which then prevailed in this country and other parts of W. Europe.*"[37] In other words, the catastrophic harvests from 1845–1847 in Western Europe caused an unprecedented demand for cereals from southern Russia, which, among other factors, were directly related to an economic

32 Sakelaropoulos, *Οι κρίσεις στην Ελλάδα*, Α', 153–54; Kardasis, *Σύρος*, 45, 49–52; The French consul in Syros reports that due to the bad diplomatic relations between the two countries, many Greek shipowners used the Russian flag, AMAE CCC, Syra, vol. 2, 18.10.1842, 332.

33 Newspaper *Ἑρμῆς*, [*Hermes*] n. 181, 5.9.1842.

34 AMAE, CCC, Syra, vol. 2, 18.10.1842, 329–31; Newspaper *Ἑρμῆς*, [*Hermes*] n. 181, 5.9.1842, n. 192, 21.11.1842, n. 195–6, 19.12.1842, n. 217, insert, 15.5.1843 «*The neighborhood of the Ipsatiots is anymore completely desert, as happens in the towns and villages during the plague*» and follows below, «*Many families originated from Crete and other parts of Turkey, not able to make a living here, they emigrate every day to their homeland, preferring the joke of the Turks, than poverty and hunger*»; Also, Kardasis, *Σύρος*, 71–72; For the statistical confirmation of the demographic loss in 1842 see Komis, *Ιστορική Δημογραφία*, 95.

35 Mc Culloch, *Dictionary, practical*, 929.

36 In Kardasis, *Ἕλληνες ομογενείς*, 181, table 6.8, in 1847 the cereals prices (shillings/quarter) in London, Marseille and Odessa reach a historical record, while the same happens to the value of exports of cereals in Odessa and Taganrog with 27.836 and 5.385 golden rubles respectively, see Moses Lofley Harvey, "The Development of Russian Commerce on the Black Sea and its Significance", (PhD diss., University of California, 1938), Table XIX a (Appendix G), 392. Patricia Herlihy, *Odessa*, 102, called the year 1847 as *annus mirabilis*.

37 Mc Culloch, *Dictionary, practical*, 929.

crisis in western markets and finally paved the way for the 'Spring of Nations' in 1848.[38]

Euphoria prevailed in the shipping market and led to an increase in investments for new sailing ships in 1848 (17,928 tons). However, this was short lived, since freight rates and shipping income decreased by approximately 50% from 1849–1852.[39] The Greek-owned fleet reached a nadir due to low demand for cereals in western markets, which in turn caused structural shocks in the entire shipping industry and undermined the credibility of the Greek-owned merchant marine due to cases of barratry with Greek captains.[40] The Greek government effectively responded to the problem with the introduction of legislative measures in 1851.[41]

The third short cycle (1853–1861) was also related directly to the grain trade in southern Russia, but mainly to structural changes following the Crimean War (1853–1856) and regional and international transport systems. The factors that influenced the political and economic situation from 1853–1857 were: a) the problems of the Eastern Question that led to the outbreak of the Crimean War, b) a deterioration of diplomatic relations between Greece and the Ottoman Empire that culminated with a severing of ties in April 1854, and c) general problems with exporting Russian grain.[42] 1853 was a recovery year after the previous three years of depression for the shipping industry and led to an increase in shipbuilding production to 9,416 tons. This amounted to an increase of 42.76% from the previous year.[43] Freight rates also reached historical highs (60.60 shillings per ton, see Figure 3.2), while shipping income doubled to about 59 million drachmae, a figure not encountered again until 1870.[44] The upward trend in the shipbuilding industry lasted until 1857, when it reached 13,600 tons. The only exception happened in 1854 (28.45% decrease in relation to 1853), which was a difficult year marked by negative political and diplomatic factors, as well as the spread of cholera in August 1854 from French troops stationed in Piraeus and Syros.[45] From 1855 cereals were imported, not

38 Hearder, *Europe in the 19th century*, 111. Hobsbawm, *The Age of Capital*, chapter A.

39 For the shipowners' tendency to overinvest in prosper periods as an endemic phenomenon in shipping industry see Stopford, *Maritime Economics*, 41–43 and Metaxas, *The Economics*, 224–28.

40 AMAE, CCC, Syra, vol. 3, 24.7.1852, 433–34, and, vol. 3, 4.10.1852, 447; Newspaper *Ἑρμῆς*, [*Hermes*] n. 416, 20.9.1850; Newspaper *Αἴολος*, [*Eolos*] n. 321, 21.4.1851 and n. 322, 3.5.1851.

41 See Chapter One, page 29.

42 Sakelaropoulos, *Οι κρίσεις στην Ελλάδα*, B′, 111; Kardasis, *Σύρος*, 82–83.

43 Newspaper *Αἴολος*, [*Eolos*] n. 470, 24.9.1853 and n. 482, 10.12.1853.

44 For the increase of cereals freight rates from southern Russia bound to Marseille and other ports of the Western Europe, see AMAE, CCC, Syra, vol. 4, 15.11.1853, 103–07.

45 See Chapter One, page 18.

from Odessa, but from the Danube Principalities due to the relocation of the war front in the Crimean peninsula.[46] This change was not temporary, as mentioned above, but shifted in a definitive way the routes of grain trade for Greek ships. The end of the Crimean War had a negative impact for Syros merchants, as well as the entire Greek merchant diaspora and the shipping industry. It led to a long recession in shipbuilding that lasted until 1861. Parallel with these events, the freight rates after the war had a downturn and the Greek-owned fleet decreased in tonnage from 1859–62.[47]

The period from 1853–1857 was perhaps the last prosperous period for the shipbuilding industry on Syros. Afterwards, changes during the second half of the nineteenth century in maritime transport and international trade affected the position of the Greek-owned fleet and the importance of wooden shipbuilding on the island. The globalization of the shipping industry expressed in the widening of the markets, in the trade routes, and in the purchasing of new and second-hand ships brought structural changes that made the shipping services of Syros less vital to a more globally integrated maritime market.[48]

Short Shipbuilding Cycles II (1862–80)

In the context of the second long shipbuilding cycle, the following three short terms are distinguishable: a) 1862–1865, b) 1866–1873 and c) 1874–1877. Data from these periods are not as extensive, being based mostly on aggregate figures. According to the processed data from the Historical Register of Shipping *Pontoporeia*, there was an increase of production from 1867–1870 that began already in 1866. However, reliable information is lacking in order to cross check the causes for this increase. Data from 1871–1880 are aggregate figures from the British consul of Syros. For an analysis of the shipbuilding cycles, the same tools for the shipping income and the prices of freight rates will be followed here, but in this instance the index of freight rates is based on the Norwegian Index created by Helge W. Nordvik covering the years from 1866–1896.[49] Figure 3.3 is complementary to Figure 3.2 and compares part of the latter with more appropriate data.

46 Kardasis, *Σύρος*, 84.

47 Kaukiainen, *A History of Finnish Shipping*, 77; Harley, "Ocean Freight Rates", 875; North, "Ocean Freight Rates", 550–51; Harlaftis, *A History of Greek-owned shipping*, 117.

48 Fischer – Nordvik, "Θαλάσσιες μεταφορές και ενοποίηση", 274–75; Kaukiainen, "Growth, diversification", 30–31; Interesting for the changes in the structure of the shipping industry, the routes and the markets is the comparison between the brigantine from Ithaki 'Odysseus' of 1837 and the barque from Syros 'Anastasia' of 1881, made by Harlaftis, *A History of Greek-owned shipping*, 148–56.

49 Fischer – Nordvik, "Θαλάσσιες μεταφορές", 293.

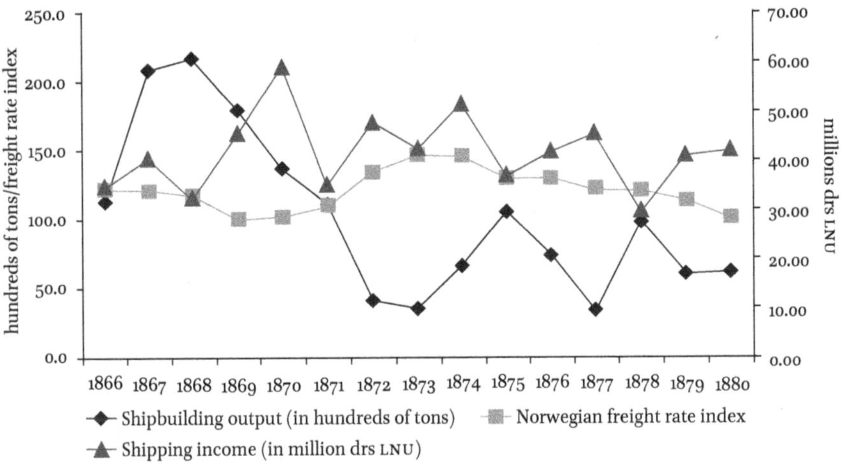

FIGURE 3.3 *Shipbuilding output/Shipping income/Norwegian freight rates index, 1866–80.*
SOURCE: APPENDIX 3.2.3.

The short cycle spanning 1862–1865 was mostly affected by external factors. The abandonment of the throne by King Otho in 1862 led to constitutional changes and the coronation of King George I in 1863. These circumstances helped improve the psychological climate in the markets. In fact, in 1863 shipbuilding output increased 58.66% compared to the previous year.[50] Shipbuilding production, after a considerable increase from 1866–1868, dropped off steadily from 1869–1873, reaching its lowest levels in 1872–1873. Freight rates were fairly stable for the entire period, but generally the last quarter of the century was a period of low prices for freight rates worldwide,[51] while shipping income fluctuated up to 1871 and then stabilized. The temporary rise of shipbuilding production from 1874–1875 was due, according to the British consul of Syros, to a Royal decree that prohibited the cutting of timber from national forests. This decision damaged the shipyards of Galaxidi, the second largest shipbuilding zone of Greece based on its vicinity to timber sources, and shifted many shipowners to the island of Syros.[52] The increased production in 1878 by 191.09% compared to the previous year was mostly due to the expectations

50 F.O. Syra, *Report by Consul Ruby*, 8.2.1873, 272; For the troubles and the fall of King Otho see Newspaper *Ἀστὴρ τῶν Κυκλάδων*, [*Cyclades Star*] n. 263, 29.4.1862, n. 264, 6.5.1862, n. 265, 13.5.1862, n. 266, 20.5.1862 and n. 287–288, 20.10.1862. For the recession in shipbuilding and shipping see idem, n. 277, 4. 8. 1862.

51 Fischer – Nordvik, "Θαλάσσιες μεταφορές", 290–91, Tables 9.6 and 9.7.

52 F.O. Syra, *Report by Consul Binney on the Trade and Commerce of the Cyclades during the Year 1874*, 21.8.1875, 1562.

TABLE 3.1 *General comparison in shipbuilding industry: Provence-Syros-Liguria.*

1835–1839, 1855–1859	Provence	Syros	1838–1852	Liguria	Syros
Number of Vessels	407	623	Number of Vessels	1,024	1,084
Tonnage	53,020	69,807.01	Tonnage	116,641.56	159,478.53
Average Tonnage	130.27	112.05	Average Tonnage	113.9	147.12

Source: Apostolos Delis "Mediterranean Wooden Shipbuilding in the nineteenth century: Production, Productivity and Ship Types in Comparative Perspective", *Cahiers de la Méditerranée*, 84, (2012), 93–4.

of shipowners after the closing of the Straits of Dardanelles during the Russo-Turkish War (1877–1878) and the rise of freight rates as usually happens in wartime.[53]

In an overall evaluation of the connection and the dependence of shipping and shipbuilding industry with the grain trade, it should be noted that a crucial factor for the rise or fall of grain exports, and in turn for the demand for maritime transport services, was the demand for cereals in Western Europe. Bad harvests in Western Europe meant a rise in demand for cereals from the Black Sea, and, as a consequence, freight rates, shipping services, and shipbuilding activity all increased as well. On the flip side, good harvests in Western Europe, and in particular England and France, caused demand for cereals from the Black Sea to decline and therefore decreased demand for maritime transport, even if the harvests in southern Russia were good.[54]

International Comparison: Classification and Evaluation of Production Level

A comparison of the production in shipyards outside of Greece aims to evaluate the dynamics of the shipbuilding industry on Syros in terms of production, productivity, ship types, and market orientation. The comparison below first examines the shipbuilding industries in Liguria and Provence.

According to Table 3.1, Syros in the middle of the century was much more productive than Provence and Liguria. From 1835–1839 and 1855–1859,

53 Harvey, *The Development of Russian Commerce*, 300–08; Metaxas, *Economics*, 184–87.

54 Καρδάσης, *Έλληνες ομογενείς*, 182; Herlihy, *Odessa*, 102.

the shipyards in Provence built 65.32% of the vessels and 75.95% of the tonnage that Syros produced during the same period. Yet as a ratio of average tonnage, Provence attained higher figures than Syros, since the French region built far more three-masted vessels than Syros. In Liguria from 1838–1852, the number of vessels and tonnage built corresponded to 94.46% and 73.13% respectively to the production of Syros. Vessels built in Syros during this so-called "golden period" in the shipbuilding industry were nearly 35 tons larger on average than those built in Liguria.

The higher average tonnage of vessels in Provence is indicative of the demand by the local shipowners, who commissioned the largest part of their clientele in Provencal shipyards. In the preceding century they had already developed business routes outside the Mediterranean in eastern and western Africa, the Caribbean, and in South America. In particular, Marseille was also a Mediterranean depot of Argentinean hides that supplied the tanneries of Syros.[55] Liguria and Syros, on the other hand, were more confined to the Mediterranean region and especially, as already mentioned, to the Black Sea grain trade. In Liguria, however, shipyards experienced a dramatic increase in the 1860s and 1870s, reaching 47,000 tons on average from 1870–1876. Before this, they hardly reached an annual average of 10,000 tons.[56]

The production of Syros shipyards was concentrated on a single location, but the shipbuilding activity in Provence and Liguria comprised 15 and 34 locations respectively. Furthermore, the two regions developed in shipping and shipbuilding with Marseille and Genoa, among the largest ports in the Mediterranean. Given this situation, Syros with a higher production than Provence and Liguria in the 1840s and 1850s, should be considered the largest wooden shipbuilding industry in the Mediterranean during this period, even though comparable evidence is lacking from shipyards in the Adriatic, North Africa, and the Ottoman Empire.

Beyond the Mediterranean, it is possible to compare the shipbuilding production of Syros with places such as Dunkirk (France), Boston (U.S.A.), Prince Edwards Island (Atlantic Canada), and Sunderland (U.K.).

According to Figure 3.4, Syros in the 1830s through the 1850s was competitive in terms of production with the major shipbuilding regions of the North

55 Roland Caty-Eliane Richard, *Armateurs Marseillais au XIXe siècle*, (Marseille: Chambre de Commerce et d'Industrie de Marseille, 1986), 47–52; Laurent Pavlidis, 'La production des bâtiments de mer en bois dans les chantiers privés provençaux au XIXe siècle', *Provence Historique*, tome LIX, fasc, 237, (Juillet-Août-Septembre 2009), 341; AMAE, CCC, Syra, vol. 4, 25.11.1848, 174b–175.

56 Luciana Gatti, *"Un raggio di convenienza". Navi mercantili, costruttori proprietari in Liguria nella prima metà dell' Ottocento*, (Genoa: Società Ligure di Storia Patria, 2008), 16–19.

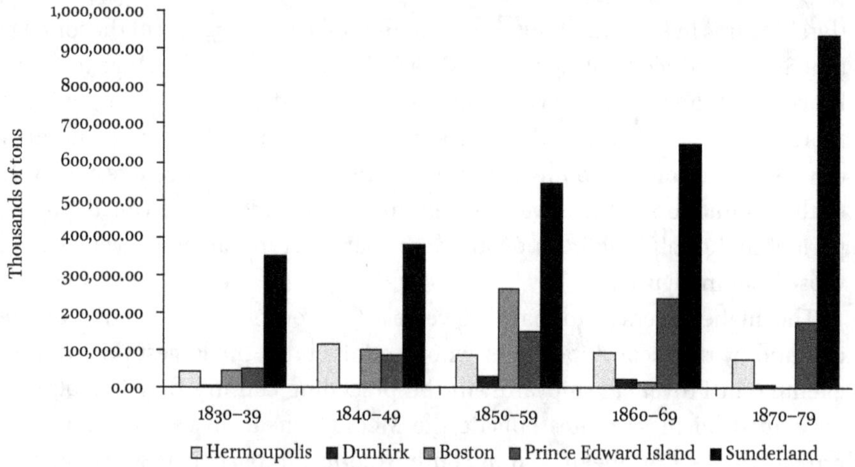

FIGURE 3.4 *Comparative shipbuilding output in tonnage capacity, 1830–1879.*
SOURCE: APPENDIX 3.2.4.

Atlantic, such as Boston and Prince Edward Island. Production levels at these two places during the 1840s were 86% and 74% of what occurred on Syros. Yet in the 1850s Prince Edward Island's output surpassed to a large extent that of Syros', and still it was the smallest shipyard in Atlantic Canada after Saint John in Newfoundland.[57] Ships from Prince Edward Island and the rest of Atlantic Canada operated in the biggest maritime market worldwide. Cargoes of timber were often sold together with the ships themselves, thus, both ships and timber became the main export commodities in this region.[58]

In America, Boston along with New York was the most important port for overseas trade and maritime commerce between the War of 1812 and the American Civil War. Boston and New York were also among the six most important shipbuilding districts in the country.[59] Medford was the most developed shipbuilding area of Boston up to 1850, but it was replaced by East Boston, which specialized in the construction of large clippers and was better

57 For the specialization of Prince Edward Island in medium size sailing ships see, Lewis R. Fischer, "The Port of Prince Edward Island, 1840–1889: a preliminary analysis", in *Ships and Shipbuilding in the North Atlantic Region* ed. Keith Matthews and Gerald Panting, (St John's, Newfoundland: Memorial University, 1978), 46.

58 Sager – Panting, "Staple Economies", 6–8; Sager – Panting, *Maritime Capital*, 34–38.

59 Fairburn, *Merchant Sail*, vol. II, 936–38. The six largest Shipbuilding Custom Districts along with Boston and New York are Philadelphia, Waldborough (Maine), Bath (Maine) and Baltimore. The three states with the most important shipbuilding production are Maine (the biggest of all), Massachusetts, and New York.

positioned in the Boston harbour.[60] The shipbuilding activity of Boston, along with the rest of the American shipbuilding industry, collapsed soon after its peak in the 1850s and never recovered.[61]

Compared to Dunkirk, the production on Syros was much larger with the average percentage of the former reaching only 16.77% from 1830–1879. A slightly better ratio is noted in the 1850s, when output at Dunkirk rose to 35.06% compared to Syros. Overall, production increased 604% compared to the previous decade. Dunkirk shipping in the nineteenth century was largely dependent on the cod fishing trade in Iceland, which represented a major source of wealth and forced shipowners and shipbuilders to adjust to this kind of market.[62]

Finally, Sunderland, along with Newcastle was one of the main shipbuilding centres in northeastern England. Sunderland and the Northeast assumed a leading position in the nation's shipping industry beginning in the late eighteenth century, producing one-third of the national shipbuilding output.[63] In the following century, Sunderland became the largest shipbuilding zone in Britain and perhaps the largest worldwide in the construction of sailing ships. Compared to areas like Newcastle, wooden shipbuilding at Sunderland was still very important up to late 1870s.[64] Sunderland played an oversize role in terms of production to the rest of the shipbuilding areas in Europe and North America. The port adjusted to technological and economic advances in shipping during the last quarter of the nineteenth century and continued to be prominent even into the twentieth century.[65]

One common feature of all the shipyards noted above is that, despite the different evolution of each, their rise and heyday was due to the production of wooden sailing ships, whose technical construction and organization were fairly standard. Differences are noticeable more in market orientation, the type and volume of demand, and the type of transport services. These were factors that influenced the volume of shipbuilding. Sunderland, Boston, and Prince Edward Island operated within the same enlarged markets of Great Britain and the ports in the North Atlantic, while Syros and Dunkirk functioned within a

60 Fairburn, *Merchant Sail*, vol. VI, 2897.

61 Safford, "The Decline of the American Merchant Marine", 81; Hutchins "The Declining American Maritime Industries", 111.

62 Christian Pfister-Langanay, *Constructeur, charpentier et navires à Dunkerque du XVIIe au XXe siècle*, (Dunkirk: Société Dunkerquoise d'Histoire et d'Archéologie, 2005), 117.

63 Ville, "Shipbuilding in the Northeast", 1; Christopher French, "Merchant Shipping of the British Empire", in *The Heyday of Sail. The Merchant Sailing Ship, 1650–1830. Conway's History of the Ship*, ed. Robert Gardiner, (London: Conway Maritime Press, 1995), 19–21.

64 Ville, "Shipbuilding in the Northeast", 3, 9.

65 Ibid., 36, Table 1.

more limited regional framework. The latter did manage, however, to integrate themselves into a wider commercial system that was dependent on international and local demand. The level of output on Syros compared to the other shipyards reveals a medium capacity shipbuilding zone for world standards, but definitely one of the largest in Mediterranean.

Repairs

Repairs were an essential business sector in the turnover of Syriot shipyards, given the strategic position of the island and the services and infrastructures offered in shipping and shipbuilding. The central position of Syros along the main sailing routes between the eastern Mediterranean, Black Sea, and Western Europe, as well as the necessity of the sailing ships for repairs in its port, gave rise to a substantial number of maritime loans to the captains of ships in route to cover the expenses for repairs and supplies. These captains often belonged to various nationalities as Table 1.3 demonstrates. Nonetheless, detailed and systematic information about ship repairs in Syros are too scant in order to assess its true size and its contribution to turnover on the island's shipyards. So far, 22 cases of ship repairs have been identified today, and from these an outline of this activity it is presented here without a systematic data series as was done for newly built ships.

From notarial records, two types of documentation regarding the ship repairs emerged. The first concerned the case of ships that needed repairs right after a second-hand purchase, an auction or their rescue after a shipwreck. The second was about ships that needed repairs due to their age and wear and tear. In the first category, the new owner in the bill of expenses appeared in the contract of completion of the works and repayment of the master shipwright, The contract was usually referred to as 'Receipt,' 'Account,' or 'Property' and included the expenditure for the purchase of the ship or for her rescue and transportation from the wreck site to the shipyard. Thus in 1857 Hadjiyannakos Dim. Kolozos spent 40,000 drachmae for the rescue, transportation, and necessary repairs of the brig *Athina* (268 tons). In addition, he spent 14,000 drachmae for the purchase of the ship, including her two masts and the bowsprit, and 16,000 drachmae for further repairs that included the cost of materials and the wages of craftsmen to the master shipwright Christofis Krystallis. The high cost of repairing the ship was directly related to the use of 1,025 kilos of copper nails and copper sheets.[66]

66 GSA, Syros, Notary Andreas David, n. 30209, 13.9.1857.

The cost of sale of the second-hand brigs *Agios Konstantinos/Eftichia* and *Elpis/Kalliarchis* (it was usual practice for the new owner to change the name of the ship) was 19.63% and 18.02% respectively of the total cost of sale and repair, while the purchase cost represented 33.33% of the total cost of the brig *Aristidis* (204 tons).[67] Works on the hull, rigging, and ship equipment as a total cost varied according to the condition of the ship and its special needs. Repairs to the hull of *Agios Konstantinos/Eftichia* covered 60% of total expenses, whereas *Aristidis* covered 28.89% and *Elpis/Kalliarchis* only 7.51%. Inversely, rigging and equipment on *Agios Konstantinos/Eftichia* was 17.88% of the total expenses and for *Elpis/Kalliarchis* 74.17%. This also explains the big difference in the wages of the master shipwright responsible for the two ships. Zannis Koufoudakis received 1,000 drachmae (2.5% of the total cost) for his supervision in repairs to the hull of *Agios Konstantinos/Eftichia*, while Pantazis Lekatzas was compensated only 50 drachmae (0.30% of the total cost) for his work on the *Elpis/Kalliarchis*. The substantial difference in their remuneration was related, in part, to Zannis Koufoudakis' reputation on the Syros shipbuilding market.

Table 3.2 estimates the percentage of reinvestment for repairs through a sample of four cases of ships. It does not show how many other repairs took place in the intermediate period or the capital reinvested. However, based on the age of vessel and the amount required for repairs it is possible to outline the condition of the ships at the time of repairs, their quality of construction, and the economic costs. The goleta *Ira* (probably a schooner) and the brig *Chrysoula* required a reinvestment of 40.43% and 22.92% respectively after 13 years of service. The amount for the goleta reached almost half of her initial building cost, but the ship required the replacement of structural parts in the hull and an entirely new deck and superstructure. On the other hand, brigs *Socratis* and *Dimitrios* required much lower sums of reinvestment after 17 and 15 years of service respectively. This was perhaps due to the quality of construction, but also to the fact that the larger the vessel, the smaller the percentage of timber costs to the total cost. In the case of *Dimitrios*, it is probable that the cost savings was related to her owner, Mikes Potous, one of the most important master shipwrights and shipowners on Syros. Although Potous commissioned

67 The brig *Agios Konstantinos/Eftichia* belonged to Dimitris Dimitrakopoulos from Hydra, but resident in Constantinople, ibid., n. 28227, 14.4.1855. The brig *Elpis/Kalliarchis* 148 tons belonged to Ioannis Kallergis from Ermoupolis, ibid., n. 24642, 22.3.1851. The brig *Aristidis*, ibid., n. 30215, 16.9.1857, bought the Ermoupolis merchant Pantazis Kaniskeris from Petros Georgios Petrospetsiotis from Hydra, see the sale contract ibid., n. 30212, 14.9.1857. The sale took place in the Greek consulate of Smyrna in 8.6.1857.

TABLE 3.2 *Estimation of reinvestment percentage through repairing to Syros built ships.*

	Goleta, *Ira*, 68 tons.	Brig *Chrysoula*, 220 tons.	Brig *Socratis*, 199 tons.	Brig *Dimitrios*, 349 tons.
Year of construction	1844	1849	1845	1848
Year of repair	1857	1862	1862	1863
Cost of construction (in drs)	11,500	48,000	34,000	100,000
Cost of repairs (in drs)	4,650	11,000	6,000	15,000
Percentage of cost of repair to the initial building cost	40.43%	22.92%	17.65%	15%

Source: processed data from GSA, Syros, Συμβ. Μιχ. Ιωαννόπουλος, ευρ. 2, αρ. 865, 20.6.1844; Συμβ. Ανδρέας Δαβίδ, Λυτά, αρ. 29666, 15.4.1857; Συμβ. Χριστ. Ιωάννου, ευρ. 5, αρ. 5746, 12.10.1849; Συμβ. Ανδρέας Δαβίδ, Λυτά, αρ. 31958, 10.8.1862; Συμβ. Μιχ. Ιωαννόπουλος, ευρ. 2, αρ. 172, 26.7.1845; Συμβ. Ανδρέας Δαβίδ, Λυτά, αρ. 31973, 21.8.1862; Συμβ. Χριστ. Ιωάννου, ευρ. 4, αρ. 4198, 28.7.1848; Συμβ. Ανδρέας Δαβίδ, Λυτά, αρ. 32129, 4.3.1863.

the work to another shipwright, Manolis Roditis, he had excellent technical and market knowledge. Finally, as far as concerns the labour costs to the total costs for repairs with the brig *Iraklis* of Leonidas K. Zalambas from Syros, labour costs covered 33% of the total. The master shipwright and carpenters wages were 22.41%, while the caulker's wages were 11.26%.[68]

The Economics of the Shipbuilding Industry

This section analyses the following: a) production cost, subdivided in total and individual cost, and the cost structure of new ships, b) income of the Syriot shipbuilding and its contribution to the national income of Greece, and c) overall productivity of Syriot shipyards, which along with income determined the economic and productive performance of the industry.

Cost of Production: Total Cost and Average Price

Estimates for the total cost are carried out by measuring the average price per ton. The monetary unit used is the Greek drachma, which along with the

68 Ibid., n. 29978, 20.4.1857.

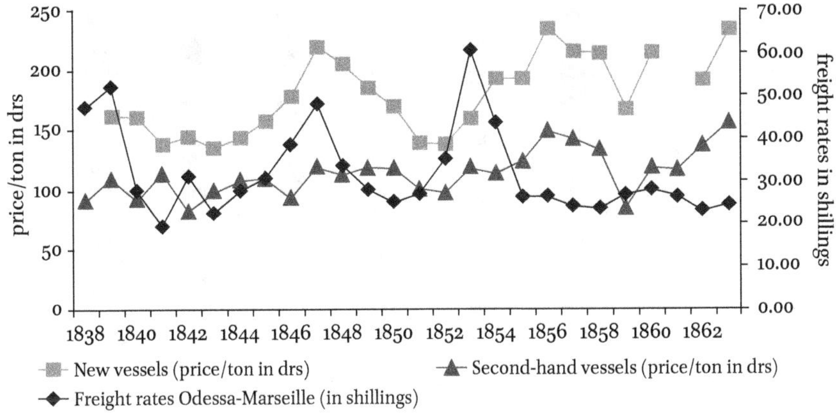

FIGURE 3.5 *New vessels prices/Second hand vessels prices/ Grain freight rates of Odessa – Marseille, 1838–1863.*
SOURCE: APPENDIX 3.3.1.

Spanish silver dollar, was one of the two currencies that appeared in most transactions. The drachma had a longer and more stable presence than the Spanish silver dollar, and it remained the only currency of shipbuilding transactions in Syros after 1850. For compatibility reasons, all prices given in other monetary units are converted to drachmae. Available data for prices spans 1838 to 1866; note that data is missing for the 1861 and 1864–1865. In order to estimate the total cost of construction, it is first necessary to translate this into its real dimension, namely the shipping market. Therefore, Figure 3.5 shows the average price per year of new ships on Syros and is related to the second-hand prices per ton and the cereal freight rates between Odessa and Marseille.

The general trend of prices among new and second-hand ships is harmonious, which also happens to be the case in today's shipping market.[69] The prices of new ships are also harmonious with freight rates, but do follow with delays (up to 1855, as explained above). However, second-hand prices sometimes were contrary to the other two series, as shipowners tended to prefer new orders when freight rates were high, a circumstance that obviously decreased the demand for second-hand ships.[70] On the contrary, the fall of freight rates and the consequent fall of prices for new ships caused an increase in the price for second-hand vessels. Therefore, in the years 1841, 1843–1844 and 1848–1851, when freight rates and new ships were in decline, prices of second-hand

69 Stopford, *Maritime economics*, 110, fig. 3.12.

70 Martin Stopford, "Shipping market cycles", in *The handbook of maritime economics and business*, op. cit., 219.

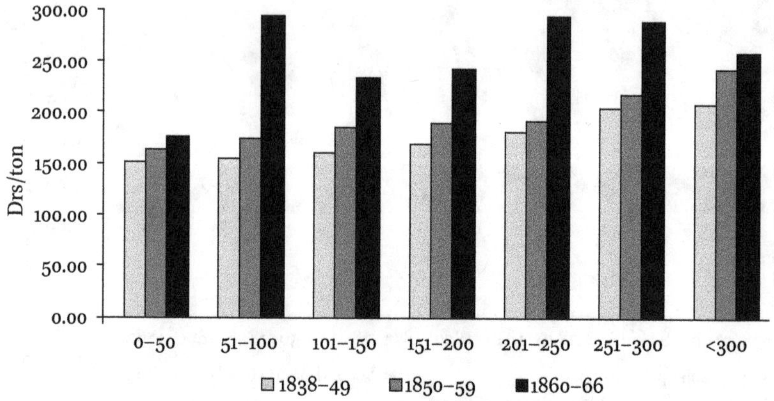

FIGURE 3.6 *Distribution of average price per tonnage class.*
SOURCE: APPENDIX 3.3.2.

vessels were on the rise. A smaller discrepancy between second-hand and new ships occurred in 1841 and from 1843–1844. On the other hand, great demand for new tonnage in 1847, 1853, and 1856, led to the rise of both markets, but at the same time also led to the greatest price divergence between them in 1847, 1856, and 1860. In this last instance, both prices followed a downward trend.

It is equally important to mention that the average price followed the capacity of production. Years when the price surpassed 200 drs/ton coincided with the peak years of production in 1847 and 1848, which reached 219.86 and 205.14 drs/ton respectively. In 1856 and 1857, production soared to 234.24 and 215.22 drs/ton after a recession of over 10,000 tons with 11,717.21 and 13,607.78 tons respectively. After the 1859–1862 depression, production rose by 58.66% in 1863 compared to the previous year and along with it the price of new ships rose to 233.49 drs/ton. The same trend happened in 1866, when, after a decline in 1864–1865, production surpassed 10,000 tons (11,269.35) and the average price reached its highest figure of 295.75 drs/ton.

Overall, the trend of both new and second-hand ships was pointing upwards, despite depressions in 1849–1852 and 1859–1862. Even when the rate of growth fell 28.45% and 49.94% in 1854 and 1858, the average price of new ships managed to remain relatively high. In 1854 it increased by 32.84% compared to the previous year, and in 1858 prices remained fairly stable (213.95 drs/ton) compared to 1857 (215.22 drs/ton). Finally, it is worth noting that, although both new and second-hand ships prices were set on an upward trend, the price difference between them increased steadily during the same period.

Figure 3.6 shows the price/ton per tonnage class, which has an upward general trend in the period under examination. However, the 1860s witnessed great price increases, when the average percentage to all tonnage classes rose by 32.54% compared to the previous decade. In contrast, prices during the 1850s increased by only 11.08% compared to the 1840s. The largest increase came in the 51–100 and 201–250 tonnage classes, with 69.42% and 53.90% respectively. Only the 1–50 class remained under 200 drs/ton (172.08), while the rest surpassed 230 drs/ton. The largest difference between 1–50 class and over 300 tons from 1838–1849 was 56.4 drs/ton, but the following decade it increased to 79 drs/ton and in 1860–1866 to 83.16 drs/ton. Smaller price divergences are noted between the 1–50, 51–100, and 101–150 classes of ships from 1838–1849 (not over 5 drs/ton) and also between the 101–150, 151–200, and 201–250 classes from 1850–1859 when price divergences were not more than 4 drs/ton.

International Price Comparison

Contemporary sources indicate that sailing ships built on Syros were cheaper than those abroad. French observers who compared prices between French and Syriot ships in the 1840s and 1850s confirmed that the latter were about 30%–50% cheaper. Greek sources characterised the price of Syriot ships as moderate.[71] The consul of Bavaria and Hannover in Athens, F. Strong, compared certain examples from shipyards in Greece and reported that the range of prices of Greek ships varied between 2 pounds and 15 shillings (75 drs/ton) for a 200 tons goleta (a schooner or a brig-schooner) built on Skiathos without copper sheathing, and up to 6 pounds and 10 shillings (180 drs/ton) for a goleta of respective size built on Aegina with copper sheathing.[72]

The international price comparison will took place with shipyards from Britain, America, and Atlantic Canada, as more data and systematic price series are available from these countries. For the sake of compatibility all prices are converted into British pound sterling.

The prices of Canadian vessels refer to those sold in the British market. Canadian sailing ships were a cheaper alternative for British shipowners up to the third-quarter of the nineteenth century, and their inflow in great numbers served the timber and cotton trade in the North Atlantic.[73] Despite their lower reputation compared to British built, sailing ships built in the British colonies numbered approximately 20% of the total registered vessels in Britain

71 Kardasis, *Σύρος*, 174–75. *Πανδώρα* [*Journal 'Pandora'*], 7, 1856–57, 165.

72 F. Strong, *Greece as a Kingdom. A statistical description of that country from the arrival of King Otho, in 1833 down to the present time*, (London: 1842), 146–48.

73 Sarah Palmer, *Politics, Shipping, and the repeal of the Navigation Laws*, (Manchester and New York: Manchester University Press, 1990), 46–47; Sager – Panting, *Maritime Capital*, 32–33.

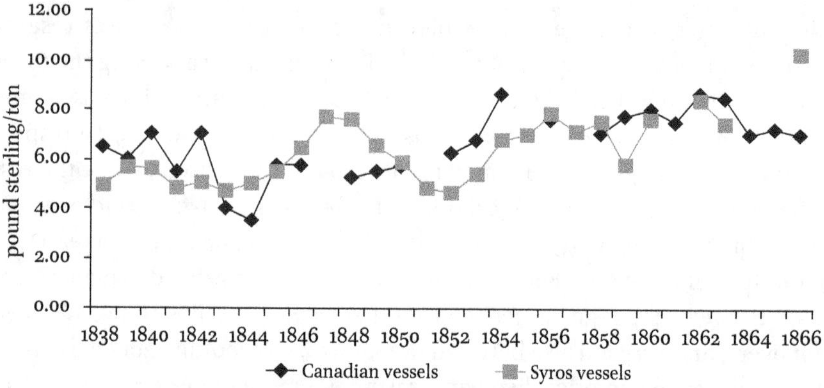

FIGURE 3.7 *Prices comparison between Syros and Atlantic Canada sailing ships (Prince Edward Island and New Brunswick), 1838–66 (in pound sterling).*
SOURCE: APPENDIX 3.3.3.

in 1846. Furthermore, 58%–70% of the ships built in Atlantic Canada were sold to British shipowners from 1820–1860.[74] According to Figure 3.7, Canadian and Syriot vessels were sold at roughly the same price. The average price was 6.62 pounds/ton for Canadian ships and 6.40 pounds/ton for Syriot ships. This represents a difference of just 0.18 British pounds. A greater price divergence occurred during the prosperous years of 1848 and 1866, when Syriot ships were 2.35 pounds/ton and 3.30 pounds/ton more expensive. However, Syriot ships when compared to British sailing ships were between 40%–160% cheaper as the price of the latter varied between 10–25 pounds/ton. The cheapest ships were built in Sunderland and cost 10–12 pounds/ton. Palmer estimates that the most affordable ships there cost only 6 pounds and 15 shillings, but the most expensive cost 25 pounds/ton and were built of oak and teak in London, Plymouth, and Liverpool.[75]

Besides the general trends of prices outlined above, it is interesting to compare more specific examples like the brig prices on Syros as the island specialised in this ship type. The brig *Tartar* (203 tons) and the barque *Crusader* (224 tons) were both built by Alexander Hall in Aberdeen in 1840 and cost 10.72 pounds/ton and 9.37 pounds/ton respectively. The average price of Syriot ships

74 John G. Hutchins, *The American Maritime Industries and Public Policy, 1789–1914*, (New York: Russell and Russell, 1941), 300–01; Sager – Panting, *Maritime Capital*, 31–32; Palmer, *Politics, Shipping*, 46, reports that the percentage of colonial built ships in 1846 was 13%.

75 Sager – Panting, *Maritime Capital*, 68–69; Palmer, *Politics, Shipping*, 48; Hutchins, *The American Maritime*, 299–300.

of the 201–250 class in 1840 was 5.20 pounds/ton. In 1857 the brig *Fearles* (240 tons) was commissioned by the J&WA Upham shipyard in Brixham, Devon and cost 10 pounds and 10 shillings, while the Syriot brig *Athina* of similar tonnage and built in the same year by the master shipwright Frangoulis Sehas cost 8 pounds/ton. In general, the average price of the 201–250 class in 1857 rose to 7.45 pounds/ton.[76] A decade later, however, the price difference evened out in certain cases, and at times completely reversed. The brig *Czarowitz* (254.5 tons) also commissioned by the J&WA Upham shipyard cost 9 pounds and 10 shillings in 1866, while the brigs *Archangelos* (253 tons) and *Agios Georgios* (250 tons) cost 11.70 and 10.45 pounds in the same year. The average cost for vessels in the 251–300 class in 1866 was almost 11 pounds/ton.[77] A downward price trend in Upham shipyard from 1857–1871 is observed in schooner prices, which fell from 10 pounds and 10 shillings in 1857 to approximately 9 pounds in 1861 and 1871.[78] In Syros, vessels of the 51–100 class in the 1850s had an average price of 5.66 pounds/ton and rose in the following decade to 9.79 pounds/ton. The schooner on Syros was also cheaper compared to American built ones, even if the difference was smaller. The average price of schooners between 40–105 tons in Woodwell Shipyard, Newburyport, MA was 6.41 pounds/ton from 1838–1849, while that of Syros in vessels of 51–100 class was 5.32 pounds/ton.[79]

Individual Cost and Cost Structure

This section outlines the cost structure and the individual costs of sailing ships on Syros. Historical sources usually mention four categories of individual costs: 1) timber and the wages of carpenters, joiners, and master shipwrights, 2) cost of material and the wages for riveting, 3) material and the cost for caulking, and 4) the master shipwright's remuneration, in case he was commissioned only to supervise the work without buying the material and paying the workers.

Other sources itemize individual costs in a different way and therefore offer more expansive evidence about the cost structure of a new ship on Syros. One such instance was the brig *Efcharistisis* (272 tons), which was built for 8,500 Spanish silver dollars (51,000 drs) in 1840 by Nikolaos Pagidas for Alexandros Georgiou, a resident in Syros originally from the island of Patmos. The cost

76 Processed data from Mc Gregor, *Merchant Sailing Ship, 1815–1850, The Supremacy of Sail*, (London: Conway Maritime Press, 1984), 116; GSA, Syros, Notary Christodoulos Ioannou, Index n. 9, n. 12084, 15.4.1857.

77 Mc Gregor, *Merchant Sailing Ship, 1850–1875*, 217–18.

78 Ibid., 218.

79 William H. Woodwell, 'The Woodwell Shipyard, 1759–1852", *Bulletin of the Business Historical Society*, vol. 21, n. 3, (June, 1947), 58–74.

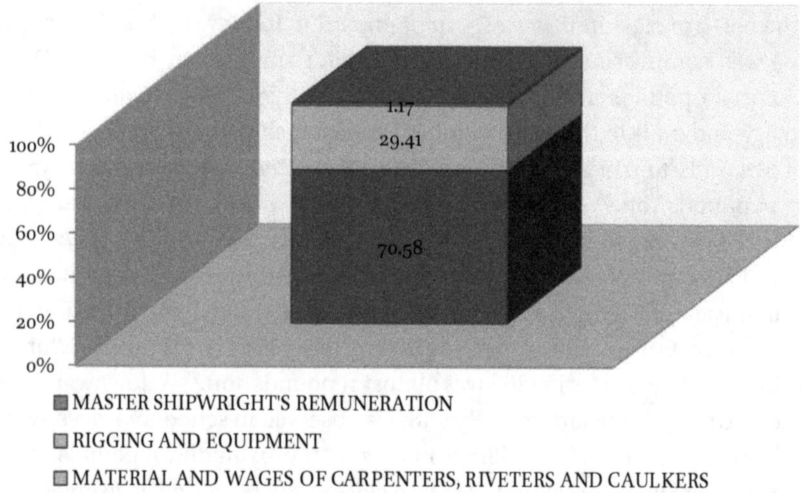

FIGURE 3.8 *Cost structure of brig* Efcharistisis, *272 tons.*
SOURCE: GSA, SYROS, NOTARY A. DAVID, N. 10730, 16.7.1840.

structure in Figure 3.8 shows that rigging and equipment were about one third of the total cost and the master shipwright's wages only 1.17%. These amounts are below the average cost category in 1840 for the 201–250 class of vessels.[80]

Another good example is the brig *Eleni* (236 tons), which was built for 19,870 drachmae in 1844 by Frangoulis Sehas for Alexandros Zarifis, an Odessa merchant represented by Nikolaos Loukas from Skopelos. It is interesting that the cost for riveting and caulking was separate from other expense categories, which amounted to 14.44% (see Figure 3.9). Rigging and equipment reached approximately the same percentage as in the brig *Efcharistisis*, while wages and timber were almost 58%. If one adds the riveting and caulking costs, this total reaches 72.31%, which is not far from the 70.58% of the cost of the brig *Efcharistisis*.

The third case is the brig *Taxiarchis* (226 tons), which was built on Samos for 50,000 drachmae in 1857 by the Syriot shipbuilder Stefanos Dimitriou for the Syriot merchant Kyriakos Charalambidis. The ship was built on Samos to obtain the flag of the Principality of Samos, a flag of convenience for Greek shipowners in the middle of the nineteenth century.[81] In this case, the cost of timber amounted to 30% and was separate from wages and other. Another 30% was paid for riveting and rigging and 35.8% for wages. The high remuneration of 4.2% for the master shipwright was above the average cost of this

80 Processed data from GSA, Syros, Notary A. David.

81 Harlaftis and Kostelenos, "International shipping and national economic growth", 1407.

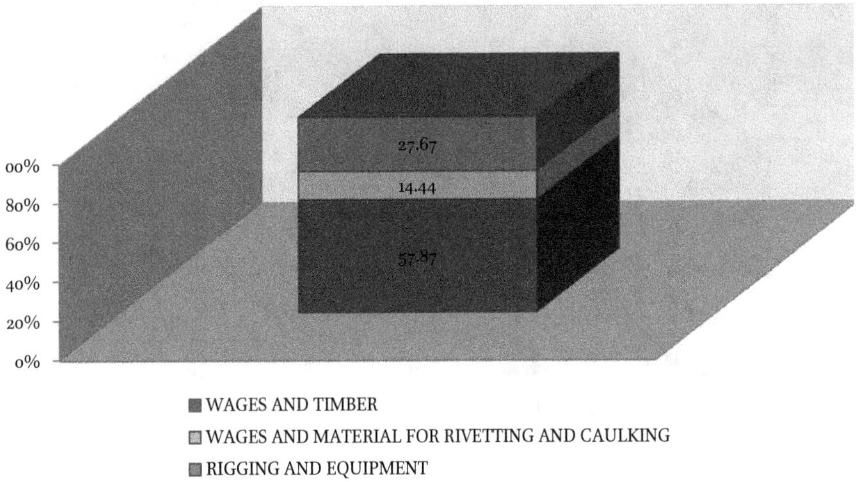

FIGURE 3.9 *Cost structure of brig* Eleni, *236 tons.*
SOURCE: GSA, SYROS, NOTARY A. DAVID, N. 16610, 11.10.1844.

category in 1857 (1.73%) for the 201–250 tonnage class. Such a discrepancy was likely due to the transfer and stay of the shipwright away from his home.

The most detailed account of expenses was outlined by the French consul of Syros regarding the brig *Koletis* (342 tons). This ship was built for 77,684.14 drachmae in 1847 by Nikolaos Pagidas for the Syros merchants Ilias Kehagias and Nikolaos Yayintzis originally from Amfissa, who each owned 25%, and the also Syros merchant Karlos Nazos originally from Tinos, who owned the other 50%.

Out of the total 77,684.14 drs, the cost for her maiden voyage amounted to 1,272.93 drs and thus her net total building cost amounts to 76,403 drs. According to Table 3.3, rigging and equipment reached about one third of the total and almost the same percentage of the brigs *Efcharistisis* and *Eleni*. Timber amounted to about 28% and was therefore close to that of the brig *Taxiarchis* (30%); however, wages were lower (23.02%) than the others, especially compared to the brig *Taxiarchis*, which was built a decade later and whose labour costs increased by 36%. The master shipwright's remuneration was higher than the average for +300 tons vessels in 1847 (1.79%). He received a pre-arranged sum of 1200 drs and afterwards a bonus of 351.90 drs. Furthermore, rivets and iron parts fabricated by blacksmiths comprised 12.82%, and 2.35% was used for guarding the ship, which must have been an essential part of the general expenses along with food and drinks for the workers. Some taxes and fees, material transportation expenses, porterage fees, and the flag were also included in the category of "general expenses."

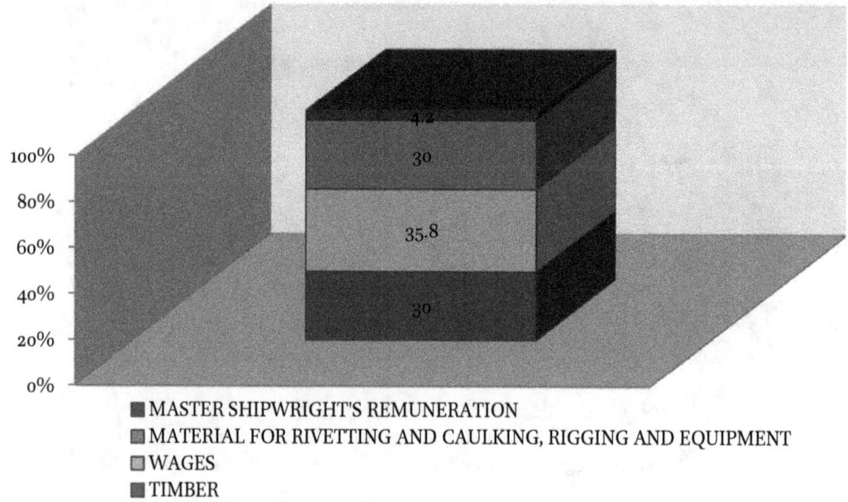

FIGURE 3.10 *Cost structure of brig* Taxiarchis, *226 tons.*
SOURCE: GSA, SYROS, NOTARY A. DAVID, N. 29873, 8.3.1857.

TABLE 3.3 *Cost structure of brig* Koletis, *342 tons.*

Cost Category	Percentage of Cost Category
Rigging and Equipment	29.60
Timber	27.67
Wages	23.02
Iron and Nails	12.82
Ship Guarding and Nutrition Expenses	2.35
Other Expenses	2.05
Master Shipwright's Wages	2.03
Tar, Pitch and Oakum	0.46

Source: processed data from Appendix 3.6.

Finally, it is necessary to consider the cost of riveting and iron parts of some ships. The brigs *Timoleon* (171 tons), built for 180.70 drs/ton and launched in 1839, and the *Adamantios Korais* (188 tons), built for 191.48 drs/ton and launched in 1840, spent 5.37% and 5.28% on riveting and iron parts. The brig *Iason* (415 tons), built for 180.72 drs/ton in 1840 was much lower at 2.65%. An exceptional case was brig *Panaya Malteza* (225 tons), which was built for only 160 drs/ton in 1839. The cost of her riveting and iron parts varied between 8.5%

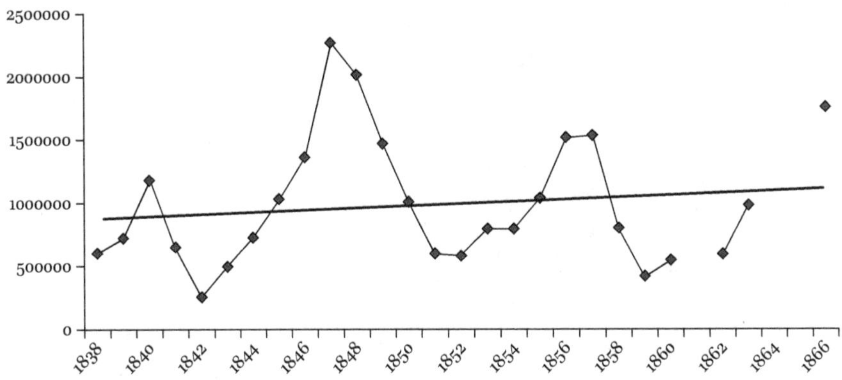

FIGURE 3.11 *Estimated value (million drs) of the ships built in Syros, 1838–66.*
SOURCE: APPENDIX 3.4.

and 9.44%. Just a few years later in 1847, the brig *Ai Patrai* (312 tons) was built for 224.35 drs/ton (a peak year, where the average price was 219.86 drs/ton) and the percentage cost of riveting and iron parts amounted to 5.66%.[82]

Revenue of the Shipbuilding Industry

Revenue from the Syriot shipbuilding industry is estimated from the total value of the ships built each year. Data covers the period 1838–1866, except for the years 1861 and 1864–1865, when a lack of data prevents one from making a systematic analysis. For ships that lack information about their value (only 1839 and 1847 are complete), an estimate was reached by multiplying their tonnage capacity with the estimated average price per ton during the year these ships were built.

The value of new ships and the gross revenue of the shipbuilding industry on the island for the entire period from 1828–1866 is estimated to be 47.599.247 drs. According to Figure 3.11, the general trend of gross revenue was upward and varied between 1,600,000 and 2,000,000 drachmae. The value was also synchronized with shipbuilding cycles and periods of prosperity and recession. Therefore, gross revenue was significantly above the general trend from 1845–1850, reaching a peak in 1847 with 4,212,820 drs. This amount represented a record and was followed in 1848 with 3,742,757.64 drs. The 1851–1854 recession, during which gross revenue was below the general trend, was followed by a period of prosperity from 1855–1857, when ship values rose above 2.5 million drs (e.g. 1857 with 2,814,284 drs). The 1858–1862 recession was overcome by the middle of the 1860s, when the value of new ships reached 3,258,729 drs in 1866, a level similar to those in the middle years of the 1840s.

82 GSA, Syros, Notary A. David, n. 19258, 6.3.1847.

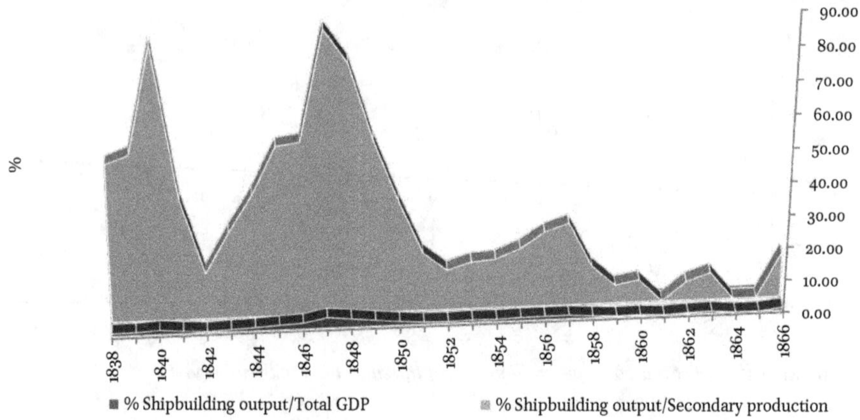

FIGURE 3.12 *Percentage of the added value of Syros shipbuilding activity to GDP, 1838–66.*
SOURCE: APPENDIX 3.4.1.

It is critical to connect the above data of gross revenue in the shipbuilding industry to the wider context of the national Greek economy. In other words, one must estimate its share to the GDP, both in the secondary sector and to the total GDP. To do this it is first necessary to estimate the added value of the shipbuilding industry. As George Kostelenos says: "*the designation of added value assess the contribution of manufacturing to the total of the production process of the country in the examined period.*" Estimates of the added value results from the deduction of the inputs of raw materials to the total value of built ships. Given that all the necessary raw materials for shipbuilding were imported, only the wages and the profits from labour made a net contribution to the GDP. After deducting the imported raw materials, the added value came to be 60.35% of the gross revenue of all shipbuilding activity. This is an identical amount to the estimates of George Kostelenos (60%), who mentions also that shipbuilding was the most expansive activity of the secondary sector up to 1858.[83]

Figure 3.12 demonstrates that the contribution of the Syriot shipbuilding industry to the secondary sector of the national economy was extremely important, its average being almost one third of the total (31.55%). Its share was particularly high in the 1840s, when it reached an average of 51.15%. For the peak years of 1840 and 1847–1848, the numbers rose to 82.35%, 85%, and 75% respectively. A subsequent decline in the importance of shipbuilding is reflected in the percentages from the 1850s and 1860s, which fell on average

83 Kostelenos et al. *Πηγές οικονομικής ιστορίας*, 91, 94.

to 15.05% and 8.65% for each decade.[84] Similar figures are noticeable in the contribution to the total GDP. The total average was 1.02%, but in the 1840s it rose to 1.49%. Afterwards, it fell considerably to 0.75% in the 1850s and 0.56% in the 1860s. One should compare this data to the peak years of 1847 and 1848 with 3.24% and 2.57%. Characteristic of the decreasing importance of the shipbuilding industry after the 1840s is that it remained below 1% even in the boom years of 1856 and 1857.

Productivity of the Shipbuilding Industry

The measurements of productivity along with the revenue of the shipbuilding are two essential indices of the economic performance of the industry. The methods followed to measure the productivity of Syriot shipyards are: a) the average tonnage and the distribution of new ships per class tonnage in the examined period, b) the delivery time of the vessels, and c) the capacity of the shipyards. The conventional formula in the shipbuilding economics tonnage/number of workers cannot be followed as data about the workforce are scarce.

Average Tonnage

Average tonnage was related to the size of the vessel as well as to its type. An increase or decrease reflected the level of demand, while the ship type might have reflected the type of trade and transport it served. In other words, average tonnage is an essential instrument of measuring the productivity in shipping.[85]

According to Figure 3.13, average tonnage was synchronised with the rise and fall of production, except in 1857 when the output increased by 16.14%, but

84 The 1860s as it was mentioned includes only 1860, 62, 63 and 66 for which available data exist.

85 North, "Ocean Freight Rates", 958; Kaukiainen, "Growth, diversification", 52–53; Sager – Panting, *Maritime Capital*, 54–58; Jari Ojala, "Productivity and technological change in 18th and 19th centruy sea transport: a case study of sailing ship efficiency in Kokkola, Finland, 1721–1913", *International Journal of Maritime History*, vol. IX, n. 1, (June 1997), 98–114; Simeon J. Crowther, "The Shipbuilding Output of the Delaware Valley, 1722–1776", *Proceedings of the American Philosophical Society*, Vol. 117, No. 2 (Apr. 10, 1973), 95–97; Christopher J. French "Productivity in the Atlantic Shipping Industry: A Quantitative Study", *Journal of Interdisciplinary History*, Vol. 17, No. 3 (Winter, 1987), 630–31; Gary M. Walton, "Sources of Productivity Change in American Colonial Shipping, 1675–1775", *The Economic History Review*, New Series, Vol. 20, No. 1 (Apr., 1967), 69–70; Starkey, "The Shipbuilding Industry", 80.

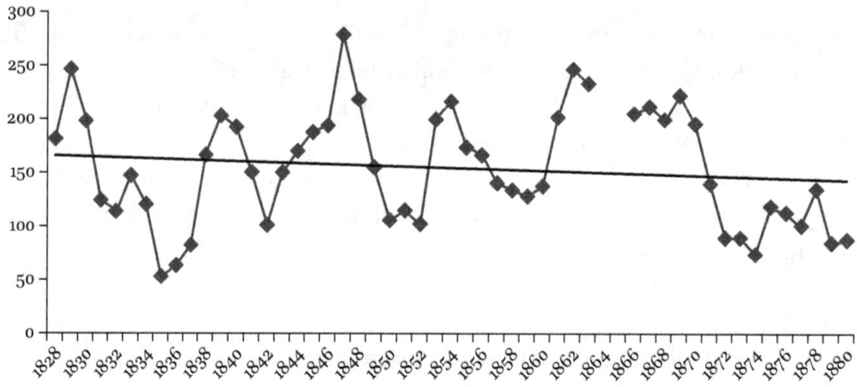

FIGURE 3.13 *Average tonnage of Syros built ships, 1828–80.*
SOURCE: APPENDIX 3.5.

average tonnage decreased from 167 tons in 1856 to 140.95. The general trend in the period under consideration is downward and varied slightly above 150 tons. Yet this downward trend was due to a decrease in average tonnage in the 1870s. Up to then, the trend was upward and varied between 150–200 tons. A downward shift in average tonnage began in 1870 and marked a turning point between the period of prosperity and the period of decline of the shipbuilding industry on Syros. Ultimately, it signifies lower demand for new seagoing sailing ships.

During the three last decades of the nineteenth century, oversupply of sailing ships and new technologies using iron, steel, and steam reduced the prices for wooden ships and forced shipowners and shipbuilders to make their sailing ship more competitive by reducing operating costs and improving the onboard technology. This effect transformed the industry from a labour intensive unit to a capital intensive one.[86] Efforts to adjust wooden sailing ship to the new realities did not take place on Syros to the same extent as in other Greek shipyards, such as Galaxidi where many large barques were built in the last quarter of the century. The general average tonnage did not surpass 200 tons and shows that Syriot shipyards focused mainly on two-masted vessels as long as these kinds of ships remained a profitable investment with high capital return. The long recession in freight rates in the last quarter of the nineteenth century, the oversupply of sailing ships, and smaller capital return eventually shifted capitals to other forms of investment.[87]

86 Sager – Panting, *Maritime Capital*, 54–60.

87 See Chapter Two, pages 52–53.

TABLE 3.4 *Comparative average tonnage, 1830–79.*

Decade	Syros	Dunkirk	Sunderland	Prince Edward Island	Medford, Boston
1830–39	129.04	38.86	265*	114.32	428.95
1840–49	180.83	91.77	274.5	121.11	463.1
1850–59	149.07	122.88	365	201.23	802.9
1860–69	208.06	157.36	391	259.84	843.95
1870–79	114.48	148.95	736	272.31	–

Source: Appendix 3.2.4.

It is important to note that the average tonnage of Syriot ships was synchronised with the international standards of the period (see Table 3.4). Average tonnage in the United Kingdom did not surpass 200 tons before the 1850s, although in Sunderland it was above the national average and similar trends occurred in Atlantic Canada.[88] Medford in Boston was an exception due to the construction of large clippers.[89] On the Italian peninsula, the average tonnage of the Austrian flag seagoing sailing ships registered in the port of Trieste was 59.47 tons in 1834.[90] In Genoa, sailing ships were below 100 tons up to 1846, but ten years later average tonnage increased to 144.53 tons and in 1859 to 166.14 tons, surpassing 200 tons only after Italian unification in 1862.[91]

Along with average tonnage, the distribution per tonnage class identifies the productivity level of the industry. According to Figure 3.14, the majority of vessels was built in the 1840s and 1850s, while vessels built over 250 tons were few in the 1830s. The most productive decade was the 1840s, as the number of vessels over 150 tons increased and comprised 55% of the total number of ships being built. Ships over 300 tons also reached their peak (74) in the same decade, amounting to 10.09% of the total and three to five times more than other decades for vessels of this class. The 1860s, although imperfect, was more level with all tonnage classes, with the 151–200 and 201–250 classes

88 Starkey, "The Shipbuilding Industry", 109; Sager – Panting, *Maritime Capital*, 55.

89 Arthur H. Clark, *The Clipper Ship Era: An Epitome of Famous American and British Clipper Ships, their Owners, Builders, Commanders and Crews, 1843–1869*, (New York and London: G.P. Putnam's sons, 1911).

90 Processed data from Sergio Anselmi, "Tipologia navale italiana in eta moderna (secoli XVIII–XIX)", in *La penisola italiana e il mare*, op. cit., 241.

91 Ibid., 243; For 1862 see, Doria, "La marina mercantile", 90.

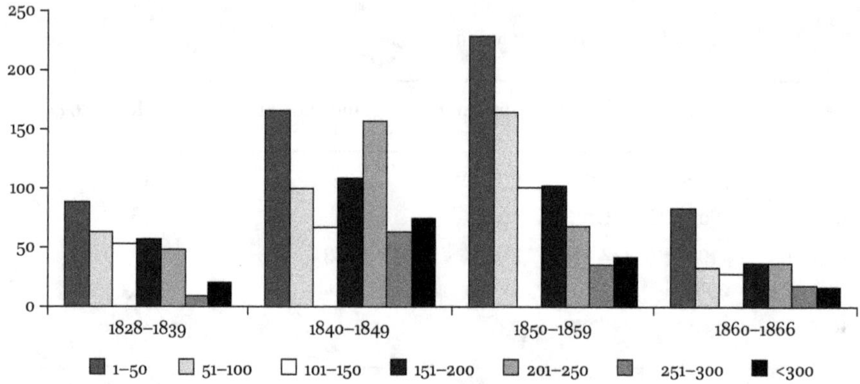

FIGURE 3.14 *Distribution of Syros ships built per tonnage class, 1828–66.*
SOURCE: APPENDIX 3.3.2.

more elevated, which also coincided with the 200 tons average capacity of this decade.

In general, the average tonnage and the distribution of tonnage class confirm that the great rise of productivity in Syriot shipyards began in the 1840s, and more precisely in 1838. On the other hand, the 1850s was a period of tribulation and intense fluctuation between boom years like 1853 and 1856–1857, and extremely difficult ones like 1852, 1854, and 1858–1859. As the 1860s progressed, shipbuilding activity recovered to levels of production last occurred in the 1840s, but it was the last glimpse before the 1870s, which defined the beginning of a general decline.

Delivery Time of Vessels

The delivery time indicates the turnover rate and the intensification of production, and is therefore an important aspect of the productivity of shipyards.[92] The time to deliver a vessel along with external factors greatly influenced the shipping business, as supply in the short-term was inelastic to the volatility of demand. Usually orders for new ships were placed when freight rates and the expectations of shipowners were high, but there was always the danger that between the time of the order and the launch of the vessel a fall of freight rates would occur, lowering the expected earnings from any new investment.[93] In Syriot shipyards, delivery times fluctuated, but improved in all classes of

92 Stopford, *Maritime economics*, 482.

93 Sager – Panting, *Maritime Capital*, 37; Metaxas, *The Economics*, 97; Stopford, *Maritime economics*, 473.

TABLE 3.5 *Delivery Time of Vessels (in months), 1828–66.*

Tonnage Class	1828–39	1840–49	1850–59	1860–63, 1866	General average time
1–50	2.25	1.82	2.1	1.72	1.97
51–100	3.25	2.74	2.67	3.09	2.93
101–150	4.7	3.31	3.7	3.47	3.79
151–200	5.15	3.86	4.03	3.2	4.06
201–250	–	4.06	4.51	4.14	4.23
251–300	4	4.1	3.69	5.3	4.27
<300	4.05	4.82	4.55	4.37	4.44

Source: processed data from GSA, Syros, Notarial records, Συμβολαιογράφου Μάξιμου Ταλασλή, Συμβ. Σκαρλάτος Μάξιμος, Κατάστιχα 1–6, 1827–1830, Συμβ. Ανδρέας Δαβίδ, Κατάστιχα 7–16, 1830–24.1.1835, Λυτά έγγραφα 1835–1862. Συλλογή Ιστορικού Αρχείου Κυκλάδων, Συμβ. Κων. Αγγελίδης, Ευρετήρια, 1–5, 1854–1863, Συμβ. Αντώνιος Αλμπέρτος, Ευρετήρια 1–2, 1853–1864, Συμβ. Μιχ. Ιωάννόπουλος, Ευρ. 1–2, 1843–1845, Συμβ. Χρ. Ιωάννου Ευρ. 1–10, 1846–1860. I/Ναυπηγικά, 1836–1866.

vessels (see Table 3.5). The average time of the 1–50 class vessels was about two and a half months and four and a half months for the vessels over 300 tons. The difference between intermediary tonnage classes was scalable as tonnage increased, but generally by only a small amount, while for larger tonnage classes, i.e. over 150 tons, the average time was slightly over four months. The short delivery times in Syros were probably due to its specialization with two-masted vessels less than 300 tons.

In the 1840s and 1850s, one notes a considerable decrease in delivery times in most tonnage classes. In 51–100 class, delivery was decreased from three months and one week in 1828–1839 to two months and three weeks in the 1840s, and in 151–200 class from slightly more than five months to less than four months. The average decrease of one month on average in the 1840s and 1850s demonstrates an increase in production and the necessity of faster delivery compared to the 1830s.

Capacity of Shipyards

A key to understand the intensification of production was the character of the Syriot shipbuilding industry. Syriot shipyards were active all year around, as shipbuilding was not a seasonal activity, and complemented the local economy. The island was the only shipbuilding centre on Greece, and one of only

TABLE 3.6 *Shipyard's capacity and distribution of the number of vessels built each month in selected years.**

	1840			1850			1857		
1/1–30/3	14 (Jan.)	17 (Feb.)	**21 (Mar.)**	15 (Jan.)	17 (Feb.)	16 (Mar.)	31 (Jan.)	31 (Feb.)	19 (Mar.)
1/4–30/6	9 (Apr.)	19 (May.)	12 (Jun.)	**29 (Apr.)**	27 (May.)	28 (Jun.)	25 (Apr.)	35 (May.)	**37 (Jun.)**
1/7–30/9	8 (Jul.)	11 (Aug.)	10 (Sep.)	18 (Jul.)	18 (Aug.)	9 (Sep.)	27 (Jul.)	29 (Aug.)	24 (Sep.)
1/10–31/12	10 (Oct.)	10 (Nov.)	7 (Dec.)	18 (Oct.)	13 (Dec.)	12 (Dec.)	15 (Oct.)	9 (Nov.)	10 (Dec.)

Source: processed data from GSA, Syros Συμβολαιογράφου Μάξιμου Ταλασλή, Συμβ. Σκαρλάτος Μάξιμος, Κατάστιχα 1–6, 1827–1830, Συμβ. Ανδρέας Δαβίδ, Κατάστιχα 7–16, 1830–24.1.1835, Λυτά έγγραφα 1835–1862. Συλλογή Ιστορικού Αρχείου Κυκλάδων, Συμβ. Κων. Αγγελίδης, Ευρετήρια, 1–5, 1854–1863, Συμβ. Αντώνιος Αλμπέρτος, Ευρετήρια 1–2, 1853–1864, Συμβ. Μιχ. Ιωάννόπουλος, Ευρ. 1–2, 1843–1845, Συμβ. Χρ. Ιωάννου Ευρ. 1–10, 1846–1860. I/Ναυπηγικά, 1836–1866. * Numbers in bold are the highest figures attained per year.

a few in the eastern Mediterranean that provided year round employment (see Table 3.6).[94]

In Table 3.7, the years 1840, 1850 and 1857 were chosen for the greatest possible range of time period, but also because a large number of vessels were built in these years. In 1840, 75 vessels were built and production surpassed 13,000 tons for first time in the history of the Syriot shipbuilding industry. One should compare this to 1850 when 102 vessels were built, a record number until then, and 1857 when the largest number of ships were built on the island (116 vessels). The intensification of activity often fluctuated between a less active period (October–December) and the busiest period between (April–June). Weather conditions and the amount of daytime working hours in each season were also crucial factors. The longer the amount of light from dawn to dusk obviously maximised the working hours. The highest capacity of shipyards, as a determining factor of productivity, was also dependent on infrastructure and the labour force.[95]

Data from the period shows an increase in the capacity of the shipyards, which culminated in 1857. The primary area of construction was a strip of land on the western coast of Syros' harbour, which today is known as the Stratarchis

94 AMAE, CCC, Syra, vol. 4, 28.6.1853, 77.

95 Stopford, *Maritime economics*, 473–74.

Papagos coastline.[96] Twenty one vessels were under construction in this section of the harbour in March 1840. This number increased to 29 in April 1850 and 37 in June 1857, when no less than 24 vessels were under construction in an eight month time period in 1857, the majority of them being brigs and schooners (60 brigs and 30 schooners out of 116 vessels). If one assumes that an average of ten workers, carpenters, and joiners were needed to build a ship's hull, then it is possible to estimate that in 1857, for example, 90 men on average were needed in November, the least busy month of that year, and 370 men for July, the busiest one. The total average for that year must have reached about 240 men.[97]

General Performance of the Shipbuilding Industry on Syros

For four decades, the construction of sailing ships was the most important activity of the secondary sector and the most industrialised zone for Syros and the entire country. Shipbuilding on Syros remained a labour intensive activity, as shipbuilders were not involved in the industrialization of production and new technologies, despite the opening of the factory of the Greek Steamship Navigation Company in 1861. However, the growth generated from the volume of shipbuilding affaires and the spinoff effects to local and regional economies reinforced the importance of the port of Syros in the Aegean and the eastern Mediterranean, as well as to the growth of other ports, like Andros, Hydra, Mykonos, and Santorini, which largely depended on the prosperity of Syros.

In quantitative terms, the shipbuilding industry on Syros built 3,178 ships of 429,301 tons from 1828–1880. The value of ships built between 1838–66 reached 48 million drs (47.599.247), corresponding to 1,782 ships of 222,787 tons. The contribution to the secondary sector up to 1850 was on average over 50% and afterward decreased to 25% as other types of production and more mechanized sectors developed. Average tonnage remained on an upward trend up to 1870 with 166.5 tons and fast delivery times. The large capacity of shipyards and the constant rates of work ensured the sustainability and competitiveness of the industry as long as demand for wooden sailing ships was the dominant investment option in maritime transports in the context of the Greek-owned merchant marine.

96 Agriantoni – Fenerli, *Ερμούπολη*, 45.

97 The average number of ten workers per hull is found on four shipbuilding contracts in Syros, two in 1832, one in 1836 and one in 1843.

CHAPTER 4

The Production Process

The Institutional Framework

Ship Construction, Institutional Process and Transaction Cost

Ship construction in nineteenth century Syros was a complex issue, which demanded not only access to the necessary capital but also specialised know-how of maritime technology, the shipping business, and the shipbuilding market. Ship construction involved interdependent institutional and technical procedures, in an articulated and enlarged market connected to other ports and maritime centres of the period. The sources of the institutional and technical procedures required in the construction of a sailing ship are the notarial acts of Syros and the certificates of ships built by Syros shipbuilders, issued from the Municipality of Hermoupolis. According the above sources, the documents that set out the institutional procedures to be followed are the following:

1) Shipbuilding Agreement
2) Agreement for the purchase of shipbuilding timber, subdivided into:
   a) Sale of shipbuilding timber to a timber merchant or a non-specialist purchaser in the Syros market.
   b) Direct sale and transportation of timber from the place of supply by chartering a ship.
3) Agreement to manufacture metal components for the vessel under construction.
4) Document of ownership.
5) Certificate of ship construction.

It has been argued that, along with technology, formal and informal institutions determine the transaction and production costs, thus shaping economic performance.[1] The analysis of the institutional procedure provides useful conclusions concerning not only economic performance but also the dominant mentalities and behavioural practices of the actors involved in shipping and shipbuilding transactions. In nineteenth century Greece, the sailing ship was a high cost capital investment with a serious capital return, protected from

1 Douglass North, 'Transaction costs, Institutions, and Economic Performance", (*Occasional Papers*, ICEGP 30, San Francisco, 1992), 5, 8–9. Ibid., *Institutions, Institutional Change*, 129.

© KONINKLIJKE BRILL NV, LEIDEN, 2016 | DOI 10.1163/9789004306158_006

a legal framework oriented towards the safeguarding of property rights.[2] Our main source for these claims is the contract stipulated in the presence of a notary, which was the official registration of formal and informal rules and institutions, and a basic instrument of the transaction process between the actors, protecting their property rights. The qualitative elements of the contract and its degree of complexity reflect the society's institutional framework, its level of market evolution, and the transaction costs.[3]

The existence of transaction costs is due to the fact that the market actors are not equally well-informed about prices, products, and other parameters. Access to necessary information costs money, time and effort, creating information and research costs. Furthermore, transactions involve a bargaining cost, needed to conclude an agreement with specific requirements such an affordable price, a monitoring cost needed to ensure that the terms of the agreement will be respected, and, in a contrary case, an enforcement cost.[4] All the above costs are due to three basic factors that influence transactions: the asymmetric information due to bounded rationality, the opportunism of those involved in the transaction, and the asset specificity.[5] Transaction and manufacturing costs are part of the production costs. The greater the specialization and division of labour (and thus the stages of production), the higher the necessary measuring and monitory costs.[6]

In the case of ship construction in nineteenth century Syros, the existence of a transaction cost fell to the investors who were interested in building sailing ships. They had to collect the necessary information from the market about shipbuilders' reputations, prices, and building costs and materials, and had to bargain with shipbuilders, other craftsmen and suppliers, and monitor the stages of construction, either directly or through an agent (an entrusted person, usually with some specific know-how, who was able to handle the task).

2 For the first attempts of the King Otho governments, already in 1833 and 1836, to create a legal framework for the protection of ship property rights see GSA, Athens, KOA, Marine, φακ. 43, Διάταγμα περί εμπορικής ναυτιλίας, 15/27 Οκτωβρίου 1833 and Διάταγμα περί εμπορικής ναυτιλίας, 14/26 Νοεμβρίου 1836.

3 North, *Institutions, Institutional Change*, 101, 111–12, 139–40.

4 Rao P.K., *The Economics of Transaction Costs. Theory, Methods and Application*, (New York: Palgrave Macmillan, 2003), 8; Gordon Boyce & Simon Ville, *The Development of Modern Business*, (New York: Palgrave Macmillan, 2002), 20; Douglass North, *Structure and Change in Economic History*, (New York: Norton, 1981), 40; Ibid., "Conference Summary", in *Merchant shipping and economic development in Atlantic Canada*, ed., Fischer L. – Sager E., (St Johns Newfoundland: Maritime History Group, Memorial University of Newfoundland, 1982), 231.

5 Rao, *The Economics*, 12; Boyce – Ville, *The Development*, 20–21.

6 North, *Institutions, Institutional Change*, 63; ibid., *Structure and Change*, 41.

On the supply side, craftsmen also had to bargain for the desired price, the delivery time, and other requirements needed to protect themselves from the client's opportunism, especially with respect to payment obligations.

The Shipbuilding Agreement

The shipbuilding agreement was the first detectable stage in the institutional procedure of ship construction, and was the final stage of the transaction process as a whole between the shipbuilder and the investors. Although little can be known about the information research and negotiations phase, its results are registered in the terms of the contractual agreement, a document which illustrates the knowledge of the market, the dominant mentalities, and the bargaining skills of both sides involved. The following stages of the transaction are also registered: the specification of the characteristics of the object of agreement, the services required, and the terms ensuring the completion of the agreement (monitoring, measurement, and enforcement).[7] The examined agreements cover the period 1830–62. To a certain degree, these have a standarised structure and form.

A shipbuilding agreement begins with general introductory data about the transaction, such as the date, the location, and the personal data of the contracted parts and witnesses. "*On September 30 1837, Thursday, before noon, in my office located in the market, in Hermoupolis of Syros, before me, the notary Andreas David, and the witnesses Dimitrios Kairis, merchant, and Vasilios Karakasis, merchant, residents here, known to me and not having ties of kinship with the contracted parts, they presented themselves, the gentlemen Stamatios Ioannis Koufoudakis, shipbuilder, resident here and known to me, and Georgios Dimitrios Thermisiotis, seafarer, resident in Andros, of whose identity I am informed by the witnesses.*"[8]

The next section details the obligations of the shipbuilder to the owner/investor, and gives a specification of the basic characteristics of the vessel, including the ship type, the duration of construction, and the three basic dimensions (length, maximum breadth, depth): "*Mister Koufoudakis confessed that he promised, within four months starting from today, to build on behalf of the aforementioned Thermiotis, here in Hermoupolis, a vessel of the brig type, twenty two shipbuilding picheis* [*picheis=πήχεις*, equal to 0.914 metres] *in length, twenty three and a half kannes* [*kannes=κάννες*, equal to 0.3048 metres] *and twelve kannes in height and depth, in accordance with the following*

7 North, "Conference Summary", 231, 233.

8 GSA, Syros, notary Andreas David, n. 6917.

agreements."[9] The subsequent section specified the nature of the shipbuilding product undertaken, and included the expenses associated with every specific stage in construction, such as timber and wages: "*The shipbuilder promises to provide, in full, the necessary quantity of timber, from pine, for the construction of the vessel. The timber must be of good quality. He further promises to pay the wages of the joiners and carpenters*." Often, these contracts mention the type of timber used, usually pine, also referred to as tame wood (*ἡμεροξυλεία*), which means softwood. The need to use good quality timber was also stated as a requirement. This was intended to protect the investor from any opportunistic behaviour by the shipbuilder. The last and often very lengthy section concerned the basic obligations of the shipbuilder, and was devoted to a technical description of the construction process, which was varied and usually very technical. The purpose of this section was to ensure that the shipowner would receive the object of the agreement, and that it would be built according to the desired specifications. These specifications included the insertion of structural pieces of hull, their measurements, and the distance between them: "*the keel will be five parmakia thick* (19 cm) [parmaki=παρμάκι, equals 0.038 metres], *the keelson will be six parmakia thick* (22.8 cm), *the frames will be double and three parmakia thick* (11.4 cm), *and the distance between them will be five and a half parmakia* (20.9 cm)".[10] Furthermore, the superstructures and the rest of ship's equipment (and sometimes the rigging) were also specified in detail, if they were included among the items deliverable by the shipbuilder: "*he will build the bitts on the bow and stern, the kadena* [a kind of beam on the prow and the stern] *with its supporters on the bulwark, the catheads for the anchor, with the scuppers on the bow and the stern, the binnacle, the galley with the belfry, the capstan, the cutwater, but without the figure.... the shipbuilder also promises to build the rudder, the single-planked bulwarks, the gunwale with holes except in the ward room, and two boats proportionate to the size of the ship*."

The section following that on the shipbuilder's obligations and the technical features of the ship specified the cost to the owner for materials, wages, and the master shipwright's remuneration: "*To the aforementioned way of construction of the hull, the said Thermiotis promises to pay to Shipbuilder Koufoudakis one thousand four hundrend spanish silver dollars in four installments, one quarter at the beginning of each month*." This method of payment was not the most typical. In most cases, owners paid the installments as the work progressed, and at specific stages of the construction process. On 8 August 1848, for the construction of the brig *Nelson*, of 216 tons, the Ipsariot captain Dimitrios A.

9 Georgios I. Kotsovillis, *Περί εξαρτισμού των πλοίων*, (Syros: 1919, (reprint), Athens: 1995), 8.

10 GSA, Syros, notary Andreas David, n. 6917.

Androulis "*promises to pay to Shipbuilder Nikolaos Georgiou Solomos the mutually agreed price of fourteen thousand seven hundred fifty drachmas, which mister Androulis promises to pay in four equal installments, one quarter today, one quarter when he* [the shipbuilder] *inserts the wales, one quarter when he starts to lay the deck, and the last when he delivers the ship to the port.*"[11] The number of payment installments varied between two and six, but was most commonly three or four. Installments to be paid when "*he inserts the wales*" or "*when he starts to lay the deck*" are very often mentioned in the agreements: these are clearly milestone phases in the construction process. Wales are the first strakes of the planking, inserted when the shipbuilder completes most of the skeleton and is about to insert the longitudinal fastenings; the laying of the deck commences when the skeleton, the inner planking, and ceiling of the hull are completed.[12]

Multiple currencies were used in the transactions covering the thirty-seven years of the examined period. From 1829 to 1833, payment for newly built ships was based on grosi (γρόσι), the ottoman gurus, while parallel to this, from 1830, finikas (φοίνικας), the first currency of the Greek National State under Governor Ioannis Kapodistrias appeared: the exchange rate between these, as specified in the transactions, was 1 finikas to 2.5 grosi. Finika's coinage was based on the Spanish silver dollar, of which it amounted to one sixth of the value. The currencies mentioned in the transactions must have been very often nominal, due to the scarcity of coins. The transactions would have been made in whatever currency was available.[13]

The drachma, which became the national currency in 1833, was also based on Spanish silver dollar, and corresponded to one sixth of the value of the latter. King Otho's governments hoped that its introduction would shakeout the damaged and counterfeit ottoman currencies and stimulate the influx of cash that the internal market required. However, this prohibition was not valid in the case of European currencies recognized by the Greek government,

---

11 GSA, Syros, notary Andreas David, n. 21283. [ΓΑΚ/ΑΝΚ Σύρου, Συμβ. Ανδρέας Δαβίδ, Λυτά έγγραφα]. The brig *Nelson* took its certificate of construction in 24.12.1848, Ibid., Ι/Ναυπηγικά n. 2858, and traced also in Harlaftis – Vlassopoulos, *Historical Register 'Pontoporeia'.*

12 Damianidis, *Ελληνική Παραδοσιακή*, 195–97, 201–02.

13 Eftichia Liata, *Φλωριά δεκατέσσερα στένουν γρόσια σαράντα. Η κυκλοφορία των νομισμάτων στον ελληνικό χώρο, 15ος–19ος αι.*, [*"Fourteen florins make forty gurus". The circulation of currencies in the Hellenic areas, 15th to 19th centuries*], (Athens: Department of Neohellenic Research Editions, 1996), 291; Nikolas Kougeas, *Η τιμή του συναλλάγματος και η νομισματική πολιτική στην Ελλάδα (1843–1879)*, [*The exchange rates and the monetary policy in Greece (1843–79)*], (Athens: Cultural Foundation of National Bank, 1992), 24, 30.

which published drachma exchange rates for many such currencies.[14] The Spanish silver dollar had a strong presence in the Syros shipbuilding market in the 1830s and 1840s, but the drachma was also used in transactions from 1833, initially to a lesser degree, but it gradually began to appear more frequently from the late 1830s, and from the 1850s it became the only currency used in contractual transactions.

The payment section of the contract follows the section that includes nailing, bolting, caulking, and launching: "*all the necessary riveting (nails, bolts, treenails, the pitch, oakum, the hole openers, caulkers, the ropes for the drags, the tallow) and the men that the shipbuilder needs to launch the ship to sea and to deliver her to Thermiotis are in charge of Thermiotis, but the drags are in charge of the Shipbuilder.*" The above case, of delivering a vessel "white", (as used to be said) was very common, and consisted in delivering the hull assembled but not nailed and caulked, leaving the owner responsible for the rest of the work needed to complete the vessel and for hiring the necessary craftsmen. The launch, the standing facilities, the grid, the transversal pieces, the drags, the necessary material for launching, the tallow and the ropes, as well as the men, were all the responsibility of the shipbuilder.

In the final section of the contract, both sides promised to abide by the agreement and gave their signature, although often shipbuilders and captains were illiterate, as declared in the document. However, the fact that they would promise to observe the terms of the agreement, without specifying further clauses in the case of the contrary, is perhaps due to a kind of "*generalized morality*". This is a system of informal but embedded values, morals, and mentalities that strenghtens confidence due to the fear of damage to the professional reputation or the social and personal ties of the parties involved.[15] However, often the fear of opportunistic behaviour outweighed the trust and values of "generalized morality", and led the parties to designate certain clauses. These could be quite generic: "*the violator of this agreement must compensate the other party for all expenses and delays*", as in the agreement for the construction of the brig *Agia Trias* of the Ipsariot captain Dimitris Ch. Filinis

14 Official Government Gazette, [*Εφημερίς της Κυβερνήσεως του Βασιλείου της Ελλάδος*], n. 3, Nafplio, 28 February 1833; Kougeas, *Η τιμή του συναλλάγματος*, 35–36, 38. The first mention of a new ship to be paid with drachma in Syros was the agreement of the brig *Themistoklis* of Nikolaos Anisis and Petros Tapontes from Andros, GSA, Syros, notary Andreas David, [ΓΑΚ/ΑΝΚ Σύρου, Συμβ. Ανδρέας Δαβίδ, Βιβλίον Μνημονικὸν ὑπὸ στοιχεῖον Η',] n. 196, 14.2.1834 and the property document ibid., [Βιβλίον Μνημονικὸν ὑπὸ στοιχεῖον Θ'], n. 1351, 20.7.1834.

15 Granovetter, "Economic action", 58–63.

and the merchants Ioannis G. Kotzas and Nikolaos Psaltoglou.[16] Clauses could also be explicit but unilateral. For instance, the shipbuilder Nikolaos Pagidas was obliged to deliver a vessel to captain Diodatos Kuekitz on April 1, 1843, or he would be required to indemnify him for five thousand drachmas. Captain Kuekitz demanded the full compensation amount from Pagidas for the delay in delivering the brig *Alexandros*, which belonged to the Odessa merchant Markos Michail Kuekitz, and was delivered few days later.[17] Finally, clauses could be also explicit but mutual, as in the agreement between the shipbuilder Zannis Koufoudakis and the captain Georgios Triantafillou, who bound themselves to pay an indemnity of three thousand drachmas in case of any violation of terms in the construction of the brig *Nea Kalliopi*, of 179 tons.[18]

Variations in the Object of the Shipbuilding Agreement

In most cases, shipbuilders worked with orders, but in some cases they also built semi-finished vessels on speculation. For instance, the Ipsariot shipbuilder Georgios Dramitzas agreed to deliver a ready to sail semi-finished *goleta* (schooner) to the Hydra captain Ioannis Balis, which was subsequently named *Agios Nikolaos*.[19] The sale of a semi-finished vessel could also concern a share of the ship, not its entirety, as in the case of the shipbuilder Ioannis Pagidas, who agreed to sell half or two-thirds of a vessel after its completion to Stamatis Dimitriou.[20] Shipbuilders also sometimes agreed only to supervise the construction of a vessel without taking charge of the material and labour expenses. The shipowners Dimitrios and Nikolaos Lykiardopoulos from Cephalonia, who represented the merchant Nikolletos Fokas (also Cephalonian but resident in Syros), commissioned the shipbuilder Frangoulis Sehas to supervise the construction of a vessel, to supply the necessary craftsmen, and to agree their wages with them, although the payments were to be made by Fokas alone.

A third variation concerns the deliverable object of the agreement. In most cases, shipbuilders delivered a "white vessel", which was not nailed and caulked. However, from the late 1840s, there was an increase in the number of cases where shipbuilders agreed to deliver a "*black vessel of a brig*", which

16 GSA, Syros, notary Andreas David n. 5997, 18.8.1837, property document, ibid., n. 6355, 10.11.1837.

17 Ibid., n. 14157, 2.11.1842, n. 14977, 14.1.1843, property document, n. 15077, 7.5.1843.

18 Ibid., n. 26315, 9.1.1853. In the property document n. 26531, 25.4.1853 it is stated that co-shipowners are the merchant Konstantinos Mistrouvakis, resident in Trieste, the brothers Triantafyllos and Konstantinos Hadjimavroudis and Garifalos Anastasiou.

19 Ibid., n. 12060, 27.6.1841, property document, n. 12245, 13.8.1841.

20 Ibid., n. 12037, 21.6.1841.

had a nailed and caulked hull, as the shipbuilder Nikolaos Pagidas agreed with the muslim captain from Crete, Pilalaga Kougimtzaki, for his brig *Aspasia*.[21] Subcontracting was rarely documented, but did occur: for instance, the shipbuilder Nikolaos Tzannes assigned the recruitment of workers and the supervision of construction to captain Dimitrios Tzentzeres.[22] In contrast, the Cretan captain Osman Beyzade prohibited the shipbuilder Nikolaos Pagidas from subcontracting the work for the brig *Amilton* to anyone else, either entirely or in part, and demanded that the ship had to be completed by Pagidas alone.[23] In order to guarantee that there would be no subcontracting, the owners of the brig *Limnos* (the Syros captain Antonios Ioannidis, the Trieste merchant Konstantinos Mistrouvakis and the Cairo merchant Nikolaos Emmanouil) prohibited the shipbuilder Koufoudakis from paying the joiners and sawyers a lump sum, and insisted upon daily wages.[24] Generally, the effort to secure that the supervision of construction was to be carried out by the master shipwright himself, and not someone else of inferior or dubious skills, can be explained as a guarantee of quality and an attempt to reduce future costs that might arise due to issues of responisibility and the need for technical corrections.

The practise of withdrawal, though not widespread, was not unknown in the Syros shipbuilding market. Nikolaos Kozadinos from Mykonos conceded an old vessel of 137.5 tons without rigging and with little equipment to shipbuilder Ioannis Pagidas, along with the money he had agreed to pay for the timber and wages on his future brig *Athina*, of 150 tons.[25] Captain Dimitrios Mantzouranis from Trikeri obtained a discount of 125 Spanish silver dollars for his new brig *Aristidis*, after he conceded his old brig of 150 tons with no rigging or equipment.[26] The case of the brig *Othon*, of 273 tons, was more characteristic. It was conceded for two thousand drachmas by its owner, the Santorini captain Konstantinos Kozaos, to the shipbuilder Zannis Koufoudakis, after 17 years of service, in order to meet the expenses for the construction of his new *Othon*.[27]

In order to guarantee the completion of the work, a timely delivery, and the quality of construction, owners sometimes set specific terms related to

21 Ibid., n. 25126, 17.9.1851, property document, n. 25373, 28.12.1851.

22 Ibid., n. 22337, 1.4.1849.

23 Ibid., n. 24770, 4.5.1851, property document, n. 25047, 14.8.1851.

24 Ibid., n. 26392, 23.2.1853, property document, n. 26711, 24.7.1853.

25 Ibid., Βιβλίον Μνημονικόν ὑπὸ στοιχεῖον Η′, n. 247, 22.2.1834, property document, Βιβλίον Μνημονικόν ὑπὸ στοιχεῖον Θ′, n. 1540, 13.8.1834.

26 Ibid., n. 5486, 15.4.1837, property document, n. 6245, 13.10.1837.

27 Ibid., n. 24741, 24.4.1851. The previous *Othon* belonged to captain Kozaos since 7.3.1834.

the use of workforce. To ensure productivity, they demanded a fixed minimum number of workmen, which served as a kind of guarantee for the timely delivery of the vessel. Thus, for the construction of the 80 ton brig *Tombazis*, the shipwright Panagiotis Karakonstantis promised the Hydra captain Mihail Kiosses to "*during all the days of work to keep eight craftsmen working on the vessel, until they lauch it at sea*".[28] The owner Efstathios Anastasiou from Samos, on the other hand, not only set the minimum limit at ten carpenters per day, but also demanded to send away anyone who was not performing well.[29] The policy of the shipbuilder Hadjidimitrios Magos of hiring fewer craftsmen from those demanded for the completion of the brig *Marigo* led the Ipsariot owners Ioannis G. Kalimeris and Ioannis D. Mamounis to remind him that if he had not recruited more craftsmen and delivered the vessel by the prescribed date, he would have to pay one thousand spanish silver dollars. Despite these warnings, the vessel was indeed delivered one month and a half after the deadline, but there is no information available regarding whether or not the shipbuilder paid the amount demanded.[30]

Contracts are "*inevitably imperfect*" and they cannot fully protect the transacting parties from opportunistic behaviour. Thus, in certain cases, the attempt was made to include as many guarantees as possible to protect the terms of agreement, which in turn increased monitoring and enforcement costs.[31] The presence of a guarantor in the shipbuilding agreements, even if this was not standard procedure, must be interpreted in accordance with the above described behavioural perception. It was more usual for there to be a guarantor present on the owner's side to ensure that the shipbuilder would respect the agreement. However, in the case of the brig *Aristidis*, both the shipbuilder Ioannis Pagidas and the captain Dimitrios Mantzouranis used their own guarantors to ensure mutual respect of the agreed terms of the contract.[32]

Supervising the phases of construction and evaluating the quality of work on a wooden sailing ship required specialised knowledge of shipbuilding and maritime technology. This, along with distance, presented serious difficulties for an owner who wished to monitor the course of the work and any possible opportunistic behavior from the shipbuilder. Therefore, the presence of an

---

28 Ibid., Βιβλίον μνημονικῶν πράξεων ὑπὸ στοιχεῖον Δ', n. 1811, property document, n. 2022, 31.10.1832.

29 Ibid., n. 4028, 17.7.1836, property document, n. 4663, 23.10.1836, the vessel was a goleta (schooner), which had not been given a name yet.

30 Ibid., n. 26867, 29.9.1853, property document, n. 27803, 16.12.1853.

31 Rao, *The Economics*, 12, 117–20; North, *Institutions, Institutional Change*, 68, 122.

32 GSA, Syros, notary Andreas David, n. 5486, 15.4.1837.

agent who had the know-how and skills needed to follow the phases of construction was essential. Nikolaos Paterakis, a Nafplio merchant, assigned this task to the Ipsariot Mikes Arvanitis, the future captain of the 155-ton brig *Arieta*, who "*promised to supervise the construction of the ship, having as assistants his father Dimitrios Arvanitis and his two brothers Georgios and Andreas Dimitrios Arvanitis, and all four will work diligently until the vessel is ready to sail, with a monthly salary of one hundred drachmas for all, or else twenty five drachmas each, up to the completion of the vessel. If two of them, or even one, is absent, the rest will receive the above twenty five drachmas per month.*"[33] However, the practise of the future captain supervising the construction of the vessel on behalf of the shipowner is a long-established and universal practice, which continues in the shipping industry today.

The agency of Ilias Vavoulas, a Chiot merchant and Nafplion resident who built the 188-ton brig *Adamantios Korais* in Syros, is a more complicated issue. He assigned the tasks of paying installments to the shipbuilder Stamatis Leriotis and of hiring a supervisor for the construction of the ship to a Chiot merchant who was resident in Syros, Stamatis Tzitzinias. However, Vavoulas also appointed two additional men as supervisors.[34] The effort of the principal to control his agent is due to the assymetric information that distance generates, and is also a way of protecting himself from the possible opportunistic behavior of the agent, usually manifested through hiding information (adverse selection) or hiding acts (moral hazard).[35]

Timber Quality Control Issues

Timber was the most essential material in shipbuilding, and its type and quality was a matter of bargain and dispute between owners and shipbuilders. Therefore, almost all contracts include paragraphs ensuring the usage of good quality timber. However, in certain cases owners had more specific demands, the most frequent being the right of the owner to replace every piece of timber that was not of good quality, for example the case of the Santorini captain

33 Ibid., n. 7878, property document, n. 8714, 1.5.1839.

34 Ibid., n. 9434, 2.9.1839, property document, n. 10099, 12.3.1840.

35 Gordon H. Boyce, *Cooperative structures in global business. Communicating, transferring knowledge and learning across the corporate frontier*, (London-New York: Routledge, 2001), 4–5; Boyce – Ville, *The Development*, 41–42; Ann Carlos – Stephen Nicholas, "Managing the Manager: An Application of the Principal Agent Model to the Hudson's Bay Company", *Oxford Economic Papers*, New Series, vol. 45, n. 2, (April 1993), 244–45.

Ruben Luigi's 281-ton brig *Kiriaki tis Vaioforou*, or the Lemnos captain Andreas Trypos's 55-ton bombarda *Voto*.[36]

Defining the provenance of the timber was the owners' second specific demand, a sort of guarantee of quality, and each part of the hull's structure required timber of a different designation of origin. For the building of the brig *Alexandros*, Captain Diodatos Kuekitz demanded from the shipbuilder Nikolaos Pagidas that "*the keel, the keelson, the stempost, and the sternpost, the strakes, the frames, as well as the wing transom, have to be made with timber from Euboea; all the rest of the timber has to be made with timber from Asia Minor.*"[37]

The description of the timber to be used in the brig *Limnos* was even more exact and detailed: "*the timber must be eighty-one logs of prime quality from Kiovata, the rest from Thasos*... [later in the document]... *the deck strakes must be made of logs from Thasos, the posts from Xiros*... *in case it is not available from Xiros but from Arcadia, these must be used for the keel, posts, keelson, clamps, waterways, decklight, wales, gunwales, rudder, and cutwater; and four rows of strakes from the garboard strake and above must be from Kiovata, the beams and strakes for the planking and the rest of the timber must be from Thasos and Xiros*".[38] The passage cited identifies four areas of provenance, of which only Arcadia belonged to the Greek state. The Gulf of Xiros (today the Gulf of Saros) in eastern Thrace, Kiovata in southeastern Asia Minor in front of the Gulf of Simi, and the island of Thasos in the northern Aegean, all then belonged to the Ottoman Empire. On the basis of this case, we can see that timber from Xiros and Arcadia was better for the construction of the skeleton of the hull, whereas the timber from Kiovata and Thasos was better for the strakes of decking and planking, as well as for long connecting timbers, such as the keel and the posts.[39]

The kind of tree timber that was used influenced both the quality of timber and the endurance of the hull. Softwood was pinewood, and hardwood oak or elm. The overwelming majority of the ships built in Syros were made of softwood, but some were built from both types of timber. Hardwood was used for the skeleton, subject to trussing and hogging, whereas softwood was used for the large surfaces of the hull, planking, and decking. The Ipsariot

36 GSA, Syros, notary Andreas David, n. 6387, 17.11.1837, property document, n. 6974, 13.4.1838, n. 29004, 14.12.1855, property document n. 29251, 6.4.1856.

37 Ibid., n. 14157, 2.11.1842.

38 Ibid., n. 26392, 23.2.1853.

39 Similar reports for the provenance of the timber are found in other agreements of 1853, see, ibid., n. 26416, 7.3.1853 and n. 26649, 27.6.1853.

Andreas Mytaras, owner of the gabara (barque) *Mytaras* demanded from the shipbuilder Andreas Livadaros that the frames, knees, breast hooks, posts, wing transom, apron and dead wood must be from hardwood, while the rest must be from softwood.[40]

Special Demands on Technical Issues

This category included technical issues, which reveal the technical knowledge required in the shipbuilding market, as well as the efforts of the shipowners to obtain as many techinal benefits for their ships as possible. The demand for specific technical requirements or characteristics was based on previous experience. Information spillover was crucial for the transmission and the appropriation of knowledge between the actors, in a market where physical proximity was a necessary condition for easier and less costly dissemination.[41]

Copying was a basic means of disseminating information. Thus, captain Nikolaos Koutzoukos from Moschonisia asked to the shipbuilder Frangoulis Sehas to make "*a keelson from wild olive, and* [asked for] *the middle thick stuff to be like in Goulandri's ship*". This confirms that he was aware of the specific technical detail of the agreement made a month before between the Andros captain Leonardos Goulandris and Frangoulis Sehas, for the construction of the 135-ton brig *Epameinondas*.[42] Copying was not limited only to the accumulated experience of shipwrights in charge, but extended to the effort to copy from other shipwrights: "*The Shipbuilder Koufoudakis furthermore promises to do in the ship whatever else the* (shipbuilder) *Nikolaos Pagidas does in the ship of Konstantinos Skandalis, which is under construction here*." This phrase demonstrates that the owner considers copying a legitimate and feasible practice.[43]

The most tangible evidence of information spillover and copying in the Syros shipbuilding market arises in the case of sister ships. This very widespread practice also confirms the degree of standardization in ship construction in Syros, and suggests that for shipowners, this was a guarantee of the quality of construction. Captain Frantzeskos Mavroudis, a Syros resident of Chiot origin

---

40 Ibid., n. 31817, 23.2.1862. Certificate of construction in 18.6.1862, Ibid., n.I/Ναυπηγικά, n. 2143.

41 Mario Forni – Sergio Paba, "Spillovers and the Growth of Local Industries", *The Journal of Industrial Economics*, vol. 50, n. 2, (June, 2002), 163, 166.

42 GSA, Syros, notary Andreas David, Βιβλίον μνημονικῶν πράξεων ὑπὸ στοιχεῖον Β′, n. 811, 2.12.1831. For brig *Epameinondas*, ibid., n. 692, 28.10.1831, property document, ibid., Βιβλίον μνημονικῶν πράξεων ὑπὸ στοιχεῖον Γ′, n. 1113, 14.3.1832.

43 Ibid., n. 21039, 4.6.1848. Certificate of construction, GSA, Syros I/Ναυπηγικά, n. 2400, 4.10.1848. Konstantinos Skandali's ship was the brig *Nikolaos*, 261 tons, ibid., I/Ναυπηγικά, n. 1911, 9.9.1848.

who built a sister ship with his countryman Nikolaos Tzouros, asked the shipbuilder Ioannis Koufoudakis to launch his own ship simultaneously (and from the same grid) as Tzouro's ship.[44] Characteristically, the building of sister ships was mostly a case of owners of common origin, or at least of the same professional milieu. This shows that information circulated more easily between groups with connecting links, continuous contact, and established relationships of trust. On the other hand, this also meant that the construction of a ship based on a previous example and owned by a person from the same place or of the same profession worked as a guarantee, and diminished the level of research, the information, and the bargaining costs demanded of the investor.

These cooperative networks based on kinship, common origin and common profession functioned as informal channels of protection from the uncertainty of transactions in the market, and mobilized human and material resources more cheaply and efficiently. Most importantly, they provided information spillover through a business network that would have cost a lot more to obtain, in terms of both time and money, through a free market.[45] Thus, the Spetses captain Stylianos Stemnitsiotis agreed with the shipbuilder Dimitrios Koufoudakis to build his brig *Agios Nikolaos* based on the agreements of two sister brigs whose captains were also from Spetses. These were the *Evangelistria* of Nikolaos Mystrakis and the *Agios Georgios* of Ghikas Kostouros, built by Zannis Koufoudakis, brother of Dimitrios.[46] The brig *Kimisis tis Panagias*, built by Nikolaos Pagidas for Georgios Papoff, a Berdiansk merchant of Russian citizenship, was a sister ship of the brig *Athina* of a Russian merchant of Taganrog who was resident in Constantinople, Konstantinos Synodis. The latter was also a deputy to Papoff in the construction of his brig, and in his turn

44 Ibid., notary Andreas David n. 9722, 23.11.1839. These are the brigs *Nisos Chios* of Mavroudis and *Leonidas* of Tzouros, both of 185 tons, property documents n. 10279 and 10280, 17.4.1840.

45 Gordon Boyce, "Network structures, processes and dynamics: Inter-firm cooperative frameworks in the shipping industry", in *International merchant shipping in the 19th and 20th centuries. The comparative dimension*, op. cit., 165–70; Mark Casson, "Entrepreneurial networks in international business", *Business and economic history*, vol. 26, n. 2 (Winter 1997), 813–17; Mary Rose, *Firms, networks and business values. The British and American cotton industry since 1750*, (New York: Cambridge University Press, 2000), 74.

46 GSA, Syros, notary Andreas David, n. 20232, 12.11.1847, property document Ibid., notary Christodoulos Ioannou [Συμβ. Χριστόδουλος Ιωάννου], Inventory 3, n. 3758, 1.4.1848. For brigs *Evangelistria* and *Agios Georgios* ibid., notary Andreas David, n. 20033, 22.9.1847 and n. 20018, 19.9.1847 and the property documents, ibid., n. 20921, 6.5.1848 and n. 20936, 8.5.1848.

commissioned captain Dimitrios Konstantis, from Koutali in the Sea of Marmara, to supervise the construction.[47]

The owners' efforts to obtain the best possible quality of work and reduce costs made them extremely meticulous and demanding as regards the phases of construction, nailing, metal component application, and caulking. In some cases, when a master shipwright undertook to complete both the nailing and caulking (or less frequently only the former), the agreements included detailed descriptions of the size of metal components, the type of material, and the size and thickness of the bolts to be used. For instance, in the agreement for the construction of the brig *Nea Kalliopi* of Georgios Triantafyllou, we find: "*The bolt of the keel must be of iron of twelve oka and thicker on the back side* [a measure of mass equivalent of 1.282 kg in Greece], *of the posts of fifteen oka, of the cutwater of eighteen oka, of the clamps of five oka, waterways of seven, for the futtocks of five oka square, for the wales and planking proportional to the size of the ship*".[48]

Caulking was a very sensitive process, as it concerned the sealing of the vessel. It was therefore a source of worry for some shipowners, to the extent that they demanded that a specific craftsman should be appointed to carry out the task. The merchant Ioannis Sinos asked the shipbuilder Frangoulis Sehas to hire the caulker Tzikourlas for his ship.[49] Some owners insisted upon specifying the exact way in which they wanted surfaces of the hull to be caulked. For instance, the Ipsariot captain Alexandros Domestinis did this for his brig *Nikolaos*, asking the shipbuilder Nikolaos Pagidas to caulk the hull inside and outside, as well as the deck and the bulwarks.[50] Others had specific technical requirements, such as as the Ipsariots, Ioannis Kalimeris and Ioannis Mamounis, who demanded that their brig *Marigo*, of 306 tons must be caulked inside and outside with the necessary oakum and spun-yarn, right up to the waterline.[51]

Rigging was a process that Syros's master shipwrights rarely undertook. However, it was sometimes the case when a shipbuilder would sell a semi-finished vessel. For instance, Frangoulis Sehas sold the 196-ton brig *Esodia tis Theotokou* to the Myconian captain Peris Markaris: "*Mister Sehas will make*

47 For brig *Athina*, ibid., n. 22786, 21.7.1849 and for *Kimisis tis Panagias*, ibid., n. 22912, 17.8.1849.

48 For the brig *Nea Kalliopi* see above.

49 GSA, Syros, notary Andreas David, n. 5729, 21.6.1837, property document ibid., n. 6010, 20.8.1837.

50 Ibid., n. 26372, 10.2.1853, property document ibid., n. 26504, 8.4.1853.

51 Ibid., n. 26722, 29.7.1853, property document ibid., n. 27503, 16.12.1853.

a bowsprit, a boom, a flying jib boom, two cat harpings from iron chain for the bowsprit, a foremast with mainsail [probably a course] *with the truss, a topsail, a topgallant and a royal, a mizzen mast, a mainsail with truss, a topsail, a topgallant, a royal, a spanker boom and a gaff, a jib, a flying jib, a fore topmast staysail, a fore sail, a fore topsail, a topgallant sail, a royal sail, a mainsail, a main topsail, a main topgallant and a main royal. The said sails, jibs, fore topmast staysail, foresail, fore topsail, mainsail, main topsail, spanker must of six sail twines, the rest five. The ropes, the shrouds, the breast backstays and the rest must be from Livorno, among the best to be found here.*"[52]

The Shipbuilding Timber Agreement

Once a shipbuilding agreement had been concluded, the first step was to collect all the materials needed for the construction of the ship. The shipbuilder or the owner, according to the type of agreement, had to make all the necessary deals for the timber supply, the iron parts, the rigging, and the rest of ship's equipment (anchors, barrels, etc.). Of these, timber was the first and most important material to assemble in order to begin the work. There were two basic ways of acquiring a timber supply. The first was to purchase it from a specialized timber merchant or whoever else had shipbuilding timber for sale, and who would be responsible for delivering the timber in the shipyard. The second was for the shipbuilder or owner to buy the timber directly from the place where it was cut. This would involve hiring a vessel to transport the timber to Syros. The differences between these two types of contract regarding timber supply are as follows: (1) the sales contract, where the timber is either in Syros or it is elsewhere, and the seller must transport it; (2) chartering agreements for the transportation of the timber between the buyer and the captain of the transporting ship. A thorough analysis of the timber trade through these two types of contract will be presented in Chapter Six. Here, our focus will be on the timber supply procedure from the shipbuilder or the owner.

In some cases, the shipbuilder undertook to cover the cost of materials and wages. Ioannis Pagidas did this for the 150-ton brig *Athina*, which belonged to Nikolaos Kozadinos, and he had to buy the timber from Evangelos Tambourlos from Mitzela (Amaliapolis).[53] Similarly, the Syros resident shipbuilder (original from Hydra) Dimitrios Leriotis bought 100 timber logs from Manolis Nikolaou from Kasos, to build the brig *Miaoulis*, of 229 tons, for Dimitrios

52 Ibid., n. 27307, 3.3.1854, property document ibid., n. 27416, 7.4.1854.

53 Ibid., Βιβλίον Μνημονικόν ὑπὸ στοιχεῖον Η', n. 343, 9.3.1834. For brig *Athina* see above.

Andreas Miaoulis.[54] Both of these belong in the first category of timber supply contracts. In contrast, the owner Diodatos Kuekitz's demand to build his brig *Alexandros* with timber from Euboea forced the shipbuilder Nikolaos Pagidas to charter the 59-ton goleta *Themistoklis*, which belonged to Mihail Aggelis from Limni of Euboea, to carry the timber logs to Syros.[55]

When the building of the ship was on speculation, then the timber supply agreement preceded the agreement for the completion and delivery of the vessel to the potential customer. This was the case of shipbuilder Panagiotis Karakonstantis, who bought a quantity of timber from Dimitrios Konstantinos Kyparissis, director of the firm *Kyparissis and Serrafis brothers* with an interest loan of 1% per month, for the brig *Agios Spyridon*, later sold to Kali, the wife of Georgios Yannikos from Spetses.[56]

When the owner undertook to cover building expenses in full, he had to do everything necessary to supply the timber from an occasional seller or a timber merchant, like Konstantinos Zanes from Santorini, who bought two hundred strakes of pine from Euboea from the timber merchant Pantelis Chrysinas from Kranidi, for his 225-ton brig *Panaya Malteza*.[57] Emmanouil Kalaris, who built his 248-ton brig *Achilleus* at almost the same time, preferred to obtain a timber supply directly from the cutting place. So, he chartered the 104-ton Goleta *Poseidon*, which belonged to Nikolaos Ghikas from Limni of Euboea, to carry 90 logs from northern Euboea to Syros.[58] One peculiar and interesting case was that of the brothers Pothitos and Loukas Mathas from Santorini, who bought 200 logs from the shipbuilder Nikolaos Pagidas, who was also in charge of building their 187-ton brig *Panaya Platzani*. The shipbuilder for the transport of timber to Syros used a ship belonging to the Mathas brothers, also named *Panaya Platzani*, of 90 Russian lasts.[59] The Mathas brothers did not demand any freight for it, but all the ship and cargo expenses, including the manning, victualing, and the hiring of a captain, were the responsibility of the shipbuilder Pagidas.[60]

---

54 Ibid., Βιβλίον Μνημονικόν ὑπὸ στοιχεῖον Ε', n. 2195, 23.12.1832, property document ibid., n. 271, 29.3.1833.

55 GSA, Syros, notary Andreas David, n. 14172, 6.11.1842. For brig *Alexandros* see above.

56 Ibid., n. 17359, 4.7.1845. Agreement of sale of a semi-finished vessel, ibid., n. 17503, 25.8.1845, property document, ibid., notary Mihail Ioannopoulos [Συμβ. Μιχ. Ιωαννόπουλος], n. 685, 28.12.1845.

57 Ibid., n. 8532, 22.3.1839, property document ibid., n. 9195, 2.8.1839.

58 Ibid., n. 8546, 23.3.1839, property document ibid., n. 9170, 28.7.1839.

59 For the *last* equal to 1.85 tons see Kaukiainen, *A History of Finnish Shipping*, 46.

60 GSA, Syros, notary Andreas David, n. 6237, 11.10.1837, property document ibid., n. 6817, 9.3.1838.

The Iron Components Agreement

Almost parallel to the timber supply procedure was the agreement for the fabrication and supply of iron components. The above-described picture for the timber supply is equally valid for the iron components. Thus, if the shipbuilder had to order the iron material he would address an ironsmith. For instance, Antonios Ioannis Karistinos agreed with shipbuilder Stamatios Koufoudakis to fabricate and supply as construction proceeded the iron parts for the hull, the rigging, and the boats for a brig of 21 metres long. These were made according to the prototype samples provided by the shipbuilder, an essential parameter in all contracts for iron parts.[61]

If the owner had to provide the iron material, which was more frequent, the deliverables in the contract could be stated in a more generic fashion, as in the agreement between Konstantinos Zanes for his brig *Panaya Malteza* (see above) and the ironsmith Dimitrios Bugiukas, who promised to fabricate all the nailing material of the brig in construction scheduled for the following week.[62] Here, the iron components agreement preceded the shipbuilding agreement by three days, which meant that Zanes had obtained an oral agreement with the shipbuilder that allowed him to proceed with other deals. However, the agreement sometimes included a detailed inventory of the iron parts to be fabricated. The ironsmith Hadjizaharias Ioannou undertook to fabricate the nails for the futtocks, the wales, the deck, the bulkwark, the large nails of the launch (the large boat), the bolts, the hooks, the thimbles, the hinges, and all the necessary wrought iron (except for the chains and the anchors, which were imported) for the brig *Rousseau* whose captain was the Ipsariot Ioannis Georgios Kalimeris.[63]

A basic and constant demand in these agreements was that the ironsmith should supply the materials promptly during ship construction, in order not to interrupt the process, as the ironsmith Bugiukas promised to captain Dimitrios Nikolaos Arapis for his 171-ton brig *Timoleon*.[64] A further guarantee of quality, as with timber, was provided by specific demands regarding the provenance of the iron. The shipbuilder Stamatios Koufoudakis asked for the wrought iron to be fabricated from English iron, but for the standing rigging and hinges to be made from Russian iron. Similarly, Kalimeris demanded English iron for all parts except the hinges, which he wanted to be made from Russian iron.

61 Ibid., n. 9477, 28.9.1839.

62 Ibid., n. 8508, 18.3.1839.

63 Ibid., n. 10823, 3.8.1840. Certificate of construction, ibid., I/Ναυπηγικά, n. 2486, 21.12.1840.

64 GSA, Syros, notary Andreas David, n. 8665, 19.4.1839, property document ibid., n. 8941, 12.6.1839.

The price of all iron components was paid in drachmas per oka (see above). The payment was made upon delivery of the parts, and a clause ensured the two parts from ex post opportunism. Thus, captain Zanes agreed to pay to Bugiukas 85 lepta (a drachma subdivision, where 100 lepta is equal to 1 drachma) per oka for all types of nailing components, and the clause was fixed at 500 drachmas.

The Property Document

The completion of the construction process and the delivery of the vessel to the owner were validated by a notarial act named *Property*, which was the final stage of a complex and sometimes lengthy procedure, which confirmed the succesful end of the agreement between shipbuilder and shipowner. This document was the legal property title, and was needed to register the ship in a Greek port registry. For this, it was necessary that at least 50% of the ship should belong to Greek citizens.[65] The importance of this document is also revealed in the shipbuilding agreements, where it is fixed that the payoff of the owner to the shipbuilder would take place after the launch of the ship and the supply of the property document.

Unlike the shipbuilding agreement, which was usually a long document, the property document in most cases consisted of only two pages, with information concerning the final technical features of the vessel (type, dimensions), the final costs, the ship's name, and the ownership pattern. Information about the construction cost appears in the contracts from 1836 onwards, and, after 1838, included additional details concerning the partial and total costs of the vessel. The document was divided into two parts. The first part concerned the deliverables, the amount the owner paid to the shipbuilder for materials and wages, the recognition of ownership from the shipbuilder to the owner, and the conclusion of the agreement: "*Mister Sehas confessed that had agreed with mister Grimaldis to build for him a brig, built here, made of softwood, with a length of twenty four picheis* [πήχεις, see above] (21.93 m), *a breadth of twenty five kannes* [κάννες, see above] (7.62 m), *and a depth or height of fourteen and a half kannes* (4.41 m). *Furthermore, mister Sehas confessed that had received from mister Grimaldis twelve thousand and seventy one drachmas for the timber consumed in the construction of the vessel and for his own wages and those of the joiners and sawyers working under him. Thus, under this document, the shipbuilder Sehas confesses that he considers mister Grimaldis the undeniable and sole owner of this vessel and that he is in receipt of the agreement made between*

65 GSA, Central Service, [ΓΑΚ/Κεντρική Υπηρεσία], Athens, King Otho Archive [Αρχείο Περιόδου Όθωνος], Ministry of Marine [Υπουργείο Ναυτικών], file 43, Decree on merchant marine [*Διάταγμα περί εμπορικής ναυτιλίας*], 14/26 November 1836. Articles 4 and 6.

them for the construction of the ship on the eighteenth of August of the previous year."[66]

The second part of the document concerned only the owner and the ship, and reported the remaining building and equipping expenses, the total value of the ship, her name and the owners, if more than one, along with their holding shares: "*Furthermore, mister Grimaldis confesses that he has additionally paid thirty thousand drachmas for the nailing of the ship, the furniture and equipment, for the wages of the caulkers and augerers, and for the consumed pitch, tar and tallow, making the whole value of the ship fourty two thousand two hundred and seventy one drachmas. Finally, mister Grimaldis confesses that the name of the ship is* Kantito."

The Four Types of Shipbuilding Product

The analysis of the first part of the property documents shows that the deliverables were not uniform, and that in most cases shipbuilders undertook only certain phases of construction. Overall, four categories of agreement can be distinguished, which coincide with four types of shipbuilding product or services.

The first category of agreement is to deliver the hull of the vessels neither nailed nor caulked: these used to be called "white vessels." In this category belongs also the previous example of the brig *Kantito*, of captain Ioannis Grimaldis from Ano Syros. In the second category, the shipbuilder agreed to deliver a nailed hull, as Nikolaos Pagidas did for the 177-ton brig *Apostolos Petros*, of captain Petros Papapetrou from Galaxidi. The hull cost 17,100 drachmas, out of a total of 30,000 that the owner paid in total.[67] In the third category, the delivered hull was nailed and caulked ("*black*", as was stated at the time), like the brig *Aspasia*, built by Nikolaos Pagidas for Pilalaga Kougimtzaki, who paid 6,800 drachmas out of the total cost of 12,000 for the above services.[68] The three mentioned practises concern the delivery of a specific shipbuilding product. Nailing and caulking, as previously mentioned, began to be included more systematically among the deliverables from 1838 onwards.

The fourth category is the supervision of construction. In this case, the shipbuilder receives remuneration for his services of supervising the construction of the vessel, but all expenses are the responsibility of the owner. The shipbuilder was therefore responsible only for the quality of work and the prompt delivery

66 GSA, Syros, notary Andreas David, n. 8221, 26.1.1839, shipbuilding agreement, ibid., n. 7568, 18.8.1838.

67 Ibid., n. 30199, 9.9.1857.

68 Ibid., n. 25373, 28.12.1851.

of the vessel: this was the case of Zannis Koufoudakis, who *"built here with workmanship and with the expenses of the said Gentlemen Dimitrios Georgios Papas and Nikolaos Georgios Papas, the hull of a brig, and received from them one thousand five hundred drachmas for the supervision of the construction of the ship named* Georgios."[69] Agreements for the supervision of the construction began to appear in large number from 1839, parallel to the more verticalized practises of the Syros shipbuilders. This also coincided with a period of take-off in production. However, according to Ugo Marchese, the undertaking of supervision in the Liguria shipyards during the nineteenth century was due to the lack of capital (on the shipuilder's side) needed to pay for materials and wages.[70]

However, in the agreements for the supervision of construction, there were a few exceptions when a shipbuilder was rewarded for his supervision services as well as for the timber he consumed in building the hull, as happened to the shipbuilder Ioannis Stamatiou, who received 1,500 drachmas for his work and the timber of the goleta *Ioniki Ellas*, of Vasilios Mouropoulos from Constantinople.[71] Another shipbuilder named Andreas Livadaros received 5,000 drachmas for his supervision and for the wages to be paid in a lump sum to the caulkers for the brig 172-ton brig *Theologos*, of Georgios Fteris from Patmos.[72]

It has already been mentioned that it was rare for a ship to be delivered with all its equipment ready to sail. In the two known cases, the ships were built by Frangoulis Sehas: the first was the previously mentioned brig *Esodeia tis Theotokou*, of Peris Markaris, and the second the 300-ton brig *Agios Georgios* of Andreas Paleologos, a Berdiansk merchant who was resident in Mariupol, and who paid 51,000 drachmas for the entire ship.[73]

Agency and Ownership

In the second part of the property document, it was very often the case that the person who made the agreement was called to reveal the property pattern. In other words, that person needed to reveal whether he was the sole owner, or if there were others (and the amount of shares they held), or if he was not

69 Ibid., n. 24398, 18.12.1850.

70 Pierangelo Campodonico, "Genoese shipbuilding in the 19th century", in *Shipbuilding and Ships in the eastern Mediterranean during the 18th and 19th century*, ed. Kostas Damianidis (Chios: Homerion Cultural Center of Chios Municipality, 1999), 169–70.

71 GSA, Syros, notary Andreas David, n. 26082, 10.9.1852.

72 Ibid., n. 32023, 24.10.1862.

73 Ibid., n. 25031, 8.8.1851.

the owner of the ship but an agent. Captain Aggelos Konstantinos Denerikos declared that he held 5/8 of the brig *Dimitrios*, of 465 tons, whereas 2/8 belonged to the commercial firm *Vouros, Damianos and Co* of Constantinople, and 1/8 belonged to the Trieste merchant Antonios Dimitriou.[74] Many of the investors, mostly merchants, who were established away from Syros, could not deal directly with shipbuilders. Even if they could, they probably lacked the knowledge needed to monitor a process as complex and specialised as ship construction. Therefore, it was often the case that the future captain (eventually also a shareholder) was appointed. For instance, the Cephalonian captain Spyridon Charalambos Rosolimos represented the above mentioned Russian citizen merchant Andreas Paleologos, and captain Theodoros Petalas from Ithaki represented Ioannis Mestakis from Rensk, Bessarabia, for his brig *Eftychia*.[75]

The Certificate of Construction

The very last stage of the institutional process was the issue of the certificate of construction by the municipal authorities of Hermoupolis. The declaration of construction was an obligation of the shipbuilder, and the certificate was needed for the registration of the ship on port registries. The certificate is a short document, in which the shipbuilder declared the place of construction, the ship type, the name of the ship, the owners, and (sometimes) their origin. In addition, it also mentions the time span of the construction and, in some cases, the tonnage, the dimensions, or the total value of the ship. From 1862, shipbuilders were also obliged to declare the commencement of construction to the municipal authorities, in order to have the right to obtain the certificate.[76]

The Technical Process

Technology and Methods of Construction in Syros Shipyards

The building of sailing ships in Syros in the nineteenth century followed methods that had been in use in the Mediterranean since Medieval times, which merged with the achievements of the northern European tradition, the square sail and the sternpost rudder, and produced through certain evolutionary

74 Ibid., n. 22862, 3.8.1849.

75 Ibid., n. 12579, 30.10.1841.

76 GSA, Syros, I/Ναυπηγικά, n. 3321/1937 and newspaper *Astir ton Kykladon*, [*Αστήρ των Κυκλάδων*], n. 285–286, 6.10.1862.

stages the dominant nautical and shipbuilding technology for wooden sailing ships, lasting from the Renaissance until the decline of sail.[77] In the nineteenth century, the two fundamental methods of ship construction in Syros and in the Mediterranean world more generally were the *skeleton-first* and *carvel* techniques.

Skeleton-first is an established term in the literature concerning a method of building the hull of a vessel in which the frames are inserted first, thereby defining the shape of the hull, followed by the planking. This method replaced the older method of *shell-first*, applied in the Graeco-Roman world as well as among the Vikings, where the hull was built by first joining the strakes with mortises and tenons. Then the frames were inserted, having a 'passive' role to the shaping of the hull, as Lucien Basch stated.[78] The proof of the earlier usage of the *skeleton-first* method comes from an eleventh century shipwreck, and there are indications of its use in the early Byzantine period, if not before.[79] *Carvel* is the method of building the planking, and has been in use in the Mediterranean from antiquity until the present. Contrary to the *clinker* built vessels of overlapping strakes, the *carvel* method consists of attaching the planks edge to edge, thereby creating a smooth surface. The *clinker* technique was outstripped by *carvel* in the construction of large sailing ships from (at least) since the beginning of the seventeenth century.[80]

Most of the hulls built in the Syros shipyards were longer than ten metres, which necessitated the use of a shipbuilding plan. Among Greek shipbuilders, this plan was called *sala* (σάλα), and was a wooden floor upon which the shipwright marked the lines of the hull in real scale. The last registered *sala* in Syros, which was active until very recently, belonged to the Mavrikos Brothers

---

77 Timothy J. Rynyan, "The Cog as a warship", in *Cogs, Caravels & Galleons. The history of sailing ship, 1000–1650. Conway's History of the Ship*, ed. Robert Gardiner, (London: Conway Maritime Press, 1994), 49–50; Cipolla, *Before the Industrial* Revolution, 227–33; Richard W. Unger, "Introduction", in *Cogs, Caravels & Galleons*, op. cit., 8–10; Cees de Voogd, "Shipbuilding, Commercial", 569–72.

78 Lucien Basch, "Ancient wrecks and the archaeology of the ships", *International Journal of Nautical Archaeology and Underwater Exploration*, 1, (1972), 16.

79 Frederick H. Van Doorninck, "Serçe Limani", in *Encyclopedia of Underwater and Maritime Archaeology*, ed. James P. Delgado (New Haven-London: Yale University Press, 1997), 367–70; Frederick M. Hocker, "Shipbuilding: philosophy, practice and research", in *The Philosophy of Shipbuilding. Conceptual approaches to the study of wooden ships*, ed. Frederick M. Hocker and Cheryl A. Ward, (College Station, Texas: Texas A&M University Press, 2004), 6.

80 Hocker, "Shipbuilding", 5; Unger, "Introduction", 10.

shipyard.[81] In the Aegean, the use of shipbuilding plans for the construction of large vessels began at the end of the eighteenth century. Nineteenth century sources report that the shipbuilder Stamatios Koufoudakis from Chios introduced sala after he had worked in the Ottoman Imperial shipyards in Constantinople: (he was the father and grandfather of the Syros Koufoudakis family shipbuilders, examined in Chapter Six).[82] In Syros, the only mention of the use of *sala* in the nineteenth century comes in the agreement for the building of the barque *Mytaras*, built by Andreas Livadaros.[83] However, it is certain that master shipwrights had to use shipbuilding plans in the construction of medium or large merchantmen ranging from 100 to 300 tons (or more). The existence of such infrastructure is therefore clear.[84]

The examined agreements do not provide a plan or any other visual evidence concerning the design of the vessels, with the exception of a detailed reference to all structural elements of the hull and their dimensions, alongside the other equipment that the shipbuilder had to construct. Specific hull types are not referred to, for instance, whether they are double ended or counter stern; instead, most ship types are defined according to the rig. The examined agreements refer to nine ship types: gabara (barque), briki (brig), lotika, goleta (schooner), bombarda, kotero (cutter), bratsera, sacoleva and malteza. The gabara is the only three-masted vessel found in any construction agreement, and the lotika must have been a two-masted vessel with a hull similar to that of a brig, as we can deduce from her dimensions, though we have no specific information about this. The brig is the most widespread ship type, as we shall see below, and most of the agreements concern this type. The rest of ship types are coasters. The only available information about the necessary quantity of timber per structural element comes from brig *Koletis*, of 342 tons, built in 1847.

81 Damianidis, *Ελληνική Παραδοσιακή*, 153–60.

82 Konstantinos Nikodimos, *Υπόμνημα της Νήσου Ψαρών*, [*History of the Island of Psara*], (Athens: 1862), 72.

83 GSA, Syros, notary Andreas David, n. 31817, 23.2.1862.

84 Angeliki Fenerli, 'Les premiers constructeurs de navires à Hermoupolis (île de Syra), 1823–1835', in *The evolution of wooden shipbuilding in the Eastern Mediterranean during the 18th and 19th centuries. First International Workshop*, ed. Kostas Damianidis (Athens: Institute of Neohellenic Research, National Hellenic Research Foundation, 1993), 31; Damianidis, *Ελληνική Παραδοσιακή*, 73, 75.

TABLE 4.1 *Quantity of timber per structural element of brig* Koletis.

Structural element	Number of pieces
Timber logs	15
Straight timbers	227
Frames	957
Wales	47
Knees	103
Breast hooks	4*
Postson	1
Strakes	824
Stanchions	81
Hatches	12

Source: processed data from Appendix 3.6.
* In the document a further reference to breast hooks is found, but not its exact quantity.

According to Table 4.1, timber logs and straight timbers were for the straight structural elements, the keel, the keelson, and the posts. Frames, knees, the breast hooks and the postson for used for the internal reinforcement of the hull, while strakes and wales were for the planking. Stanchions could be used either as internal supporting structural elements or as stockings that supported the hull during its construction.

The Phases of Construction

The construction of the hull followed three separated phases, corresponding to three categories of structural elements of the vessel: (1) the skeleton, (2) planking and decking, and (3) superstructures and equipment.

The Skeleton

The skeleton elements are divided in two broad categories: (a) the longitudinal structural elements and (b) the vertical structural elements,[85] which according to the sources consulted are the following:

85 The distinction of the structural members belongs to Damianidis, *Ελληνική Παραδοσιακή*, 214–15.

Longitudinal elements	Vertical elements
Keel [karina, καρίνα]	Frames [postes, stravoxyla, πόστες, στραβόξυλα]
Stem and sternpost [podostama tis ploris kai tis primnis, ποδόσταμα της πλώρης και της πρύμνης]	Beams [kamaria, καμάρια, kadenes, καδένες and pagatses, παγκάτσες]
Keelson [sotropi, σωτρόπι]	Knees [bratsolia, μπρατσόλια]
Lower thick stuffs [stragalies, στραγαλιές]	Carling [pikeria, πικεριά]
Waterway [kourzeto tis kouvertas, κουρζέτο της κουβέρτας]	
Clamp [kourzeto tou kouradourou, κουρζέτο του κουραδούρου]	
Middle thick stuffs [louros, λούρος]	
Breasthooks [fournistes, φουρνιστές] and distuffs [ntoufekia, ντουφέκια].	

Keel, Stempost, Sternpost and Stern

The first timber laid was the keel. The laying was applied over the cleats to facilitate the construction and the subsequent launch.[86] The keel was the foundation of the hull, and was the timber that defined the ship's length; many documents therefore specify the length of the keel rather than the overall length. The keel of Syros built ships varied between one and three pieces, depending on the vessel's length. The minimum cross section of a brig's keel was made of two pieces. It measured 16.9 metres in length (henceforth L.K.), had a maximun breadth (henceforth M.B.) of 6.1 metres, and a depth (henceforth D) of 3.2 metres, and measured 17.1 centimetres in height per 20.9 centimetres in width (henceforth as follows: 17.1 × 20.9 cm), and belonged to

86 Damianidis, *Ελληνική Παραδοσιακή*, 183.

the brig *Agios Nikolaos* of the merchant Ioannis Sinos.[87] The maximum cross section of another two piece keel belonged to the brig *Maris Ath. Vallianos*, which belonged to the Cephalonian Aggelis Dion. Kambitzis. Its measurements were L.O. (overall) 31.08 × M.B. 7.3 × D 4.2. metres, 26.6 × 30.4 cm.[88] The keel's crossection minimum dimensions, in vessels made of three pieces, was 19 × 28.5 cm, and belonged to three sister brigs of Spetses shipowners. The measurements were L.K. 19.5 × M.B. 7.3 D 4.11 metres, while the maximum was 30.4 × 34.2 cm, on the brig *Zagora* of Ioannis Kassavetis, which measured L.K. 28 × M.B. 9.14 × D 5.48 metres.[89] On smaller ship types, such as the cutter, the measurements were L.K. 13.75 × M.B. 5.18 × D 2.6 metres, and the keel cross section was 13.3 × 19 cm.[90] Two sister bombardes of 30 tons, *Polyxeni* and *Panaya*, measured L.K. 11.88 × M.B. 4.87 × D 2.2 metres, had a keel cross section of 11.4 × 17.1–19 cm., and the sacoleva *Agios Spiridon* of Anastasios Halikiopoulos from Naxos, measured L.O. 10.96 × M.B. 3.96 × D 1.82 metres, and had a keel breadth of 9.5 cm.[91]

After the keel had been laid, the stempost and sternpost were attached. The stempost usually in vessels of over ten metres in length, was made of two pieces. Posts were reinforced with knees, called akrapi (ακράπι=apron) in the stempost, and skorpios (σκορπιός=inner sternpost) in the sternpost. Sometimes, skorpios was used for both the stemson and the postson, as in the brig *Agia Ekaterini* of Ioannis A. Tziros, where the horizontal (lower) leg measured 1.82 metres, and the vertical (upper) leg measured 1.37 metres. In larger vessels like brigs, this was straight timber on which the entire skeleton of the stern was attached, shaping along with the wing transom and the quarter timbers a kind of Ψ. The dimensions of the cross sections of both posts were the same as the keel.[92] There were two basic types of stern, the square or transom stern and the elliptical or counter stern. According to Mystic shipbuilders, an elliptical stern was stronger and less expensive than a transom stern. The elliptical or counter stern replaced the transom stern and became widespread in the

87 GSA, Syros, notary Andreas David, n. 5729, 21.6.1837, property document ibid., n. 6010, 20.8.1837.

88 Ibid., n. 30178, 14.8.1857, property document ibid., n. 30436, 22.4.1858.

89 Ibid., n. 24859, 2.6.1851, property document ibid., n. 25284, 17.11.1851.

90 Ibid., Βιβλίον Μνημονικόν ὑπὸ στοιχεῖον Ζ΄, n. 1029, 22.8.1833.

91 For *Polyxeni* ibid., n. 23398, 20.1.1850, property document ibid., n. 23579, 30.3.1850. For *Panaya* ibid., n. 23541, 15.3.1850, property document ibid., n. 23824, 13.6.1850. For *Agios Spiridon* ibid., n. 7094, 13.5.1838, property document ibid., n. 7446, 28.7.1838.

92 Efthimios Gourgouris, *Το Γαλαξείδι στον καιρό των Καραβιών*, [*Galaxidi in the age of sailing ships*], (Athens: 1983), 470; Damianidis, *Ελληνική Παραδοσιακή*, 184–86; GSA, Syros, notary Andreas David, n. 21039, 4.6.1848.

third quarter of the nineteenth century.[93] Most of the hulls built in Syros in the examined period must have been built with transom sterns. The wing transom, a founding element of the transom stern, was sometimes double, which mean that an extra timber, also called a counter wing transom, was inserted above the wing transom over the deck level, as in the brig *Agioi Apostoloi* (L.O. 23.16 × M.B. 8.07 × D 4.41) of the Cephalonians Achilleas Metaxas, resident in Syros, and Dionisios Karousos, resident in Trieste.[94] The only documention about the dimensions of the wing transom comes from the agreement of the brig *Aspasia*, which belonged to the merchant Georgios Iliadis, resident in Hermoupolis and originally from Samos. The ship's dimensions were L.O. 16.76 × M.B. 6.4 × D 3.35, and the wing transom measured 4.87 metres in breadth.[95]

The Frames

The next step was the insertion of the frames, which determined the lines of the skeleton and its resistance. The frames had an absolutely 'active' role, which is proven by the importance given to them in the agreement terms.[96] In larger vessels, the frames were composed of three, five, or nine pieces, depending upon the size of the hull. Shipbuilders first started to insert the frames in the midship section of the hull, which determined the maximum breadth, then used ribbands to shape the lines of the hull, thereby also defining the curvature of the rest of the frames.[97]

An 1834, a two-masted vessel, probably a brig (with dimensions of L.K. 17.36 × M.B. 6.4 × D 3.42 metres) required 46 frames, except the hawse pieces on the prow and the wing transom.[98] For an 1834 brig, *Agios Dionisios*, which belonged to Evangelos Karavias from Zakynthos and measured L.O. 19.2 × M.B. 6.7 × 3.35, it was agreed to insert 50 frames, with hawse pieces included.[99] The same number of frames is reported four years later in the agreement of the brig

93 William N. Peterson, *"Mystic Built". Ships and shipyards of the Mystic River, Connecticut, 1789–1914*, (Mystic, Connecticut: Mystic Seaport Museum, 1989), 95; Harold A. Underhill, *Deep-Water Sail*, (Glasgow: Brown Son & Ferguson, 1952), 48; Damianidis, *Ελληνική Παραδοσιακή*, 77; Campodonico, "Genoese shipbuilding", 171; Carlo De Negri, *Vele italiane del XIX secolo*, (Milano: Mursia, 1974), 51.

94 GSA, Syros, notary Andreas David, n. 26416, 7.3.1853, property document ibid., n. 26713, 25.7.1853.

95 Ibid., n. 18336, 18.5.1846, property document ibid., n. 18586, 23.7.1846.

96 Basch, "Ancient wrecks".

97 Damianidis, *Ελληνική Παραδοσιακή*, 186–88, 194.

98 GSA, Syros, notary Andreas David, Βιβλίον Μνημονικόν ὑπὸ στοιχεῖον Η', n. 196, 14.2.1834.

99 Ibid., n. 907, 25.5.1834, property document ibid., Βιβλίον Μνημονικόν ὑπὸ στοιχεῖον Θ', n. 1631, 27.8.1834.

Dimitrios, of 156 tons, which measured L.O. 18.28 × M.B. 6.85 × 3.8 and belonged to the Hermoupolis merchants Panagiotis Geralopoulos, Ioannis Amvrosios Rallis, and the captain Ioannis Mavroukos.[100]

In many cases, owners demanded double frames up to the wales, the waterway, the deck, or even up to the gunwale, as in the brig *Kiriaki tis Vaioforou* (see above, in *Timber quality control issues*). The dimensions and spacing between the frames were important factors in determining the strength of the hull. The smallest frames had dimensions of 7.6 cm thick × 10.15 cm wide, as in the sister ships the brig *Amilton* and the goleta *Panaya Mirtidiotissa* (L.O. 18.28 × M.B. 6.43 × D 3.048), built by Nikolaos Pagidas for the Cretan Osman Beyzade and Vassilios Kritikos from Kythira respectively.[101] However, in the 1830s, brig hulls were between 16.96 and 21 metres long, and had frames of 11.4 cm thick on average. Four brigs built in 1846–47, and measuring L.O. 21.9–25.6 × M.B. 7.77–8.5 × D 4.36–4.87, had frames 30.4 cm thick.[102] The largest frame dimensions were found on the brig *Limnos* (L.O. 26.51 × M.B. 8.83 × D 5.18), of 455 tons, at 45.6 cm thick, whereas the cross section of the frames varied from 26.6 × 30.4 cm on the brig *Kimon* (L.K. 20.71 × M.B 7.46 × D 4.26), of 206 tons, of Georgios Ioannis Kalaris built in 1842, up to 34.2 × 38 cm on the brig *Maris Ath. Vallianos* (L.K. 25.6 [L.O. 31.08] × M.B. 7.3 × D 4.2), built in 1857 (See above *Keel, stem and sternpost and stern*). In a cutter built in 1833, measuring L.K. 13.7 × M.B. 5.18 × D 2.6 (see above *Keel, stem and sternpost and stern*), the frames cross section dimensions were similar to an average brig (11.4 × 11.4 cm). In a 1849 built Goleta, with dimensions of L.K. 12.79 × M.B. 4.5 × D 2.13, the frames cross section measured 10.45 × 15.2–17.1 cm, and on two 1850 built sister bombardas (see *Keel, stem and sternpost and stern*), with dimensions of L.K.11.88–12.48 × M.B. 4.87 × D 2.2, the frames cross section measured 9.5 × 13.3 cm.[103]

The spacing between the frames on most brig hulls in the 1830s varied from 15.2 to 19, and reached up to a maximum 20.9 cm. The only exceptions were the more dense frames arrangement of an 1831–32 built vessel, measuring L.K. 16.45 × M.B. 6.096 × D 3.048, on which frames were spaced 12.69 cm apart and the brig *Kantito* (see THE PROPERTY DOCUMENT), of 253 tons, built in 1838 and measuring L.K. 21 × M.B. 7.62 × D 4.26 metres, where the spacing

100 Ibid., Andreas David, n. 7090, 13.5.1838, property document ibid., n. 7687, 13.9.1838.

101 Ibid., n. 24770, 4.5.1851, property document ibid., n. 25047, 14.8.1851 and ibid., n. 24920, 22.6.1851, property document ibid., notary Christodoulos Ioannou, Inventory 6, n. 7443, 20.10.1851.

102 GSA, Syros, notary Andreas David, n. 18791, 16.9.1846, n. 19115, 24.1.1847, n. 19206, 21.2.1847, n. 19657, 27.6.1847.

103 GSA, Syros, notary Andreas David, n. 23150, 15.10.1849.

was 13.3 cm.[104] In most of the brig hulls in the 1840s and 1850s, the average spacing was 15.2 cm, although in the three sister brigs of Spetses shipowners (see *Special demands on technical issues*), measuring L.K. 19.5 M.B. 7.3 × D 4.11 metres, the frame spacing was between 11.4 and 13.3 cm, and in the brig *Agioi Apostoloi* (see *Keel, stem and sternpost and stern*) it was 11.4 cm. Generally, frames were less densely arranged on smaller vessels. In the 1833 built cutter, the frames spacing was 19 cm, the same as in the sacoleva *Agios Spiridon* (see *Keel, stem and sternpost and stern*), while in the 1844 built sacoleva-bombarda *Agios Nikolaos*, measuring L.O. 12.18 × M.B. 4.72 × D 1.98, the frames spacing was 20.9 cm[105] In malteza, also named *Agios Nikolaos*, belonging to Georgios Hadjigrigoriou from Sfakia and measuring L.K. 13.25 × M.B. 4.19 × D 1.37, the spacing was 22.8 cm. This vessel's frames were the smallest to be found, with cross section dimensions of 7.6 × 7.6 cm.[106]

Longitudinal Fastening Elements

The reinforcing element of the frames to the keel was keelson, which ran lengthwise, binding the floors to the keel.[107] An average cross section dimension, in vessels of up to 20 metres in length, was 22.8 × 22.8 cm. In vessels larger than 22 metres in length, the dimensions reached 30.4 × 30.4 cm, while in the brigs *Zagora* and *Limnos*, the cross section dimensions were 45.6 × 45.6 cm. In smaller vessels, such as the bratsera *Arhagelos Mihail tis Ionias* (L.K. 12.33 × M.B. 4.26 × D 2.05), the keelson was 15.2 cm thick, in the 1850 built bombardas the thickness varied between 11.4 and 13.3 cm. In even smaller vessels, like the sacoleva-bombarda and malteza (see previous paragraph), it was 9.5 and 8.5 cm respectively.[108]

From the 1850s, in larger hulls such as on the *Zagora*, a sister keelson was inserted on each side of the keelson. In a brig measuring 18.28 metres in length, these timbers were 15.2 cm thick, in two sister lotikas measuring L.K. 20.11 metres they were 19 cm thick, while the largest were in the brigs *Limnos* and *Neon Taganrog*, 24.7 × 24.7 cm).[109] In some cases, two rows of sister keelson were inserted, in the brig *Marigo* (23.46 metres long, see *Special demands on*

104 Ibid., Βιβλίον μνημονικῶν πράξεων ὑπὸ στοιχεῖον Β', n. 811, 2.12.1831.

105 GSA, Syros, notary Andreas David, n. 15977, 10.2.1844.

106 Ibid., n. 31004, 30.9.1859, property document ibid., I/Ναυπηγικά, n. 3659, 31.12.1859.

107 Damianidis, *Ελληνική Παραδοσιακή*, 194–95.

108 GSA, Syros, notary Andreas David, n. 25317, 8.12.1851, property document ibid., notary Christodoulos Ioannou, Inventory 6, n. 7695, 20.2.1852.

109 GSA, Syros, notary Andreas David, n. 26649, 27.6.1853, property document ibid., n. 26888, 3.10.1853.

technical issues), measuring 19 cm, the same as in the brig *Thessaloniki*, measuring L.O. 19.5 × M.B. 5.48 × D2.13 and in *Maris Ath. Vallianos*; however, in this latter sister ship, the keelsons were thicker at 22.8 cm.[110]

The next longitudinal fastenings were the lower thick stuffs (stragalies, στραγαλιές), attached to the joints of the frames, which were placed on both sides of the keelson in different rows on the inner part of the skeleton.[111] In vessels up to 20 metres long, three or four rows of lower thick stuffs were usually inserted. In three row hulls, the thickness of these timbers was 5.7 cm, whereas in those that had four rows, the thickness reached 7.6 or even 8.5 cm, with the exception of the brig *Agios Dionisios* (see *the frames*), in which the lower thick stuffs were 10.45 cm thick. In vessels longer than 20 metres, there were five to six rows ranging from 7.6 to 13.3 cm thick, as found in the large hulls of *Limnos* and *Neon Taganrog*. The bratsera *Arhagelos Mihail tis Ionias* had four rows of lower thick stuffs of 5.7 cm thick, the same size as the three rows found in the bombarda *Panaya Mirtidiotissa* belonging to Athanasios Nikolaos Koroneos from Kythira,[112] whereas in the sacoleva–bombarda *Agios Nikolaos* they were 3.8 cm thick, and in the malteza *Agios Nikolaos* they were 2.85 cm thick.

After the keelson and the lower thick stuffs, craftsmen inserted the wales [tsapes=τσάπες]. These were external planks that, unlike the rest of the planking timbers, had an active role in the stability of the skeleton and determined the shaping of the gunwale, the deck, and the rest of the planking strakes. Wales, which were also called thick stuffs, [zonaria=ζωνάρια], as in the agreements of the sister brigs from Spetses, were inserted under the tripito [τρυπητό], a pierced waterway timber of the deck, and were thicker than the rest of the external planking strakes.[113] The insertment of wales was, as we have seen (THE SHIPBUILDING AGREEMENT), also a nodal phase of construction in terms of payment installments. Vessels of up to 20 metres long rarely had more than six rows of wales, and the average thickness was 7.6 cm. Instead, the number of rows in vessels longer than 20 metres increased proportionally, reaching eleven rows in the *Limnos, Neon Taganrog* and *Agioi Apostoloi*, of 11.4 and 13.3 cm thick. The thickest wales were found on the *Zagora*, reaching 15.2 cm. In smaller vessels, like the 1833 built cutter, the bombarda *Panaya Mirtidiotissa*, or the bratsera *Arhagelos Mihail tis Ionias*, there were three rows of wales of 5.7 cm thick, whereas in the sacolevas, the wales were one centimetre thinner.

110 Ibid., n. 30489, 19.5.1858, property document ibid., n. 30562, 23.7.1858.

111 Damianidis, *Ελληνική Παραδοσιακή*, 197.

112 GSA, Syros, notary Andreas David, n. 23738, 19.5.1850, property document ibid., n. 24024, 8.8.1850.

113 Damianidis *Ελληνική Παραδοσιακή*, 195–96.

After the wales, longitudinal fastenings such as the waterways, clamps and middle thick stuffs (louroi, λούροι) were inserted. In traditional boatbuilding, the waterway is also called the tripito=pierced, as we have already seen, with holes that "*passed through the frames onto the deck beams and the tsapa* [τσάπα=wales] *and were placed at the level of the deck planking*".[114] However, in the Syros shipbuilding agreements, tripiti or frakaristi [φρακαριστή] were terms used to define the type of gunwale, which will be discussed below. Instead, it is sometimes referred to as harakto [χαρακτό] kourzeto, meaning "incised waterway", and its notches were fitted into the spaces between the frames and attached under the deck beams. Waterways could be double on each side, as in *Thessaloniki*, or triple as in *Maris Ath. Vallianos*. Cross sections ranged from 11.4 × 19cm, as in the sister brigs *Leonidas* and *Agios Nikolaos* (L.K.18.28 × M.B. 6.7 × D 3.65–3.5), which belonged to Andros shipowners, up to 24.7 × 30.4 cm on the brig *Marida*, of 360 tons, belonging to captain Santorini Anagnostis N. Eleftheriou.[115] An exceptional case was that of the brig *Kiriaki tis Vaioforou*, with five rows of waterways all incised tangentially to one another, and measuring 30.48 × 30.48 cm.

Clamps, like waterways, were double, as in *Zagora, Thessaloniki* and *Maris Ath. Vallianos*, while in the three sister brigs from Spetses (see *Special demands on technical issues*) they were incised and inserted one above and the other below the hold beam. The cross section ranged from 11.4 × 15.2 cm, as in the brigs *Leonidas* and *Agios Nikolaos* (see previous paragraph) and up to 20.9X24.7 cm, as in the brig *Panaya tis Kimiseos*, 314 tons belonging to the Santorini shipowners Dimitrios Sirigos and Dimitrios Nomikos, and the brig of the Santorini shiponwer Georgios Antonios Alafouzos.[116] Other types of complementary longitudinal fastenings were the incised timbers [harakta= χαρακτά] and half waterways or half clamps [misokourzeta=μισοκούρζετα], which ran from the bow to the stern, and were placed on both sides of the keelson between the lower thick stuffs and the orlop deck and, even higher, were attached to the beams between the orlop deck and the upper deck.

The second type of stringers after the lower thick stuffs [stragalies], which were placed below the waterline, were the middle thick stuffs [louroi=λούροι].

114 Tassos Leontidis, "Longitudinal fastenings in traditional Greek wooden boats", in *Shipbuilding and Ships in the eastern Mediterranean during the 18th and 19th century*, op. cit., 285.

115 GSA, Syros, notary Andreas David, n. 19657, 27.6.1847, property document ibid., notary Christodoulos Ioannou, Inventory 3, n. 3339, 23.12.1847.

116 Ibid., notary Andreas David, n. 18791, 16.9.1846, property document ibid., n. 19207, 21.2.1847 and n. 19115, 24.1.1847.

These were placed above the waterline. There were two types of these, incised and glued (probably meaning they were attached to the frames). Their position varied, and they were placed either under the upper deck, above and below the orlop deck, or between the two decks. Their thickness ranged from 5.7 to 11.4 cm, whereas the largest cross section was found in the hull of *Kiriaki tis Vaioforou* (11.4 × 26.6 cm).

On the bow and stern, reinforcing timber breasthooks and distaffs were inserted that extended horizontally over the posts and the futtocks in a form of a knee shaped Λ. In the agreement of the brig *Aristidis* (see *Variations in the object of the shipbuilding agreement*), breasthooks extended over three futtocks, whereas in the agreement of the brig *Kantito* they were required to extend up to the bulkhead of the bow. Breasthooks were placed over the entire height of the vessel or, alternatively, as stated in the agreement of the goleta of Efstathios Anastasiou, the five breasthooks of the bow had to be placed from the keelson up to the parapet.[117] Larger hulls such as brigs usually had six to seven breasthooks on the bow and three to five on the stern, with the exception of the strong hull of *Agios Dionisios* (19.9 metres long), which had nine breasthooks from the bowsprit to the hold and seven on the stern. The very large and well-built hulls of *Agioi Apostoloi, Zagora* and *Maris Ath. Vallianos* had ten, eleven and twelve breasthooks on the bow, and four, six and five on the stern respectively. Smaller vessels like bombardas and bratseras had four breasthooks on the bow and either two or three on the stern.

Distaffs were essentially the extensions of the breasthooks, but were thinner, as is recorded in the agreements for the goleta *Athina*, 53 tons, belonging to the Chiot-Hermoupolis captain Frantzeskos Mavroudis and the brig *Kantito*, where the breasthooks were 19 cm thick and the distaffs 15.2 cm.[118] The distaffs were notched to the frames. In the brig *Aristidis* they extended over nine futtocks, whereas in the goleta *Athina* they were 3.65 metres long. Vessels less than 20 metres long usually had two pair of distaffs on the wing transom, whereas those longer than 20 metres had three or four pairs of distaffs, on the bow and the stern.

Vertical Fastening Elements

Three main categories of beams supporting the upper and the orlop deck have been identified: kamaria, pagatses and kadenes. The latter two were used interchangeably, which leads us to believe that the difference between them

117 Ibid., n. 4028, 17.7.1836.

118 For goleta *Athina* see ibid., notary Andreas David, Βιβλίον Μνημονικόν ὑπὸ στοιχεῖον Η', n. 114, 27.1.1834, property document ibid., n. 810, 14.5.1834.

was perhaps merely nominal. Pagatses and kadenes were larger than kamaria (the conventional type of beams), and were placed at the points where they were required as major reinforcements, such as the hatches and mast steps. In the agreement of the brig *Dyo Adelfoi*, of 186 tons and 20.1 metres long, as well as the nine kadenes of the orlop deck, it was planned to build six more, two on the foremast, two on the mainmast, and two on the hold.[119] In the three Spetses sister brigs, the kadenes placed in the hatches and the mast steps were 3.8 cm thicker than those placed of the upper deck. The brig *Agia Ekaterini* (see *Keel, stem and sternpost and stern*), which measured L.K. 22.25 × M.B.7.9 × D4.41, had the largest number of kadenes, 37 on the upper deck, 22 on the orlop deck, and one more in the bow between the orlop and the upper deck.

Kadenes were supported by knees, usually four for each kadena, placed on both sides at each end. In the brig *Zagora*, the kadenes and kamaria on the upper deck were inserted alternately, supported by four wooden and two iron knees. The spacing of the kadenes on the upper deck ranged from 30.48 cm in the three Spetses sister brigs, 61 cm in the *Limnos*, and up to 76.20 cm in the *Agioi Apostoloi* and *Maris Ath. Vallianos*. Vessels longer than 20 metres (for instance the *Zagora* and the *Maris Ath. Vallianos*) had between 10 and 15 kadenes on the orlop deck, with the exception of the previously mentioned extraordinary case of the *Agia Ekaterini*, which had 22. The main cross section of the kadena in the orlop deck was 22.8 × 22.8 cm, but *Zagora* had the largest, at 26.6 × 30.48 cm.

Pagatses were probably made of the same timber as kadenes, as previously mentioned. The two terms never both appear in the same agreements. It is characteristic that the agreement of the Andros sister brigs *Agios Andreas* and *Tychi*, built in 1837, mentions only pagatses, whereas the rest of Andros sister brigs built in that same year mention only kadenes, and in all cases these timbers had the same dimensions and were supported by four knees each. In the brig of the Santorini captain Georgios Alafouzos, pagatses and kamaria alternate in equal number, but the pagatses were larger. According to Damianidis, the pagatsa was a large beam placed on the bow supported by lodging knees that were placed horizontally. This arrangement was found only in two brigs, the previously mentioned one of Georgios Alafouzos, and the 220-ton *Panaya tis Akathistou*, of the Santorini captain Marinos Alafouzos.[120]

---

119 This brig belonged to Hermoupolis captain Konstantinos Sakkas and Efstratios P. Petrokokkinos see Ibid., notary Andreas David, n. 10670, 4.7.1840, property document ibid., n. 11207, 4.11.1840.

120 Damianidis, Ελληνική Παραδοσιακή, 202, 204; for the brig of George Alafouzos see ibid., n. 19115, 24.1.1847, and for the Panaya tis Akathistou n. 19206, 21.2.1847, property document n. 19717, 11.7.1847.

Kamaria were placed alternately with kadenes and pagatses, fastened to the frames supported by knees, and sometimes notched and fastened inside the waterways and clamps. The beams placed under the hatches, mast steps and canopy were larger, and called maggiora [μαγγιόρα], like those in goleta *Voto*, of 55 tons, where the major beams were 9.5 × 19 cm and the rest 7.6 × 19 cm.[121] Beams in vessels less than 20 metres long measured 7.6 × 19 cm up to 7.6 × 22.8 cm, but in larger hulls, like that of the brig *Alexandros* of captain Kuekitz, which was 25 metres long, the beams measured 12.69 × 22.8 cm, and in Georgios Alafouzos brig of 25.6 metres long they measured 11.4 × 28.5 cm. The average spacing of the beams was between 26.6 and 30.4 cm, with the surprising exception of the goleta *Marikaki*, 14.16 metres long, which had a much denser arrangement of 20.9 cm.[122]

Knees supporting the beams were attached to the frames and the longitudinal fastenings as waterways and middle thick stuffs.[123] In Syros hulls, five to seven hanging knees were inserted under the upper deck on each side, whereas the brig *Eftichis*, of 16.45 metres in length, had eight each side of the keel, and the gabara *Mytaras* was unique in having 18 iron knees, 9 on each side.[124] Carling was a reinforcing timber placed under the beams and under the sides of the hatch openings, supported by the stanchions on both the upper and orlop deck, and was also supported by knees, as in the brig *Zayoru*, where an iron knee of 1.5 metres long was placed. The cross section of carling ranged from 7.6 × 19cm, as found in the brig of Spyros Mousouris, and up to 19 × 19 cm, as in the brig *Panaya tis Kimiseos*.[125]

Covering of the Hull

The laying of the deck and the external planking followed the completion of the skeleton and the ceiling or inner planking, The making of the gunwale took place during these stages, either after the laying of the deck or before (for the further stability of the frames and beams).[126]

121 Ibid., n. 29004, 14.12.1855, property document ibid., n. 29251, 6.4.1856.

122 Ibid., n. 17200, 18.5.1845, property document ibid., notary Mihalis Ioannopoulos, inventory 2, n. 305, 1.9.1845.

123 Damianidis, *Ελληνική Παραδοσιακή*, 200.

124 GSA, Syros, notary Andreas David, Βιβλίον Μνημονικόν ὑπὸ στοιχεῖον Ε΄, n. 488, 17.5.1833, property document ibid., Βιβλίον Μνημονικόν ὑπὸ στοιχεῖον Ζ΄, n. 1212, 20.9.1833.

125 Ibid., notary Andreas David, n. 14630, 4.2.1843.

126 Damianidis, *Ελληνική Παραδοσιακή*, 202.

The Ceiling

For the inner planking of the hull, strakes of cheap quality called farsia (φάρσια) were used. These were placed between the lower thick stuffs or other inner longitudinal fastenings. The limber boards placed on the keelson and floors were called paniola (πανιόλα), and for better fitting, notched timbers were inserted on both sides of the keelson on which the limber boards were stepped, as in the case of the brig of captain Dimitrios Valavanos from Chalkida.[127] It also seems that Syros shipbuilders used these two terms to define the inner strakes interchangeably, as is revealed in the Hydra captain Manouil Antonios Kriezis's demand for his brig *Miltiadis*, of 102 tons, to extend paniola right up to the orlop deck.[128] In most cases, ceiling strakes were laid from the keelson, the lower thick stuffs or the limber boards, up to the orlop deck or the larger beams (kadenes and pagatses). Ceiling right up to the upper deck was found only in the agreement of the brigs of Nikolaos Koutzoukos and *Thessaloniki*.[129] The ceiling strakes in vessels of less than 20 metres in length had a minimum thickness of 3.8 cm, in those longer than 20 metres the thickness was 5.7, and only *Limnos* and *Neon Taganrog* reached 7.6 cm.

Decking and Bulwark

Laying the strakes of the deck followed the ceiling. This started from the middle outwards, by following the sheer of the beams, whereas the joints of the strakes (sokoro, σόκορο) stepped on the beams for the purpose of further strengthening.[130] The average thickness of the deck strakes was between 4.7 and 5.7 cm in larger vessels. However, in the brigs *Kiriaki tis Vaioforou* and *Marida*, and the sister lotikas *Kleopatra* and *Prevesa*, the strakes were 6.65 cm thick, and in the even larger brigs *Marigo* and *Agioi Apostoloi* the deck strakes were 7.65 cm thick, in *Maris Ath. Vallianos* and *Limnos* they were 8.55 and 9.55 cm respectively, and in *Zagora* they were 11.4 cm.[131] In smaller crafts, bombardas and the goleta *Athina*, the deck strakes were 3.8 cm thick.

In the bulwark construction, there were two types of gunwales, the upper gunwale (or the gunwale of the parapet as it is referred to in the agreement

---

127 Ibid., and GSA, Syros, notary Andreas David, n. 24144, 16.9.1850.

128 Ibid., notary Andreas David, Βιβλίον Μνημονικόν ὑπὸ στοιχεῖον Η', n. 585, 14.4.1834, property document ibid., Βιβλίον Μνημονικόν ὑπὸ στοιχεῖον Θ', n. 1564, 17.8.1834.

129 Ibid., Βιβλίον Μνημονικόν ὑπὸ στοιχεῖον Β', n. 811, 2.12.1831.

130 Damianidis, *Ελληνική Παραδοσιακή*, 202.

131 For *Kleopatra* see GSA, Syros, notary Andreas David, n. 26236, 22.11.1852, property document ibid., n. 26385, 20.2.1853. For *Prevesa* ibid., n. 26305, 31.12.1852, property document ibid., n. 26478, 2.4.1853.

of *Agioi Apostoloi*) and the lower gunwale, a pierced timber [tripiti, τρυπητή] that was passed through the frames or notched [harakti, χαρακτή or frakaristi, φρακαριστή] to fit between them. The length of pierced or notched (lower) gunwale run along the entire side, from the "*shroud of the bow down to the counter of the stern*", as in the brig *Aspasia*, or "*from the gunport of the bow to the transom stern*", as in *Maris Ath. Vallianos*. A pierced or notched gunwale was thicker by 2 to 6 cm than the upper gunwale, which ranged between 7.6 to 11.4 cm thick in brig hulls around 20 metres long, but increased up to 13.3 and 15.2 cm in larger ones. In smaller craft, such as the malteza *Agios Nikolaos* and the bratsera *Arhagelos Mihail tis Ionias*, the thickness was 6.65 cm, and in the goleta *Pinelopi* (which was 13.71 metres long) thr thickness was 4.7 cm.[132] The upper gunwale in the brig *Dyo Adelfoi* was 5.7 cm thick, in the larger *Neon Taganrog* and *Agioi Apostoloi* it was 8.55 cm. The maximum thickness of 11.4 cm was in the brig *Panaya tis Akathistou*, which was also the only case found where the upper and the lower gunwale had the same thickness.

The strakes of the bulwark or parapet could be single or double, or single in the middle of the sides and double at the ends. When double, no caulking was required. The height of the parapet ranged from 0.76 to 1.06 metres, as far as we know according to the sparse information available. After the inner ceiling of the parapet, the upper gunwale was placed and the external planking followed, composed of a few rows of strakes, which numbered a total of six in the only known case, that of the three Spetses sister brigs. These strakes were placed between the lower and the upper gunwale, the largest being the zonari (ζωνάρη), a wale that was 1 or 2 cm thicker or even double the thickness of the rest of the strakes of the parapet, as in the case of the brig of Georgios Alafouzos. The bulwark strakes were between 2.5 and 3.8 cm thick on average, and in brigs longer than 25 metres they reached 4.75 or even 5.08 cm, whereas in the brig *Tilemachos*, of 167 tons, with L.K.18.28 metres, the double parapet was 9.5 cm thick.[133] The scuppers opened in the lowest part of the bulwark at deck level, six of them in brig or lotika hulls, whereas the goleta *Evangelistria*, which was 14 metres long belonged to the Trikeri captain Hadjimanolis Hadjianagnostou, had four, which were lead made in all cases.[134]

Planking

The last stage in completing the hull started from the wales down to the keel. In large hulls, strakes were attached from the stempost to the counter stern. In

132 Ibid., n. 23150, 15.10.1849, property document ibid., n. 23481, 17.2.1850.

133 Ibid., n. 20422, 12.1.1848, certificate of construction, ibid., I/Ναυπηγικά, n. 983, 3.6.1848.

134 Ibid., n. 25153, 26.9.1851, property document ibid., n. 25374, 28.12.1851.

double ended and transom stern hulls of coasters, planking also started from the wales, but stopped around the waterline, restarting from the keel. Strakes were attached lengthwise, first at the ends, then in the middle.[135] The average thickness of planking strakes (mostly on brigs, as we have seen) was 4.7 to 5.7 cm. Some hulls, either longer than 25 metres such as *Neon Taganrog, Agioi Apostoloi* and *Marigo*, or less than 25 metres such as *Agios Dionisios* and *Thessaloniki*, had strakes 7.6 cm thick. The largest were on *Maris Ath. Vallianos* (8.55 cm), *Limnos* (9.5 cm), and *Zagora* (11.4 cm). In bombardes, sacolevas, the malteza *Agios Nikolaos* and bratsera *Arhagelos Mihail tis Ionias*, strakes were 3.8 cm thick, whereas in the small bombarda *Panaya Mirtidiotissa*, which was 10 metres long, they were only 2 cm.[136]

Subdivision of the Ship's Hold

The hold of a ship was subdivided vertically between the upper and the lower (orlop) deck, and horizontally on the ends by the bulkheads (bulmedes, μπουλμέδες). As well as storage on the fore and aft bulkheads, there were also the bilge bulkhead and the prison bulkhead, as found in the three Spetses sister brigs. In the compartments fore and aft, the accommodation spaces were formed in the forecastle (kabuni, καμπούνι) for the seamen and in the quarterdeck (kasaro, κάσαρο) for the captain. Under the captain's cabin, there was also the provision store room or the steward's room (despentsa, δεσπέντσα). The anchor and chain pit (stritzi, στρήτζι) on the bow was a further space, which in the brig *Aristidis* was a lockin with a port lid (portelo, πορτέλο).

Superstructures

The main superstructures were the quarterdeck, built after the mainmast, and the canopy (tabuki, ταμπούκι) fore and aft, giving access to the forecastle and to captain's cabin respectively. On top of the canopy the skylight (spirayo, σπιράγιο) was opened, whereas the binnacle (grizola, γριζώλα) was placed on the canopy or nearby. In large brigs, such as *Limnos, Agioi Apostoloi* and *Neon Taganrog*, the binnacle was made of walnut, whereas in the brig *Aspasia* there was room for two compasses.

Ladders completed the necessary elements needed for access to the various spaces on deck and underneath. In the previously mentioned *Zagora*, there were two ladders on deck, and eventually on each end of the quarterdeck, two fore and aft, perhaps those of the canopies and one more outboard, which

135 Damianidis, *Ελληνική Παραδοσιακή*, 203–10.

136 GSA, Syros, notary Andreas David, n. 15252, 11.7.1843, property document ibid., n. 15559, 24.8.1843.

might be the accomodation ladder of the ship, removed when the ship was afloat. The two ladders of the parapet mentioned in the agreement of *Limnos* present a similar case. Between the foremast and the fore canopy, the galley (magirio, μαγειρίο) was built, and next to it the belfry. The two of these were sometimes demanded in the agreements. In the brig *Aristidis*, one was to be placed after the foremast and one next to the galley, and in the goleta *Voto*, a single one was to be placed near the bowsprit.

The deck opened the hatches (kuvusia, κουβούσια) lengthwise to the hold and also to the bilge pumps, such as on the brig *Miltiadis*, which had two of these. On some vessels, port lids opened on the sides. The brigs *Aristidis* and *Aspasia* of Georgios Iliadis had five on each side, plus two abaft, *Adamantios Korais* had six on each side plus two abaft, the larger brigs *Limnos, Neon Taganrog* and *Agioi Apostoloi* had seven, eight and nine respectively, and the owner of the brig *Dynamis* demanded only two abaft, and for those on the sides to be false.[137]

Ship's Equipment

The first set of equipment was the mast steps (skantza, σκάτζα), reinforced with knees. On the brig *Eftychis*, the bowsprit mast step was 14.25 cm thick. A large transverse board called a kadena was also placed on the bowsprit and reinforced with knees, four on the brig *Eftychis*, measuring 8.55 × 23.75 cm, and six on the goleta *Athina*, which were in addition reinforced with bowsprit cheeks. On the sides, on the gunwale or projecting outboard, were placed the channels or chain wales (paraxartes, παραξάρταις) for the lower shrouds, giving additional side support on the masts. On the goleta *Evangelistria* and the sister lotikas *Kleopatra* and *Prevesa*, channels were made of iron chains, whereas on the brig *Dyo Adelfoi*, which was 18.28 metres long, four racks and four channels were placed.[138] A further element in the rigging handling were boards (no specific name is given) placed horizontally on the inner part of the parapet, on which to attach various ropes. On the *Maris Ath. Vallianos* there were two of these made of hard wood, and on the *Limnos* there were four, one on each side from the anchor's cathead to the bitt of the bow, and two more forward for the sail ropes.

Similar mooring posts on deck and on other parts of the vessel were the bitts (babades, μπαμπάδες, or bintes, μπήντες). These must have been of various sizes, as they are mentioned as being fore and aft on deck, on the

137 Ibid., n. 25918, 14.7.1852, property document ibid., notary Christodoulos Ioannou, Inventory 7, n. 8257, 16.10.1852.

138 Ibid., n. 19930, 28.8.1847, certificate of construction, ibid., I/Ναυπηγικά, n. 190, 11.2.1848.

gunwale or bulwark, for the anchor, the bowsprit, the stern fast, and the cable. On the brig *Panaya tis Kimiseos*, and on that of Georgios Alafouzos, the bitts measured 30.4 × 30.4 cm in cross section, and on the brig *Agia Trias* there were eight bitts, two on the anchor, two abaft, and a pair on each side of the gunwale. Sometimes bitts were reinforced by knees, as on the brigs *Panaya tis Kimiseos* and *Kantito*. Catheads (kaponia, καπόνια) were also placed in different pairs fore and abaft for the anchor and the boats. On the lotika *Prevesa*, the side catheads were made of iron.

There were usually two hawse holes (okkia, όκκια, from the Italian *occhio*, meaning eye) on each side of the bow, but on the goleta *Evangelistria* and the lotika *Kleopatra* four are mentioned, and six on the brig *Zagora*: two fore, two on the deck, and two abaft. Cutwater (taliamas, ταλιαμάς, from the Italian word *tagliamare*, meaning exactly cutwater) was initially concave, but from the middle of the nineteenth century it became convex, following the clippers design. Cutwater was framed by headrails (saites, σαΐτες), which on the goleta *Voto* had a grid shape, and were normally reinforced by knees. There were four on the brig *Panaya tis Akathistou* and on that of Georgios Alafouzos, and two on the brig *Agia Ekaterini*, in addition to a net underneath to collect the jibs. On top of the cutwater and under the bowsprit a figure was placed. This is rarely mentioned, except in five cases: on the brig *Amilton* the figure was a violin, and on the goleta *Panaya Mirtidiotissa* it was a woman, and in three further cases, it is not known what there figure was.

The sternpost rudder was larger in its lower part and narrower in the upper part, and was fastened to the sternpost with iron hinges. In Syros, brigs used three to four such hinges, usually copper plated. Most Syros built hulls carried a tiller and not a wheel, and on the brig *Zagora* the tiller was, exceptionally, iron made. Capstan (ergatis, εργάτης) was one of the two basic mechanical devices onboard, and was placed after the bowsprit hole and between the catheads. On an average Syros brig, the capstan had eight bar holes, but larger vessels such as *Agioi Apostoloi* had nine and *Zagora* had ten. The brig *Marigo*'s drum head was made of walnut and iron fastened, on *Limnos* it was made of apple tree, and on *Panaya tis Akathistou* it was made of elm. The second mechanical device was a windlass (boba, μπόμπα), placed before the fore canopy. The only example of a windlass on a Syros vessel is that of *Zagora*. It had a diameter of 55.85 cm and was made of soft and hard wood.

Syros built brigs usually had two boats, one larger and one smaller. Sometimes the smaller one was called a skabavia (σκαμπαβία), or else on the *Limnos* the smaller boat was called a pasara (πάσαρα) and the larger one a skabavia. The one case of carrying three boats was found on the brig *Alexandros*, whereas smaller vessels had only one boat. A small brig, which belonged to

Konstantinos Eleftheriou and measured L.K. 13.7 × M.B. 5.18 × D 2.75, had a boat 6.39 metres long, the same dimensions as that of the larger (L.K. 16.76 m) brig *Aspasia* of Georgios Iliadis, which also carried a smaller feluca of 4.57 metres.[139] The even larger *Panaya tis Akathistou*, of 220 tons, was an exception, having only one boat of 7.3 metres, whereas the goleta Voto, of 55 tons, had two, the larger being 5.18 metres.

Caulking

When the hull was completed, the caulking followed. The first part to be caulked was below the waterline, before the launch, and the process continued above the waterline once the ship was launched into the water. It was easier for the caulkers to work on special rafts called salia (σάλια) to careen the ship on one side then the other, using scaffolds to reach the upper part of the hull. Cauking was done from left to right for the external planking, as well as for the deck.[140] The only existing documentation about caulking on Syros's newly built ships concerns the already mentioned brigs *Nikolaos* and *Marigo*. In the latter case, it was demanded that the shipbuilder Magos must careen the ship at his own expense.[141]

Launching

The main launching infrastructure of a shipyard, as mentioned in the agreements, included the cradle (schara, σχάρα), the drags (vazia, βάζια) and the transversal pieces (falagia, φαλάγγια).[142] The cradle was a kind of ladder, part of which was in the water and which allowed the hull to float more easily. Drags were squared timbers, transversally inserted below the hull on both sides, and stepped on the longitudinal timbers of the cradle. According to nineteenth century sources, they were introduced to the Aegean by Stamatios Koufoudakis at the end of the eighteenth century, as an element of further security in the launching of ships.[143] Transversal pieces were large timber logs that had a similar role to the drags. The tallow applied on drags and transversal pieces and the ropes completed the running material necessary for the launching.

139 Ibid., Βιβλίον Μνημονικόν ὑπὸ στοιχεῖον Δ', n. 1929, 4.10.1832.

140 Dimitris K. Dervenis, « Τα παραδοσιακά εργαλεία του ξυλοναυπηγού », ["The traditional tools of the shipwright"], in *Shipbuilding and ships in the eastern Mediterranean in the 18th & 19th centuries*, op. cit., 292–93; Damianidis, *Ελληνική Παραδοσιακή*, 211–12.

141 For details on caulking see also page 107.

142 GSA, Syros, notary Andreas David, n. 6197, 30.9.1837.

143 Damianidis, *Ελληνική Παραδοσιακή*, 123; Nikodimos, *Υπόμνημα της Νήσου*, 72.

Ship Types

The classification of the vessels built in the Syros shipyards in the period 1828–66 is based on three criteria: (1) the number of masts; (2) the hull or the rigging, and (3) the Mediterranean or northern European shipbuilding tradition to which each vessel belongs. In the first type of categorization, ships are classed as one, two, or three-masted, following the historical evolution of the sailing ship up to the last quarter of the nineteenth century. Additional masts in merchant ships were introduced in the very last period of sail, when the competition with steamships led to the perfection of the sailing ship in terms of its rigging and hull, especially the multimast American schooners.[144]

TABLE 4.2 *Classification of Syros built ships according the number of masts (1828–66).*

Single-masted	Two-masted	Three-masted
tserniki (τσερνίκι)	tserniki (τσερνίκι)	polaca (πολάκα)
trehandiri (τρεχαντήρι)	trehandiri (τρεχαντήρι)	barque, gabara (γαβάρα)
perama (πέραμα)	perama (πέραμα)	full rigged ship, nava (νάβα)
sacoleva (σακολέβα)	sacoleva (σακολέβα)	mistico (μίστικο)
bellou (μπελού)	bellou (μπελού)	felucca (φελούκα)
trata (τράτα)	mistico (μίστικο)	
malteza (μαλτέζα)	felucca (φελούκα)	
skabavia (σκαμπαβία)	trabacolo (τραμπάκολο)	
lemvos or varka (λεμβος ή βαρκα)	brig, briki (μπρίκι)	
felucca (φελούκα)	schooner, goleta (γολέτα)	
martingana (μαρτιγάνα)	brig-schooner, goletobriko (γολετόμπρικο)	
	bratsera (μπρατσέρα)	
	martingana (μαρτιγάνα)	
	cutter, kotero (κότερο)	
	bombarda (μπομπάρδα)	

144 W.J. Lewis Parker, "The Schooner in America", in *Sail's Last Century. The Merchant Sailing Ship, 1830–1930*, op. cit., 118–31.

According to Table 4.2, the largest number of ship types fell within the category of the two-masted ship, and as we shall see below, this category also dominated in terms of number of vessels and in tonnage. Some types, like the sacoleva, felucca, tserniki, or perama could fall within more than one category, depending on their size. The classification of a ship type as single or two-masted is based on general knowledge about it, as our data does not always inform us about the number of masts. Thus, for example, the trehandiri is classified as single and two-masted based on acquired knowledge about the craft, not because data describe the ship as having one or two masts. Furthermore, the number of masts is not always proportionate to the size of the vessel. For example, a brig, a two-masted vessel, was always much larger than a mistico, and in a few cases also had a higher tonnage capacity than a barque, which is generally classified as a larger merchantmen.

A ship type always refers either to a type of hull or a type of rigging fashion. Sometimes this distinction is not easy, as a term (e.g. bombarda) is used either for a type of hull or for rigging.[145] Also, in sources, a craft might be named

TABLE 4.3 *Classification of Syros built ships according hull or rigging (1828–66).*

Ship types according the hull	Ship types according rigging
bombarda (μπομπάρδα)	barque, gabara (γαβάρα)
martingana (μαρτιγάνα)	brig, briki (μπρίκι)
cutter, kotero (κότερο)	schooner, goleta (γολέτα)
trabacolo (τραμπάκολο)	brig-schooner, goletobriko (γολετόμπρικο)
tserniki (τσερνίκι)	full rigged ship, nava (νάβα)
trehandiri (τρεχαντήρι)	polaca (πολάκα)
perama (πέραμα)	bratsera (μπρατσέρα)
trata (τράτα)	sacoleva (σακολέβα)
mistico (μίστικο)	
bellou (μπελού)	
malteza (μαλτέζα)	
felucca (φελούκα)	
skabavia (σκαμπαβία)	
lemvos or varka (λεμβος ή βαρκα)	

145 Damianidis, *Ελληνική Παραδοσιακή*, 65–66, 80–82.

ILLUSTRATIONS 1 AND 2 *Two brigs moored in the port of Chania,* photographed by Giuseppe Berinda around 1870 (courtesy of the *Hellenic Literary and Historical Archive-Cultural Foundation of National Bank of Greece*).

after its type of hull, e.g. perama, and thus little is known about the rigging, which could be bratsera, schooner, or even brig-schooner. In very rare cases, both types are mentioned, like the sacoleva-bombarda or goleta-bombarda. However, for certain hulls, it is possible to speculate about rigging based upon more general knowledge, like tserniki, which was usually rigged like a sacoleva.

According to Table 4.3, there were more hull types than rig types, but rig types concern larger vessels. Unfortunately, for rig types such as the brig, we have no specific knowledge about which type of hull was built, and thus it is posssible to reconstruct the hull features only indirectly based upon descriptions in shipbuilding agreements. These are similar to what has been called

karavoskaro (καραβόσκαρο), the hull of a ship, a denomination used among twentieth century shipwrights in Greece.

A third distinction of ship types is based on the shipbuilding tradition to which each type belonged and originally developed. According to Table 4.4, Syros vessels are distinguished according to two broad categories, Mediterranean and North European ship types. The former were much more numerous that the latter, but Northern ship types were built in far greater numbers and were more important in terms of aggregate tonnage. Furthermore, the Mediterranean types were mainly small coasters or fishing vessels, hardly exceeding 50 tons on average, whereas the Northern types were mostly seagoing ships (brigs, barques) or larger coasters, like the schooner (goleta) and the cutter (kotero). Among the Mediterranean types, there were boats originally from the Aegean Sea, like the trehandiri and the perama, from the Black Sea, like the tserniki and the sacoleva, and from the Adriatic Sea, like the bratsera

TABLE 4.4 *Classification of Syros built ships according shipbuilding tradition (1828–66).*

Ship types	Minimum-maximum tonnage	Average tonnage	Number of vessels	Period
Mediterranean Types				
trabacolo (τραμπάκολο)		87.61	1	1837
bombarda (μπομπάρδα)	18–96.76	50.53	156	1834–66
martingana (μαρτιγάνα)	33.26–47.12	38.31	6	1830–36
sacoleva (σακολέβα)	4–56.75	29.97	40	1831–66
bratsera (μπρατσέρα)	7.75–62	25.48	75	1835–66
malteza (μαλτέζα)	5.76–43.28	19.07	11	1835–58
tserniki (τσερνίκι)	3–71.74	16.99	149	1831–64
perama (πέραμα)	7–38.09	16.11	36	1841–65
bellou (μπελού)	9.91–20.94	15.43	9	1843–63
mistico (μίστικο)	9.4–15.65	12.99	3	1835–41
trehandiri (τρεχαντήρι)	2–35.7	12.23	49	1840–66
trata (τράτα)	6–22.74	11.88	13	1838–61
felucca (φελούκα)	3.36–14.11	8.73	2	1835–52
skabavia (σκαμπαβία)		4.81	1	1830
lemvos or varka (λεμβος ή βαρκα)	0.22–4.30	2.62	50	1840–65
North European Types				
barque, gabara (γαβάρα)	200.87–519	367.49	23	1833–66
brig, briki (μπρίκι)	64–533	208	1154	1828–66
brig-schooner, goletobriko (γολετόμπρικο)	87.61–205.88	118.83	9	1828–1853
schooner, goleta (γολέτα)	20.95–203	73.65	293	1829–66
cutter, kotero (κότερο)	20.57–119.35	54.93	33	1830–44
Archetypal Type				
full rigged ship, nava (νάβα)		556	1	1844
Hybrid Types				
polaca (πολάκα)		120	1	1835

Ship types	Minimum-maximum tonnage	Average tonnage	Number of vessels	Period
Mixed Types				
goleta / bombarda		55	2	1848–56
tserniki / martigos		49	1	1832
sacoleva / bombarda		34.18	1	1837
sacoleva / martigos		27.79	1	1831

Source: Processed data for the years 1828–66 from GSA, Syros, Αρχείο Συμβολαιογράφου Μάξιμου Ταλασλή, Συμβ. Σκαρλάτος Μάξιμος, Κατάστιχα 1–6, 1827–1830, Συμβ. Ανδρέας Δαβίδ, Κατάστιχα 7–16, 1830–24/1/1835, Λυτά έγγραφα 1835–1862. Συλλογή Ιστορικού Αρχείου Κυκλάδων, Συμβ. Κων. Αγγελίδης, Ευρετήρια, 1–5, 1854–1863, Συμβ. Αντώνιος Αλμπέρτος, Ευρετήρια 1–2, 1853–1864, Συμβ. Μιχ. Ιωάννόπουλος, Ευρ. 1–2, 1843–1845, Συμβ. Χρ. Ιωάννου Ευρ. 1–10, 1846–1860; I/Ναυπηγικά, 1836–1866; Kardasis, *Σύρος*, 180–81.

and the trabacolo (though only one vessel of this type was built). The mistico came from North Africa, and the martingana and feluca came from the Tyrrhenian Sea. Most of the Northern types were two-masted vessels (brigs, brig-schooners and schooners), and only one full-rigged ship and a few barques were built in the examined period.

Similar tendencies are observed in other Mediterranean shipyards. In Provence and Liguria during the same period, Northern type, like the brig, the barque and the ship were the main types of seagoing merchantmen, whereas local crafts of smaller tonnage were used in the coastal trade. In fact, in Provence, brigs and full rigged ships covered 77.28% of the total tonnage in the period 1835–39, 1855–59, and in Liguria the brigantino (or the brig), covered 58.06% of the total tonnage built in 1838–52. Generally, northern ship types represented more than 90% of total tonnage.[146] The dominance of northern maritime technology in the Mediterranean had become quite clear as early as the last quarter of the eighteenth century. In the period of great expansion of eastern Mediterranean commerce during the French Wars, the larger units of the Mediterranean fleets were ships, brigantines and brigs, whereas Mediterranean types like *polacca* and *pinco* were transformed into square riggers and assumed some characteristics derived from northern technology in their hull design.[147] This

146 Delis, "Mediterranean Wooden Shipbuilding", 360–66.

147 Ibid., "From Lateen to Square-Rig: The evolution of the Greek-owned merchant fleet and its ships in the eighteenth and nineteenth centuries", *Mariner's Mirror*, 100, 1, (February 2014), 43–57.

adjustment to northern European types must have been an indispensable condition for the control of the main Mediterranean trade routes by local fleets, like the Ottoman-Greek or the Ragusan, which experienced considerable growth during the French Wars thanks to their status as neutral carriers. The superiority of northern maritime technology over the more obsolete Mediterranean one is also an indication of the superiority and the penetration of North European economies in Mediterranean markets, through a powerful tool such as the sailing ship.[148] This is part of a longer process that started in the fourteenth century with the introduction of the square sail and the sternpost rudder in the Mediterranean, and which later saw the affirmation of Northern ship types like the cog, the carrack and finally the full rigged ship as the ocean and seagoing cargo carrier *par excellence*.[149] In the nineteenth century, the supremacy of northern maritime technology through the use of its ship types is an interesting aspect of integration in the standards of the dominant economies of the time, a sort of maritime globalization.

According to Table 4.4, certain ship types had a continuous presence throughout the examined period, such as the brig. Others with a strong presence include the schooner, barque, bombarda, bratsera, tserniki and sacoleva, whereas the perama, trehandiri, bratsera and bombarda start to appear in a more systematic way only from the beginning of 1840s. Other types like the cutter, mistico, trata, polacca, nava, martingana and felucca had a very limited presence, and were built only in very small numbers. This is particularly true of the mistico, polacca, felucca and martingana, which were mostly built in the early 1830s, as survivors of previous traditions.

The type of vessel that enjoyed the greatest demand over the entire period was the brig: 1,154 brigs were built between 1828 and 1866, or an average of almost thirty brigs per year, which is quite an impressive figure. Brigs represented 53% of the number of vessels built, and 81.46% of the total tonnage produced in Syros. This tendency was strictly connected with the position of the brig as the backbone of the Greek-owned sailing merchant fleet in the

---

148 Harlaftis – Laiou, "Ottoman state policy"; Robin Harris, *Dubrovnik: a history*, (London: SAQI, 2006), 353; Harriet Bjelovučić, *The Ragusan Republic: victim of Napoleon and its own conservatism*, (Leiden: E.J. Brill, 1970), 41; Fanfani, "Lo scenario generale", 4–6.

149 Cipolla, *Before the industrial revolution*, 229–33. Richard W. Unger, *The Ship in the Medieval Economy, 600–1600*, (Montreal and London: McGill-Queen's University Press, 1980), 163–67, 183–84; Ian Friel, "The Carrack: The Advent of the Full Rigged Ship", in *Cogs, Caravels* & Galleons, op. cit., 77–103; Jacques Heers, *Gênes au xve siècle. Activité économique et problèmes sociaux*, (Paris: SEVPEN, 1961), 271–72.

nineteenth century, as we shall see below. Despite the overwhelming presence of brigs, the shipyards in Syros also built a large quantity of other types, the most widespread after the brig being the goleta (schooner, 293 units, 7.31% in tonnage), the bombarda (156, 2.61% in tonnage), the tserniki (149, 0.87% in tonnage) and the bratsera (75, 0.77% in tonnage). This is an indication that demand was varied, and that the shipbuilders had the know-how to respond satisfactorily to this demand.[150]

A good number of ship types built in Syros were also common to other shipbuilding areas in the Mediterranean. In Table 4.5, Northern and Mediterranean ship types are compared to their tonnage.

TABLE 4.5 *Common ship types and average tonnage in comparison.*

Common ship types	**Syros** 1828–1866	**Liguria** 1838–1852	**Provence** 1835–1839, 1855–1859
Northern common types			
μπρίκι/brig /brick	208	190,56	142,38
γολετόμπρικο/brick scooner, brick goletta/brig goelette	118,83	96,40	94,00
γολέτα, σκούνα/goletta, scooner/ goelette	73,65	88,49	91,18
γαβάρα/barck scipp	367,49	277,03	–
νάβα/nave/trois mats	556*	373,08	350,45
κότερο/cutter	54,93	18,36	48,00
Mediterranean common types			
βομβάρδα/bombarda/bombarde	50,53	77,98	78,20
φελούκα/filuca	8,73	14,27	–
μίστικο/mistico/mistic	12,99	38,34	79*
tartana/tartane		32,77	46,9
πολάκα/polacca	120*	–	–

Sources: Delis "Mediterranean wooden shipbuilding", 93–4. * Only one example of this ship type.

150 See Appendix 4.2.

A first conclusion is that there are more common Northern types than Mediterranean ones. Among the latter, the filuca, mistico, tartana and polacca were built in very few numbers, and should be considered merely as survivors of the eighteenth century, when they had a very strong presence in the Mediterranean. A second conclusion is that a common feature in all the three shipbuilding areas is that the majority of ship types built, especially for the seagoing trade, belonged to the northern tradition (ships, barques, barquentines, brigs, brig-schooners, schooners and cutters). These were employed in many other areas outside the Mediterranean, and represented the basic ship types in the sailing fleets of the most advanced economies worldwide. Among the Northern types, brigs and brig-schooners were larger in Syros, but schooners and the Mediterranean bombarda were larger in Liguria and Provence, whereas cutters were much smaller in Liguria as compared to the other two areas. In the category of three-masted vessels, ships were almost absent in Syros, while in Liguria they were slightly larger than in Provence; and barks were about 90 tons larger in Syros than in Liguria. However, the fact that the construction of these ship-types was widespread throughout the Mediterranean did not prevent the existence of specific local ship types.

Brig: The Barometer of Syros Shipbuilding Industry

The brig was adopted by Greeks in the second half of the eighteenth century and became a popular rig among seafarers in the Ionian Sea and Western Greece, Zante, Cephalonia, Messolonghi, and Galaxidi. Furthemore, in the second decade of the nineteenth century, the brig replaced the polacca, previously the most widespread ship type in the Greek fleet, on a massive scale. The brig became the basic fighting unit in the Greek War of Independence (1821–29), and during the period 1830–80 constituted the backbone of the Greek-owned merchant fleet.[151]

Figure 4.1 further proves this monopolized use of the brig among Greek shipowners. It was used as the main cargo carrier in the grain trade, the area of specialization of Greek-owned shipping. This trade demanded sufficient carrying capacity, a moderate size for the often rudimentary infrastructures of the traffic-jammed Black Sea and Mediterranean ports, and properly rigged ships as square riggers for long distance routes, such as between the Black Sea and the Western Mediterranean.

---

151 Delis, "From Lateen to Square-Rig".

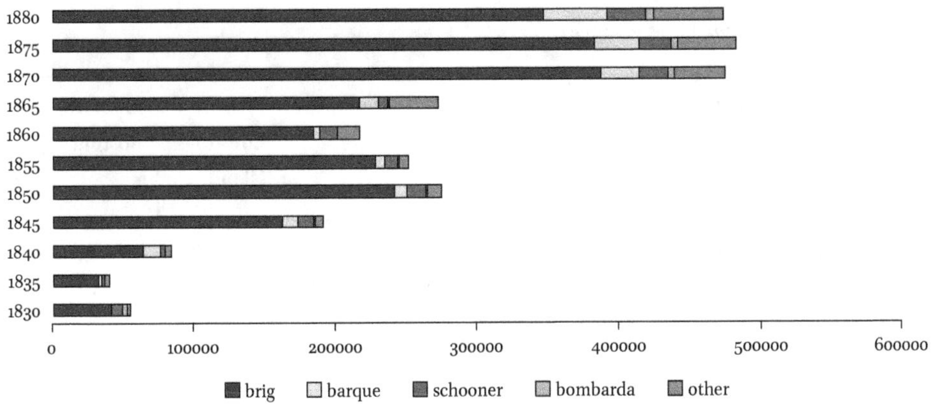

FIGURE 4.1 *Distribution per ship type of the registered greek-owned ships (in thousand tons), 1830–1880.*
SOURCE: PROCESSED DATA FROM HARLAFTIS – VLASSOPOULOS, *HISTORICAL REGISTER 'PONTOPOREIA'*, TABLE A.4, MB'.

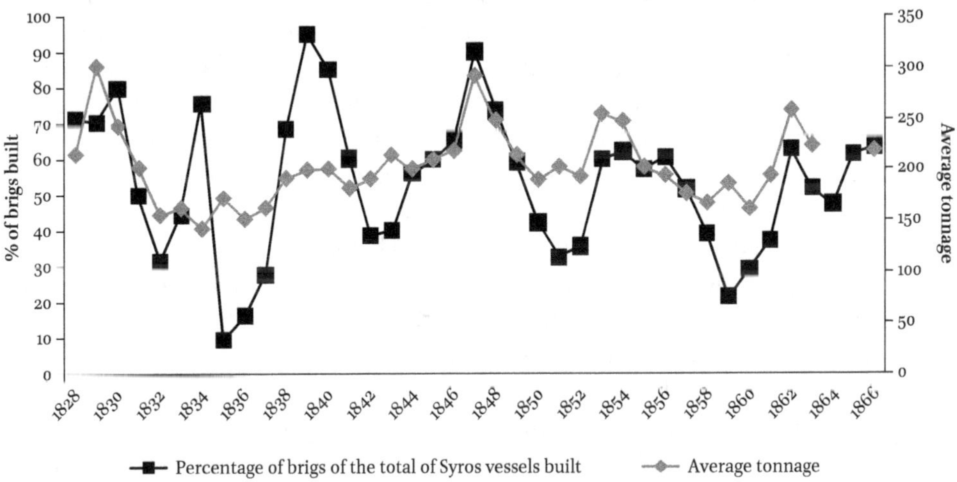

FIGURE 4.2 *Average tonnage and percentage of brigs built in Syros, 1828–1866.*
SOURCE: APPENDICES 3.5 AND 4.1.

Thus, the brig, as the dominant ship type of the sailing merchant fleet of the Greeks, was also the barometer of the shipbuilding output in Syros, the major shipbuilding centre of Greek-owned shipping. In Figure 4.2, the combined data concerning the average tonnage and the percentage of brigs of the total vessels built in Syros in the period 1828–66 provides a useful indicator of the productivity of the Syros shipbuilding industry and of Greek-owned shipping.

TABLE 4.6 *Comparative tonnage of brigs.*

Compared areas	Syros	Saint Tropez	Liguria	Dunkirk	Prince Edward Island	Medford, Boston
Period	1828–66	1828–68	1838–52	1855–69	1840–69	1830–69
Average tonnage	208	144.93	190.56	197.57	215.33	215

Source: Appendix 3.2.4 and Delis "Mediterranean wooden shipbuilding".

Generally, the two variables follow the same trend and suggest that an increase in the percentage of brigs is accompanied by an increase in average tonnage. After the period 1828–31, when brigs reached an average of 301 tons (1829), during the rest of the 1830s until 1838, the average tonnage fell to below 200 tons. Similarly, the percentage of brigs, with the exception of 1834, was not very high, and only started to increase considerably in 1838. In the peak years such as 1840, when production surpassed 10,000 tons, the brig's average tonnage also surpassed 200 tons, and in 1847 the brig reached 292 tons on average, and its percentage reached 90.14%, the second best year after 1839 (95%). Similarly, falling trends for both variables are observed in the trough years (1841, 1849 and 1858–59), demonstrating that brig trends are perfectly harmonious with Syros shipbuilding production, that they clearly reflect shipbuilding and shipping productivity, and that they justify the definition of the brig as the barometer of the Syros shipbuilding and Greek-owned shipping industry.

Syros brigs had a large tonnage variation, ranging from 64 to 533 tons, whereas the average tonnage in the above examined period was 208 tons. According to Table 4.6, the average tonnage of Syros brigs was at the same level as (if not higher than) other shipyards beyond the Mediterranean, in the North Sea and the Atlantic.

In the first half of the nineteenth century, the brig was the most widespread medium size merchantmen in the fleets of the Mediterranean, Northern Europe and North Atlantic. However, from 1870, it was gradually replaced by the barque, due to the advantages offered by the latter, namely its larger tonnage capacity and its addition of the mizzen and the fore-and-aft-rig mast, which increased the sail area without increasing labour costs.[152] Similar

152 Sager, *Seafaring Labour*, 35–36; Sager – Panting, *Maritime* Capital, 54–55.

considerations of labour cost reduction led to the replacement of the brig by the topsail schooner in the fruit trade.[153] So, although the brig was "*the most efficient and powerful rig for deepsea work, as well as the handiest of all square-riggers*", it was replaced with more economic and flexible rig types, for reasons of operational cost and the demand for higher speed and turnover, as opposed to carrying capacity, in the second half of the nineteenth century. It may have been the low labour costs of Greek-owned shipping that led to Greek shipowners not shifting to other rig types until 1870.[154]

153 Underhill, *Deep-Water*, 64–65; Mc Gregor, "The Wooden Sailing Ship", 50.

154 Harlaftis, *Ιστορία της Ελληνόκτητης*, 311–12.

CHAPTER 5

The Demand: Shipowners and Investors

According to Greek law in the examined period, the co-ownership of ships was not a stock company, and each shareholder preserved the right to sell his share at any time without the consensus of the rest of shareholders.[1] The division of the ship into 24 shares was probably due to a practice that had prevailed in the Italian Peninsula dating back to fifteenth century Genoa.[2] The fact that a ship investment was flexible, of relatively moderate cost, and often a profitable investment option, attracted investors of all kinds of professional occupations and socio-economic strata. The limited liability that ship investors enjoyed made it easier to enter and leave the industry, and it created a basic distinction between active and passive shareholders. The latter were those who did not participate in the management and operation of the ship, which were tasks undertaken by captain or other shareholders in the shipping business.[3]

This distinction between permanent and occasional investors also applied in the Syros shipbuilding market, with active investors being those who were engaged in shipping activities as captains, seamen or shipbuilders, as well as merchants, who were either more actively involved in shipping affairs or were just interested in a good investment or in transporting their commodities more cheaply. Furthermore, the passive investors were those who, more often, were individuals outside the shipping industry who were interested in a profitable investment, as shipping was considered to be profitable in pre-industrial societies. The investors in the Syros shipbuilding market in the period 1828–66 will be analyzed through (a) their group of geographic origin, (b) their occupational groups, and (c) the trends in distribution and concentration of ship ownership. Each of these aspects will be measured according to the following

1 Rallis G.A., *Ερμηνεία του Ελληνικού Εμπορικού Δικαίου*, [*Interpretation of the Greek Commercial Law*] vol. B', (Athens: 1865), 73–74.

2 Ibid., 74. Annunziata Berrino, "I sorrentini e il mare", in *A Vela e a* Vapore, op. cit., 36; Giovanni Carosio, "La costruzione navale ligure nell' Ottocento: solo tradizione?", in *Dal Mediterraneo all' Adriatico. La marineria ligure nei mari del mondo*, ed. Pierangelo Campodonico, (Genoa: Tormena, 1993), 317; Heers, *Gênes*, 288–91.

3 Simon Ville, *English Shipowning during the industrial revolution. Michael Henley and son, London shipowners, 1770–1830*, (Manchester: Manchester University Press, 1987), 2; Palmer, *Politics, Shipping*, 10.

© KONINKLIJKE BRILL NV, LEIDEN, 2016 | DOI 10.1163/9789004306158_007

three factors: (a) the number of investors, (b) the percentage of the holding in tonnage capacity, and (c) the percentage of the holding in terms of the value of the ship.

Geographic Origin and Ownership Distribution of Investors

Distribution per Number of Investors

A first distinction to be drawn among Syros shipbuilding investors is between those who were resident in Hermoupolis and those from outside. As mentioned in the first chapter, the new town of Syros, to which the island owned its prosperity, was a large and well-articulated international shipping market, with a very active and wealthy entrepreneurial class of merchants, shipowners and shipbuilders, who represented a constant source of capital investment.

According to Table 5.1, these two main categories are fairly evenly represented, whereas a third category of investors whose origins cannot be identified emerges, representing almost one in six investors. As mentioned in the first chapter, the population of Hermoupolis was divided according to groups of origin. These groups often lived in separate neighborhoods bearing the name of their place of origin, like psariana (from Psara) or hydreika (from Hydra). The breakdown of these groups, which characterized Hermoupolis during the first decades of its existence, is presented in Figure 5.1. We shall see below how this relates to further socio-economic and occupational specialization.

Figure 5.1 represents only eleven of the sixty places of origin registered by the investors of Hermoupolis, and includes only those places represented by ten or more individuals. The largest share goes to those from Chios and Psara, standing at 303 and 291 individuals respectively. The numerical superiority of investors from these areas, as will be demonstrated below, was not only due to the fact that they were the largest communities in the town.[4] The third largest investor group consisted of individuals about whom no further information was found as regards origin. The remaining groups of investors in the town range from Hydra, with 27 individuals, down to groups of 10 individuals each with origins in Cephalonia, Lemnos and Samos.

4 Kolodny, "Hermoupolis-Syra", 200–04.

TABLE 5.1 *Distribution of Hermoupolis residents and outside Hermoupolis new ships investors, 1828–66.*

	Total number	Percentage (%)
Hermoupolis residents	1,020	42.39
Outside Hermoupolis	999	41.54
Not identified	387	16.09
Total	2,406	100.00

Source: processed data from Appendices 5.1 and 5.2.

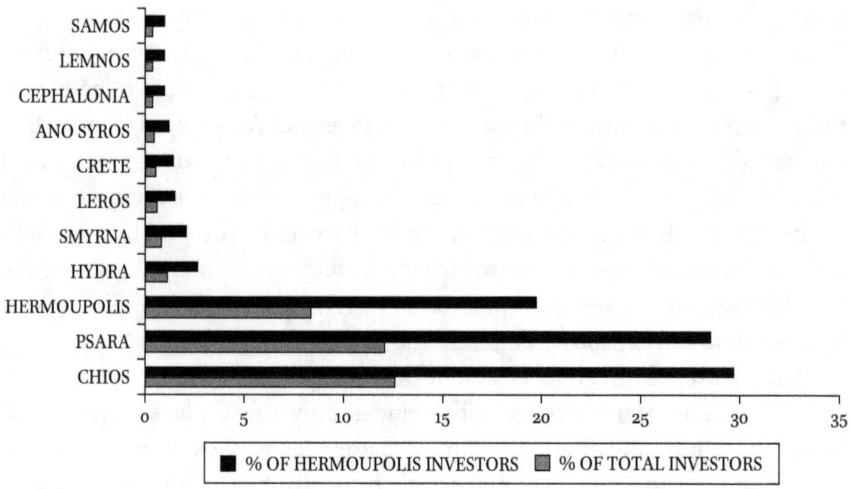

FIGURE 5.1 *Percentage distribution of number of Hermoupolis investors (1828–1866).*
SOURCE: APPENDIX 5.1.

Groups of investors from outside Hermoupolis are much more numerous, 108 in total, and their geographic diversification is much greater. The largest percentage originate from the Aegean, an area represented by individuals from 37 islands, and with the exception of Euboea and Crete, which are very large, specific location of provenance are mentioned, including Limni in Euboea and Sfakia in Crete. Furthermore, most of the Cretans who migrated to the islands of Milos, Ios, and Sifnos during the Greek War of Independence were from

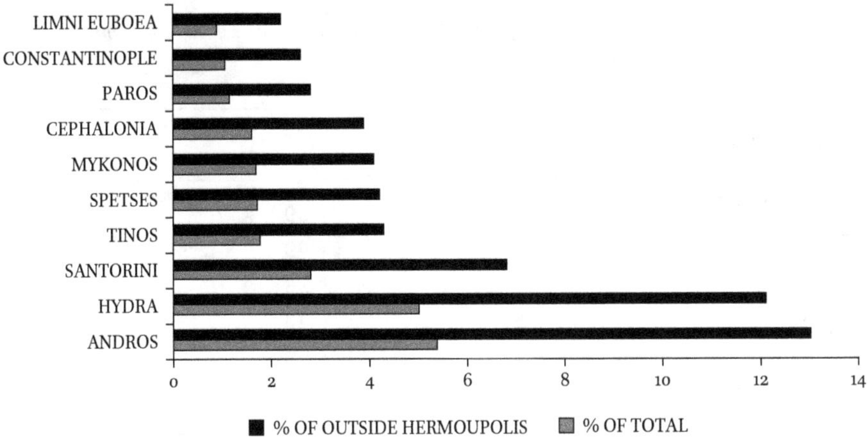

FIGURE 5.2 *Percentage distribution of number of investors outside Hermoupolis (1828–1866).*
SOURCE: APPENDIX 5.2.

Sfakia, an area with a tradition of shipping and privateering.[5] Other investors were from continental Greece, Asia Minor, and the Ionian Sea, but also from the Greek diaspora communities in the Black Sea, the Danube area, the eastern Mediterranean, Western Europe, Odessa, Berdiansk, Mariupol, Taganrog, Galatz, Braila, Constantinople, Trieste, Livorno, and even London.

Figure 5.2 shows 10 of the 108 most important places of origin for investors outside Hermoupolis. Cyclades and the islands of Argolic Gulf, which both had a long maritime tradition, dominate this category. Andros (130 individuals), Hydra (121), and Santorini (68) together constitute almost one third of the investors outside Hermoupolis. There was a more limited presence in the shipbuilding market of Syros from investors who originally came from the islands of Cephalonia and Spetses, which also had a developed shipping industry. In the latter case, however, this is due to its competitive shipyards, developed prior to Greek Independence.

5 Andreas Drakakis, « Η πειρατεία εις τάς Κυκλάδας κατά την Επανάστασιν του 1821 », ["Piracy in Cyclades during the Greek War of Independence"], *Μνημοσύνη* [*Mnemosyni*], vol. 5, (1974–75), 337–40.

TABLE 5.2 *Percentage distribution of the most important in numbers groups of origin of investors, 1828–66.*

Group of origin	% of total
Chios (Hermoupolis)	12.59
Psara (Hermoupolis)	12.09
Hermoupolis	8.35
Andros	5.40
Hydra	5.03
Santorini	2.83

Source: Appendixes 5.1 and 5.2.

Table 5.2 records the largest groups of investors in terms of origin, from both Hermoupolis and outside it. It includes all the groups holding more than 2% of the total amount of investments. Residents in Hermoupolis represent almost 33% of this total, whereas the collective total for Andros, Hydra and Santorini stands at above 13%. Investors from these areas were the main protagonists in the Syros shipbuilding market, a result of their embedded know-how and specialization in shipping business, the roots of which will be examined below.

Distribution of Investors per Tonnage Capacity

The number of individuals engaged in ship investment from each geographic area is a demographic indicator of the population's involvement and participation in shipping. However, the tonnage capacity and value of ships provides a more qualitative image of the impact on the shipbuilding market of investors from each area. In terms of tonnage capacity, during 1828–66 the percentage of Hermoupolis residents investing in new ships was 53.64%, and for those from outside Hermoupolis the total was 46.35%.

Table 5.3 lists the nine groups of investors above 2% of the total. Investors from Psara and Chios hold two digit numbers in percentage, with the former surpassing one fifth of the total. Generally Hermoupolis investors held the largest share of the shipbuilding market. Andros, Hydra and Santorini, all from outside Hermoupolis follow, as in the case of the previous category (the number of investors). Cephalonia and Mykonos, however, even though represented by fewer investors than Tinos and Spetses (Figure 5.2), both built more in terms of tonnage.

TABLE 5.3 *The most important groups of origin of investors in tonnage capacity, 1828–1866.*

Group of origin	Tonnage capacity of new ships	% of tonnage capacity
Psara (Hermoupolis)	58,530.08	21.22
Chios (Hermoupolis)	43,748.91	15.86
Hermoupolis	21,360.07	7.75
Andros	16,580.87	6.01
Hydra	13,372.52	4.85
Santorini	9,916.85	3.60
Cephalonia	6,463.73	2.34
Mykonos	6,413.75	2.33
Spetses	5,608.99	2.03

Source: Appendix 5.3.

TABLE 5.4 *Coefficient tonnage/number of investors, 1828–66.*

Group of origin	Coefficient tonnage/Number of investors
Psara (Hermoupolis)	201.13
Cephalonia	165.74
Mykonos	156.43
Santorini	145.84
Chios (Hermoupolis)	144.39
Spetses	133.55
Andros	127.55
Hydra	110.52
Hermoupolis	106.27

Source: processed data from appendixes 5.1, 5.2 and 5.3.

In Table 5.4, the coefficient tonnage/number of investors offers the quality rate of investments in relation to the concentration of ownership (the larger the tonnage and the fewer the investors, the higher the coefficient) and, to a certain extent, the average tonnage of vessels. Investors from Psara (Hermoupolis), Cephalonia, Mykonos and Santorini tended towards a more concentrated ownership and generally built larger vessels, with the exception of Spetses, which has a lower coefficient but a higher average tonnage (184.09 tons) than Cephalonia (176.38), Mykonos (161.97), and Santorini (169.70). The Hermoupolis investors, without further specification of origin, have the lowest coefficient and the lowest average tonnage (110 tons), as they were mostly represented by the *petite bourgeoisie* of the town, composed of shopkeepers, craftsmen, fishermen and seamen.[6]

A similarly high rate in the quality relation is observed in Ithaki investors, who numbered just 18 but who built 2,972.73 tons, which represents 1.08% of the total. The southern Russia merchants were scattered throughout various cities, but if aggregated as an occupational group from a specific wider area, represent 2.04% of the total. Relatedly, the Constantinople merchants built 3,386.18 tons, making up 1.3% of the total.

Distribution per Values of Ships

The second qualitative indicator after tonnage, the financial contribution of investors, is estimated according to the value of the ships built. However, in Table 5.5, the lack of total cost for all built vessels lead us to indicate the tonnage corresponding to the estimated values for each group of origin. Before analyzing Table 5.5, it is important to mention that Hermoupolis investors held 58.87% of the total, almost 3/5 of the total as compared to those outside Hermoupolis.

Table 5.5 mentions the groups of origin with investment levels higher than half a million drachmae. Investors originating from Chios and Psara again held the largest share, more than 2/5 of the total. In the category of those outside Hermoupolis, Andros investors were the most important, with more than 7% of the total. As with the previous categories, Hydra and Santorini follow, but Mykonos and Spetses owners invested more in terms of value, even if they built less in terms of tonnage than Cephalonia (Table 5.3). The Cephalonians are also surpassed by the Constantinople merchants, even if the latter held only half of tonnage of the former. Table 5.6 offers a more qualitative view of the financial volume of investments in relation to the tonnage to which these values correspond.

Investors from Andros built more expensive ships, especially in comparison to those from Hydra and Spetses, but Psara, Chios and Constantinople investors follow, and this can be explained as being due to the availability of funds from Syros and Constantinople, which were important commercial, maritime and financial centres in the eastern Mediterranean. Perhaps the most important

6 Crossick – Haupt, *The petit bourgeoisie*, 1–15.

TABLE 5.5 *Total value of new built ships per group of origin (over 500.000 drachmae), 1828–66.*

Group of origin	Values of ships	% of values in the total	Tonnage corresponding in the value of ships	% tonnage
Psara (Hermoupolis)	8,414,178.44	22.68	40,976.55	21.10
Chios (Hermoupolis)	7,260,618.16	19.57	35,529.65	18.30
Hermoupolis	3,315,077.87	8.94	18,677.20	9.62
Andros	2,708,707.65	7.30	12,504.86	6.44
Hydra	1,560,159.99	4.21	9,042.37	4.66
Santorini	1,400,921.42	3.78	7,738.21	3.99
Mykonos	1,062,705.32	2.86	5,904.85	3.04
Spetses	905,850	2.44	5,578.33	2.87
Constantinople	657,150.36	1.77	3,344.24	1.72
Cephalonia	656,379.98	1.77	3,431.25	1.77
Ithaki	515,800	1.39	2,706.97	1.39

Source: Processed data from Appendix 5.4.

TABLE 5.6 *Coefficient values of ships/tonnage.*

Group of origin	Coefficient values of ships/tonnage
Andros	1.13
Psara (Hermoupolis)	1.07
Chios (Hermoupolis)	1.07
Constantinople	1.03
Cephalonia	1.00
Ithaki	1.00
Santorini	0.95
Mykonos	0.94
Hermoupolis	0.93
Hydra	0.90
Spetses	0.85

Source: Processed data from Table 5.5.

name among them was that of the Constantinople merchant George Zarifis, the elder brother of Alexandros Zarifis of Odessa and the founder of the firm 'Zafiropoulos and Zarifis', who in 1847 built the 400-ton brig *Omonoia* through his agent George Ioannis Voulgaris.[7] Other Constantinople Greek merchants with Russian citizenship and business cooperation ties with Black Sea commercial houses were Zaharias Zaharov and Dionysios Kountouris, the first class Taganrog merchants, and Ioannis Deltas, the first class Berdiansk merchant.

The southern Russia merchants were an important group of investors, as they built ships of 419,614 drachmae, representing 1.13% of the total. Greeks were in the majority, such as Markos and Kosmas N. Varvakis, grandsons of Ioannis Varvakis from Psara, who settled in Astrakhan after the Russo-Turkish War of 1768–74, and then moved to Taganrog in 1812. He was among the first Greeks to create an enormous fortune there.[8] In addition, there was Ioannis Zaharov from Taganrog, Andreas Paleologos, a first class merchant from Berdiansk who was resident in Mariupol, Kosmas Zaharov, Dimitrios Paleologos and Grigorios Maraslis, merchants who had settled before 1820 in Odessa, and Theodoros Rodokanakis and Alexandros Zarifis, who both settled there after 1820.[9]

However, Greeks were not the only investors from southern Russia. Aivas Isaak Jufutovik from Eupatoria, represented by Georgios Th. Kazantzis from Tripolis of Pontos and Ionas Megoubi from Odessa, who built the 350-ton ship *Tsar Solomon* and were represented by the Mykonos captain Synevis Drakopoulos, were probably Jews.[10] Furthermore, there was Frangiskos Laura from Odessa, represented by Diodatos Kvekia, and the second class merchant Markos Mihail Kuekitz, represented by Diodatos Kuekitz; all probably of Dalmatian origin.[11] A last group of origin worth mentioning is the Muslim investors. The data confirming this religious identity in the documents are the names of the investors, the names of the ships, the signatures at the end of the contract, and the mention of a Hijra date along with a Christian one. Of the 25 Muslim investors, all ottomans, 14 were from Crete, from which 8 from Chania, 5 from Cesme and 2 from Constantinople. In total, they built

7 GSA, Syros, notary Christodoulos Ioannou, Inventory 2, n. 2635, 23.6.1847; Kardasis, *Έλληνες ομογενείς*, 218–19.

8 Kardasis, *Έλληνες ομογενείς*, 228–29.

9 Ibid., 89, 132, 140, 202, 218–19. Apostolos Delis, "Rodokanakis family", *Encyclopaedia of the Hellenic World, Black Sea* URL: http://blacksea.ehw.gr/Forms/fLemma.aspx?lemmaid=11590&contlang=58, 2007.

10 GSA, Syros, notary Andreas David, n. 8803, 16.5.1839, and ibid., I/Ναυπηγικά, n. 1121, 11.6.1843.

11 Ibid., n. 964, 13.6.1835 and n. 15077, 7.5.1843.

1,639.38 tons of 173,850 drs. The only case of a joint venture between Muslims and Christians was that between Markis Bratsanos from Psara and Abuhara Hadji Mehmet and Kafedji Ahmet Kapitan from Constantinople, who built the 189-ton brig *Dimosthenis*, of which 50% belonged to Bratsanos and 25% to each of the two Muslim investors.[12]

The Making of Shipping Knowhow of the Groups of Origin

The Hermoupolis Groups of Origin—The Psariots

The Psariots were the second largest population group in Hermoupolis. Their neighbourhood was on the western side of the Syros harbour just behind the shipbuilding zone, and bore their name of origin, Psariana, which is still in use today. Along with Hydra and Spetses, they formed the fleet of Independence (1821–29).[13] Psara was located in a strategic position in the Northeast Aegean, and was initially inhabited by Christians and Muslims, but in the seventeenth century, as the Muslims abandoned it, Psara was colonized by the Greek speaking population from Magnesia of Thessaly and Euboea.[14] The crucial event in the island's history occurred in 1770, when they sided with the Russian fleet operating in the Aegean during the Russo-Turkish War of 1768–74. Some years later joined the corsair fleet of Lambros Katsonis (1787–92), which allowed them to accumulate experience in nautical warfare that proved to be very useful during the Greek War of Independence.[15]

The growth of Psara's merchant marine followed the Russo-Turkish War of 1768–74. The financing of neighbouring Chios was a decisive factor, especially for the building of large merchantmen.[16] Psara was located next to Chios, and seemed almost to be an extension of the latter, and was a relatively inconspicuous market when compared to Chios, which was a large maritime centre at the time. A kind of specialization and division of activities developed between the two places. Shipping as a complementary activity of trade was in large part

12 Ibid., n. 8825, 20.5.1839.

13 Tryfonas Konstantinidis, *Καράβια, Καπεταναίοι και Συντροφοναύται 1800–1830*, [*Ships, Captains and Fellow seamen 1800–30*] (Athens: 1954), 318–48.

14 Nikodimos, *Υπόμνημα*, 12–13.

15 Nikodimos, *Υπόμνημα*, 21, 34–35, 42; Konstantinidis, *Καράβια, Καπεταναίοι*, 18–24, 56, 516–21.

16 Ibid., p. 64, Georgios Leon (Leontaritis), "Ελληνική Εμπορική Ναυτιλία", [Greek Merchant Marine], in *Ελληνική Εμπορική Ναυτιλία, 1453–1821*, [*Greek Merchant Marine, 1453–1821*], ed. S. Papadopoulos (Athens: National Bank of Greece, 1972), 41; Traian Stoianovich, "L'espace maritime segmentaire de l'empire ottoman", in *Actes du IIe Colloque International d'Histoire*, Tome I, op. cit., 213.

served by Psariots in cooperation with the Chios capitalists, who mostly specialized in trade. The fleet of Psara upgraded in the mid-1790s when the small sacolevas were replaced by three-masted polaccas, in order to respond to the increase of demand for foodstuffs during the French Wars, and the routes were extended to the western Mediterranean, Lisbon, and beyond.[17]

The partnership between Chios's funds and Psara's nautical know-how seems to have continued later in Hermoupolis, where not even the emigration that followed the massacres on both islands (Chios 1822, Psara 1824) during the Greek War of Independence disturbed the entrepreneurial mechanisms that had previously developed between them. Interesting proof of this comes from a liquidation letter stipulated between the Chios merchant Efstratios Dimitrios Petrokokkinos, a representative of the firm *Petrokokkinos & Co* of Livorno, and the sons of the late captain from Psara, Georgios Apostolis, for funds and interest invested in his two ships to cover the expenses of fighting operations during the Greek War of Independence.[18] The Psariots who settled in Hermoupolis in their own neighborhood continued to work in the shipping business as captains and shipowners, assisted by the funds of Chiot merchants, in a new framework of the Greek National State and, more importantly, within the internationally expanded network of the Greek Diaspora, which controlled the trade between the Black Sea, the Eastern Mediterranean and Western Europe.[19]

This continuity is also confirmed by the actors themselves. An important number of Psara investors on the Syros shipyards have been found to be members of the families of captains and shipowners involved in the maritime business at least since 1780. Thus, the family names of Androulis, Apostolis, Velissariou, Vourekas (Bourekas), Vratsanos (Bratsanos), Yannitsis, Diakoyannis, Diasakis, Kavilias, Kalaris, Kalimeris, Kabouris, Katzoulieris, Kontos, Kotzias, Koutsodontis, Kyparissis, Loumakis, Mamounis, Milaitis, Mitilias, Mikaros, Papanikolis, Sarris and Filinis continued, as very active shipowners in Hermoupolis.[20] Further, it has been confirmed that some members

17 Delis, "From Lateen to Square-Rig", 49–52.

18 GSA, Syros, notary Andreas David, n. 26695, 15.7.1853, attached to the above was the liquidation letter stipulated by the Syros notary Skarlatos Maximos dated 15.4.1830.

19 Gelina Harlaftis, "Mapping the Greek Maritime Diaspora", in *Diaspora Entrepreneurial Network. Four centuries of History*, ed. Ina Banghdiatz Mc Cabe, Gelina Harlaftis and Ioanna Pepelasi-Minoglou (Oxford-New York: Berg, 2005), 154–61.

20 Database Amphitrete, 'Pythagoras' I, Research Programme, 2004–07, financed from the European Union and the Greek Ministry of Education, Department of History, Ionian University, *The Maritime History of the Greeks, 1700–1821*.

of these families participated in the Greek War of Independence, such as Andreas and Dimitrios Arvanitis, Ioannis Kabouris, Georgios Kalaris, Andreas Katzoulieris, Georgios Dimitrios Koutsodontis, Nikolaos Kyparissis, Dimitrios Loumakis, Anagnostis Bourekas, Mikes Filinis and Georgios Chilas.[21] Some of these families also managed to continue working in steamship navigation until the twentieth century, such as Domestinis, Kalimeris, Kalafatis, Kotzias, Filinis and Hadjikiriakos, whereas the Kotzias family is still active in shipping today, specialized in chartering, and with headquarters in Piraeus.[22]

The Chiots

The Chiots were the most numerous and economically powerful group, and had the greatest influence in the city's affairs. They had a long experience in shipping and trade, and the richest and most powerful members of the city's merchant class were among them. Their most important capital was the strong network of ties they maintained with other members of the Chios diaspora in the commercial and maritime centres of the Mediterranean, the Black Sea and Western Europe, thus forming what Gelina Harlaftis defined as the 'Chios Network', an informal cooperative business network based on common origin, kinship, and marital strategies. These ties strengthened the relationships of trust between the network members, which, along with obedience and discipline in a strictly defined hierarchy, were the necessary preconditions of harmonious cooperation, commercial information exchange and mutual support, and the key of their success.[23] Therefore, the cooperation mechanisms, the rate of penetration into the international markets, and the availability of funds from their partners abroad were decisive factors in the dominant socio-economic position of the community of Chiots in Hermoupolis.[24]

Chiots were conscious of their particularity, and they defined themselves and were recognized by others as a distinct business community, based

21 Maria Christina Chatziioannou, «Οι εμποροκαπετάνιοι μετά την Επανάσταση. Μερικές παρατηρήσεις» [The merchant captains after the Revolution. Some observations], *Η Επανάσταση του 1821. Μελέτες στη μνήμη της Δέσποινας Θεμελή-Κατηφόρη*, [*The 1821 Revolution. Studies in the memory of Despoina-Themeli Katifori*], (Athens: EMNE, 1994), 157–72.

22 Gelina Harlaftis, Helen Beneki and Manos Haritatos, *Ploto, Greek shipowners from the late 18th century to the eve of WWII*, (Athens: ELIA/Niarchos Foundation, 2003), 285–99; Ioannis Theotokas and Gelina Harlaftis, *Leadership in World Shipping: Greek Family Firms in International Business*, (London-New York: Palgrave/Macmillan, 2009), 279.

23 Harlaftis, *A History of Greek-Owned Shipping*, 40–67.

24 Kardasis, *Σύρος*, 23–24, 295–96.

on their origins and their unique characteristics.[25] Thus, as a compact and distinct community, they divided the rest of the population of Hermoupolis into two 'camps', the Chiot and the Anti-Chiot parties, which competed for local political power and control. The municipal elections became the main field of these antagonisms. This dualism within the Greek communities is also reported in other diaspora communities, such as London.[26] Even the gentlemen's clubs in Hermoupolis were divided according to the two parties: the *Hermes* was founded in 1836, and belonged to the Chiot party, and the *Hermoupolis citizen's Club* was founded in 1838 by their opponents (see Chapter 1).

However, the particularly developed business know-how of the Chiots and the competitive advantage they gained through their network cannot be explained simply as a consequence of the general rise of the Western European economy and its penetration into the markets of the Mediterranean and Levant, as was the case with the maritime communities of the Aegean, such as Hydra and Spetses. Instead, the economic know-how of the Chiots seems to have involved a long-lasting and continuous process, and to have been a complex phenomenon which integrated Chios society into capitalist economic practices much earlier, having its roots in the Genoese dominion of the island (1346–1566).[27]

Genoa, along with other Italian city-states (Venice, Florence, Milan) preceded the rest of Europe in the transformation of economic and social life from the Late Middle Ages to the Renaissance. Many of the main achievements of the European economy and society in the Modern Period, such as the monetization of the economy, bank credit, the commercialization of goods, manufacturing, seagoing shipping and urbanization started in these societies, and much of it was also transplanted to their colonies.[28] Chios was not a simple part of the economic empire of Genoa in the Eastern Mediterranean. Venetians used to call it the '*right eye of Genoa*', and Heers defined its status as follows: '*Tout d' abord Chio est une île exclusivement génoise, une colonie au sens complet du terme, où l'autorité s'exerce sans aucune restriction.*'[29] It became an international centre of the transit trade, a departure point and

25 Maria Christina Chatziioannou "Greek Merchant Networks in the Age of Empires (1770–1870)", in *Diaspora Entrepreneurial Network*, op. cit., 374.

26 Kardasis, *Σύρος*, 35–37; Chatziioannou, *Οικογενειακή στρατηγική*, 124–25.

27 Philip Argenti, *The Occupation of Chios by the Genoese and their administration of the island 1346–1566*, (Cambridge: Cambridge University Press, 1958).

28 Cipolla, *Before the Industrial Revolution*, 117–208; Fernand Braudel, *The Mediterranean and the Mediterranean World in the Age of Philip II: Volume I*, (Berkeley-Los Angeles: University of California Press, 1995), 390–91.

29 Heers, *Gênes*, 385.

final destination of the Genoese routes between the Eastern and Western Mediterranean, as well as for the long distance routes to the North, Flanders and England, a crossroad that all major trading axes of the Levant, such as the Bursa, Thessaloniki, and Alexandria passed through. Under these circumstances, Chios also became the most important shipping and ship repairing centre of the Eastern Mediterranean.[30]

It was also an exporting centre of local commodities, a result of commercialized methods of production. Mastic, along with silk, fruits and wine, created the character of an agriculture economy '*spéculative et "colonial"*.' However, due to its strategic position next to the Asia Minor hinterland and its commodities cereals, cotton, resin, and most of all alum, Chios played a crucial role in the economic importance of the island for Genoa and in the growth of its commercial activities.[31]

Chios was a place of great importance for Genoa, and adopted the structure, mechanisms, institutions and innovations of the Genoese capitalist economy in full, which was by then well-advanced. Monetization and bank credit were the main instruments of transaction, processing and the use of *cambiali*, the bills of exchange, was widespread, whereas payments were made on an exchange rate based on the golden ducat of Chios.[32] On the other hand, the commercial methods used by Maona, the society that controlled all its revenues and possessions and essentially ruled Chios during the two centuries of Genoese occupation, were fully aligned with the latest developments in commercial capitalism. The creation of a commercial corporation with shares "a carati", usually divided into 24 parts as in the ships, but which also included the administration of corporation through a board of shareholders that took decisions based upon the majority view of its members and asset management partnership, were innovative methods by the standards of the period.[33] In shipping, the marine insurance sector was very developed, whereas an important element in progress was the distinction that arose between the merchant and the shipowner. The commercial trading houses of Chios did not own their own ships, but instead hired the services of shipowners, who functioned as transporters of goods in exchange for a fare (*noli*).[34]

---

30 Ibid., 298, 388–402, 405–06, 456; John Dotson, "Economics and logistics of Galley warfare", in *The Age of the Galley. Mediterranean oared vessels since pre-classical times. Conway's History of the Ship*, ed. Robert Gardiner, (London: Conway Maritime Press, 1995), 218–22.

31 Heers, *Gênes*, 390–91, 394–98, 406.

32 Ibid., 76–78.

33 Ibid., 200–03, 288–91, 386.

34 Ibid., 211–14, 309–10.

The eminent economic position of Chios continued during the Ottoman period, given the previously developed commercial ties of the island with Ottoman areas and its strategic geo-economic importance. This prosperity and privileged position within the Ottoman Empire, along with its Genoese past, had a significant effect on every aspect of everyday life and culture. Chios was very different to other Ottoman areas, and its prosperous, westernized and almost Genoese outlook upon the elements of material life (architecture, gardens, costumes), as well as the mentality of its inhabitants, are reported by many European travelers.[35] In terms of the economy, mastic was a protected good destined only for internal consumption, especially in the Sultan's harems, whereas silk manufacture maintained the island's thriving export trade. Vlastos mention that in 1770, Chios had 1200 silk manufacturing establishments exporting to Smyrna, Constantinople, and Alexandria, where Chiots held their own trading stores.[36] Furthermore, the trade of *sevigliana* or Spanish silver coins was another very profitable sector in which Chiots distinguished themselves, given the chronic lack of currency in the Ottoman Empire and the prohibition of the circulation of foreign currencies, except *sevigliana*, issued in the late seventeenth century. Generally, in the Ottoman period, Chiots were the main money brokers, and they traded, recast and redistributed European currencies (phony or not) to the markets of the Levant.[37]

In Smyrna, at the end of the eighteenth century Chiots dominated trade among other Orthodox merchants from Peloponnese, Ioannina, the Aegean Sea, and Ambelakia. They owned the overwhelming majority of the biggest trading houses, such as *Dimitrios Rodokanakis and Co, Ralli, Sechiari and Argenti, Ralli, Petrokokkinou and Argenti*, the *Vlastos Brothers*, and so on.[38] Smyrna must be considered the departure point in the expansion of the Chios merchants to the markets of the Eastern and Western Mediterranean and the Black Sea in the first decades of the nineteenth century.[39] In the same period, Chios merchants were seriously engaged in shipping finance with shipowners from Psara and Hydra, an extremely profitable investment, especially during

---

35 Alexandros Vlastos, *Χιακά ἤτοι Ἱστορία τῆς νήσου Χίου*, [*History of the Island of Chios*] (Hermoupolis: 1840), 83–84; Georgios Zolotas, *Ιστορία της Χίου*, [*History of Chios*], vol. A1, (Athens: 1921), 252–53; ibid., vol. A2, (Athens: 1923), 128, 148, 223.

36 Hélène Pigné, "Εξωτερικό και διανησιωτικό εμπόριο στη Χίο τον ιη' αιώνα", ["Overseas and inter-island trade in Chios in the eighteenth century"], *Τα Ιστορικά-Historica*, 8, (1988), 117, 119–20; Zolotas, *Ιστορία της Χίου*, vol. A1, 56–257; Vlastos, *Χιακά*, 175.

37 Liata, *Φλωριά δεκατέσσερα*, 50–51, 153, 178, 183; Pigné, "Εξωτερικό και διανησιωτικό εμπόριο", 117–21.

38 Elena Frangakis-Syrett, *The commerce of Smyrna in the 18th century (1700–1820)*, (Athens: Center of Asia Minor Studies, 1992), 110.

39 Kardasis, *Έλληνες ομογενείς*, 135–37.

the French Wars, where, after breaking the blockaded ports, the latter sold cereals at exorbitant prices to the starving population.[40]

The actors themselves confirm the continuity and the transfer of business know-how from Chiots of previous periods to those of Hermoupolis. The families that established and dominated economic life in the new town were, to a large extent, descendants of the same elites formed in Chios by the Genoese and Greeks of the fourteenth century. A list written in the eighteenth century by Skarlatos Konstantinos Mavrokordatos comprised the 37 noblest Chios families, of whom twelve had Genoese origins, such as the Salvago family, one of the most powerful, who belonged to the party of 'black' (or *Guelfi*) during the dispute between the Pope and the Holy Roman Emperor during the Late Middle Ages.[41] Members of many of these families, which formed the socio-economic elite of Hermoupolis, belonged to the families of Argentis, Salvago, Prassakakis, Petrokokkinos, Rodokanakis, Rallis, and so on. Of the 37 above mentioned noble families, members of 19 invested in the Syros shipbuilding industry, whereas members of 4 families that did not invest in shipbuilding were seriously engaged in shipping transactions. Some had a more occasional presence, but Loukas Koressis, Amvrosios Damalas and Ioannis Rodokanakis were involved in shipowning, as to a lesser extent were members of the Agelastos, Negrepontes, Petrokokkinos, Rallis and Salvagos families.

In Hermoupolis, however, outside the members of the Chios merchant elite with a long tradition, the first pure group of Chiot shipowners formed, with connections to their motherland and Oinousses, a small island to the northeast of Chios that had been colonized by Chiots. These shipowners held a considerable share in new ships and developed into the most dynamic shipowning group, which made the transition to steamship navigation and is today perhaps the most important shipowning group in Greek-owned shipping. The group includes the families of Andreadis, Mihalinos, Palios and Fafalios.[42] The mighty Lemos family had established Mihail, Nikolaos and Konstantinos in Hermoupolis, whereas the family founder Diamantis remained in Oinousses.[43] The Chios and Oinousses families that invested in Syros built ships were Lo, Lyras and Pateras.[44] With the exception of the Mihalinos family, all the

40 Vlastos, *Χιακά*, 129; Georgios Zolotas, *Ιστορία της Χίου*, vol. Γ1, (Athens: 1928), 312; Stoianovich, «L'espace maritime segmentaire», 213.

41 See Appendix 5.5; Heers, *Gênes*, 569–70, 586.

42 Harlaftis, Beneki and Haritatos, *Ploto*, 239–83.

43 Ibid., 267.

44 Ibid., 247, 274–76.

previously mentioned families continue their shipping activities today, and have become an important point of reference for Greek-owned shipping.[45]

The Outside Hermoupolis Groups of Origin-Andros

Andros shipowners, as the above results show, were among the most important investors in the Syros shipbuilding market during the nineteenth century. From the early years of the 1830s, they built large sailing ships such as brigs, and smaller ones such as tsernikia. However, the rate of shipping development before 1830 was not such as to predispose the very rapid and massive growth that followed, despite the relative growth noted since the late-eighteenth century, following the trends of the Greek-Ottoman merchant marine.[46] According to Pouqueville's table on Greek shipping development in 1813, Andros had 40 ships of 70 tons on average, far below the average tonnage of important maritime places such as Hydra, Spetses, Psara, Galaxidi, Skopelos and Mykonos. However, the high number of seamen (400) might be confusing, or perhaps be an indicator of a future dynamic perspective in shipping.[47] The fact that the majority of the captains were from *Chora*, the capital and most urbanized place on the island, characterizes the rest of its purely agricultural economic landscape and explains the limited impact of shipping upon economic life.[48]

Continuity is also an indicative issue in the development of shipping. Quite a large number of Andros shipowners who were already engaged prior to 1830 appear to build systematically in Syros, such as Goulandris, Empiricos, Zarbis, Thermiotis, Anysis, Loukissas, Grafas, Kostis, Paschalis, Polemis, Rallias, Tatakis, Fakis and Hadoulis. After Greek Independence, the number of Andros shipowners grew. Individuals who appeared as seamen in the Greek fleet during the war were among the Andros investors in the Syros shipyards, such as Stamatis Voulgaris and members of the Astras, Maris, Balkas and Piagos families.[49] New and important investors, as compared to the pre-war period, were members of Palaiokrassas, Moraitis, Dabasis and Sigalas families.[50] Finally, members of the pre-war elite with no previous engagement in shipping entered in a dynamic way, such as the Kabanis family.[51] The Goulandris, Empiricos,

45 Theotokas – Harlaftis, *Leadership in World Shipping*, 101–321.

46 Harlaftis, Beneki and Haritatos, *Ploto*, 131.

47 Dimitrios I. Polemis, *Τα ιστιοφόρα της Άνδρου*, [*The Andros sailing ships*], (Andros: Agra Publishers, 1991), 23; Leontaritis, "Ελληνική Εμποριχή Ναυτιλία", 46.

48 Polemis, *Τα ιστιοφόρα της Άνδρου*, 23–24.

49 Ibid., 24–26 and Appendix 5.1.

50 Harlaftis, Beneki and Haritatos, *Ploto*, 139, 149–54 and Appendix 5.1.

51 Polemis, *Τα ιστιοφόρα*, 29; Harlaftis, Beneki and Haritatos, *Ploto*, 146.

Dabasis, Kabanis, Moraitis, Paleokrassas, Polemis and Hadoulis families, who built sailing ships in Syros, belonged to those who made the transition to steamship navigation.[52] Of these, the Goulandris, Empiricos, Dabasis, Polemis, Kabanis and Paleokrassas families became some of the most important Greek shipowning firms in the entire twentieth century: the first four continue up to the present day, and the sons of Nikolaos I. Goulandris took on the management of Syros's Neorion Shipyards in 1970.[53]

Andros shipowners had close ties of cooperation with the Koufoudakis family of shipbuilders, which had Chiot origins. Of the 123 ships built for Andriots in the period 1831–66, 57 were built by Ioannis and his sons Zannis and Stamatis Koufoudakis. The Andriots were Stamatisis's most important customers, as he built 23 of their 57 ships, and one more with his father. Furthermore, in the years 1842, 1846, 1848 and 1850, Stamatis worked in Andros, where he built 22 vessels, most of them coasters, of a total of 51 built in the island's shipyards between 1835 and 1850.[54]

The close interdependence of the Andros sailing merchant marine and the Syros shipping and shipbuilding centre, especially as a source of shipping finance, is further highlighted by other contemporary sources. In its meeting of 8 January 1843, the Andros provincial council supported Syros's case to be granted free-port status by the Greek government, and asked to the latter to grant this: "*without granting the same privilege to any other port... considering that after the center of Greek trade is established after so many surmounted difficulties in this nearby island* [Syros] *offers thousands of facilities and assistance to the newly founded Andros merchant marine, as many capitalists always minister funds to Andriots, especially when they build ships with the purpose of a commercial enterprise, and there* [in Syros] *the Andros captains easily derive funds in the form of maritime loans to complement their commercial enterprises... thanks to the trade and industry that concentrated in the nearby island of Syros, the Andros merchant marine has grown and flourished.*"[55]

Hydra

Hydra was the most developed maritime community of the Greek-owned merchant marine before the War of Independence. They developed considerably in the last quarter of the eighteenth century, and their fleet was the

52 Harlaftis, Beneki and Haritatos, *Ploto*, 131–58.

53 Theotokas – Harlaftis, *Leadership in World Shipping*, 166.

54 Polemis, *Τα ιστιοφόρα της Άνδρου*, 47; Demetrios I. Polemis, "Shipbuilding on Andros during the period 1830–1850", in *The evolution of wooden shipbuilding*, op. cit., 45–53.

55 Newspaper *Ἑρμῆς*, [*Ermis*], n. 203, 6.2.1843.

largest among the Greeks. Hydriots were among the richest shipowners, and they played a decisive role in naval and political leadership during the War of Independence.[56] Their fleet grew from approximately 17,000 tons in 1802 to 45,000 tons in 1813, before decreasing to 27,000 tons in 1821 due to the shipping crisis after the end of Napoleonic Wars.[57] From 1790, Hydriots upgraded their fleet from lateeners to brigantines and polaccas before their main competitors from Spetses and Psara. This development is related to the increase in demand during the French Wars and the expansion of the routes beyond Malta and Trieste towards Genoa and Marseille. From 1783 to 1814, Hydriots held 50% of the arrivals of Greek-owned ships in the port of Genoa, and they sailed mostly with brigantines and polaccas.[58]

After Independence, Hydra maintained a considerable fleet, which reached 20,000 in the period 1850–70, but had lost its eminent position of the pre-War period.[59] In the newly founded Greek Kingdom, a large part of Hydra's population was unemployed, due to the relative decline of the island's shipping business, and sought better opportunities in the large Greek ports of Syros and Piraeus.[60] A very interesting fact is that many Hydriot shipowners/investors in Syros were not involved in shipping during the pre-War period. However, especially in the early years, some members of the great shipowning families of Hydra built ships in Syros, such as Georgios and Lazaros Kountouriotis, Manouil Antonios Kriezis, Kosmas Tsamados, Andreas and Georgios Th. Sachtouris, Theofanis and Antonios I. Vokos, along with others who, while not members of Hydra's elite, were seriously engaged in shipping during the pre-War period. These included Mihail and Nikolaos Emmanouil Kiosses, Ioannis A. Zakas, Vasilios N. Kaminis, Georgios Vasilios Kaminis, the brothers Ioannis and Georgios A. Kaloyannis, Lazaros Negas, Georgios P. Politis and Georgios Revidis.[61]

56 Delis, "From Lateen to Square-Rig", 53.

57 Vassilis Kremmydas, *Ελληνική Ναυτιλία, 1776–1835.Οι Μηχανισμοί*, [*Greek Shipping, 1776–1835. The mechanisms*], vol. B′, (Athens: Historical Archive of the Commercial Bank of Greece, 1986), Table 7, 45.

58 Harlaftis, "The fleet 'dei Greci". Table 8; Delis, "From Lateen to Square-Rig", 50–51.

59 Harlaftis, Beneki and Haritatos, *Ploto*, 419.

60 Ibid., 422; Vasias Tsokopoulos, *Πειραιάς 1835–1870. Εισαγωγή στην ιστορία του ελληνικού Μάντσεστερ*, [*Piraeus 1835–70. Introduction to the history of Greek Manchester*], (Athens: Kastaniotis, 1984), 57; Matina Malikoutis, *Η εξέλιξη του αστικού Πειραιά, 1834–1922*, [*The development of Urban Piraeus, 1834–1922*], (Athens: Efesos, 2000), 147.

61 Database Amphitrete, op. cit.

Santorini

The case of Santorini shipping has common features with the development of other Cyclades islands, such as Andros and Mykonos. The first period of considerable growth began in the last decades of the eighteenth century, and was based mainly on wine exports, cotton fabrics, volcanic earth, and wax.[62] More frequent reports on Santorini ships following the typical routes of the Greek-owned shipping between the Mediterranean, the Black Sea and the Sea of Azov ports began in 1780. This fleet consisted mainly of large vessels like polaccas, brigs and brigantines. According to Pouqueville, in 1813 Santorini had 32 ships of 2,560 tons in total, with an average tonnage of 80 tons.[63]

After Independence, Santorini shipping experienced considerable growth, like the maritime centre of Syros and other Greek seafaring communities that participated in the Greek-owned shipping routes between the Black Sea and the Mediterranean, carrying wine on the outward leg of the voyage and cereals on the homeward leg.

TABLE 5.7 *Capacity of Santorini fleet in the nineteenth century (Ships above 30 tons).*

Year	Number of ships	Tonnage capacity	Average tonnage
1848(1)	78	11,276	144.56
1850(2)	16	4,084	255.25
1852(3)	74	13,661	184.60
1855(4)	69	12,630	183.04
1855(2)	12	3,220	268.33
1858(5)	61	11,951	195.91
1860(2)	16	3,395	212.18

Source: (1) AMAE, CCC, Syra, vol. 3, 20.4.1849. (2) Harlaftis, Beneki and Haritatos, *Ploto*, 129. (3) AMAE, CCC, Syra vol. 4, 28.6.1853, Mémoire sur la Statistique, la navigation, le commerce et l'industrie de Syra et des autres îles Cyclades pendant l'année 1852, (4) ibid., vol. 4, 17.7.1856, (5) ibid., vol. 5, 27.4.1858.

62 Harlaftis, Beneki and Haritatos, *Ploto*, 177. Maria Spiliotopoulou, *Η Σαντορίνη στην Τουρκοκρατία. Κοινωνικές και οικονομικές πρακτικές στο πλαίσιο της οικογένειας*, [*Santorini during the Ottoman Period. Social and economic practices within the family context*], (Ph.D diss., University of Crete, 2005), 68.

63 Database Amphitrete, op. cit.; Leontaritis, "Ελληνική Εμπορική Ναυτιλία", 46.

Table 5.7 compares the data on the capacity of the Santorini fleet, based on the reports of the French consul of Syros and the historical shipping register *Pontoporeia*. There is a great divergence between these two sources, the data of *Pontoporeia* amounting to only one fourth of that presented by the French consul. However, it is worth noticing the high average tonnage of the Santorini ships: of the 58 ships built in Syros between 1833 and 1866, there were 43 brigs, 1 gabara (barque), and 11 schooners, bombards and other smaller craft.[64]

Santorini also had also its own shipyards where, between 1843 and 1858, 79 vessels were built, mostly coasters (sacoleva, mistico, bratsera, trehandiri, tserniki and only three brigs) of which the total capacity reached 1,598 tons, with an average tonnage of 20 tons.[65] In Santorini, there was significant continuity with shipowning in the pre-War period, as was also the case in Barbarigos, Nomikos and Syrigos. Therefore, the great shipowning families of the island, such as Alafouzos, Zanes, Barbarigos, Manolessos, Nomikos, Sarris, Syrigos and Mavrommatis, but also others of lower rank like Platis, Karras and Mathas, systematically built their ships (mostly brigs) in Syros.[66] Of the above families, only Alafouzos and Nomikos made the transition to steamship navigation, and their shipping firms flourished throughout the twentieth century. They continue to manage high capacity fleets to the present day.[67]

Mykonos

Mykonos shipowners had been engaged in shipping from the first half of the eighteenth century, when they sailed up to Ancona, and later expanded their routes to Malta. Its port (along with Milos in the eighteenth century) was a notorious centre of piratical preys in Cyclades.[68] In 1813, the Mykonos fleet was composed of 22 ships of 3,300 tons, with an average tonnage of 150 tons, almost double that of Andros and Santorini.[69] After 1830, Mykonos followed a path like that of Andros and Santorini, benefited by its proximity to Syros.

---

64 Database Amphitrete, op. cit.

65 Harlaftis, Beneki and Haritatos, *Ploto*, 179; Kardasis, *Σύρος*, Table 26, 182–83.

66 Harlaftis, Beneki and Haritatos, *Ploto*, 180–93.

67 Ibid., 180–81, 186–88; Theotokas – Harlaftis, *Leadership in World Shipping*, 103, 243–46.

68 Harlaftis, Beneki and Haritatos, *Ploto*, 167; Leontaritis, "Ελληνική Εμπορική Ναυτιλία", 41. Database Amphitrete, op. cit.

69 Leontaritis, "Ελληνική Εμπορική Ναυτιλία", 46.

TABLE 5.8 *Capacity of Mykonos fleet in the nineteenth century (Ships above 30 tons).*

Year	Number of ships	Tonnage capacity	Average tonnage
1848(1)	40	6,023	150.57
1850(2)	16	3,588	224.25
1858(1)	37	6,821	184.35
1860(2)	9	2,021	224.55

Source: (1) AMAE, CCC, Syra, vol. 3, 20.4.1849. vol. 4, vol. 5, 27.4.1858. (2) Harlaftis, Beneki and Haritatos, *Ploto*, 129.

As in the previous table, the data in Table 5.8 presents a great divergence between the two sources. However, similarly with the previous table, the high average tonnage of Mykonos ships is indicative of the orientation of its shipping to long distance trade. Of 40 vessels built in Syros in the period 1834–63, of which 35 belonged to a sole owner, 24 were brigs, whereas of 10 schooners, 5 ranged between 85 and 134 tons. As is to be expected, Mykonos shipping firms also had a continuous tradition, and Barberis (Varveris), Drakopoulos, Yannou, Konstantinou, Bonis and Skordilis were among the shipowners who invested in Syros ships, and who had already been active in the period prior to the Greek War of Independence.[70] Among the most active Mykonos investors in the Syros shipyards were the Drakopoulos family, Peris Markaris, and, most importantly, Antonelos Bonazountas. However, the latter two did not manage to make the transition to steamships, whereas the Drakopoulos family did so, developing into one of the most flourishing shipowning firms represented by *Empros Lines*.[71]

Spetses

Spetses, along with Hydra and Psara, was one of the most developed Greek maritime communities, and formed the Fleet of Independence. The rise of its shipping activity dates back to after 1770, when the town was destroyed by the Ottomans as a reprisal for supporting the Russian admiral Orloff in his naval

70 Database Amphitrete, op. cit.

71 Harlaftis, Beneki and Haritatos, *Ploto*, 170; Theotokas – Harlaftis, *Leadership in World Shipping*, 139–40.

TABLE 5.9 *Capacity of Spetses fleet in the nineteenth century (Ships above 30 tons).*

Year	Number of ships	Tonnage capacity	Average tonnage
1838(1)	82	13,557	165.32
1840(2)	26	5,597	215.25
1845(2)	60	12,586	209.76
1850(2)	102	19,992	196
1853(3)	208	37,209	178.88
1855(2)	92	17,987	195.5
1855(4)	151	24,775	164.07

Source: (1) GSA, Athens, KOA, Marine file, 42. (2) Harlaftis, Beneki and Haritatos, *Ploto*, 419. (3) GSA, Athens, KOA, Marine, file, 41. (4) AMAE, CCC, Syra, vol. 4, 17.7.1856, 470.

campaign in the Aegean during the Russo-Ottoman War of 1768–74.[72] From 1780 to the mid-1790s, the Spetses fleet was composed mainly of lateeners, and was only later upgraded to larger polaccas, due to the investment of Peloponnese merchants, when it expanded its routes to Genoa, Marseille, Barcelona and Lisbon. Interestingly enough, for the Genoa routes, Spetsiot shipowners, like their neighbours from Hydra, used large vessels, polaccas and brigantines, even before 1796.[73] Estimations of the capacity of the pre-War fleet show that in the biennium (1807–08), Spetses had 23,000 tons, which decreased to 19,500 in 1813, and then fell further to 16,000 tons in 1821, due the recession that followed the Napoleonic Wars.[74] After the 1830 period, shipping continued to be the most flourishing economic activity in Spetses, although, like Hydra, it had lost its former supremacy, in the face of competition from the emerging Cyclades maritime communities.

Table 5.9 shows the capacity of Spetses fleet after 1830. The data are drawn from different sources, as with previous tables, and this explains the divergences between them. However, all sources suggest an increase in the general trend in tonnage during the period 1838–55, with the exception of the years 1850–53 and 1855, probably due to the 1849–52 recession and the troubles caused to Greek shipping by the Crimean War (1853–56). The Spetses shipyards, which had been very active since the pre-War period, continued to be among

72 Anargyros Andreou Hadjianargyros, *Τα Σπετσιωτικά*, vol. 2, (Piraeus: 1925), 54–68.

73 Database Amphitrete, op. cit.

74 Kremmydas, *Ελληνική Ναυτιλία*, vol. B′, Table 8, 47.

the most productive in the Greek Kingdom, second only to those of Syros, producing 643 vessels in the period 1843–58 of 44,337 tons.[75] Despite this, many Spetses shipowners preferred to build in Syros, such as members of families engaged in pre-War shipping like Andrianos, Androutsos, Lazarou, Boukouris, Raptis, Sklias and Tzoupa Ghikas, and those who were new, like Pnevmatikos, Lebessis, Stemnitsiotis, Kastriotis and others.[76] Interestingly, with the exception of Lazarou and Boukouris, no other member of the shipowning elite, for instance Koutsis, Mexis, Goudis or Hadjianargyros, invested in Syros's ships.[77]

The Ionians (*Cephalonia and Ithaki*)

Ionian shipping flourished almost half of a century earlier than Aegean shipping, and major areas of this development were the islands of Cephalonia and Ithaki. From the early eighteenth century, Ionian seafarers were active on Adriatic routes up to Malta as part of the shipping activity of the Venetian State, especially after the loss of Crete (1669), when Ionian Isles became the base of commercial affairs in the Levant.[78] However, the intrusive control of the Venetian authorities led many of the Ionian capitalists, shipowners and shipbuilders to transfer their activities to the Ottoman Messolonghi, Aitoliko and Prevesa, and to contribute to the development of shipping in Western Ottoman Greece.[79]

Unfortunately, no systematic data about the size of the Ionian fleet before 1821 exists. After 1830, some estimations show an upward trend in the Cephalonian fleet, from 19,709 in 1830 to 24,632 in 1870, with a recession in the years 1835–45 and 1860–65, whereas similar trends present the Ithaki fleet with much lower figures, from 4,746 tons in 1830 to 9,195 tons in 1870.[80] However, the above figures cannot capture the range of maritime activity and the expansion of Ionian shipowners that was widespread in the great ports of the Danube, the Sea of Azov, the Black Sea, the Eastern Mediterranean, and Western Europe. There, they formed a powerful business group who controlled a large part of the grain trade and international shipping, and which included tycoons like the Vagliano Brothers. These groups were based, as the

---

75 Kardasis, *Σύρος*, Table 26, 182–83.

76 Database Amphitrete, op. cit.

77 Harlaftis, Beneki and Haritatos, *Ploto*, 436–45.

78 Helene Yannakopoulou, "L'architecture navale en Grece de l'Ouest", in *Shipbuilding and ships in the eastern Mediterranean*, op. cit., 48.

79 Leontaritis, "Ελληνική Εμπορική Ναυτιλία", 30; Yannakopoulou, "L'architecture navale en Grece", 51–55.

80 Harlaftis, Beneki and Haritatos, *Ploto*, 51.

Chiot groups had previously been, on the entrepreneurial networks founded upon the common origin of their members.[81]

Continuity is also a very notable characteristic of Ionian shipping, lasting from the beginning of eighteenth century up to the present day, as can be observed by looking at the families involved in the maritime business. In the Syros shipyards, the majority of Cephalonian investors were members of families engaged in shipping since the eighteenth century, like Antoniou, Vaglianos, Igglesis, Karantinos, Kokolis, Koupas, Lykiardopoulos, Mousouris, Rosolimos, Frangopoulos, Fokas, and Helmis. Some Ionian shipowners were also established in Syros, like Spyridon Metaxas, Spyridon Svoronos, Spyridon Potamianos and Fillipos Kalligas. Similarly, the Ithaki shipowners with a long tradition who built in Syros included Vlassopoulos, Dendrinos, Maratos, Petalas, and Tantarias.[82]

A large number of the shipowners of both islands who built ships in Syros continued into the age of steamship navigation. As well as those already mentioned, this category includes the mighty Vagliano Brothers, who had a crucial role in ship finance for many other Ionian shipowners, the families of Metaxas, Lykiardopoulos, Svoronos, Fokas, Koupas and Rosolimos from Cephalonia, and Vlassopoulos and Petalas from Ithaki.[83] Of the above families, Lykiardopoulos and Vlassopoulos managed to become major players in Greek shipping in the twentieth century, and their firms are still active now.[84]

The Occupational Groups of Investors

The profession of the investors is not given with all types of source, and is often problematic, as individuals tended to declare different occupations from those they originally exercised. Thus, some merchants and shipowners prefer to declare themselves as landowners, and some shipbuilders declare themselves as carpenters, captains, or simply seafarers. As with the groups of origin, occupational groups will be analyzed according their numbers, the tonnage, and the value of ships. Of 2,407 investors in the period 1828–66,

81 Harlaftis, *A History of Greek-Owned Shipping*, 70–103; Ibid., "From Diaspora Traders to Shipping Tycoons: The Vagliano Bros", *Business History Review*, 81 (Summer 2007), 237–68.

82 Database Amphitrete, op. cit.

83 Harlaftis, Beneki and Haritatos, *Ploto*, 60–87. Delis Apostolos, "Lykiardopoulos family", *Encyclopaedia of the Hellenic World, Black Sea*, URL: http://kassiani.fhw.gr/blacksea/forms/fLemma.aspx?lemmaId=11583.

84 Delis, "Lykiardopoulos family"; Theotokas and Harlaftis, *Leadership in World Shipping*, 217–18.

we know the professions of 1,462, while 945 cases are unknown. 82 types of profession have been discovered and classified into more generic occupational categories. Among maritime occupations, there are eleven such types of profession. Most of these involve seagoing shipping, such as captains (πλοίαρχος, εμποροπλοίαρχος), seafarers (ναυτικός, θαλασσινός), or seamen (ναύτης). Seafarer (ναυτικός) was the most frequently mentioned, appearing in 854 of 1,081 cases. Maritime occupations also included boatmen, bargemen and fishermen, who were mostly from Hermoupolis and belonged to its lower social strata, as well as a few Greek Navy officers, such as the Rear Admiral/Senator and national hero Konstantinos Kanaris.

In the mercantile occupations, 22 types of professions are found. One subgroup is composed of 40 investors and consists of retailers from Hermoupolis, milkmen, fishmongers, butchers, coffee shop owners and others, which represent a small share and invest mostly in small coasters. Merchants (έμποροι), who form the majority (186), mainly invest in seagoing ships. The secondary sector occupations included craftsmen, who were mainly from Hermoupolis. In this category, of a total of 69 investors, 43 were in the shipbuilding professions, and of these 25 were shipwrights (ναυπηγός), and the rest carpenters, caulkers, sawyers, pulley makers and others.

The administrative profession included state officials, such as the secretary of the Cyclades Prefecture, the Port Authorities, the Transit Stores or the Post Office, but also those of higher rank, such as the Psariot Senator Anagnostis Monarchidis, the harbour master Andreas Koskorozis, and the Hydriot magistrate Petros Petrospetsiotis. The primary sector professions include two farmers from Ikaria and nine landowners from Hermoupolis, Ano Syros, Andros, Mykonos and Santorini. It is very probable that the term landowner indicates property holders engaged in business ventures, rather than individuals whose income depended upon the exploitation of their land. The acquisition of landed property and the transition from the mercantile professions to the category of rentier involved integration into a more prestigious social group, and this became quite obvious among many former merchants and entrepreneurs in the second half of the nineteenth century in Hermoupolis, as well as in other Greek cities and Greek diaspora communities.[85] The service occupations were very varied, such as the Hermoupolis interpreter Efstratios Kantartzoglou from Kydonies/Aivali, who also appears as captain, the Hermoupolis doctor Nikolaos Velissariou (likely from Psara), and the Paros priest Nikolaos Kontaratos. This

85 Yannis Yannitsiotis, *Η κοινωνική ιστορία του Πειραιά. Η συγκρότηση της αστικής τάξης, 1860–1910*, [*Social History of Piraeus. The making of the bourgeois class, 1860–1910*], (Athens: Nefeli, 2006), 55–57; Loukos – Samiou, *Οικονομικές συμπεριφορές*, 19–24; Kardasis, *Έλληνες ομογενείς*, 236.

category also includes the professions of guardian, servant (generally meaning employee), and musician.

Women, although not an occupational category, are classified as a separate social group, who were unemployed and dependent upon their fathers or husbands, as explicitly stated in the documents. Only the women of lower strata, such as factory workers, would later in the nineteenth century have an occupational identity. Thus, women shipowners are referred to as daughters, wives or widows, and in their majority were of maritime families from Psara, accustomed to managing the household and business family affairs during men's absence at sea.

According to Table 5.10, maritime professions amount to three quarters of the total in all three categories: number of investors, tonnage, and values of ships. The remaining occupational categories percentages range from one sixth to one seventh of the total. The secondary sector profession (which, as already mentioned, are dominated by shipyard craftsmen) percentages are double in terms of tonnage and values of ships, as compared to the number of investors. This more qualitative relation is explained by the large shares of some Syros shipbuilders in tonnage and values of ships, as will be examined below. Women, as members of the mercantile-maritime families, also held also an important share after that of the secondary sector professions, whereas the percentages for the remaining categories are negligible.

It is interesting that specific professions or entire occupational groups are largely represented by specific groups of origin. The maritime professions,

TABLE 5.10 *Distribution per occupational category of investors in Syros shipyards, 1828–66.*

Occupational categories	Number of investors	%	Tonnage	%	Values of ships	%
Maritime Professions	1,081	73.94	133,441.61	69.73	20,275,091	69.24
Mercantile Professions	246	16.83	31,098.9	16.25	4,970,698	16.98
Secondary sector professions	69	4.72	18,474.32	9.65	3,029,144	10.35
Women	36	2.46	4,189.35	2.19	449,125	1.53
Administrative Professions	11	0.75	1,635.82	0.85	294,008.3	1.00
Primary sector professions	11	0.75	1,448.17	0.76	218,400	0.75
Services professions	8	0.55	660.78	0.35	25,275	0.09

Source: Processed data from Appendixes 5.5–5.11.

although investors came from many different places, are massively represented by specific groups of origin like Psariots, Andros, Hydra, Spetses, Santorini, Mykonos, Cephalonia, Ithaki and Mitzela (Amaliapolis). Chiots, on the other hand, although to a large degree identified with the wealthy merchant class, generally represent the most diversified range of professions, but in terms of the number of investors most belong to the maritime professions. Mercantile professions are largely identified with Chiots, Smyrna and Hermoupolis, as well as diaspora merchants from Trieste, Constantinople and Southern Russia. In general, the non-maritime professions are represented by Hermoupolis investors, with the exception of the Psariots, who in their overwhelming majority were seafarers.

Most Important Individual Investors: A Socio-Economic Profile

The criteria for membership of this category is to have built ships valuing more than 100,000 drachmas, either as a sole owner or in partnership. Thirty seven such individuals were found in total, and the value of the ships they built reached 7,901,282.28 drachmas, which represented 16.60% of the total value of new ships and 20.04% of the estimated tonnage capacity of these ships. As there is not information available about all built ships, it is possible that there were more investors who passed the 100,000 drachmas limit. This is the case of the Chiot merchant Ioannis D. Rodokanakis and the Andros origin Hermoupolis shipowner Leonardos I. Vatis, whose registered investments amount to 97,000 drachmas, but who also invested in more new ships who values is unknown.

Of the 37 investors, only 5 are not from Hermoupolis; the Andros shipowners Mihail and Nikolaos Empirikos, the Mykonos Antonelos Bonazountas and Peris Markaris, and Georgios Zarifis, a merchant and banker from Constantinople. The latter had only an occasional presence, as he invested in only one ship in 1847, costing 120,000 drachmas. Of those from Hermoupolis, 18 are Psariots, 10 Chiots, 1 was from Smyrna, Panagiotis Geralopoulos, 1 was from Crete, Konstantinos I. Volanakis, 1 was Hydriot, Andreas Kosmas, and the last, Sterios Kontos, was of unknown origin. Of the total Hermoupolis and non Hermoupolis residents, 23 belong to maritime professions, 9 were merchants, 4 were shipbuilders, and 1 was the landowner Andreas Kosmas. Almost every Psariot was a maritime professional, whereas Chiots were merchants, shipbuilders, and 1 was a captain, Tomasos Kokkinos. All the investors from Andros and Mykonos were seafarers.

According to Table 5.11, the three most important investors were Chiot shipbuilders, who controlled a large part of the shipbuilding production and together held 5.53% of the total value in new ships, which corresponds to 2,181,526.28 drs. Thus, they were also very important shipowners, with a fleet

TABLE 5.11 *Most important individual investors in Syros shipyards 1828–66. (Investments over 100,000 drachmas).*

Classification according the values of ships	Origin	Profession	Values of ships (in drs)	Tonnage corre- sponded to the values of ships	Total tonnage	% of Values in the total of ships built
Potous Mikes	Chios (Hermoupolis)	Shipbuilder	790,466.66	3,734.13	4,448.07	2.01
Maskas Pantelis	Chios (Hermoupolis)	Shipbuilder	771,168.32	4,319.37	4,748.81	1.96
Sehas Frangoulis	Chios (Hermoupolis)	Shipbuilder	619,892	2,905.16	3,094.27	1.57
Volanakis I. Konstantinos	Crete (Hermoupolis)	Merchant	307,000	1,541.59	1,541.59	0.78
Kalimeris Dimitrios	Psara (Hermoupolis)	Seafarer	276,000	1,189.65	1,189.65	0.70
Kalimeris G. Ioannis	Psara (Hermoupolis)	Seafarer	272,666.66	1,127	1,127	0.69
Aggelikaras G. Nikolaos	Psara (Hermoupolis)	Seafarer	270,000	939	1,152	0.68
Chilas Georgios	Psara (Hermoupolis)	Seafarer	246,000	1,533.21	1,533.21	0.62
Empirikos Nikolaos	Andros	Seafarer	226,000	1,027.87	1,332.37	0.57
Kefalas Andreas	Psara (Hermoupolis)	Seafarer	216,000	1,070.08	1,070.08	0.55
Empirikos Michail	Andros	Seafarer	210,000	688	688	0.53
Psychas Pantelis	Chios (Hermoupolis)	Merchant	199,500	861.66	1,055.66	0.51
Yannaris N. Georgios	Psara (Hermoupolis)	Navy Office/Seafarer	195,800	675	875.72	0.50
Diakoyannis N. Ioannis	Psara (Hermoupolis)	Seafarer	187,000	521	736	0.47
Koressis Loukas	Chios (Hermoupolis)	Merchant	177,000	683.67	697.17	0.45
Pagidas Nikolaos	Chios (Hermoupolis)	Shipbuilder	165,591.66	1,152.14	1,247.59	0.42
Chilas G. Dimitrios	Psara (Hermoupolis)	Seafarer	160,000	463	463	0.41
Eleftheriou G. Andreas	Psara (Hermoupolis)	Seafarer	156,000	416.33	625.65	0.40
Kosmas Andreas	Hydra (Hermoupolis)	Landowner	150,625	583.75	729.21	0.38
Domestinis G. Alexandros	Psara (Hermoupolis)	Seafarer	150,000	584.79	584.79	0.38
Androulis G. Nikolaos	Psara (Hermoupolis)	Seafarer	150,000	620	620	0.38
Mitaras Georgios	Psara (Hermoupolis)	Seafarer/Third Commander of Greek Navy	149,000	1,072.03	914.24	0.38

Classification according the values of ships	Origin	Profession	Values of ships (in drs)	Tonnage corresponded to the values of ships	Total tonnage	% of Values in the total of ships built
Vafiadakis Dimitrios	Chios (Hermoupolis)	Merchant	146,916.66	697.66	707.66	0.37
Bonazountas Antonelos	Mykonos	Captain	142,663.32	954.42	1,104.42	0.36
Kois A. Ioannis	Psara (Hermoupolis)	Seafarer	142,000	440	440	0.36
Kalaris Dimitrios	Psara (Hermoupolis)	Seafarer	140,600	742.65	1,005.17	0.36
Markaris Peris	Mykonos	Seafarer	138,000	546	546	0.35
Kapparis Stef. Alexandros	Chios (Hermoupolis)	Merchant	127,500	570.33	570.33	0.32
Hadjikiriakos N. Konstantinos	Psara (Hermoupolis)	Seafarer	126,000	769.25	887.25	0.32
Geralopoulos Panagiotis	Smyrna (Hermoupolis)	Merchant	124,100	773.16	1,047.16	0.31
Zarifis Georgios	Constantinople	Merchant	120,000	400	400	0.30
Pappas Dimitrios	Chios (Hermoupolis)	Merchant	111,192	661.6	547.1	0.28
Kotzias Andreas	Psara (Hermoupolis)	Seafarer	110,000	597.58	597.58	0.28
Kontos Sterios	Hermoupolis	Merchant	109,000	540.02	540.02	0.28
Diasakis D. Georgios	Psara (Hermoupolis)	Seafarer	108,000	452	452	0.27
Mikaros Ioannis	Psara (Hermoupolis)	Seafarer	106,475	563.75	901.25	0.27
Kokkinos Tomazos	Chios (Hermoupolis)	Captain	103,125	363.43	363.43	0.26
Total of the 37 Investors			7,946,282.28	37,013.28	40,816.45	20.04
General Total			39,419,319*	194,167.25	275,777.90	100.00

Sources: Processed data from GSA, Syros, Αρχείο Συμβολαιογράφου Μάξιμου Ταλασλή, Συμβ. Σκαρλάτος Μάξιμος, Κατάστιχα 1–6, 1827–1830, Συμβ. Ανδρέας Δαβίδ, Κατάστιχα 7–16, 1830–24/1/1835, Λυτά έγγραφα 1835–1862. Συλλογή Ιστορικού Αρχείου Κυκλάδων, Συμβ. Κων. Αγγελίδης, Ευρετήρια, 1–5, 1854–1863, Συμβ. Αντώνιος Αλμπέρτος, Ευρετήρια 1–2, 1853–1864, Συμβ. Μιχ. Ιωάννόπουλος, Ευρ. 1–2, 1843–1845, Συμβ. Χρ. Ιωάννου Ευρ.1–10, 1846–1860. I/Ναυπηγικά, 1836–1866.

analogous to those of the great Greek shipowners of the time, as we shall see in detail in the following chapter, and as is crosschecked by many notarial documents concerning their ship management.

The next most important investor was the merchant of Cretan origin Konstantinos Iakovos Volanakis, who was unique in having surpassed 300,000 drs in new ship investments. During 1840–54, he invested in 6 brigs and 2 schooners: he was the sole owner of 5, he held three quarters of 2, and one third of 1. His most active period was 1849–54, when he built 7 out of 8 of his ships, whereas in the period 1853–56 he had a strong presence in the second-hand vessels market. Konstantinos Volanakis was among the major shareholders and was a board member of the *Hellenic Steam Navigation Company*. According to the 1860 census, he lived in Agios Nikolaos, the wealthiest district of the town, with his five children Achilleas, Efrosini, Iakinthia, Iakovos and Chrissiida (listed in order of their age) and three servants from Paros, two women and one man. He named his ships after his children, whereas his wife was no longer living. We assume she must have been called Polyxeni, after a ship he named thus in 1849.[86]

Of those in the seafaring professions, the most important investor was the Psariot Dimitrios Kalimeris, with a total of 276,000 drs. In the years 1846–62, he built 3 brigs and 1 barque, of which he shared only the 245-ton brig *Xenophon* with the Psariot captain Andreas Georgios Kotzias. Kalimeris, as stated in his will in 1849, lived in the Psariana neighbourhood with his wife Maria, his sons Georgios and Ioannis, his younger daughter Kalliopi and an adopted daughter; his elder daughter Aghelika was already married. He owned two houses and a store at the junction of today's Stamatios Proios and Kythnos streets, at the limit between the Market and Psariana neighborhoods.[87] We know from his later will in 1870 that the only change in his real property was the addition of 7 consecutive newly built warehouses in Posidonia Avenue, estimated at 86,000 drs. Of the ships, the only one that remained in his property was the barque *Amphitriti*, the last he had built, in 1862. Dimitrios Kalimeris died on 18 March 1873.[88]

86 Kardasis, *Σύρος*, 141–42; Database, Hermoupolis Censuses, 1860, number of family, 2633, Project: The City in Modern Times, ed. Christos Loukos, IMS/FORTH, Rethymnon, Crete, (http://cities.ims.forth.gr/recordview.php?l=1&id=47557&type=census&search_term=).

87 GSA, Syros, notary Andreas David, n. 22361, 12.4.1849; Agriantoni – Fenerli, *Ερμούπολη-Σύρος*, 60.

88 Christos Loukos, *Πεθαίνοντας στη Σύρο τον 19° αιώνα*, [*Dying in Syros in the nineteenth century*], (Iraklion: Crete University Press, 2000), 82; Pepi Gavala – Eleni Garezou, *Τα γλυπτά μνημεία του κοιμητήριου του Αγίου Γεωργίου. Ερμούπολη Σύρου (19ος–20ος αιώνας)*,[*The sculptures of the St George Cemetery. Hermoupolis, Syros. (19th–20th centuries)*], (Athens: Ministry of Aegean, Municipality of Hermoupolis, Gnosis Editions, 1994), 482–83, 528–29.

Of the rest of the Psariot shipowners in this category, Ioannis G. Kalimeris, who follows immediately after Dimitrios Kalimeris, bequeathed to his 2 daughters and 1 son a property worth 80,000 drs and only 750 drs for bequests. In 1860, Georgios N. Yannaris had a property worth 10,000 drs, and in 1874 had a house with a storeroom, three consecutive warehouses, and a plot. In 1871, Ioannis A. Kois in 1871 had an annual income of 20,000 drs and, in 1878, his property was estimated at 35,000 drs.[89] Ioannis Mikaros and his wife Margarona had a son Georgios and a daughter Zoi, married to Ar. Chilas, also from Psara. He died in 1851, aged 60, and today a two-storey building, a house and a warehouse belonging to him survives at the junction between Port Avenue and Sifnos Street.[90]

The Chios merchants group of ship investors is represented by Pantoleon Psychas, Dimitrios Vafiadiakis, Alexandros Stefanos Kapparis and Dimitrios Pappas. All of these were involved in intense and continuous activity in other shipping affairs, as well as the second-hand vessels market. There is not much information available concerning Psychas and Pappas, except that the former was a shareholder to the *Hellenic Steam Navigation Company* in 1857, and that he lived in the Agios Nikolaos district in 1860 and was unmarried.[91] Loukas Koressis (1793–1882) was a descendant of a noble family of Chios, the son of Pantelis and Konstantina Negreponte, and he settled in Hermoupolis in 1824. He was married to Kalliopi I. Sigala from Tinos in 1844 and had three daughters, of whom only the younger two survived, and a son, Ioannis, who married Marietta Ioannis Skaramangas (another old Chios family) from Taganrog in 1866.[92] He built his first ship in 1840, the brig *Polyxeni*, but his activity intensified in the 1850s, in parallel with his involvement in the second-hand vessels market. His last investment was the brig *Pantoleon* in 1863, and he invested in 4 brigs and 1 perama in total, in all as a sole owner except of the brig *Kassandra*, of 211 tons, in which he held 50%. He was also among the major shareholders of the *Hellenic Steam Navigation Company*.[93]

The entrepreneurial spirit of Chiots and Hermoupolitans is concentrated in the person of Dimitrios Vafiadakis. He was the most emblematic figure of the town, the peak of his activity was the mayor's office and his contribution

---

89 Loukos, *Πεθαίνοντας στη Σύρο*, 280, 303–04, 314.

90 Gavala – Garezou, *Τα γλυπτά μνημεία*, 608–09; Agriantoni-Fenerli, *Ερμούπολη-Σύρος*, 44.

91 Kardasis, *Σύρος*, 142; Database, Hermoupolis Censuses, 1860, number of family, 3356.

92 Database, Hermoupolis Municipal Rolls, catalogue number, 1194, Project: The City in Modern Times, ed. Christos Loukos, IMS/FORTH, Rethumnon, Crete, (http://cities.ims.forth.gr/recordview.php?id=11786&type=population&search_term=&l=1); Gavala – Garezou, *Τα γλυπτά μνημεία*, 488.

93 Kardasis, *Σύρος*, 142.

to the building of the impressive town hall, and he was engaged in every type of business transaction in nineteenth century Hermoupolis.[94] In shipbuilding, except two early investments in 1835 and 1843, he invested systematically in the period 1846–49, and for the last time in 1863. His percentage never exceeded 50% in any ship, whereas in 1846 his activity was connected to his friendship with the shipbuilder Pantelis Maskas. He only invested in ships built by and shared with him, and the names of the ships he participated in are indicative of this, such as *Maskas, Neos Maskas*, and perhaps the most representative of this cooperation, the brig *Dyo Filoi* (Two Friends), of 277 tons, built in 1849.[95]

Alexandros Stefanos Kapparis (1814–70) settled at a young age in Hermoupolis (1827). He invested in three brigs, the *Marigitsa* (1847), named after his mother Maria Xanthakis, *Smaragda* (1849) named after his wife Smaragda Pantia Rallis, by whom he had three boys, Stefanos, Alexandros and Amvrosios, and *Stefanos* (1854), named after his elder son. The two younger sons married daughters of important Hermoupolis families, Alexandros to Argyri Ioannis Krinos (a doctor) and Amvrosios to Maria Elpidoforos Ladopoulos (a merchant, banker and industrialist).[96]

Finally, the non-Chiot Hermoupolis investors of this category were represented by Andeas Kosmas and Panagiotis Geralopoulos. The profile of the former, a Hydriot 'landowner', reflects the making of the city by the first generations of Hermoupolis settlers. He fought as a sea captain in the War of Independence and in 1825 was appointed head of security of Hermoupolis. His role was of crucial importance, especially in the first turbulent decade of the city until the coming of King Otho. He was also elected as alderman.[97] Parallel to his involvement in the city's affairs, he also invested very early in real property and ships. Of his real properties, two were on the eastern side of Syros harbor in the old Lazaret Square (today Kanaris Square), one workshop and the other a coffee-house, a popular one, outside of which many ship or cereal cargoes auctions took place.[98] He invested in six brigs in the period 1830–63, while he had a limited presence in the second-hand vessels market. He married

94 Loukos, *Πεθαίνοντας στη Σύρο*, 75–76; Agriantoni – Fenerli, *Ερμούπολη-Σύρος*, 67; Harlaftis, Beneki and Haritatos, *Ploto*, 206–07.

95 GSA, Syros, notary Andreas David, n. 22563, 27.5.1849.

96 Database, Hermoupolis Municipal Rolls, catalogue number, 2476; Gavala-Garezou, *Τα γλυπτά μνημεία*, 686.

97 Drakakis, *History of the settlement*, 186–89; Travlos – Kokkou, *Hermoupolis*, 220; Ambelas, *History of the Island of Syros*, 519–39.

98 GSA, Athens, Αρχείο Σχεδίων Πόλεων, f. 51. n. 212. GSA, Syros, notary Andreas David, n. 28495, 7.7.1855, n. 29246, 4.4.1856.

Komna Tsamadou, from a very important shipowning family of Hydra, and had two sons, Ioannis and Dimitrios. He died aged 77, on 5 November 1863.[99]

Panagiotis Geralopoulos and his brothers Konstantinos and Pantoleon moved to Syros from Smyrna in 1823, where they had previously held a commercial house, through Tinos. They had initially settled there, as many refugees did at the time, but had abandoned it due to the plague that struck the island the same year.[100] Panagiotis Geralopoulos was perhaps the son of Dimitrios and Marigo from Smyrna, and his mother came with him to Hermoupolis, where she died in 1851. Geralopoulos had two sons, Dimitrios, who died in Alexandria in 1850, and Alexandros.[101] In the 1850s or earlier, Konstantinos went to London, where he found another branch of their family firm. Panagiotis was involved in shipping very early, and in maritime loan operations and marine insurance.[102] However, the most tangible evidence of this engagement was his coffee house on the ground floor of the two storey house built in 1843 on the eastern side of Syros harbor, where the Hotel Aktaion (*Ακταίον*) stands today.[103] The coffee house, located in a central position in the port, was perhaps (along with Andreas Kosma's coffee house) a hot spot of business and shipping transactions, and most of the announced ship auctions took place outside it.[104] In the period 1838–52, Geralopoulos built five brigs with different partners, such as the Chiot merchant Ioannis Amvrosios Rallis, the Hydriot captain Ioannis Mavroukos, and the Serres merchant Argyrios Tarpochtsis and his brother Konstantinos. He was the sole owner of the brig *Sokratis*, built in 1844.

Towards a Concentrated Ownership: Specialization and Shipowning

The third aspect to examine is the distribution of ownership per number of investors or, in other words, the rate of concentration of ship ownership. To do this, it is necessary to take into consideration the three previous factors, the number of investors, the tonnage, and the values of the ships.

99 Gavala – Garezou, *Τα γλυπτά μνημεία*, pp. 368–371.

100 Drakakis, *History of the settlement*, p. 26. Database, Hermoupolis Municipal Rolls, catalogue number, 15.

101 Gavala – Garezou, *Τα γλυπτά μνημεία*, 613–14.

102 Kardasis, *Σύρος*, 195–98.

103 Agriantoni – Fenerli, *Ερμούπολη-Σύρος*, 40.

104 Newspaper *Αίολος*, n. 63, 27.10.1845, n. 411, 28.6.1852. GSA, Syros, notary Andreas David, n. 16651, 21.10.1844, n. 24986, 22.7.1851.

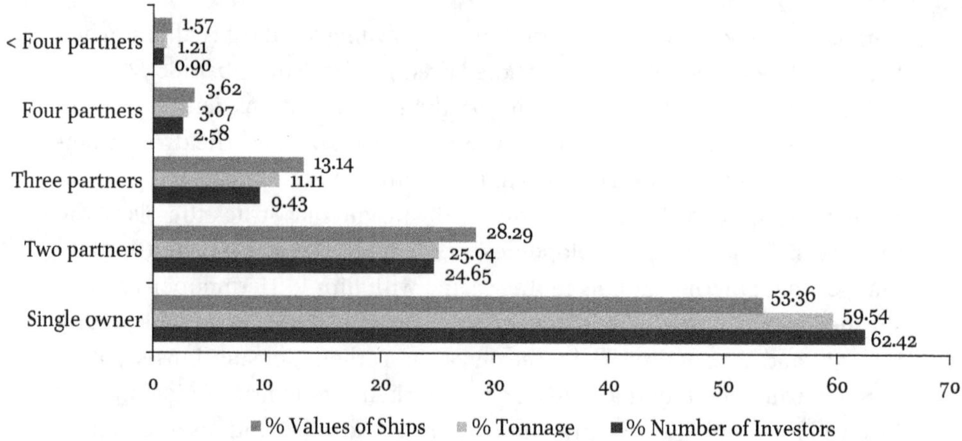

FIGURE 5.3 *Percentage distribution of concentration in ship ownership of new built ships, 1828–66.*
SOURCE: APPENDIX 5.12.

According to Figure 5.3, Syros's newly built ships had a high concentration of ownership in all three categories. Single-owned ships dominated, since they exceeded 62% in terms of the number of investors, whereas in terms of tonnage, single-owned ships stood at almost 60% and more than 50% in terms of value. Percentages tend to decrease considerably and inversely, relative to the increase in the number of partners. It is important to note that in all categories except for single-owned ships, the percentage in the number of investors is lower than the tonnage and the value of ships. In practical terms, this means that the gap between single-owners and the rest, even if large, tends to decrease in the categories of average tonnage and the value of ships, which corresponds to the larger and more expensive ships.

The above analysis of the three aspects, groups of origin, occupation and distribution of ownership, show that the high concentration of ownership was a necessary condition for the distinction between merchant and shipowner and a further specialization in this profession, that created a distinct professional group that earned its living exclusively by providing transport services in shipping and sought high profits through the payment of freight rates.[105] This specialization trend towards exclusive shipowning, expressed in the concentration of ownership, was also helped by the massive presence in Syros

105 Palmer, *Politics, Shipping*, 13–14; Ville, *English Shipowning*, 3.

of a population that depended exclusively upon maritime professions. These occupational categories built the largest and most expensive ships, proving their deeply rooted belief that ship investment was fundamental not only to their business survival and the reproduction of their socio-economic group, but also the only means of increasing shipping productivity and ensuring higher profits.

However, other factors contributed to this evolution as well. In summarizing them, we should mention the reduction of the risks on the seas after the wiping out of corsairs and piracy, and the colonization of the Barbary Regencies in the Mediterranean by the Western Powers and the end of long wars in Mediterranean and Atlantic after 1830. In addition, the development of marine insurance made the practice of shared ownership even less necessary for the purpose of risk reduction.[106] Thus, in contrast with Syros where single ownership dominated, in the pre-War Greek merchant marine, the joint ownership of as many as five to eight partners on average for the building of a ship was customary.[107] Typical entrepreneurial behavior of this kind is that of the Peloponnese merchant Hadjipanayotis Politis, whose percentage in any of the 26 Spetses ships he invested in between 1783–1821 never exceeded 50%.[108]

The high ownership concentration and the further specialization in shipowning can also be identified with certain groups of origin. Psariots were perhaps the most typical example, and it is interesting that they never participated with more than three partners. A small presence in ships shared by more than two partners meant that seafarers from Andros, Hydra, Santorini, Spetses, and especially the Ionians, were fully integrated into the shipping market and depended on the course of freight rates. Exceptions to this scheme were investors from Limni of Euboea, who were mainly seafarers, but, likely due to the lack of capital, participated as many in the building of a ship, continuing their pre-War practices. Finally, the Chiots, representing a broad range of professions, were single-owners as well as engaging in large partnerships, confirming the customary choice of many outside shipping that buying ship shares was a profitable form of investment.[109]

106 Ville, *English Shipowning*, 3.

107 Kremmydas, *Ελληνική Ναυτιλία*, B′, 20.

108 Ibid., *Αρχείο Χατζηπαναγιώτη. Χατζηπαναγιώτης-Πολίτης* (*Hadjipanayotis Archive. Hadjipanayotis-Politis*) (Athens: 1973), 31–32, 67–69.

109 Syngros, *Απομνημονεύματα*, Τόμος A′, 132. Syngros' father was doctor, who held shares in an Andros ship in 1847.

CHAPTER 6

Factors of Production

This chapter will examine the organization, structure and function of supply forces. Firstly, we will analyze the forms of organization of production, along with the level and the characteristics of entrepreneurship. Then, the analysis will continue with an examination of inputs, labour, capital, land, raw materials, and auxiliary activities developed around shipbuilding.

Organization of Production

The Shipbuilding Enterprise

The main institution dealing with the organization and functioning of shipbuilding production is the shipbuilding enterprise, which concentrates and coordinates production factors. During the Age of Sail, a shipbuilding enterprise was usually represented by a master-shipwright, who was not only a specialized artisan but also the holder of the means of production. He was a kind of contractor, who provided a labour force of specialized craftsmen, carpenters, joiners and, in certain cases, included riveters and caulkers. He also owned the fixed capital, the warehouses, the workshops, the tools and the shipyard infrastructures (such as the slip yards) and, of course, the land on which the ships were constructed. He also controlled the working capital for the purchase of timber and other prime materials (which sometimes included nailing and caulking material) as well as the wages of his workers.

However, for a successful shipbuilding enterprise, the above does not suffice. In order to secure the sustainability and profitability of his business, a master shipwright needed more specific skills, of the following two general kinds: (a) skills internal to the business, such as the organization, coordination and successful monitoring of the work process, which as well of specific technical knowledge also required human and material resource management skills; (b) skills directed towards the external environment, which require knowledge of the market, of current prices, and bargaining and decision-making skills, which are especially in a contracting business, such as shipbuilding, which depends on the fluctuation of demand.[1]

1 Geoffrey Jones, *Merchants to Multinationals: British Trading Companies in the Nineteenth and Twentieth Centuries*, (New York: Oxford University Press, 2000), 229–49; Mark Casson et al.

© KONINKLIJKE BRILL NV, LEIDEN, 2016 | DOI 10.1163/9789004306158_008

Structure and Characteristics of the Shipbuilding Enterprise in Syros in the Nineteenth Century

Shipbuilding enterprises in nineteenth century Syros were single or family-owned businesses. This is due to the following two characteristic elements; firstly, many of the shipwrights were sons of shipwrights, who had been trained in the profession through the family business; secondly, there is evidence of a few cases (we suspect there were more but lack the evidence to prove it) of a ship built by two master shipwrights who were either father and son or brothers. It is also reasonable to assume that some male family members, when not master shipwrights, were paid a salary or were remunerated in some other way through building contracts undertaken by another family member. The term 'family' used here does not denote the nuclear family of modern western society, but rather the extended family, which might comprise more than one household.[2] Therefore, single-owned and family business are inter-related and identified through a nexus of informal but substantial relations.

According to the family business theory, Syros shipbuilding enterprises can be classified as belonging to the 'dynastic' type. These firms are characterized by a traditional and conservative management and business strategy, and their sustainability and continuity is identified with the continuity of the family.[3] Therefore, it is a fundamental policy of 'dynastic' family firms to trust family members only, who are provided with an appropriate education and whose succession can be planned. Family firms of this 'dynastic' type are mostly identified with small scale craft and labour-intensive businesses, such as the Syros shipbuilders.[4]

These types of small to medium scale enterprise usually belonged to non-mechanized industry sectors. These did not have a verticalized organizational structure, but were instead structured on the basis of flexibility and cooperation with other enterprises, with each one specializing in a different phase of production. This complementarity was obtained through a network of contacts

---

"Introduction", in *The Oxford Handbook of Entrepreneurship*, ed. Mark Casson et al (New York: Oxford University Press, 2006), 3–4; Mark Casson & Andrew Godley, "Entrepreneurship and historical explanation", in *Entrepreneurship in Theory and History*, ed. Youssef Cassis and Ioanna Pepelasis Minoglou (New York: Palgrave Macmillan, 2005), 28–33; Lewis S. Summers, "The Prediction of Shipyard Costs", *Marine Technology*, 10, n. 1, (January 1973), 8–9.

2 Andea Colli – Mary Rose, "Family Business", in *The Oxford handbook of Business History*, ed. Geoffrey Jones and Jonathan Zeitlin (Oxford-New York: Oxford University Press, 2007), 197.

3 Colli – Rose, "Family Business", 196–197.

4 Mark Casson, "The economics of the family firm", *Scandinavian Economic History Review*, 47, (1999), 11, 20–21; Andrea Colli, *The history of family business, 1850–2000*, (Cambridge: Cambridge University Press, 2003), 75.

and the exchange of ideas and both material and human resources, for which spatial proximity was a basic precondition. Cluster theory, which concerns the concentration of many related enterprises within a specific geographical area, creating industrial districts of a particular kind, seems to fit well with the development of the shipbuilding enterprises in Syros.[5] One characteristic of the flexibility of the enterprises acting in this context (which contributes to a reduction in transaction costs) is the predominantly informal cooperation agreements between them. For example, in nineteenth century Syros, there is no evidence in the notarial records for a single agreement between a master shipwright and a caulker or any other artisan, with the exception of a very small number of agreements between shipwrights and ironsmiths. As it is certain that many artisans were hired or contracted by shipwrights for specific tasks in the ship construction process, the absence of relative documentation indicates the development of a nexus of professional relationships which frequently had social extensions, especially through intermarriages, which integrated the participants into a system of values and a common culture that informally (but essentially) protected from opportunism and made a written agreement of any sort unnecessary.[6]

The small or medium scale individual or family firm that characterizes the Syros shipbuilding industry was also found in other countries, until the second half of the nineteenth century and beyond. In Sunderland, up to approximately 1860, shipbuilding enterprises were of a small scale and many were short-lived: they had no verticalized organization structure, they favoured easy access to low initial capital business activity, and their strategy depended largely upon economic conjuncture.[7] During the same period, on the east coast of the U.S., shipbuilding enterprises were of a similar scale, and the master shipwright (like in Syros) was a central figure who had all the necessary skills as regards both craftsmanship and the marketing strategy of the enterprise.[8] East coast American shipbuilding enterprises were family firms, like those in Syros, and their longevity was based upon training family members within the firm and the transmission of a culture which was embodied in specific values and

5 Colli, *The history of family*, 55–58.

6 Ibid., p. 57, Andea Colli – Mary Rose, "Families and Firms: The Culture and Evolution of Family Firms in Britain and Italy in the Nineteenth and Twentieth Centuries", *Scandinavian Economic History Review*, 47, (1997) 1, 28–29; For intermarriages between family members of shipbuilding and auxiliary industries in Syros see GSA, Syros, notary Andreas David, n. 12887, 3.2.1842, 26296, 23.12.1852 and 31425, 2.12.1860.

7 Ville, "Shipbuilding in the Northeast", 21–25.

8 Hutchins, *The American Maritime*, 103–04, 112.

practices that characterized the shipbuilding community and served to maintain its cohesiveness.[9] Similar examples from Mediterranean shipbuilding enterprises, especially in Italy, conform to the model of small to medium scale enterprises with a flexible infrastructure and training in the art of shipbuilding within the context of family firms.[10] In general, it seems that the nature of the wooden shipbuilding business determined these sharing characteristics across different countries. Entry into the industry demanded a small level of initial capital; the cost of the necessary infrastructure and land was similarly low, and working capital could be supplied on credit from a local network of associates and suppliers. The contractual nature of the activity and the volatility of demand resulted in the exit and re-entry into the market when conjuncture favoured. On the other hand, a shipwright could work as a salaried worker for another shipwright when he was unable to undertake the business himself.[11]

Shipbuilding Enterprises and Shipbuilders in Syros: Origin and Know-how

In the period 1828–66, there were 150 cases of master shipwrights undertaking the construction of at least one vessel. In 94 (63%) of these cases, their origin is known, whereas for the remaining 56 cases (37%) no information about their origin was found (see Table 6.1). In total, 24 areas of origin of Syros shipbuilders are known, among which (with the exception of two which refer to Syros as Ano Syros and Hermoupolis), the rest mainly originate on the Aegean islands, especially from areas that developed shipping as Hydra, Spetses, Mykonos, Santorini, but also Crete, Peloponnese and places in the Eastern Aegean such as Chios, Lesvos and Moschonisia. As shown in Table 6.1, Chiots were the dominant category, numerically represented by 44 individuals (29.33% of the total). Immediately after the Chiots are the Hydriots, with 7 individuals (4.67%). However, this predominance tends towards a monopoly when it comes to tonnage and values of ships, with Chiot shipbuilders building 85.86% of all tonnage and 87.62% of the total value of newly built ships. Hydriots and Lesbians (among whom Nikolaos Solomos is a prominent example) follow, but these groups account for only 4.27% and 2.49% respectively in terms of tonnage, and 4.24% and 2.11% in terms of the value of ships.

9 Thiesen, *Industrializing American Shipbuilding*, 46–49.

10 Massimo Maresca, "Cantieri navali in penisola sorrentina nell' Ottocento. Il costruttore Aniello Castellano", *Estratto da Navis*, 3, (2006), 22–23.

11 Colli – Rose, "Family Business", 196; David S. Landes, "French entrepreneurship and industrial growth in the 19th century", in *Family Business*, ed. Mary Rose (Aldershot: Edward Elgar, 1996), 45–61.

TABLE 6.1 *Distribution per geographic origin of Syros shipbuilders, 1828–1866.*

Origin	Number of shipbuilders	% of the total	Tonnage	% of the total	Values of ships	% of the total
Ano Syros	2	1.33	142.00	0.05	24,372	0.05
Gytheio	1	0.67	17.85	0.01	–	–
Hermoupolis	6	4.00	1,534.63	0.54	282,44871	0.54
Kasos	1	0.67	30.52	0.01	3,000,00	0.01
Cephalonia	1	0.67	715.15	0.25	–	–
Kranidi	1	0.67	188.70	0.07	70,538.19	0.14
Crete	3	2.00	122.14	0.04	15,310.00	0.03
Kythira	1	0.67	200.54	0.07	15,641.19	0.03
Leros	1	0.67	283.00	0.10	–	–
Lesvos	3	2.00	7,058.18	2.49	1,099,944.73	2.11
Malta	1	0.67	91.00	0.03	22,000.00	0.04
Moschonisia	4	2.67	3,493.54	1.23	492,713.73	0.95
Mykonos	2	1.33	138.44	0.05	13,300.00	0.03
Patmos	1	0.67	0.22	0.00	–	–
Rhodes	1	0.67	28.28	0.01	3,000.33	0.01
Santorini	2	1.33	42.01	0.01	1,400.00	0.00
Serifos	1	0.67	21.46	0.01	5,500.00	0.01
Skopelos	4	2.67	1,259.36	0.44	313,396.15	0.60
Spetses	3	2.00	3,535.58	1.25	581,123.64	1.11
Tinos	2	1.33	140.46	0.05	24,360.00	0.05
Cesme	1	0.67	183.74	0.06	19,980.00	0.04
Hydra	7	4.67	12,099.50	4.27	2,210,963.79	4.24
Chios	44	29.33	243,246.35	85.86	45,679,691.86	87.62
Psara	1	0.67	942.07	0.33	121,101.29	0.23
Total of identified origin	**94**	**62.67**	**275,515.72**	**97.25**	**50,999,785.61**	**97.82**
Total of non-identified origin	**56**	**37.33**	**7,793.44**	**2.75**	**1,136,601.08**	**2.18**
General Total	**150**	**100.00**	**283,309.16**	**100.00**	**52,136,386.69**	**100.00**

Source: Appendixes 6.1 & 6.2.

The great predominance of Chiots is not only due to the population factor. Also Psariots, who were also numerous in Hermoupolis, were never engaged seriously to shipbuilding, but were almost exclusively involved in shipping transports. As shown in Chapter 5, during the Genoese period, Chios was a great crossroad of the eastern Mediterranean, and its port became an important maritime centre and a necessary port of call for ships sailing in the Levant. The situation remained unchanged until the second half of the eighteenth century,[12] and there must, therefore, have been an increasing demand for repairs as well as for new ships, and this demand would have justified the existence of an important shipbuilding and ship-repairing unit. Notarial records from Chios mention the names of ten caulkers in the period 1457–74, and eleven shipwrights in the period 1449–67.[13] Shipbuilding, which according to Zolotas had been developed by the Genoese to exploit the island's timber resources, was organized in Chios in the area below town under the castle, in locations which until very recently were called *tarsanas* (shipyards). The shipyard in Langada was sixteen kilometres north of Chios town, and the one in Vrontado six kilometres north of Chios.[14] The excellent reputation of the craftsmen working in the shipyards of Chios is reflected in the continuous requests from the Ottoman authorities for these craftsmen to work in State Ottoman shipyards. These requests began before the Ottoman conquest of the island in 1566. In 1468, the Ottoman authorities asked Maona to send sixty caulkers to the shipyards of Gallipoli. In 1496, Bayezid II asked for twenty carpenters to build large ships (*navas*) in Constantinople, and the following year he demanded that Chiot caulkers be sent in Gallipoli to repair the Ottoman fleet's galleys. A few years later, in 1502, he demanded the dispatch of twenty carpenters and twenty caulkers to Constantinople, and in 1505 the number of craftsmen he demanded had risen to one hundred. Over the course of the fifteenth century, the craftsmen of Chios were called to work in Ottoman State shipyards on many occasions, in Gallipoli, Constantinople, Bodrum and elsewhere. In fact, in 1714, during the reign of Ahmet III, the foreman of the Constantinople *Tersane*, a Chiot named Georgios asked (on behalf of the Sultan) for all the craftsmen in Chios to be dispatched to the imperial shipyard in the capital. This practice continued throughout the age of sail up to the

12 Panzac Daniel, 'L'escale de Chio: un observatoire privilégié de l'activité maritime en mer Egée au XVIIIe siècle.' *Histoire, économie et société*, 4e année, n°4, (1985), 541–61.

13 Argenti, *The occupation*, 646, 648.

14 Zolotas, *Ιστορία της Χίου*, vol. A1, 253–54. Aikaterini Exadaktylou-Bekiaroglou, "Μετακινήσεις τεχνιτών από τη Χίο στο ναυπηγείο της Κωνσταντινούπολης", in *Shipbuilding and ships in the eastern* Mediterranean, op. cit., 40.

nineteenth century; in 1830, Mahmud II asked for craftsmen from Chios to be sent to the shipyards of Bodrum.[15] The dominance of Chiots in the shipyards of Syros has a long history, and is connected to the position of the island in the economic geography of the Genoese and Ottoman period. Although Chios didn't develop a sizable merchant fleet until the mid-nineteenth century, its growth can be attributed to general economic prosperity and the special position of the island in the eastern Mediterranean.[16]

Productivity and Classification of Master Shipwrights and of Shipbuilding Enterprises

Among the 150 master shipwrights, there was a great diversity in performance, based on the number of ships they built, the tonnage and values of these ships, and the duration (continuous or not) of their professional activity. As shown in Table 6.2, 63 out of 150 (42%) built only one ship over the course of their professional lives. 119 shipbuilders (79.33%) built between 1–9 ships, whereas only fourteen shipbuilders built more than 50 vessels (9.33%). The only shipbuilder who built more than 200 ships was Nikolaos Pagidas from Chios. Of those shipbuilders who built over 100 vessels, Pantelis Maskas, Zannis Koufoudakis and Frangoulis Sehas were all Chiots, while Nikolaos Solomos was from Lesvos.

On the basis of these variations in performance, we can distinguish three broad categories of master shipwright. The first are those who had a continuous presence as holders of the means of production and always worked on their own. The second includes those who occasionally, but systematically in certain periods and in relation to the economic situation, undertook the building of several vessels, and who presumably worked as salaried workers when not working alone. The third and largest category consists of those who worked mainly as salaried workers in the shipyards, and only rarely managed to undertake the building of a vessel by their own means. Access to the capital, technical skills, reputation and social networking must have been the distinctive professional and socio-economic features which distinguished the most successful from the rest. This pattern can also be seen elsewhere, such as the U.S. east coast shipbuilding market.[17]

Table 6.3 concerns the 17 most productive master shipwrights and shipbuilding enterprises of Syros in the period 1828–66, based on the criteria that all built ships of more than 500,000 drachmas in value. Of the 17, only three (Emmanouil Frangos, Petros Boumis and Emmanouil Tzitzinias were from

15 Bekiaroglou, "Μετακινήσεις τεχνιτών", 41–44.

16 Vlastos, *Χιακά*, 129.

17 Hutchins, *The American Maritime*, 104.

TABLE 6.2 *Distribution in number of ships per shipwright.*

Number of ships	Master shipwrights
1	63
2	15
3	14
4	9
5	5
6	1
7	4
8	4
9	4
10–49	17
50–99	9
<100	4
<200	1

Source: Appendix 6.1.

Hydra, and Nikolaos Solomos was from Lesvos; the rest were all Chiots. 11 of them, all Chiots, built vessels of more than one million drachmas, thus confirming the domination of the shipbuilding market by the Chiots in Syros.

TABLE 6.3 *The most productive master shipwrights in Syros, 1828–66.*

Shipbuilders	Estimated values of ships	% of the total values	Tonnage	% of the total tonnage	Number of ships	% of the total number of ships	Period of activity
Pagidas Nikolaos	9,934,885.65	19.06	50,770.23	17.92	275	13.22	1828–66
Koufoudakis Zannis	5,585,577.69	10.71	26,368.75	9.31	145	6.97	1842–66
Maskas Pantelis	4,557,976.88	8.74	27,263.40	9.62	152	7.31	1828–62

TABLE 6.3 *The most productive master shipwrights in Syros, 1828–66* (cont.)

Shipbuilders	Estimated values of ships	% of the total values	Tonnage	% of the total tonnage	Number of ships	% of the total number of ships	Period of activity
Sehas Frangoulis	4,054,838.32	7.78	22,507.59	7.94	123	5.91	1829–60
Krystallis Christofis	3,280,722.55	6.29	13,815.02	4.88	66	3.17	1845–66
Koufoudakis Stamatios	2,996,016.39	5.75	12,047.30	4.25	82	3.94	1835–66
Koufoudakis Ioannis	2,459,280.85	4.72	13,271.26	4.68	81	3.89	1831–48
Potous Mikes	2,183,108.56	4.19	13,258.95	4.68	82	3.94	1829–63
Maskas Stamatios	1,985,918.75	3.81	10,497.54	3.71	58	2.79	1833–66
Levadaros Andreas	1,441,379.22	2.76	7,141.64	2.52	51	2.45	1859–66
Pagidas Ioannis	1,337,859.29	2.57	11,387.38	4.02	55	2.64	1828–47
Solomos Nikolaos	972,301.72	1.86	6,037.17	2.13	113	5.43	1833–66
Kokkinakis Charalambos	828,281.84	1.59	4,075.15	1.44	45	2.16	1850–66
Frangos Emmanouil	760,088.92	1.46	3,798.75	1.34	18	0.87	1853–61
Boumis Petros	640,000.00	1.23	1,910.91	0.67	8	0.38	1866
Magos Hadjidimitrios	592,892.70	1.14	3,129.80	1.10	20	0.96	1850–66
Tzitzinias Emmanouil	552,569.96	1.06	3,172.13	1.12	18	0.87	1847–63
GENERAL TOTAL	52,136,387	–	283,309.16	–	2,080	–	–

Source: Appendixes 6.1 & 6.2.

Nikolaos Pagidas was the most productive shipbuilder in Syros at every level. In 38 years of continuous activity (our data ends in 1866, so it is possible that he continued to work until his death in 1871) he built 275 vessels, which makes an average of 7.23 ships per year, a performance that no-one else has ever come close to matching; Pantelis Maskas worked for 34 years and built 152 vessels (4.47 vessels per year, on average); Zannis Koufoudakis worked for 24 years and built 145 vessels (5.17 vessels per year, on average); Frangoulis Sehas worked for 31 years and built 123 vessels (3.96 vessels per year, on average). The total tonnage of vessels built by Nikolaos Pagidas is estimated at slightly more than 50,000 tons, whereas the estimated value of ships he built approaches ten million drachmas, which corresponds to one fifth of the entire value of ships built in Syros. Pantelis Maskas and Zannis Koufoudakis built approximately half of tonnage of Nikolaos Pagidas, whereas Zannis Koufoudakis built ships that correspond to one tenth of the total value and Pantelis Maskas to 8.74% of the total. The performance of all these shipbuilders is extremely positive in in relation to other international examples. For example, in the period 1848–80, Aniello Castellano (the most important shipbuilder in the Sorrento Peninsula and the Gulf of Naples, who worked in location of Cassano) built sixty ships, most of them barques, with a total capacity of 24,370 tons, and an average tonnage of 434.61 tons.[18]

In the period 1833–76, "George Greenman & Company", a Mystic River firm in Connecticut, built sixty-six sailing ships with a capacity of 28,312 tons, and an average tonnage of 429 tons.[19] The three most important shipbuilders in East Boston in the period 1835–58, Donald McKay (who along with Isaac and William W. Webb was one of the most famous American shipbuilders in the age of sail) Samuel Hall and Paul Curtis had built 49, 53 and 22 ships respectively, with a total tonnage of 68,978, 30,186 and 26,954 tons, and an average tonnage 1,407, 570 and 1,225 tons.[20]

Among the most long lasting Syros shipbuilding enterprises were those of Nikolaos Pagidas, Pantelis Maskas, Mikes Potous, Frangoulis Sehas, Nikolaos Solomos, Stamatios Koufoudakis and Stamatios Maskas, who each lasted longer than a single generation (for thirty or forty years). All the above mentioned master shipwrights, along with Zannis Koufoudakis, Ioannis Pagidas and Ioannis Koufoudakis, were always the holders of the means of production and never hired as employees.

---

18 Processed data from Maresca, "Cantieri navali", 29.

19 Fairburn, *Merchant Sail*, vol. VII, 2853.

20 Ibid., 2910.

TABLE 6.4 *Indices of performance of Syros master shipwrights, 1828–1866.*

Value/Tonnage (average price per ton)		Tonnage/Number of ships (average tonnage)	
Boumis Petros	334.92	Boumis Petros	238.86
Koufoudakis Stamatios	248.69	Frangos Emmanouil	211.04
Krystallis Christofis	237.48	Krystallis Christofis	209.32
Koufoudakis Zannis	211.83	Pagidas Ioannis	207.04
Kokkinakis Charalambos	203.25	Pagidas Nikolaos	184.62
Levadaros Andreas	201.83	Sehas Frangoulis	182.99
Frangos Emmanouil	200.09	Koufoudakis Zannis	181.85
Pagidas Nikolaos	195.68	Maskas Stamatios	180.99
Magos Hadjidimitrios	189.43	Maskas Pantelis	179.36
Maskas Stamatios	189.18	Tzitzinias Emmanouil	176.23
Koufoudakis Ioannis	185.31	Koufoudakis Ioannis	163.84
Sehas Frangoulis	180.15	Potous Mikes	161.69
Tzitzinias Emmanouil	174.20	Magos Hadjidimitrios	156.49
Maskas Pantelis	167.18	Koufoudakis Stamatios	146.92
Potous Mikes	164.65	Levadaros Andreas	140.03
Solomos Nikolaos	161.05	Kokkinakis Charalambos	90.56
Pagidas Ioannis	117.49	Solomos Nikolaos	53.43

Source: Processed data from Appendix 6.2.

To supplement the previous data on number, tonnage and values of ships in estimating productivity, in Table 6.4 we employ two more indices which help to assess the qualitative aspects of shipbuilders' performance; the first concerns the relation between values/tonnage (the average price), which reflects the cost level of the ships built per master shipwright; the second indicates the average tonnage and, indirectly, the typology of vessels in which each shipwright specialized. For example, Charalambos Kokkinakis rates highly in terms average price (203.25), which means that for the volume of production, the ships he built were expensive. On the other hand, in terms of the average tonnage of vessels built, he ranks among the lowest (90.56 tons).

Petros Boumis, who ranks first according to both indices, is a special case who built eight sailing ships in only one year (1866); the capacity was 1,910.91 tons, with an average capacity of 238.86 tons and cost of 640,000 drachmas.

Stamatios Koufoudakis, although low in the average tonnage index (146.92), built ships at a high cost (248.69). It seems that over 21 years, Christofis Krystallis performed better than the much longer engaged (34 years) Mikes Potous, as he built 13,815 tons compared to Potous' 13,258 tons, and his ships were worth 1,100,000 drachmas more than the latter. As regards Nikolaos Solomos, he is ranked fifth with 113 ships built, although many of these vessels were coasters, which explains why both the average capacity (53.43 tons) and the index of the value of ships are low (161.05).

Shipbuilding Enterprises and Entrepreneurship—the Making of a Shipbuilding Elite

Although a large number of individuals were involved as master shipwrights, the core of the shipbuilding enterprises, which controlled the largest share of production, was formed in the period 1828–66. This core can be identified with specific families whose members, as previously mentioned, maintain a closer cooperation and mutual support between themselves which allows us to define them as family business, even if they sometimes acted as autonomous entrepreneurs and to a certain extent followed different strategies in shaping their social profiles. For example, Stamatios Maskas built sixteen ships for his brother Pantelis; Ioannis Koufoudakis was co-owner of two ships built by his son Stamatios, while Frangoulis Sehas owned five ships built by his relatives Ioannis Sehas, Dimitrios Ioannis Sehas and Dimitrios Frangoulis Sehas. Furthermore, the brothers Zannis and Stamatios Koufoudakis built the 304 ton brig *Aggeliki*, which belonged to Ioannis G. Kalimeris; Ioannis Koufoudakis built the 165 ton brig *Sokratis* (which belonged to Ioannis and Nikolaos Goulandris from Andros) with his son Zannis, and with his other son Stamatios he built the 229 ton brig *Afriki* 229, which belonged to the shipowners Yannoulis, Nikolaos and Dimitrios Piagos, who were also from Andros.[21] However, on some occasions, there was also a practice of joint construction by shipbuilders who had no family ties, for instance Nikolaos Solomos and Hadjioannis Zafiris, who built three ships together in the period 1833–34. From the evidence presented above, we can conclude that the role of the family in the shipbuilding enterprises of Syros was crucial as a resource for human capital, skills development and training and labour force, and was embedded within the values of trust, devotion and cooperation as well as mutual support

21 GSA, Syros, notary Andreas David, n. 29266, 12.4.1856, ibid., notary Mihail Ioannopoulos, inventory, n. 172. 26.7.1845, n. 479, 22.10.1845.

TABLE 6.5 *Classification of the core of the most important shipbuilding family enterprises of Syros, 1828–66.*

Families	Ship values	% of the total	Tonnage	% of the total	Number of ships	% of the total
Koufoudakis	11,316,230.62	21.71	53,340.75	18.83	316	15.19
Pagidas	11,272,744.93	21.62	62,157.61	21.94	330	15.87
Maskas	6,543,895.63	12.55	37,760.94	13.33	210	10.10
Sehas	5,206,579.75	9.99	28,038.06	9.90	148	7.12
Krystallis	3,280,722.55	6.29	13,815.02	488	66	3.17
Potous	2,606,331.56	5.00	15,041.66	5.31	97	4.66
General Total	52,136,387	77.16	283,309.16	74.18	2,080	56.11

Source: Appendix 6.2.

in the face of an external environment characterised by uncertainty and strong competition.[22]

The core of the elite family businesses that shared the largest part of shipbuilding production includes the families of Pagidas, Maskas, Koufoudakis, Sehas, Potous and Krystallis, who were all of Chiot origin. In Table 6.5, the eleven master shipwrights who built ships valued over one million drachmas all belong to the above families, with the exception of Andreas Levadaros.

According to Table 6.5, these families were responsible for 77.16% of the total production in terms of ship values, 74.18% in terms of tonnage, and 56.11% in terms of the of vessels, which gives a perfect illustration of their control of the shipbuilding market in Syros. Furthermore, the fact that the percentage of number of ships they built is 20% lower than in the other two categories shows that these families built the largest and the most expensive ships. The Koufoudakis and Pagidas families (with only a slight difference between them) managed to surpass the ten million drachmas limit in the category of ship values. However, the fact that the Pagidas family built 10,000 tons more indicates that Koufoudakis built more expensive ships. The same applies to Christofis Krystallis who, in comparison with the Potous family, built 1,200 tons less, although Krystallis' ships cost 800,000 drachmas more in total.

22 Colli – Rose, "Family Business", 207; Carole Howorth, Mary Rose & Eleanor Hamilton, "Definitions, diversity and development: key debates in family business research", in *The Oxford Handbook of Entrepreneurship*, op. cit., 230.

Koufoudakis Family

This was perhaps the family that bears the most celebrated name in the Syros shipbuilding market. The father of Ioannis and the grandfather of Stamatios Koufoudakis (also named Stamatios), was the shipbuilder who, according to Konstantinos Nikodimos, diffused the shipbuilding plan (sala, σάλα) in the Aegean at the end of the eighteenth century, after having worked in the Ottoman Imperial shipyards of Constantinople. He arrived and settled at Syros a year after the destruction of Psara (1824) with his son Ioannis, but it is not known how long he lived, and there is evidence that he worked in the shipyards of Syros.[23] The members of the family involved in shipbuilding were Ioannis and his three sons Stamatis, Zannis and Dimitrios. Of the sons, the most productive was Zannis, even though he became master shipwright in 1842, seven years later than his elder brother Stamatios. It is probable that in the 1830s he was building ships in Kherson in the Black Sea, as a person named Ioannis Koufoudakis is mentioned as having worked there; the person mentioned could not be his father, who worked continuously in Syros from 1831, but was probably Zannis (a nickname of Ioannis) himself.[24]

Over 24 years of activity, Zannis built 145 vessels totalling over 26,000 tons, and over 31 years, Stamatios built 81 vessels totalling approximately 12,000 tons. He also worked in Andros for a few years, building mostly coasters. Dimitrios, who appeared only in the favourable conjuncture of 1847–48, built eight ships of 1,653.44 tons. Generally, the Koufoudakis' entrepreneurial strategy was more orientated towards a scale development, with little diversification into other sectors, such as trade and shipping. Zannis was the sole owner of the brig *Kalliopi*, and he had a share in the goleta *Katigo* and the brigs *Marigo* and *Ioannis*.[25] His father Ioannis was the sole owner of brig *Nea Tychi*, and he had shares in the perama *Epaminondas* and the bombarda *Ekaterini*.[26] His brother Stamatios (together with the Andros captain Petros Tsamis) had a share in the 280 ton brig *Mihail*.[27]

The Koufoudakis enterprise enjoyed great popularity in local society according to the newspaper *Enosis*, which included Stamatios and Zannis among

---

23 Nikodimos, *Υπόμνημα*, 157–58; Fenerli, "Les premiers constructeurs", 26.

24 Kardasis, *Έλληνες ομογενείς*, 295.

25 GSA, Syros, notary Andreas David, n. 30592, 8.8.1858, n. 304747, 13.5.1858, ibid., notary Christodoulos Ioannou, Inventory 4, n. 4692, 6.11.1848, ibid., I/Ναυπηγικά n. 2592, 18.9.1861.

26 Ibid., notary Andreas David, n. 19215, 23.2.1847, n. 14311, 26.11.1842, notary Mihail Ioannopoulos, inventory, n. 540, 8.11.1845.

27 Ibid., notary Christodoulos Ioannou, Inventory 4, n. 4331, 24.8.1848.

the most important Syros shipbuilders in 1855.[28] Zannis, the most productive of the family, also enjoyed a high reputation according a list of jurors in 1852 and in that same year he actively participated in local politics.[29] In 1860, he lived in Metamorphosis, a middle class district in the town, with his wife Sevasti and his four daughters (all of whom were minors) Ekaterini, Filia, Kalliopi and Maria, his 19-year old son Ioannis (who probably worked in the shipyards) and Konstantinos (a minor), and his mother in law.[30] On the other hand, Stamatios lived in the more folk district of Psariana, where many seamen and shipbuilding craftsmen lived, with his wife Viola, his three sons Ioannis, Dimosthenis and Mihail and his daughters Anezia and Ekaterini, all of whom were minors.[31]

In 1842, the third brother Dimitrios was declared to be a seaman in the civil register of the city. However, in 1845 in a dowry agreement for his imminent wedding with the sister of tanner Ioannis Marinakis, Argiro, declared himself to be a carpenter.[32] Five years later he agreed, under the supervision of his father Ioannis, to build a ship (as shipbuilder and carpenter) in Tulcea of Danube. The ship was owned by the Cephalonian merchant Dionysios Kountouris, who had settled in Constantinople.[33] Finally, in 1836 their father Ioannis lived near the shipbuilding zone and in 1841, as a dowry, he gave a single-storey house worth 50 Spanish dollars and 300 dollars in cash to his son-in-law Pantelis K. Magos, a seafarer. To his other daughter Triantafyllia, who married the Peloponnese tavern-owner Georgios Frangopoulos in 1848, he gave a dowry of 7,900 drachmas.[34]

Pagidas Family

Only two members of the family were involved in shipbuilding, Ioannis and his son Nikolaos. During the Greek War of Independence, Ioannis Pagidas was at

28 Newspaper *Ένωσις* [*Enosis*], n. 176, 30.9.1855.

29 Φ.Ε.Κ. [Hellenic Government Gazette], n. 64, 18 December 1852; Newspaper *Ένωσις*, n. 270, 16.10.1852.

30 Database, Hermoupolis Censuses, 1860, number of family, 1951, Project: The City in Modern Times, ed. Christos Loukos IMS/FORTH, Rethymnon, Crete, (http://cities.ims.forth.gr/recordview.php?l=1&id=45004&type=census&search_term=).

31 Ibid., number of family, 4215.

32 Database, Hermoupolis Municipal Rolls, catalogue number, 4388, Project: The City in Modern Times, ed. Christos Loukos (IMS/FORTH, Rethymnon, Crete, (http://cities.ims.forth.gr/recordview.php?id=14981&type=population&search_term=&l=1); GSA, Syros, notary Andreas David, n. 17683, 27.10.1845.

33 GSA, Syros, notary Andreas David, n. 23595, 3.4.1850, n. 23592, 3.4.1850.

34 Ibid., n. 4751, 10.11.1836, n. 12058, 6.6.1841, n. 21792, 15.11.1848.

Psara (Chios was destroyed in 1822), where, according his headstone, '*he built many fast ships and he provoked terror in the fleets of Turks*', which implies that he is likely to have built fire ships, a very widespread method of offensive warfare among the Greeks during the war.[35] In 1825, he was in Tinos, where there were many war refugees, where he built different ships up to 1828, when he eventually settled in Syros.[36] His son Nikolaos had settled in Syros before his father, and he had been building ships at least since 1828. The business orientation of the Pagidas family was towards scale development, similar to the Koufoudakis family. However, Nikolaos Pagidas expanded into shipowning, as well as investing in several ships of 1,225 tons and an estimated value of 165,000 drachmas, the majority of which he built by himself. However, Pagidas intention, in contrast with other shipbuilders (we shall see below), was not to become a shipowner; rather, he took shares in the ships which he had built as a method of payment, and he would later sell these when the opportunity arose.

During the difficult conjuncture for Greek-owned shipping in 1851 he encountered serious financial difficulties, and he borrowed the sum of 71,600 drachmas, with monthly 1% interest, from the Chiot merchant Nikolaos Z. Vlastos. To secure the loan, he had to mortgage all his real property, land and buildings in the shipbuilding area, after obtaining the consent of his three sisters (who did not, however, lose their equal inheritance rights insofar as this land was paternal inheritance).[37] To repay the loan, Pagidas sold all the shares he owned to eleven ships, eight brigs, two schooners and one bombarda, to a total value of 37,100 drachmas. Four years later, he took out another loan, from the Psariot shipowner Dimitrios Kalimeris, again by mortgaging his paternal inherited properties in the shipbuilding zone with the consent of his sisters, which he paid back in full.[38]

Nikolaos Pagidas was the most popular shipbuilder from Hermoupolis, and his fame was a decisive factor in his cooperation with the *Hellenic Steam*

35 Gavala – Garezou, *Τα γλυπτά μνημεία*, 202–03.

36 To terminus ante quem for his settlement in Tinos is a document of ownership of goleta *Panaya tis Idras*, 30 tons belonged to Lambros Dimas and built between 16.8 and 28.10.1825, GSA, Syros, notary Skarlatos Maximos, *Πωλητήρια καραβίων καὶ ἄλλων πλοίων καὶ ναυλοσυμφωνητικὰ καὶ ἄλλα θαλασσινὰ τοῦ Δημοσίου Ὑπογραφέως τῆς νήσου Σύρας βιβλίον 1827, Τόμος α. Ὁ δημόσιος ὑπογραφεὺς τῆς νήσου Σύρας Σκαρλάτος Μάξιμος. Ἀρ.1.*, n. 1962, 22.8.1828. The first ship he built in Syros was *Bella Katerina*, 304 tons of Cephalonian Gregorios Fokas, ibid., n. 1714, 9.7.1828.

37 GSA, Syros, notary Andreas David, n. 25323, 11.12.1851, n. 25339, 17.12.1851.

38 Ibid., n. 25342, 17.12.1851, n. 28261, 25.4.1855, n. 28266, 27.4.1855, Newpaper *Αίολος* [*Eolos*] n. 483, 17.12.1853.

Navigation Company on the construction of the first wooden dock for the repair of steamships in 1857. Local newspapers remarked upon his skills, the fine quality of his ships, and his innovative technical spirit, as was displayed in his construction of the first and only steamship launched in Syros shipyards, *Aspis*, which belonged to a French engineer living in Smyrna named Eugene Amat.[39] However, despite the size of his business and his reputation, Pagidas never managed to raise his social status to become a member of the local elite, as had other shipbuilders from Hermoupolis or abroad.[40] According to the 1860 census (held at a time when he was the most acclaimed shipbuilder in the port), he lived in the district of Agios Georgios, near the municipal cemetery and the shipbuilding zone, an area inhabited mainly by craftsmen and members of the most popular classes.[41] He lived with his wife Eleni and his minor sons Ioannis and Georgios, his minor daughter Domna and his mother Maria, a widow (as his father Ioannis had died in 1849).[42] However, in 1852 his elder daughter Marigo married a very wealthy timber merchant, the Chiot Mihail Pissias, and received a dowry of 6,000 drachmas.[43] In 1870, Pissias lived in Vaporia, the Agios Nikolaos district and the richest neighbourhood, with his family and two female servants from Naxos.[44] His younger daughter Domna married the painting colour maker Georgios Valmas in 1864, and received a dowry in objects and cash of 14,600 drachmas. Furthermore, Pagidas allowed the couple to stay in his house in the shipbuilding zone for two years without demanding any rent.[45]

Maskas Family

If Nikolaos Pagidas was the most acclaimed shipbuilder of his age from a technical and a productive point of view, Pantelis Maskas was certainly the most

39 Newpaper *Αίολος* n. 452, 22.4.1853, n. 499, 8.4.1854; GSA, Syros, notary Andreas David, n. 26413, 6.3.1853, n. 26804, 4.9.1853, n. 27386, 29.3.1854; Aggeliki Fenerli, "Η υποδοχή του ατμού στην Ερμούπολη από τους παραδοσιακούς ναυπηγούς τον ΙΘ' αιώνα" [The reception of steam by the traditional shipbuilders in Hermoupolis in the nineteenth century], in *Shipbuilding and ships in the eastern Mediterranean*, op. cit., 121–27; Kardasis, *Σύρος*, 187.

40 Richard F. Welch, *An Island's Trade. Nineteenth century shipbuilding on Long Island*, (Mystic, Connecticut: Mystic Seaport Museum, 1993), 71–79.

41 Agriantoni – Fenerli, *Hermoupolis-Syros*, 150.

42 Database, Ermoupolis Censuses, 1860, number of family, 3905, Project: The City in Modern Times, ed. Christos Loukos IMS/FORTH, Rethymnon, Crete, (http://cities.ims.forth.gr/recordview.php?l=1&id=52132&type=census&search_term=).

43 GSA, Syros, notary Andreas David, n. 26296, 23.12.1852.

44 Database, Ermoupolis Censuses, 1870, number of family, 277.

45 GSA, Syros, notary Andreas David, n. 32480, 16.10.1864.

socially successful, and he enjoyed a higher social status, almost equal to that of the members of the local elite. After the massacre of Chios, he escaped to Psara, and with other Chiot craftsmen such as Ioannis Pagidas, he built several fire ships. Among these were those used by Konstantinos Kanaris to burn down Kapudan's Pasha flagship in June 1822, and a two-decked Ottoman warship which saw service in the battle of Tenedos in the same year.[46] He eventually settled in Syros after the destruction of Psara (1824), although the Hermoupolis Municipal Rolls mentions that he settled there in 1825. His activity starts in 1828 at the earliest, although by 1827 he already owned a cutter.[47] His brother Stamatios, who settled at the same time as him in Syros, does not appear as master shipwright until 1833.[48]

Pantelis Maskas is the embodiment of all the characteristics of a portfolio entrepreneur, according to modern theories of entrepreneurship, a businessman who simultaneously invests and manages diverse economic ventures and who has a major talent for foreseeing and exploiting business opportunities.[49] He expanded his business into different fields, but mainly in shipbuilding and shipowning. As is stated on his headstone: '*Master shipwright, he built hundreds of many ships. He was also a shipowner of tens of merchantmen and of a fleet, all made of sailing ships*'.[50] He was among the most important investors in new built ships in the Syros shipyards, and in the period 1828–66 he invested the sum of 770,000 drachmas (see Table 5.11). His shipowning activity in the same period can be compared only to very big names in Greek-owned shipping, like Empiricos, Goulandris, Vaglianos and Lykiardopoulos which continue to the present day.

According to Table 6.6, Pantelis Maskas managed a fleet larger than those managed by the Lykiardopoulos and Goulandris families, and which was not much smaller than those of shipowning 'tycoons' such as Vaglianos from Cephalonia or Empiricos, perhaps the greatest family in Greek-owned shipping, in diachronic terms.[51] He also diversified into other fields of shipping, such as financing (through maritime loan transactions) people such as Ioannis

46 Drakakis, *History of the settlement, 1826–1827*, vol. B', 195.

47 Database, Ermoupolis Municipal Rolls, catalogue number 1947; Drakakis, *History of the settlement, 1826–1827*, vol. B', 151.

48 Database, Ermoupolis Municipal Rolls, catalogue number 3163 and Appendix 6.1.

49 Deniz Ucbasaran, Paul Westhead and Mike Wright, "Habitual Entrepreneurs", in *The Oxford Handbook of Entrepreneurship*, op. cit., 463–67.

50 Gavala-Garezou, *Τα γλυπτά μνημεία*, 270.

51 Harlaftis, "From Diaspora Traders" 237–68; Theotokas and Harlaftis, *Leadership in World Shipping*, 33–34, 79–80, 147–49.

TABLE 6.6 *Comparison of Pantelis Maskas sailing fleet in tonnage 1828–66.*

Maskas Family	Empiricos Family	Vaglianos Family	Goulandris Family	Lykiardopoulos Family
4,748.81	6,701.00	5,492.00	4,018.69	1,816.00

Source: Table 5.11 and processed data from Harlaftis – Vlassopoulos, *Historical Register 'Pontoporeia'.*

Alexandrou, the captain of the bombarda *Evagelistria*, owned by the Chiot Efstratios G. Galatis resided in Odessa.[52] He was also a shareholder in the Syros insurance companies *Enossis, Ellas* and *Karteria*.[53] In January 1850, when Syros, along with Piraeus, were blockaded by the British fleet under Vice Admiral Parker, Maskas sold 480 tons of coal to Pio Terenzio, an agent of the Austrian Steam Navigation Company *Lloyd* and the Russian subject Hermoupolis and the resident merchant Sterios Kontos.[54] However, Pantelis Maska's greatest success was in the exploitation of social capital.[55] He maintained a constant network of access and contacts with the local elite, and his best friend and associate was Dimitrios Vafiadakis, a Chiot merchant and Mayor of Hermoupolis (1870–87, 1895–98), with whom he built and owned several ships. However, a basic strategy of social networking, and an epitome of his recognition by the local upper class, was his engagement in politics. In the period 1853–62, he was elected to the municipal council under Mayor Amvrosios Damalas, a Chiot merchant. This period is associated with the construction of many of the most important of the city's infrastructures. In his first election in 1852 he received 506 votes and was classified 15th among the elected chancellors, who belonged to the socio-economic elite and included lawyers, merchants, bankers and shipowners.[56] His involvement in politics was continued by his son Alexandros, a

52 GSA, Syros, notary Andreas David, n. 20313, 29.11.1847.

53 Ibid., n. 18990, 22.11.1846, n. 30729, 31.1.1859, n. 31747, 26.11.1861.

54 Ibid., n. 23390, 18.1.1850, n. 23422, 27.1.1850; Thomas Gallant, *Modern Greece*, (New York: Bloomsbury USA, 2001), 42–3.

55 Pierre Bourdieu, "The forms of Capital", in *The sociology of economic life*, op. cit., 97–98, 102–05; Alejandro Portes and Julia Sensenbrenner, "Embeddedness and Immigration: Notes on the Social Determinants of Economic Action", in *The sociology of economic life*, op. cit., 114–17; Amir N. Licht – Jordan Siegel, "The social dimension of entrepreneurship", 524–30.

56 Ambelas, *Ιστορία της νήσου Σύρου*, 673–87; Newspaper *Ένωσις*, n. 289–72, 29.10.1852.

lawyer, who became Mayor of Hermoupolis (1899–1903) and who also enjoyed great popularity.[57] Pantelis Maskas was perhaps the only shipbuilder who resided in the Agios Nikolaos district. He lived there with his wife Maria, his minor daughters Chrysanthi, Eleni and Kalliopi, his son Alexandros and two female servants.[58] In contrast (although he expanded his business in terms of scale) his brother Stamatios did not follow these diversification strategies or use aspects of social capital. In 1860, he lived in the Psariana neighbourhood with his wife Anitsa, his son Alexandros, a seafarer, and a servant, and in 1853 his daughter Marigo married the Psariot shipowner and captain Andreas A. Babalos.[59]

Sehas Family

The brothers Frangoulis and Dimitrios Sehas, sons of Ioannis, settled in Hermoupolis in 1823 and 1824 respectively.[60] Frangoulis distinguished himself as a dominant figure in the family, and he built the overwhelming majority of ships of the family enterprise. His brother, a captain according the municipality rolls, built only nine vessels of 1,778.51 tons, valued at 293,000 drachmas, between 1833–54. During the golden period of Syros shipbuilding industry, (1845–52), the son of Dimitrios, Ioannis, built eleven ships of 2,437 tons valued at approximately 450,000 drachmas. Dimitrios, the son of Frangoulis, seems to have worked under his father's orders most of the time, and it was only in the period 1855–59 that he built five vessels, of 1,305 tons and valued at 277,000 drachmas.[61]

Frangoulis Seha's enterprise followed a strategy of growth in scale as well as in scope. He was the third most important investor in new ships in the period 1828–66, valued at 620,000 drachmas.[62] He also managed a fleet of 3,100 tons, although in the period 1852–53 he sold many of his shares or entirely owned ships. From the social point of view, like most of the craftsmen of his age, Frangoulis Sehas remained outside the upper class of Hermoupolis, and a decisive factor in this exclusion was his illiteracy. In 1860, widowed, he lived in the Agios Georgios district, next to the municipal cemetery, with his sons

57 K. Gerasimidis – E. Monoyios, *Το Πανόραμα της Σύρου*, (Syros: 1933); Newspaper *Ήλιος* [*Ilios*], n. 880, 20.8.1903 n. 882, 16.9.1903, newspaper, *Θάρρος* [*Tharos*], n. 74, 6.5.1925, n. 75, 9.5.1925.

58 Database, Ermoupolis Censuses, 1860, number of family 4087.

59 Ibid., 4250. GSA, Syros, notary Andreas David, n. 26621, 12.6.1853.

60 Database, Ermoupolis Municipal Rolls, catalogue number 628 and 1834.

61 See Appendix 8.2.

62 See Table 7.11.

Dimitrios, who worked in the shipyard, and Ioannis and Georgios, both seamen, Nikolaos, a schoolboy (although he was 19 years old) and his daughter Kokkona, who was fifteen years old.[63] His elder daughter Smaragda was married to the Chiot captain Zorzis Antonios Orietas, and received a dowry of 15,100 drachmas. He allowed the couple to live on the upper floor of his house rent-free for two years. He owned a house located in Psariana, which had been the home of Frangoulis and his wife Marigo since 1841, and he eventually sold this to his daughter Smaragda two months after the dowry contract, on the two conditions: firstly, the difference between the dowry and the value of the house, which amounted to 10,900 drachmas, had to be paid to the minor Kokkona; secondly, he reserved the right to live on the ground floor.[64]

Krystallis Family

This is a case of a rapidly developed enterprise, in terms of scale. In 1840, Christofis Krystallis was a joiner, according the Municipality rolls.[65] Five years later, he started as a master shipwright and between then and 1866, he became one of the fifth busiest shipbuilding enterprises, alongside established names like Koufoudakis, Pagidas, Maskas and Sehas. In a newspaper publication of 1855 he was mentioned as being among the most important shipbuilders of Hermoupolis.[66] Krystalli's enterprise was not expanded to other sectors, and his descendants followed the profession of shipbuilder and seaman. Alexandros became a seaman, Emmanouil became a carpenter, and Sokratis became a shipbuilder.[67] In 1924, the textile factory of Krystallis-Tsagarakis was founded by Georgios Tsagarakis, Spyridon Krystallis and his son Christofis, who was an engineer.[68] Very little is known about the social life of Christofis Krystallis; he made a marriage contract in 1842 with the chain maker Georgios Mavroudoglou who committed himself to marrying Krystalli's daughter Irini the following year.[69] In 1860, he lived in the Agios Georgios district with his minor daughters, Franga, Patra, Angelika and the four-year-old Spyridon, who would later co-found the Krystallis-Tsagarakis textile factory.[70]

---

63 Database, Ermoupolis Censuses, 1860, number of family, 16508.

64 GSA, Syros, notary Andreas David, n. 30792, 16.3.1859, 30856, 5.5.1859.

65 Database, Ermoupolis Municipal Rolls, catalogue number, 3290.

66 Newspaper *Ἕνωσις*, n. 176, 30.9.1855.

67 Database, Ermoupolis Municipal Rolls, catalogue number, 16847, 17096; Sokratis died in 1887 age 42 according to Gavala – Garezou, *Τα γλυπτά μνημεία*, 96–97.

68 Agriantoni – Fenerli, *Hermoupolis-Syros*, 131; Database, Ermoupolis Municipal Rolls, catalogue number, 32945.

69 GSA, Syros, notary Andreas David, n. 12887, 3.2.1842.

70 Database, Ermoupolis Censuses, 1860, number of family, 16994.

TABLE 6.7 *Comparison of Mikes Potous sailing fleet in tons, 1828–66.*

Potous Family	Empiricos Family	Vaglianos Family	Goulandris Family	Lykiardopoulos Family
4.448,07	6.701,00	5.492,00	4.018,69	1.816,00

Source: Table 5.11 and processed data from Harlaftis – Vlassopoulos, *Historical Register 'Pontoporeia'*.

Potous Family

Mikes Potous, from Kardamyla of Chios, can be characterized an exemplary case of a portfolio entrepreneur, to an even greater extent than Pantelis Maskas. From the first years in which he settled in Hermoupolis, in parallel to shipbuilding he was involved in all sectors of shipping industry. He was the most important investor in new ships in all of Syros, in terms of values (790,000 drs).[71] His fleet was by 300 tons less than that of Pantelis Maskas and comparable to the greatest shipowning families of his time.

Mikes Potous had largely participated in the second hand vessels market, in maritime loan operations as a lender, in marine insurance, and also the shipbuilding timber trade. He often appeared in different transactions, as a guarantor for loans and as a procurator for debt settlements between third parties. In the period 1833–59 he was involved in more than thirty cases of sales and purchases of sailing ships and he was a shareholder in the insurance companies "Filemporiki" («Φιλεμπορική»), "Enossis" («Ένωσις») and "Karteria" («Καρτερία»).[72] He also owned also a large amount of property and land, such as two warehouses which he rented to the baker Ioannis Leonis, or land in the shipbuilding zone which he sold in 1859 to another shipbuilder Andeas Levadaros, and where the latter built his house.[73]

Like Pantelis Maskas, he was also involved in politics as a councilman, from 1852 up to the end of his life. According to his headstone he had three sons and three daughters.[74] His eldest daughter married Ioannis P. Rapitis, a Chiot captain and shipowner, and son of the shipbuilder Petros Rapitis. His second daughter Athina divorced in 1856 and four years later married the ironsmith

71 See Table 5.11.

72 GSA, Syros, notary Andreas David, n. 24711, 12.4.1851, n. 18990, 22.11.1846, n. 31747, 26.11.1861.

73 Ibid., n. 24922, 23.6.1851, n. 31025, 13.10.1859.

74 Gavala-Garezou, *Τα γλυπτά μνημεία*, 647–48.

Dionysios Giatras, who took a dowry of 16,500 drs and a two storey house.[75] His youngest daughter Vrissiida married Ioannis Kosmas, son of Andreas, one of the most eminent figures in Hermoupolis, who took a dowry of 23,150 drs and a single storey house with land in the Psariana district.[76] In 1860, Mikes Potous lived in Psariana with his wife Despinou, his son Ioannis, who was 25 years old and a seaman, and Dimitrios, who was ten years old. He had two more elder sons, Andreas and Alkiviadis, the first a known shipbuilder, but both are referred to as seamen.[77] This data is not confirmed by his headstone, where it is mentioned that he had three sons and not four. This is because Despinou was not the mother of the three daughters and three adult sons mentioned, but probably only of the young Dimitrios. In fact, in his 1850 will, his wife is named as Marigo, which is also confirmed by his headstone; but, in 1858, Mikes named a brig of 168 tons after his new wife, Despinou.[78] Newspapers report that he expelled his second wife (Despinou?) for a young servant of the family. This decision caused serious problems between him and his sons; in fact, he was murdered by his sons on the morning of July 25th 1867 on his ship, as reported in his death certificate, although according to newspaper reports the ship belonged to his sons, and Mikes went on the ship, where his sons were, to punish them for their reactions of the previous day to the servant issue.[79] It is also noteworthy that in his headstone, made by the heirs of Andreas Potous, Mikes' son, it is simply stated that he died on July 24th 1867 prematurely in his 66th year, and there is not a single mention to Despinou.

His son Andreas, as previously mentioned, became a shipbuilder and in the period 1856–59 built fifteen ships of 1,782.71 tons, and an estimated value 423,223 drs. However, what makes the case of the Potous enterprise more interesting is its longevity, up to the present day. Panagiotis M. Potous (1893–1951), the fourth generation of the family and probably the son of Mikes Potous and the grandson of Andreas, was the owner of the steamships *Michalis Potous, Aris* and *Kiriaki*, the latter two being sunk in 1939 and 1941 by torpedos and

75 GSA, Syros, notary Andreas David, n. 29666, 17.9.1856, n. 31425, 2.12.1860.

76 Ibid., n. 29533, 21.7.1856.

77 Database, Ermoupolis Censuses, 1860, number of family, 11140; Database, Ermoupolis Municipal Rolls, catalogue number,7478 and 10452.

78 GSA, Syros, notary Andreas David, n. 30479, 14.5.1858.

79 GSA, Syros, ΙΑΔΕ, Δ/Ληξιαρχείο (Ε), Θάνατοι, Ληξιαρχικά βιβλία αποβιώσεων, [Registry office, deaths, registry books of deaths], n. 368. Newspaper *Ερμούπολις* [*Hermoupolis*], n. 149, 27.7.1867, *Εθνικόν Μέλλον* [*Ethnikon Mellon*], n. 9, 29.7.1867, n. 10, 5.8.1867, *Πατρίς* [*Patris*] n. 76, 29.7.1867, n. 78, 12.8.1867.

air bombings respectively.[80] Panagiotis M. Potous was related by family ties with Michail M. Xylas in 1931, also from Kardamyla of Chios, and they became associates; thus, the two families joined and continued their shipping activities successfully into the 20th century, and are today represented by *Pyrsos Managing Company*, part of *Pyrsos Shipping Company Ltd.*[81]

Cooperative Forms of Production—Partnerships of Shipbuilding Craftsmen

The shipbuilding enterprises discussed above have not included any cooperative forms, except in those cases of informal cooperation between members of the same family. However, cases of partnerships such were found in other specializations of shipbuilding craftsmen, such as caulkers and pulley makers. Between 1828 and 1831, there were at least three such companionships of caulkers; the first was formed by two Psariot caulkers who had a shop (which probably also served for storage) composed of three punts (floating rafts used as working platforms) and four cauldrons for boiling the basic substances, tar, resin and tallow. One of the partners sold his share for 1,350 gurus in 1832, after he bought a share in another partnership with two more partners at slightly less than 50% of its initial value. The initial capital required to enter this partnership was 15,000 gurus, and comprised a shop, a capstan, five punts, seven hooks, and other equipment. In June 1832, a third partnership was formed by seven men of which six were capital providers and one who assumed book keeping duties (and was perhaps not a caulker). The partnership was formed for one year, its initial capital was 3,000 gurus, and the partners rented two buildings belonging to one of them for eighty gurus per month. A basic term of the partnership was that any price agreed between a customer and a partner had to be respected by the other partners, and there should be no competition between them. Furthermore, all profits and damages had to be shared equally, and if anyone wished to withdraw from the partnership, it would suffice to sell his share to someone else, with priority given to existing partners. Similar terms are found in the agreement for the formation of a partnership between pulley makers in 1841. In both the case of caulkers and the case of the pulley makers, the clause for not respecting the terms of agreement was a fine,

80 Private Collection of Documents of Mikes Potous Family. I would like to express my sincere thanks to Eleanna Vlachou for her valuable help to the access to this material.

81 Ibid.; Theotokas and Harlaftis, *Leadership in World Shipping*, 316–18.

payable to the town's hospital, an extraordinary case of social solidarity by members of working class and the petit bourgeoisie.[82]

Labour

Specialization, Division of Labour and Hierarchy

The nature of shipbuilding activity led from the outset to a specialization of work and a division of labour, which inevitably created a hierarchy between the master shipwright (as the holder of the means of production with responsibility for the design and completion of the ship) and the rest of the craftsmen. Especially in large shipyards, whether state owned or private, specialization and division of labour were greater, and thus the hierarchy was more clearly defined. The master shipwright was at the top of this hierarchy, as the craftsman with the greatest level of knowledge in ship construction, able to design the ship, supervise the works and with responsibility for safe launching. According to sources, the specializations that compose a master shipwright's working group are carpenters and joiners, with the two terms sometimes indicating the same tasks. The carpenters and joiners had to assemble the hull, and smooth and finish the timbers. A carpenter or joiner is a potential shipwright and an experienced craftsman, who needs knowledge of ship design and the way of controlling the means of production in order to become a shipwright. Sawyers another specialized group midway between craftsman and unskilled worker. Sawyers had to cut the logs of timber for joiners and carpenters with an appropriate cutting tool called a *piski* (πισκί), and for that reason they were also known as *pisketzides* (πισκετζήδες). Logs had to be cut properly, in a way that would ease the application of planks for joiners and carpenters, and for this it was necessary to have sound knowledge of shipbuilding timbers and a good technique in cutting, in order to reduce wastage.[83] Augerers, called *bourgoutzides* (μπουργουντζήδες), were craftsmen who specialized in drilling the holes through which clench nails and treenails were driven by using hand drills. Caulkers, along with sawyers, were considered the most independent categories of craftsmen in the shipyard workforce.[84] As an art, caulking is separated from the rest of shipbuilding, and is a very specific,

82 GSA, Syros, notary Andreas David, *Βιβλίον Εἰσερχομένων*, n. 414, 14.8.1831, *Βιβλίον μνημονικῶν πράξεων ὑπό στοιχείον Γ'*, n. 1018, 4.2.1832, n. 1048, 25.2.1832, n. 1623, 21.7.1832, n. 11622, 12.3.1841.

83 Damianidis, *Ελληνική Παραδοσιακή*, 132–33.

84 Ibid., 132.

as well as sensitive, phase of construction; its inherent features made caulkers a wholly diversified and independent professional category at a technical, economic and hierarchic level. This is why (as we have seen in Chapter Four) caulking was often not included in the shipbuilding agreement, and caulkers collaborated with shipwrights but were not subordinates. Some of them were, like shipwrights, holders of the means of production who directed their own businesses.

Workforce Capacity and Wages

The estimation of the shipyards workforce is not an easy task, as our main sources mention only the names of master shipwrights. Municipality Rolls are an alternative source which must be used with caution, as some shipyard workers were not registered, and for some of the professions declared in that register, such as carpenters, is not always easy to distinguish if they worked in ship construction or in other fields of carpentry, such as house building. From the 150 master shipwrights encountered in our sources in the period 1828–66 (see Table 6.1), only 57 are cross-referenced in Municipality Rolls. Of these, sixteen were declared as profession shipbuilders, twenty one as carpenters, four as joiners, one as a sawyer, one as a marine carpenter, one as a hewer, seven as seamen (among them Zannis Koufoudakis, Stamatios Maskas and Andreas Potous), one as a captain, one as a fisherman, one as caulker and one as an architect (Mikes Potous).

The total of 711 workers in shipbuilding professions comprises a long time span of almost fifty years and thus cannot offer a precise picture of workforce capacity in specific years. Also some of the denominations of professions might indicate the same specialization, like that of the sawyer. Also some itinerary journeymen or temporary settled in Syros escape of this attempt to capture the size of workforce in a determined period. Similar problems face also the effort to find data about the wages, which are very few and scattered. From Table 6.9 it is clear that wages fluctuate according periods of increase of production and vice versa. Also some remuneration concern works to be carried out outside Hermoupolis, as the sawyers that agreed to work in Skopelos shipyards in 1827 and the caulkers that had worked at Chios in 1847.[85]

In addition to remuneration through daily wages, there were cases of remuneration by monthly salary as well. In 1850, the master shipwright Ioannis

85 GSA, Syros, notary Maximos Talaslis, *Πωλητήρια καραβίων καὶ ἄλλων πλοίων καὶ ναυλοσυμφωνητικὰ καὶ ἄλλα θαλασσινὰ τοῦ Δημοσίου Ὑπογραφέως τῆς νήσου Σύρας βιβλίον 1827, Τόμος α. Ὁ δημόσιος ὑπογραφεὺς τῆς νήσου Σύρας Σκαρλάτος Μάξιμος. Ἀρ.1.*, n. 69, 4.2.1827; ibid., notary Andreas David, n. 19266, 8.3.1847.

TABLE 6.8 *Categories of shipbuilding professions according Municipality Rolls of Hermoupolis, 1822–70.*

Categories of shipbuilding professions	Number
Shipbuilder (*Ναυπηγός*)	32
Shipbuilding carpenter (*Ναυπηγομαραγκός*)	1
Sawyer (*Ξυλοκόπος*)	2
Sawyer (*Ξυλοσχίστης*)	1
Joiner (*Λεπτουργός*)	49
Carpenter (*Ξυλουργός*)	63
Carpenter (Μαραγκός)	381
Sawyer (*Πριονιστής*)	107
Hewer (*Πελεκάνος*)	13
Augerer (*Πουργουτζής, Μπουργουτζής, Τρυπανιστής*)	8
Caulker (*Καλαφάτης*)	54
Total	711

Source: processed data from Database, Hermoupolis Municipal Rolls, ibid. and Katerina Anagnostaki "Creation, growth and decline of Hermoupolis through the professions registered in Municipality Rolls", MA essay, University of Crete, 2007.

TABLE 6.9 *Wages of specialized professions in Syros shipyards in 19th century (in drs).*

Specialization	1827	1831	1834	1839	1846	1847	1851	1852	1853	1874
Journeyman					3.35–9.2	4.8–10.6		4	5	9
Caulker						3–9.52	3.6–4.95			
Augerer						4.79	2.97–3.46			
Carpenter			5.5				1.48–3.96			
Shipbuilder			7							
Sawyer	3.6	3.2	5			10.6	2.97–3.96			
Hewer						6.85				
Carpenter							1.35–3.6			

Source: GSA, Syros, notary Maximos Talaslis and Andreas David; AMAE, CCC, Syra, vol. 3, 20.4.1849; Βασίλης Kardasis, *Σύρος*, 177, 342; Agriantoni, *Οι Απαρχές*, 90, 93.

Koufoudakis agreed to being paid 50 golden pieces of twenty of Constantinople (corresponding to 384 drs per month) to supervise the construction of a brig in Tulcea of Danube; his son Dimitrios agreed to work as a shipbuilder and carpenter for 35 gold pieces or 268.80 drs per month. In 1847, carpenters and joiners from Spetses received 20 to 30 golden pieces for the same work in Dulcea.[86]

Capital

In the shipbuilding enterprises of Syros, we can distinguish two kinds of capital: fixed capital and working capital. Fixed capital in the wooden shipbuilding consisted of low-cost pre-industrial technology and included land, barracks (which also functioned as warehouses for tools and material) and the infrastructure for the launching of vessels. Working capital was to a large degree provided by the consignors who ordered the construction of the ship. However, in a few cases, shipbuilders built ships on the basis of speculation and then needed to find financial sources. In November 1846, Nikolaos Sviros started building a brig 24.67 meters long and needed to borrow 6,000 drs from the Police Officer Konstantinos Petsalis, for the purchase of timber and the wages of journeymen. The loan was interest-free for the first five months, but after that period incurred interest of 1% per month. The shipbuilder mortgaged the shipbuilding timber, and if the shipbuilder had not repaid the lender when the vessel was completed, the latter had the right to put the ship in auction. Ultimately, Sviros repaid the loan, as in April 1847 he sold the brig *Agios Efstathios* to Nikolaos M. Paschalis from Andros for 65,000 drs.[87]

On the other hand, Dimitrios Leriotis did not often succeed in repaying his debts. Three days after Sviros had done so, and under the same terms, he also borrowed 4,300 drs from Petsalis for the purchase of the timber for a brig measuring 23.76 metres in length. Ultimately, the construction of this brig was completed by another shipbuilder, Emmanouil I. Tzitzinias, in June 1847, after having purchased her semi-finished by the merchants Sterios Kontos and Nikolaos Savvas and named *Agios Georgios*. Four years later, Leriotis borrowed 12,200 drs from Kontos, for the construction of a brig 21.94 metres in length,

86 Ibid., notary Andreas David, n. 23592, 3.4.1850, n. 23595, 3.4.1850; Archive of Spetses, notary of Spetses, n. 46 and 146 (the material from Spetses was provided to me by Dr. Alexandra Papadopoulos, to whom I express my gratitude).

87 GSA, Syros, notary Andreas David, n. 18971, 15/11/1846; ibid., notary Christodoulos Ioannou, Ευρετήριο 2, n. 2298, 9.4.1847.

and the loan matured on July 3rd 1853. The vessel was sold at auction on August 30, 1853, bought by the lender himself and completed by Nikolaos Betsanis on November 19 1853. The next day, Kontos sold 50% of the 190 ton brig named *Efrosyni*.[88]

Land

The Old Shipbuilding Area

The western coast of Syros harbour was the shipbuilding zone of the port from the mid-1820s until to the end of 1860s. This strip of sand beach, which extended from where it stands today, from the Southern Aegean Region building down to Neorion, the modern shipyards which up to 1840 stood the quarantine, was the exact area occupied by shipbuilders.[89] From the 1871 plan, we can learn of the exact position of three eminent shipbuilding enterprises one next to the other (Pagidas, Sehas and Potous), together comprising a front 107 meters long, coincident with Papagou Square in front of the modern ferry boats quay.[90] In general, the cost of land in Hermoupolis was not high and did not affect the fixed costs of shipbuilding enterprises. The arrival of a vast number of refugees after 1822 who settled on the land created a special status quo in terms of real estate, according to which someone could build on someone else's land by paying rent without needing to purchase the land. In fact, many houses, stores and warehouses were built under this system: for example, in 1840 Ioannis Koufoudakis paid 1,95 drs per month, payable every three months to the local Antonios Salachas, for the land which he used for the purpose of shipbuilding.[91] Another source reports that an owner/investor paid rent of 15 to 20 drs, as long as he occupied a piece of land on which built his ship, which also depended upon the extent of the land surface he occupied.[92] Gradually, as we have seen in the case of Pagidas, Sechas and Potous, the most important shipbuilders managed to purchase the land they used, and to build barracks and warehouses which they also rented to other professionals.

---

88 GSA, Syros, notary Andreas David, n. 18955, 12.11.1846, n. 19575, 5.6.1847, I/Ναυπηγικά, n. 877, 7.6.1847; Ibid., notary Andreas David, n. 23815, 10.6.1850, n. 26992, 19.11.1853, n. 26993, 20.11.1853.

89 Agriantoni – Fenerli, *Hermoupolis – Syros*, 40, 45, 114; Travlos-Kokkou, *Ερμούπολη*, 110, 112, Table 6 and 7β.

90 Agriantoni – Fenerli, *Hermoupolis – Syros*, 45.

91 GSA, Syros, notary Andreas David, n. 11315, 9.12.1840.

92 Kardasis, *Σύρος*, 170.

The New Shipbuilding Area

The need to transfer the shipbuilding zone to its present location was being discussed as early as 1861. The main reasons were that the entire existing shipbuilding area consisted of private properties, and that the town was extending further towards the southwest. Thus, a committee composed of shipbuilders, shipowners and merchants began to search for an appropriate new site for the shipyards.[93] The area chosen was the coastal area south of the old quarantine, where Neorion stands today, which was conceded by the State to the Municipality of Hermoupolis with the law ΣΣΤ′ of 9 April 1867.[94] On 30 September 1866, a Royal Decree approved the foundation of a joint stock company named «*Έταιρία τοῦ Ναυπηγείου Ἑρμουπόλεως*» [Company of Hermoupolis Shipyards], which inaugurated its activity on 23 July 1866, after a public invitation from Mayor of Hermoupolis to future shareholders.[95] The creation of joint stock companies for the funding of construction and management of municipal projects was a long established practice in Hermoupolis. The Fish and Meat market, the Grocery market, the Municipal coffee-house, the "*Apollo*" Theatre and the Gentlemen's Club "*Hellas*" were all built following this practice. Shareholders received all the revenues of these municipal enterprises until the funds they had invested were repaid with additional interest; thereafter, their shares were transferred to the Municipality, which gradually assumed total ownership of its enterprises.[96] The earliest known list of shareholders of the company for the new shipyards, which dates from 1870, comprised 23 individuals. Of these, the major shareholder was the Chiot merchant Stamatios K. Proios, who held 99 out of 350 shares, followed by Stylianos Kasimatis (23 shares), the Chiot merchant Zorzis Negrepontes (22 shares), the doctor Achilleas Katakouzinos (20 shares) and the Chiot merchants Stamatios I. Proios, Dimitrios Lestos and Zannis Vouros, who each held 18 shares.[97]

However, transferring from the old to the new site presented several problems. In 1863, the ten metre strip of coast facing the old shipbuilding area, which belonged to the State, was divided into four plots which were put to auction. This decision caused several problems for the shipbuilding industry, as the sale of this land from the State to privates, in order to develop the buildings

---

93 GSA, Syros, I/Ναυπηγικά, 6, 1861, αρ. πρωτ. 1752.

94 Ibid., Υπουργείο Οικονομικών προς Νομάρχη Κυκλαδων και Οικ. Έφορο Σύρου, n. 47631, 30.9.1866.

95 Ibid., Β.Δ., συνημμένο σε έγγραφο του Υπουργείου Εσωτερικών προς Νομαρχία Κυκλάδων, n. 27585, 4.10.1866. Έντυπη ανακοίνωση του Δημάρχου Ερμουπόλεως, n. 2432, 23.7.1866.

96 Fenerli, "Ο καλλωπισμός της πόλης", 177–82.

97 Ibid., ΙΑΔΕ, I/Ναυπηγικά, f. 6.

before the transfer to the new site could be finalised, would suspend or prevent any shipbuilding work. In an address to the Prefecture of Cyclades in 1866, the Mayor of Hermoupolis warned that shipbuilding was the major industry, and that any obstacle to this activity was a serious threat to the economic life of the city. He tried to suspend the proposed liquidation of the land until the new site was ready. The only effective solution proved to be the purchase of the land by the Municipality itself; after 1871 until the end of the 1880s, the exploitation of this land became a major concern, and the objective was the construction of warehouses.[98]

A second major issue was raised by the dispute between the Company of New Shipyards and tanners and other manufacturers situated nearby. In 1867, the committee of representatives of the company complained (unsuccessfully) about the impurities of the tanneries in the shipyard area, which obstructed work, damaged materials, and demanded the construction of dikes to stop the flow of sewage.[99] On the other hand, tanners and other manufacturers also complained about the construction of a wall that impeded the natural flow of water wastage into the sea, created stagnant water and infective foci, and demanded the modification with fenders and the opening of waterways through the shipbuilding area. In 1870, their committee obtained a Royal Decree to open two waterways in the shipyards, which provoked a strong reaction from the entire shipbuilding sector, timber merchants and similar professions, who all complained to the Mayor as well as to the Prefecture, on the grounds that this decision raised costs and disrupted the working unity of the area. It is not known whether this decision was eventually agreed upon and implemented.[100]

A third issue was related to the practice of depositing shipbuilding timber outside the limits of the shipbuilding zone, which provoked complaints from the Director of the spinnery "*Omonoia*" in 1870. Despite the prohibitions of the police, in place since April 1868, this phenomenon continued until at least 1874, while timber merchants also complained about the scarcity of timber storage space in the predefined areas in the new shipyards, and the erroneous policy of renting the space to certain individuals who would sublet it afterwards for profit. On 10 May 1867, within the space of fifteen days, the Mayor of Hermoupolis invited the owners of shipbuilding timber to declare that the sites were occupied or soon to be, in order to collect the rent. This inaugurated the practice of allocating a predefined space for the storage of shipbuilding

98 Ibid., Τ/Δημοτικά Έργα/77, Τ/Δημοτικά Έργα, 230, Ι/Ναυπηγικά/6.

99 Ibid., Ι/Ναυπηγικά/6.

100 Ibid.

timber within the boundaries of the new shipyards. Almost simultaneously, from the beginning of July 1867, the construction of new ships in the new shipbuilding area had begun. The transfer to a new space had a dramatic impact upon management practices, as well as on the procedures involved in shipbuilding. Investors intending to build a ship had to submit an application to the committee of the new shipyards company, in order to obtain permission. Similar processes also had to be followed by those who intended to rent space for the storage of their shipbuilding timber, though in such a case, the shipyards committee had to obtain further approval from the Prefecture in order to issue the permission.[101]

Shipbuilding was no longer the city's only industry. It had to compete with other manufacturers and factories which, in the 1860s and 1870s, were spreading in areas which were already very space-restricted, and there was an urban expansion in the only geographically possible direction, namely west-southwestwards. The city was changing slowly but irreversibly in terms of its role, needs and priorities. The management of the shipyards by a joint stock company in a narrowly delimited space, and under specific procedures, brought structural changes to the shipbuilding industry as well as to the more 'fluid' use and exploitation of space which had been a characteristic of the industry in previous years.

The Ship Repairing Zone

The ship repairing area was initially on the north side of the western coast, between the buildings of the Southern Aegean Region and the former warehouses of the *Hellenic Steamship Navigation Company* (which is today a fast food restaurant).[102] This location soon became problematic, due to the urban zone expansion and the dangers of the exposed inflammable caulking materials. A fire occurred on 7 August 1839 without serious consequences, thanks to the prompt intervention of firemen.[103] Since 1848, the reports of the Police and the Prefecture had been demanding a move to a new repairing zone, as the area occupied was not only exposed to the dangers of fire, but also obstructed the circulation of people and the commercial activities of shops and warehouses. Seven years later, in its correspondence to the Prefecture of Cyclades, the Chamber of Commerce raised the problem of congestion of the loaded ships at anchor next to those under repair, and the danger of fire spreading to

---

101 Ibid., I/Ναυπηγικά/6, 7.

102 Travlos-Kokkou, *Ερμούπολη*, Table 6. Agriantoni-Fenerli, *Hermoupolis-Syros*, 39.

103 Newspaper *Έλλάς*, n. 18, 11.8.1839.

the entire harbour.[104] In 1852, a commission (made up of the Mayor Amvrosios Damalas, the harbour master Andreas Koskorozis, the merchant and shipowner Stefanos Kapparis and the engineer G. Metaxas) had chosen the southern bay of the promontory of the old quarantine (where Neorion stands today). In its report, the commission recommended the construction of a stone mole with a capacity of four medium size ships eighty meters long and five meters wide, and a budget of 57,672.67 drs. Finally a Royal Decree of 9 June 1856 approved the construction of a ship repairing zone in the old quarantine bay at a cost of 46,909 drs, and the transfer took place towards the end of 1857.[105]

Although the new ship repairing site solved the problem of fire risk, on the other hand was not adequate to cover ship repairing needs. In 1868, a commission of 70 shipowners, captains and those of similar professions complained to the Mayor about it and the hazardous winds blowing in that anchorage, along with the problems caused by the proximity of the *Hellenic Steam Navigation Company*, which did not allow the anchorage of sailing ships within its own area. They complained that this situation led to the loss of earnings in the ship repairing business, as many captains were forced to address themselves elsewhere in order to repair their ships. They demanded an extension to the existing mole, and the abolition of the jurisdiction of the *Hellenic Steam Navigation Company* in the ship repairing zone. Similar complaints followed in 1875, but this time the representatives who signed this petition to the Mayor comprised 552 professionals from the shipping and shipbuilding sector.[106]

Auxiliary Trades-Raw Materials

Organization of Timber Trade

Timber was the most basic raw material and had the most important cost and quality factor in sailing ship construction. However, Syros was a small and arid island without any timber resources. Therefore, all the necessary timber had to be imported, and the trading and transport of timber to Syros created very significant linkages in local and regional economy, as well as mobilizing a lot of human resources, tradesmen, workers and sea transporters from Syros and from both coasts of the Aegean and its islands. The existing sources for the

104 GSA, Syros, Τ/Δημοτικά Έργα/6.

105 Ibid., and Τ/Δημοτικά Έργα/80.

106 Ibid.

organization of timber trade are of two kinds; firstly, the agreements for the transport of timber to Syros through charter parties; secondly, the bills of sale of shipbuilding timber. Both of these types of documentation belong to the category of notarial acts.

Charters Transportation

Charterers were usually timber merchants, but they could be shipbuilders or captains who bypassed Syros timber merchants and transported the necessary timber for the construction of their ships themselves. Shipbuilders and captains tried in this way to reduce costs. There were also cases of joint ventures for the transport of timber cargoes, such as between Ioannis Katolios and Michail Mantras in 1839, for the transport of 30 logs and 400 frames from the Gulf of Xiros in eastern Thrace, or between Ioannis K. Stylianou and Nikolaos Baoulos in 1844, again from the Gulf of Xiros.[107] However, in most cases these were family businesses. When they freighted a ship for the transport of timber, one member of the enterprise was sent in advance, as a correspondent in the place where the timber was to be collected; the correspondent had to ensure that the cargo was ready to load by the time the ship arrived. He could be a family member, such as Ioannis and Konstantinos Pissias, who were sent to Cyzicus in the Sea of Marmara on behalf of their relatives Michail and Nikolaos, or a trusted partner such as Georgios Sideris, who was sent on behalf of Georgios Pissas to the Gulf of Xiros in 1839, and to the Gulf of Simi in 1847.[108]

Captains chartered their ships for the transport of timber by receiving a lump sum or by fixing a price per piece of log or frame. The choice of paying a lump sum was, in most cases, the option chosen when the exact quantity of timber was not fixed in advance, and the ship had to be loaded to its maximum capacity; the sum thus depended upon the size of the ship as well as on the quantity of cargo. For schooners from 45 to 85 tons in the period 1838–47, the lump sum for freight was between 500 and 950 drs, whereas in ships between 100–200 tons in the period 1840–53, the amount ranged between 960 and 6,000 drs. In the agreements for a determined quantity of timber, the prices per piece offer a more detailed picture of freight rates. However, from what is known about the freight rates for logs in the years 1838–43, it is not clear precisely which factors affected them. For example, in 1839, in nine cases of charters examined, the price of logs fluctuated between 7 and 14.25 drs. The only factor that certainly seems to have affected the price of logs was when

107 GSA, Syros, notary Andreas David, n. 9815, 22.12.1839, n. 16082, 4.3.1844.

108 Ibid., n. 26865, 26.9.1853, n. 9693, 17.11.1839, n. 9820, 28.12.1839, n. 19641, 20.6.1847.

the cargo frames were also included. In such cases, prices ranged between 5.5 and 7.75 drs per log. In cases when the cargo consisted only of logs, prices rose to between 8.25 to 16.5 drs. On the other hand, the freight rates for frames was fairly stable in the period 1838–43, ranging between 50 to 80 lepta of drs per piece (100 lepta = 1 drs). The captain also had to pay an amount to the charterer before his departure; this was a kind of loan without interest, or a fund on the cargo as it was called, which charterers returned along with the freight when the transaction was closed.

As regards chartering agreements, a basic issue concerned the time taken for the delivery of timber. Shipbuilders needed the timber as quickly as possible in order to start work on their orders, and they demanded a delivery deadline. Over six agreements between 1828 and 1832 Mikes Potous, always fixed a deadline with the captains ranging between 40 and 71 days for the transportation of the timber from Asia Minor or Karpathos. In contrast, timber merchants did not insist on such deadlines, as the timber they ordered was not for immediate use but rather for future sale. In chartering agreements without a delivery deadline, laytime was fixed instead, where laytime was the time required to load the ship, as well as the demurrage and the extra time required to load or unload the ship, which included the charges paid by the charterer to the shipowner for extra use of the ship. According to our sources, laytime was ranged between three and twenty-one days, depending on the volume of cargo and the location of loading, which in certain cases was more than one location. Kiriakos Kouronis, who in 1843 had to load 150 logs and 200 frames in three different small ports in the Gulf of Xiros, agreed a laytime of ten working days, whereas in 1840 the Amorgos captain Michail Oikonomidis agreed to a laytime of 21 days to load 300 logs and 150 frames from a location on the southern Asia Minor coast called Kiovata, with an additional ten days for 400 logs and 200 frames.[109] The contracting parts did not always use demurrage, but if they did, this lasted between two to ten days and daily charges ranged from 15 to 36 drs, or 2% of the total freight.

The captains chartered to transport timber to Syros were from different areas such as Enos, Kasos, Ios and Kastellorizo as well as from Syros, but the great majority were from Limni of Euboea. Some captains managed to be hired on a constant basis, such as Antonios Maniadis from Kasos and his schooner *Themistoklis*, 49 tons, who transported timber for the whole first semester of 1832 from Asia Minor, on behalf of Mikes Potous. The vessels used in the timber trade were medium to small sized, ranging from 40 to 150 tons, but most of

109 Ibid., n. 14999, 21.4.1843, n. 10400, 8.5.1840.

them were below 100 tons, and were mostly schooners of 68 tons on average, with few *bombardes* and *martigoi* and brigs of an average 126 tons.

Sales

The sales of shipbuilding timber in Syros were not only a case of specialized timber merchants, but also of occasional sellers, captains, shipbuilders and others. Those who intended to build ships bought timber from local timber merchants such as Xenos Katolios, who in 1840 sold floors, knees, breast hooks, aprons and a stempost to the Chiot merchant Ioannis Amvrosios Rallis, probably for the construction of his 174 ton brig *Aristidis*, or Ioannis Stylianou and Michalis Sideris, who in 1838 sold 80 logs from Thasos to Andros captain Konstantinos Birikos (Empiricos), who took responsibility for transporting them himself.[110] However, in Syros timber merchants from other areas were active as well, such as Pantelis Chrysinas from Kranidi, who in 1839 sold 200 planks of Euboean pine to Santorini captain Konstantinos G. Tzanes, or Zanes for the construction of his 225 ton brig *Panaya Malteza* (see Chapter Four) or Ioannis G. Kitzos from Athens, who in 1840 sold a large quantity of timber, also from Euboea, for the skeleton of the hull to Mykonos captain Antonios Bonazountas.[111] Even local timber merchants were sometimes supplied by occasional timber sellers, such as Hadjimichail Pissas, who bought 400 knees from a Niokastro (Pylos) carpenter named Anastasios Moraitis, with the Syros merchant of Peloponnese origin Efstathios Bobolas acting as guarantor.[112] Shipowners also frequently bought shipbuilding timber from non-specialized merchants, such as Mavrianos Milionis, who bought timber from Manolis N. Magasianos from Kasos (not a timber merchant) for the construction of the 86 ton schooner *Rodos*, and Mykonos captains Ioannis Drakopoulos and Petros Xydakis, who intended to build in their homeland and bought directly from the shipbuilders Mikes Potous and Pantelis Maskas respectively.[113]

Shipbuilders were supplied with timber either directly from its place of origin, without the mediation of timber merchants (as we have seen in the charter agreements) or by purchasing it from timber merchants and other occasional sellers. Mikes Potous bought from locals such as Konstantinos Pissias or Stylianos Michail, as well as from professionals outside Syros like

110 Ibid., n. 17813, 19.12.1845, n. 10950, 28.8.1840, n. 8048, 9.12.1838.

111 Ibid., n. 8532, 22.3.1839, n. 9291, 23.1.1840.

112 Ibid., 10211, 2.4.1840.

113 Ibid., *Βιβλίον μνημονικῶν πράξεων ὑπὸ στοιχεῖον Γ'*, n. 1550, 4.7.1832, *Βιβλίον Μνημονικόν ὑπὸ στοιχεῖον Ζ'*, n. 1548, 23.11.1833, notary Andreas David, n. 5197, 18.2.1837, n. 6922, 29.3.1838.

Alexandros Skaventzos from Skiathos, and Ioannis Ilias from Karpathos. Similarly, Nikolaos Pagidas bought floors, knees, breast hooks and frames from Karpathos from Amorgos captain Georgios Kabourakis in 1839.[114] However, the number of bills of sale or charter parties in notarial acts regarding shipbuilding timber on behalf of shipbuilders and shipowners was disproportionally low relative to the number of ships built, which indicates that in most cases, timber was supplied by local timber merchants, in which case this did not require a notarial act and therefore left no traces.

For the shipbuilders who did not keep any timber stock, the quantity they purchased was calculated every time for the precise purposes of the construction of the ship they had received the order to build. For the hull of a vessel 22 meters long, Ioannis Pagidas bought (from the Karpathos merchant Hadjinikolaos Androulis) 800 frames of 9.14–11.88 meters in length, 15–19 cm wide and 11–17 cm in height, 150 floors symmetrical to the frames, 100 knees and ten breast hooks.[115] Captain Georgios Ioannis Vratsanos ordered from the Karitena timber merchant Georgios Tzinis a conspicuous quantity of "wild timber", perhaps oak or a similar hardwood from Euboea, every piece of which was designed by the shipbuilder Nikolaos Pagidas; it seems that Tzinis had a precise plan for each structural member when he was going to cut the wood, and this was a very common practice among shipwrights, to ensure the right cutting of the pieces.[116]

Over the examined period, the prices of logs was subject to mild fluctuations. In August 1827 the price was 66 gurus per piece. Subsequently, there was a continuous downward trend until July 1832, when the price had fallen to 40 gurus per piece; however, from December 1832 to September 1833, the price rose again to 60 gurus per piece. In 1831–32, when the price per log was fell to 52, 50 and 40 gurus per piece, the shipbuilding production in terms of tonnage was reduced to half that of previous years, whereas in 1833 production tripled when compared with 1831–32. In the recession years 1834–37, the price of logs fell to one third of the 1833 price. The price had risen again in 1838, when it reached 56 gurus per log, related to the rise of production that year and the upward trend in the following years. In 1845, the price was 23.5 drs per piece, and by October 1854 the price had risen to 60 drs per piece for Euboea timber. In the same year, the price of hardwood for keel and keelson was at 120 drs per piece, but had fallen to 90 drs per piece in April 1855.[117] In the following year,

114 Ibid., n. 13700, 17.7.1842, n. 17172, 10.6.1845, n. 5670, 4.6.1837, n. 8492, 17.3.1839.

115 Ibid., n. 4847, 30.11.1836.

116 Ibid., n. 27814, 18.10.1854.

117 Ibid., n. 27814, 18.10.1854.

the Euboea prices fluctuated between 50 and 60 drs, in Asia Minor 100 drs, and in the Gulf of Xiros only 15 drs. This rapid price increase cannot be related to the course of production but, according to a source, rose by 35% in the period since 1853 as a result of the agreement of the Syros timber merchants to establish a uniform policy regarding sales price.[118]

According to our sources, nineteen individuals appear as timber merchant or lumberjacks in Syros, most of them belonging to specific families, all originally from Chios, who largely controlled the timber trade and who represent continuity in this profession across the entire nineteenth century. According to Municipality Rolls in the period 1830–80, there were 54 timber merchants in Syros, but it is also necessary to take into account those who declare themselves as lumberjacks, because timber merchants do not originate from the traditional class of merchants, but from the groups of lumberjacks. Initially, they were specialized woodcutters with specific knowledge of shipbuilding timber and its cutting methods, who verticalized their activities in trade and became timber merchants. A characteristic feature that confirms the above is that most of the timber merchants were illiterate. The largest amount of timber was imported from the Ottoman Empire, Asia Minor and Sea of Marmara, Gulf of Xiros, Thassos, Karpathos and the peninsula of Chalkidiki, whereas in Greece the supply areas were mainly Euboea and Attica. The import of timber from the Ottoman Empire was a basic factor in the Syros shipbuilding industry. The local press, in various circumstances, raised the issue on the occasion of an increase in timber prices and with export prohibitions of the Ottoman authorities. Compensation, in the case of not obtaining the authorization to export timber from the Ottoman authorities, was a constant issue raised in the agreements for the transport of timber to Syros. The cause of the problem was the inability to exploit national forest resources which would facilitate the transport from inland to the coasts, due to the lack of road infrastructures. Syros shipbuilders and the press repeatedly raised the only suggested solution with the government, which was the construction of a road system that would connect forests and coasts, thereby facilitating the transport of timber to the loading places.[119]

Sources are not very eloquent concerning the details as regards the type of trees used for shipbuilding. The main generic distinction is between softwood and hardwood vessels built or used in some parts of the hull. Softwood is mostly identified with pitch pine. Hardwood is identified with oak, yew, elm or even olive tree, and usually used for the skeleton parts that needed to be more

118 Newspaper *Ἕνωσις*, n. 233, 23.11.1856.

119 Ibid., n. 191, 13.1.1856, newspaper *Ἑρμούπολις*, n. 4, 12.9.1864.

resistant, with natural curved shape as knees and breast hooks. The two basic types of pine used in shipbuilding up to the present day in Greece are Turkish Pine (Pinus Brutia) and Aleppo Pine (Pinus Halepensis). Turkish Pine is heavier than Aleppo and, thanks to the greater quantity of resin, is more water resistant. It reaches greater height, and its straightforward logs are considered more appropriate for planking, whereas Aleppo Pine is better suited for the structural members of the hull, due to its greater natural curvature. According to a contemporary forest map, pine imported to Syros mainly from Asia Minor, Thasos and Karpathos must be Turkish Pine, whereas that imported from Euboea and Attica is Aleppo Pine.[120]

Metallurgy and Ironsmith Workshops

Metallurgy was an important linkage created by the necessity for metallic parts in the ship, and the prosperity of the industry strongly depended upon the course of shipbuilding production. There were no large manufacturing units in Syros, and production was instead organized in small workshops run by individual craftsmen, most of these established near the shipyards; many served demand from the nearby islands, and were hired, as were shipwrights, to work abroad, for example in Mykonos and Amorgos.[121] Data about the manufacturing of iron components for ships is scarce, and covers the period from 1837–47, and mainly the period 1837–40. During this short period, manufacturing prices observed a downward trend from 81 lepta/oka in March 1837 to 70 lepta/oka in November 1840, and to 66 lepta in March 1847. Pig iron was imported mostly from England and Russia, with the English iron used for most of the metal components and the Russian iron for specific components such as the hinges and the rigging equipment.[122]

Other Shipbuilding Material and Maritime Stores

All the necessary shipbuilding material and maritime stores were available in the '*entrepot*' of the eastern Mediterranean, serving not only the small ports and maritime communities of Greece, but also those of the Ottoman Empire: as also the Syros French consul reports: «*Une vaste depôt de bois de construction et de mâture, d'ancres et de chaines, de toiles à voile et de cordages, fournent à tous les besoin des chantiers et aux demandes des îles et du bâtiments de la Grèce aussi bien que des îles et du littoral de l'empire ottoman.*».[123] In 1835, Antonios

120 Damianidis, *Ελληνική Παραδοσιακή*, 170, 172–73.

121 GSA, Syros, notary Andreas David, n. 5269, 11.3.1837, n. 11218, 6.11.1840.

122 Delis "Ερμούπολη: Σύρος", 365–66; Kardasis, *Σύρος*, 88, Table 6.

123 AMAE, CCC, Syra, vol. 3, 20.4.1849, p. 265; Agriantoni, *Οι Απαρχές*, 84.

Georgios Ghinis from Spetses (acting as an agent for his brother Vassilios G. Ghinis, who had built in Rhodes a brig named *Eleni*) bought all the necessary maritime stores for the ship in Syros. He bought sails for 772 drs and 60 lepta from the Chiot merchant Alexandros Z. Petrokokkinos & Co, an anchor from the Chiot merchant Georgios Kalvokoressis for 34 Spanish silver dollars (204 drs), and a cable from a merchant originally from Smyrna named Nikolaos Letzos for 80 Spanish silver dollars (480 drs). This purchase was made on credit, by issuing a bond of 91 days for the two first merchants and five months for the third, guaranteed by the merchant of Cretan origin, Konstantinos Papadakis.[124] Sales of maritime stores on credit must have been a widespread practice in the market of Syros. The Andros captain Ioannis Leonardos Zografos bought two chains and anchors from Konstantinos Kotzifakis & Co. for 1,360 drs and 91 lepta, with interest-free repayment after four months and interest of 1% after that date, also under the guarantee of an Andros captain, Michail Federikos Kabanis.[125]

Anchors, chains and wrought iron were imported from England. The existence of a workshop manufacturing medium size anchors from wrought iron, more appropriate for smaller sailing vessels is reported in 1853 by the Syros French Consul. Ropes were imported from Ancona, Trieste, England, France and Russia. The only known rope factory was that of G. Glykas created after 1853. However, according to the Municipality Rolls, there were only three rope makers in Syros, among them two who settled in Syros during the 1820s. In the town plan created in 1837 by the Bavarian engineer Weiler, the position of a rope factory behind the shipyards is marked; hemp imports had begun many years previously, and we can assume these were for the purpose of rope-making, though this cannot be confirmed. In 1875, the only rope factory in Syros was that of Dimitrios and Antonios G. Glykas, who were probably the sons of G. Glykas, and the British consul reports that this rope factory was steam powered.[126] It is mentioned that pulleys were imported from England, but very soon, demand led to the creation of workshops in Syros. According to the Municipality Rolls, there were 32 pulley makers registered in the nineteenth century, mainly from Hydra; in 1841, as already mentioned, some

124 GSA, Syros, notary Andreas David, n. 4, 19.2.1835.

125 Ibid., n. 19077, 2.1.1847.

126 AMAE, CCC, Syra, vol. 4, 28.6.1853, 77, 79; Newspaper *Αἴολος*, 2.9.1844; Boukas, Miltiadis, *Οδηγός Εμπορικός, Γεωγραφικός & Ιστορικός του έτους 1875*, [*Commercial, Geographic and Historical Guide of the year* 1875], (Athens: 1875), 361; F.O. Syra, *Report by Consul Binney on the Trade and Commerce of the Cyclades during the Year 1875*, 11.6.1876, 1278–279; Kardasis, *Σύρος*, 88–9, 173; Agriantoni, *Οι Απαρχές*, 93, 150.

of them created a partnership. According to Syros French Consul pulleys made in Syros enjoyed a very high reputation among Greek seafarers, who considered them of better quality even to those imported from England. Other maritime stores like sails were imported from Malta and England, and pitch and tar from Russia.[127]

127 AMAE, CCC, Syra, vol. 4, 28.6.1853, 77–79; Kardasis, *Σύρος*, 173.

Conclusions

Conditions existed in Hermoupolis for the formation and growth of sailing ship construction from the very beginning of the nineteenth century, and on a scale hitherto unprecedented in the Aegean and in the eastern Mediterranean. The first such condition to be fulfilled was the concentration of a large and specialized labour force, dependent upon wages. This labour force, which had arrived mainly from Chios, had experience and know-how in ship construction that dated back to the period of prosperity of the Ottoman Greek merchant marine (1780s–1815). The craftsmen who settled in Hermoupolis were of the generation following that which had built the Ottoman Greek fleet in Chios, Hydra, Spetses and elsewhere, during the just-mentioned period. Some members of that earlier generation, in an advanced age, had also settled in Hermoupolis. Capital availability and the flow of funds from the port's entrepreneurial class, who had connections with an international business network, were the other fundamental supply factors in the shipbuilding industry.

On the demand side, the position of the port of Syros as one of the most important transit trade and maritime centres of the eastern Mediterranean largely determined the volume of the demand and the extent of the work carried out in the shipyards. Moreover, as the centre of the Greek-owned fleet, the production of the shipyards was to a large extent dependent upon the Black Sea grain trade in which the Greeks specialized. The trump and general cargoes carried on Greek bottoms boosted the demand for new sailing ships, the majority of which were built in Syros. Furthermore, the development of activities and services around shipping and shipbuilding differentiated Hermoupolis from the rest of the shipyards in the Greek Kingdom and the Levant. For captains and shipowners, Hermoupolis was a central market for the construction and repair of ships, as well as for the supply of raw materials and maritime stores. The shipbuilding market of Hermoupolis, an integral part of the maritime centre, covered the needs of the protagonists of the shipping trade over a wide geographical area. It attracted investors from the Aegean, the Ionian and the Black Sea, as well as the Greek communities in western Mediterranean ports such as Trieste. This, in turn, reflected the dependence upon the market of Hermoupolis of the shipping affairs of many ports and seafaring communities of the Aegean and Ionian Seas.

All the above made shipbuilding and ship repair in Hermoupolis a full year activity, in contrast to the seasonality of many other shipbuilding areas, as indicated by the fast and continuous delivery of vessels. This intensity, continuity and high volume of output entitles us to characterize Syros shipyards

© KONINKLIJKE BRILL NV, LEIDEN, 2016 | DOI 10.1163/9789004306158_009

as the first labour-intensive industry of the Greek Kingdom. The Syros shipbuilding industry also created important forward and backward linkages to local, national, and transnational economies. At the local level, the need for ship components and equipment led to the spread of workshops related to shipbuilding, like black smithies, pulley making workshops, and roperies. At the national and transnational level, the need to import shipbuilding timber created a network of cutting, transportation, and disposal in the shipbuilding market. The lumberjacks-traders from Hermoupolis involved in this network controlled the whole process, from the cutting of the timber to its transportation from Ottoman areas to Syros, on ships from Kasos, Limni of Euboea, Skiathos and other minor ports, which found systematic employment in this trade.

The contribution of the shipyards to the Greek economy during the examined period is estimated to be considerable, particularly during the period of King Otho (1833–62). Its high percentage in the share of secondary production confirms it to be the most important manufacturing activity of the Greek Kingdom in economic terms. Although the percentage of Syros's shipbuilding output to total GDP was relatively low (around 1% on average, from 1838–66), the disparity in size between the primary and secondary sectors in the Greek economy of the period needs to be taken into consideration. Therefore, the average gross value of the shipbuilding output, between one and a half to two million drachmas during 1838–66, should be considered a high profile annuity, given the level of the Greek economy during the period.

In the heyday of the 1840s–60s, its output volume can be compared to the big shipyards of the UK, France, Canada, and the USA. Despite the different market orientation of the ships built in Hermoupolis, the context of the organization of the business, and the methods used to build wooden ships, did not seem very different. Relative to the size of the industry in the countries mentioned above, the Syros shipyards were ranked as being of medium to large capacity. Hermoupolis was one of the largest in the Mediterranean during the middle of the century, in terms of tonnage surpassing entire regions such as Provence and Liguria, which had long-established shipping and shipbuilding traditions.

A great variety of ships types were built in Syros, from small coasters to large merchantmen, incorporating elements of the Mediterranean as well as the North European shipbuilding traditions. However, the Syros shipyards specialized in the construction of brigs, the most widespread type of merchantmen in the Greek-owned fleet in the nineteenth century. The brig was an ideal vessel for the type of trade in which Greeks specialized, such as the transport of cereals across medium distance routes like those between the Black Sea and the Mediterranean. Brigs and other ship types that followed in terms of popularity, like schooners, confirm that the Syros shipyards were not in the avant-garde from the technological point of view, but does demonstrate that they were fully integrated in the necessities of the international seaborne trade, as their dominant types, brigs, schooners and barks, were the standard types of sailing merchant ships worldwide.

To build a ship in Hermoupolis, it was necessary to follow a procedure that demanded specialized knowledge of the subject and of the market. Often, the agreements were stipulated before a notary, and these reveal a standardization which confirms a high frequency of formal transactions of this kind. The terms and conditions and the clauses in the agreements demonstrate the efforts of the parties to reduce transaction costs. The terms of the contractual agreements eloquently reflect the norms, behaviors, mentalities, and practices of the actors involved in shipping during the age of sail. They also highlight the culture and the system of values of maritime people and communities, during the period of transition from merchant to industrial capitalism.

The organization of production conformed to the characteristics of other international shipbuilding centres during the same period. The shipbuilding enterprises specializing in wooden ship construction were mostly individual/family business types demanding only small levels of capital, and were very flexible, thanks to the proximity of other similar trades in the sector. Thus, to enter, leave, and reappear in the industry was a common phenomenon, whereas there was not any one type of company ownership. However, a distinction formed between master shipwrights: the first and largest category, whose participation in the construction of the ship was minimal or negligible; a second category, whose participation in construction as master shipwrights was frequent but not constant; finally, the last category, who were relatively few in number, was comprised of those who were holders of the means of production during the entire period under examination. Those in this last category formed a kind of shipbuilding elite, controlling the largest part of production. Almost all of them originated from Chios, which had a long tradition in shipbuilding and strong connections with the merchant class of the city.

This flourishing industry experienced a gradual decline, alongside the decline of Hermoupolis as a centre of transit trade. In addition, the advent of the steam into markets and routes previously dominated by sail, and the influx of numerous second-hand sailing ships from abroad, mainly from the UK after 1870, dealt a fatal blow to the Syros shipbuilding market. Furthermore, the development of the new big port of Greece, Piraeus, in the last quarter of the nineteenth century, shifted capital and entrepreneurship from Hermoupolis to the capital's port. Further evidence of this is provided by the transfer, in 1867, of the shipyards from their previous location to where they still stand today, and the antagonisms with other manufacturing and industrial activities. The shipyards were no longer the most important industry in the city. New types of secondary activities shifted capital and resources away from shipbuilding, following the changes that occurred in the second industrial revolution during the second half of the nineteenth century.

In Hermoupolis, the shipyards were for almost four decades among the most productive in the Mediterranean, contributing significantly to the growth of the Greek-owned sailing fleet. Their marginalization in the later part of the nineteenth century is due to the continuous and irreversible decline of the sailing ship, a phenomenon that occurred simultaneously on an international scale, and affected many European and North American areas with long traditions of wooden shipbuilding. However, despite the eclipse of the sailing ship, wooden shipbuilding left an important legacy to the port of Syros, which, until World War II, managed to maintain a relative importance as a maritime centre and industrial district, including the Arsenal for the repair and construction of steamers and several other factories.

Appendices

Chapter 3—Production, Productivity and Performance of the Shipbuilding Industry

APPENDIX 3.1 *Syros shipyards production in number of vessels, 1828–1880.*

Year	Number of vessels	Year	Number of vessels
1828	7	1854	37
1829	17	1855	63
1830	20	1856	81
1831	18	1857	116
1832	19	1858	74
1833	43	1859	65
1834	29	1860	72
1835	57	1861	35
1836	43	1862	27
1837	29	1863	50
1838	54	1864	40
1839	41	1865	39
1840	75	1866	63
1841	63	1867	98
1842	31	1868	108
1843	60	1869	80
1844	73	1870	70
1845	85	1871	79
1846	89	1872	45
1847	71	1873	39
1848	91	1874	89
1849	96	1875	88
1850	102	1876	65
1851	80	1877	33
1852	73	1878	72
1853	50	1879	71
–	–	1880	70

Source: Processed data for the years 1828–66 from GSA, Syros, Αρχείο Συμβολαιογράφου Μάξιμου Ταλασλή, Συμβ. Σκαρλάτος Μάξιμος, Κατάστιχα 1–6, 1827–1830, Συμβ. Ανδρέας Δαβίδ, Κατάστιχα

© KONINKLIJKE BRILL NV, LEIDEN, 2016 | DOI 10.1163/9789004306158_010

7–16, 1830–24/1/1835, Λυτά έγγραφα 1835–1862. Συλλογή Ιστορικού Αρχείου Κυκλάδων, Συμβ. Κων. Αγγελίδης, Ευρετήρια, 1–5, 1854–1863, Συμβ. Αντώνιος Αλμπέρτος, Ευρετήρια 1–2, 1853–1864, Συμβ. Μιχ. Ιωάννόπουλος, Ευρ. 1–2, 1843–1845, Συμβ. Χρ. Ιωάννου Ευρ. 1–10, 1846–1860. Ι/Ναυπηγικά, 1836–1866.
For the years 1864 and 1865: from Kardasis *Σύρος*, Table 25, 180–81.
For the years 1867–70: processed data from Harlaftis – Vlassopoulos, *Historical Register 'Pontoporeia'*.
For the years 1871–1880: Foreign Office/Annual Series, *Diplomatic & Consular Reports on Trade & Finance, Greece, Syros*, 1871–1880.

APPENDIX 3.2 *Syros shipyards production in tonnage, 1828–1880.*

Year	Tonnnage based on sources	Vessels with known tonnage/ Total vessels built	Estimated tonnage*
1828	1273.68	7/7	1273.68
1829	3828.74	16/17	4109.94
1830	3779.23	18/20	4022.06
1831	1247.21	16/18	1651.35
1832	2169.25	19/19	2169.25
1833	6354.74	43/43	6354.74
1834	3504.23	29/29	3504.23
1835	3024.79	57/57	3024.79
1836	2480.09	40/43	2532.56
1837	1898.87	23/29	2032.86
1838	6341.25	36/54	7746.17
1839	8354.74	41/41	8354.74
1840	12,164.29	63/75	13,237.57
1841	7547.85	50/63	8367.19
1842	2944.35	28/31	3044.88

* Estimated tonnage for each year came out with the following method: for the vessels that there are no available data for their capacity in the sources, the average tonnage of their type (e.g. brig) was attributed to each of them, and if there was not such figure for that same year, then the closest chronologically average tonnage was attributed to them (e.g. of the previous year). Then, the sum of this estimated tonnage was added to the tonnage of vessels known from the sources.

Year	Tonnnage based on sources	Vessels with known tonnage/ Total vessels built	Estimated tonnage*
1843	5281.82	35/60	6743.85
1844	7856.50	46/73	9397.01
1845	9410.42	50/85	12,073.58
1846	11,288.14	58/89	14,488.10
1847	18,463.73	65/71	19,112.11
1848	12,718.74	58/91	17,928.09
1849	12,134.15	78/96	13,800.43
1850	10,413.61	98/102	10,479.00
1851	6460.35	56/80	8109.79
1852	5119.91	50/73	6596.02
1853	6410.89	32/50	9416.35
1854	5215.25	24/37	6737.07
1855	8499.50	47/63	9390.95
1856	9309.21	55/81	11,717.21
1857	11,118.10	79/116	13,607.78
1858	5022.47	34/74	6862.42
1859	2849.57	23/65	4537.53
1860	2765.36	20/72	4600.54
1861	1821.00	9/35	3345.57
1862	4455.51	18/27	4885.17
1863	6559.00	28/50	7750.65
1864	–	–	–
1865	2556.50	–	2556.50
1866	9474.90	46/63	11,269.35
1867	20,831	–	–
1868	21,644	–	–
1869	17,586	–	–
1870	13,756	–	–
1871	11,088	–	–
1872	4049	–	–
1873	3499	–	–
1874	6622	–	–
1875	10,483	–	–
1876	7359	–	–
1877	3343	–	–

APPENDIX 3.2 *Syros shipyards production in tonnage, 1828–1880* (cont.)

Year	Tonnnage based on sources	Vessels with known tonnage/ Total vessels built	Estimated tonnage*
1878	9731	–	–
1879	6041	–	–
1880	6168	–	–

Source: Processed data for the years 1828–66 from GSA, Syros, Αρχείο Συμβολαιογράφου Μάξιμου Ταλασλή, Συμβ. Σκαρλάτος Μάξιμος, Κατάστιχα 1–6, 1827–1830, Συμβ. Ανδρέας Δαβίδ, Κατάστιχα 7–16, 1830–24/1/1835, Λυτά έγγραφα 1835–1862. Συλλογή Ιστορικού Αρχείου Κυκλάδων, Συμβ. Κων. Αγγελίδης, Ευρετήρια, 1–5, 1854–1863, Συμβ. Αντώνιος Αλμπέρτος, Ευρετήρια 1–2, 1853–1864, Συμβ. Μιχ. Ιωάννόπουλος, Ευρ. 1–2, 1843–1845, Συμβ. Χρ. Ιωάννου Ευρ. 1–10, 1846–1860. I/Ναυπηγικά, 1836–1866.

No data are available for 1864. For 1865 a handwritten notice with total tonnage capacity of that year was found in the serie I/Ναυπηγικά/6 n. 159.

For the years 1867–70: processed data from Harlaftis – Vlassopoulos, *Historical Register 'Pontoporeia'*. For the years 1871–1880: Foreign Office/Annual Series, *Diplomatic & Consular Reports on Trade & Finance, Greece, Syros*, 1871–1880.

APPENDIX 3.2.1 *Syros shipyards output in tons and total tonnage of Greek-owned shipping, 1830–1879.*

Decade	Syros	Total of Greek-owned fleet
1830–39	42,340.75	–
1840–49	118,137.04	343,518
1850–59	87,403.11	308,071
1860–69	94,738.79	487,418
1870–79	75,971	584,317

Source: For Syros: processed data from Appendix 3.2. For the total of the Greek-owned fleet: Harlaftis – Vlassopoulos, *Historical Register 'Pontoporeia'*.

APPENDIX 3.2.2 *Syros shipbuilding output in tons/freight rates Odessa – Marseille/shipping income of the Greek-owned fleet, 1835–1880.*

Year	Shipbuilding output (in hundreds of tons)	Freight rates Odessa – Marseille (in shillings)	Shipping income (in millions drs LMU)*
1835	30.24	27.06	39.40
1836	25.30	32.44	39.43
1837	20.32	37.88	37.76
1838	77.46	47.12	52.56
1839	83.54	52.02	55.80
1840	132.3	27.77	25.10
1841	83.67	19.33	29.47
1842	29.89	31.10	35.84
1843	67.43	22.55	21.67
1844	93.97	27.72	26.06
1845	120.73	30.44	34.98
1846	144.88	38.54	62.76
1847	191.12	47.99	62.53
1848	179.28	33.34	36.05
1849	138.00	27.94	29.90
1850	104.79	25.20	26.15
1851	81.09	27.00	39.63
1852	65.96	35.03	33.75
1853	94.16	60.60	59.66
1854	67.37	43.43	37.49
1855	93.91	26.25	26.58
1856	117.17	26.25	39.11
1857	136.07	23.85	33.41
1858	68.11	23.48	28.86
1859	45.37	26.63	29.51
1860	46.00	28.05	25.50
1861	33.45	26.25	36.60
1862	48.85	23.10	27.28
1863	77.50	24.53	30.75
1864	–	23.85	39.91
1865	25.56	26.25	33.93

* Drachmas of Latin Monetary Union.

APPENDIX 3.2.2 *Syros shipbuilding output in tons/freight rates* (cont.)

Year	Shipbuilding output (in hundreds of tons)	Freight rates Odessa – Marseille (in shillings)	Shipping income (in millions drs LMU)*
1866	112.69	24.53	34.68
1867	208.30	22.43	40.36
1868	216.40	21.38	32.42
1869	178.56	27.06	45.31
1870	137.50	22.05	59.00
1871	110.88	21.38	35.02
1872	40.49	20.33	47.75
1873	34.99	22.43	42.24
1874	66.22	19.65	51.42
1875	104.80	17.18	36.89
1876	73.59	17.18	41.70
1877	33.43	21.30	45.41
1878	97.31	21.53	29.63
1879	60.41	12.90	40.71
1880	61.68	13.20	41.93

Source: For the shipbuilding output: processed data from Appendix 3.2. For the freight rates and the shipping income G. Harlaftis and G. Kostelenos 'Services and economic growth: estimating shipping income in the 19th century Greek economy', Greek Economic History Society working paper, http://hdoisto.gr/gr/library/seminar-proceedings, Appendix 4, 38–39 and Appendix 7, 45–46.

APPENDIX 3.2.3 *Syros shipbuilding output, Norwegian and Isserlis freight index and shipping income of the Greek-owned fleet, 1866–1880.*

Year	Shipbuilding output (in hundreds of tons)	Norwegian freight index	Isserlis freight index	Shipping income (in millions drs LMU
1866	112.7	122	–	34.68
1867	208.3	121	–	40.36
1868	216.4	118	–	32.42
1869	178.6	100	100	45.31
1870	137.5	102	103	59.00
1871	110.9	110	102	35.02
1872	40.5	134	103	47.75

Year	Shipbuilding output (in hundreds of tons)	Norwegian freight index	Isserlis freight index	Shipping income (in millions drs LMU
1873	35.0	147	117	42.24
1874	66.2	146	108	51.42
1875	104.8	130	99	36.89
1876	73.6	130	98	41.70
1877	33.4	122	99	45.41
1878	97.3	121	91	29.63
1879	60.4	114	85	40.71
1880	61.7	101	87	41.93

Source: Appendix 3.2.2. For the Norwegian and Isserlis freight index data from Lewis R. Fischer – Helge W. Nordvik, "Θαλάσσιες μεταφορές", 271–99, Tables 9.6 και 9.7.

APPENDIX 3.2.4 *Comparative output at international level, 1830–1879.*

Decade	Syros	Dunkirk	Boston	Prince Edward Island	Sunderland
1830–39	42,340.75	3563.1	46,326	51,200	350,650
1840–49	118,137	4353.42	101,323.5	88,400	377,200
1850–59	87,403.11	30,651	260,153	148,300	542,215
1860–69	94,738.92	21,663	14,832.77	236,500	646,435
1870–79	75,791	10,365	–	173,600	935,315

Source: Appendix 3.2. For Dunkirk processed data from Pfister – Langanay, *Constructeurs, charpentiers*, 55–61.
For Boston processed data from William Armstrong Fairburn, *Merchant Sail*, Vol. VI, 2905, 2908. Note: the data of the decades 1830–39 and 1860–69 concern only the area of Medford. For the rest of the decades the data of areas from Medford and East Boston were added up.
For Prince Edward Island processed data from Matthews – Panting, *Ships & Shipbuilding in the North Atlantic Region*, 149–50.
For Sunderland processed data from Ville, "Shipbuilding in the NE of England", Table 1, 36.

APPENDIX 3.3 *Average price/ton of vessels built in Syros, 1828–1866.*

Year	Average price/ton	Number of vessels providing data for average price/ton	Total number of vessels built
1828	–	–	7
1829	124.079	1	17
1830	115.38	1	20
1831	26.98	1	18
1832	157.48	1	19
1833	119.298	1	43
1834	–	–	29
1835	119.31	3	57
1836	–	–	43
1837	82.76	2	29
1838	141.65	15	54
1839	161.45	41	41
1840	160.5	56	75
1841	138.25	39	63
1842	144.47	28	31
1843	134.9	32	60
1844	143.24	38	73
1845	157.22	48	85
1846	178.61	57	89
1847	219.86	66	71
1848	205.14	51	91
1849	184.74	73	96
1850	169.59	98	102
1851	138.49	57	80
1852	138.28	50	73
1853	160.18	30	50
1854	193.02	23	37
1855	192.98	40	63
1856	234.24	50	81
1857	215.22	60	116
1858	213.95	28	74
1859	167.21	5	65
1860	214.56	7	72
1861	–	0	0

Year	Average price/ton	Number of vessels providing data for average price/ton	Total number of vessels built
1862	243.74	10	27
1863	233.49	28	50
1864	–	–	–
1865	–	–	–
1866	295.75	45	63

Source: Processed data from Appendices 3.2 and 3.6.

APPENDIX 3.3.1 *Comparison of the average price of ships in the market of Syros and the freight rates Odessa – Marseille, 1838–1863*

Year	Freight rates Odessa – Marseille (in shillings)	Average price/ton of new ships (in drs)	Average price/ton of second hand ships (in drs)	Difference of the price between new and second hand ships
1838	47.12	141.65	91.53	50.12
1839	52.02	161.45	109.28	50.79
1840	27.77	160.5	92.59	67.91
1841	19.33	138.25	112.84	25.41
1842	31.10	144.47	82.23	62.24
1843	22.55	134.9	98.32	36.58
1844	27.72	143.24	107.68	35.56
1845	30.44	157.22	110.11	47.11
1846	38.54	178.61	93.11	85.50
1847	47.99	219.86	118.81	101.05
1848	33.34	205.14	112.53	92.61
1849	27.94	184.74	117.76	66.98
1850	25.20	169.59	117.77	51.82
1851	27.00	138.49	100.61	37.88
1852	35.03	138.28	97.47	40.81
1853	60.60	160.18	118.38	41.80
1854	43.43	193.02	114.08	78.94
1855	26.25	192.98	123.65	69.33
1856	26.25	234.24	148.70	85.54

APPENDIX 3.3.1 *Comparison of the average price of ships* (cont.)

Year	Freight rates Odessa – Marseille (in shillings)	Average price/ton of new ships (in drs)	Average price/ton of second hand ships (in drs)	Difference of the price between new and second hand ships
1857	23.85	215.22	142.14	73.08
1858	23.48	213.95	133.51	80.44
1859	26.63	167.21	84.98	82.23
1860	28.05	214.56	118.26	96.30
1861	26.25	–	116.49	–
1862	23.10	243.74	137.15	54.03
1863	24.53	233.49	155.60*	77.89

Source: For freight rates appendix 3.2.2, and for average price/ton of new ships appendix 3.3. For second hand ships processed data from GSA, Syros, notarial acts from από Αρχείο Συμβολαιογράφου Μάξιμου Ταλασλή, Συμβ. Ανδρέας Δαβίδ, 1838–1863.
* The average price/ton of 1863 is based only on two sale transactions of ships.

APPENDIX 3.3.2 *Distribution of average price/ton in classes of tonnage per decade*

Class of tonnage	1838–49	1850–59	1860–66
1–50	148.27	159.90	172.08
51–100	151.87	170.61	289.04
101–150	156.92	181.63	230.88
151–200	165.33	185.61	240.89
201–250	177.23	188.06	289.43
251–300	200.58	213.66	284.48
<300	204.67	238.97	255.24

Source: Process data from Appendix 3.3 and from GSA, Syros, Αρχείο Συμβολαιογράφου Μάξιμου Ταλασλή, Συμβ. Σκαρλάτος Μάξιμος, Κατάστιχα 1–6, 1827–1830, Συμβ. Ανδρέας Δαβίδ, Κατάστιχα 7–16, 1830–24/1/1835, Λυτά έγγραφα 1835–1862. Συλλογή Ιστορικού Αρχείου Κυκλάδων, Συμβ. Κων. Αγγελίδης, Ευρετήρια, 1–5, 1854–1863, Συμβ. Αντώνιος Αλμπέρτος, Ευρετήρια 1–2, 1853–1864, Συμβ. Μιχ. Ιωάννόπουλος, Ευρ. 1–2, 1843–1845, Συμβ. Χρ. Ιωάννου Ευρ. 1–10, 1846–1860. I/Ναυπηγικά, 1836–1866.

APPENDIX 3.3.3 *Comparison of prices of new ships between Prince Edward Island and new Brunswick and Syros in pound sterlings, 1838–1866*

Year	Prince Edward Island and New Brunswick	Average price of Canadian vessels	Syros	Difference of price
1838	6.50	6.50	4.97	1.53
1839	6.00	6.00	5.66	0.34
1840	6.00–8.00	7	5.63	1.37
1841	4.00–7.00	5.5	4.85	0.65
1842	7.00	7.00	5.07	1.93
1843	4.00	4.00	4.73	−0.73
1844	3.50	3.50	5.05	−1.55
1845	5.5–6	5.75	5.52	0.23
1846	5.5–6	5.75	6.45	−0.70
1847	–	–	7.71	–
1848	4.00–6.5	5.25	7.60	−2.35
1849	5.50	5.50	6.51	−1.01
1850	4.5–7	5.75	5.89	−0.14
1851	–	–	4.83	–
1852	5.5–7	6.25	4.67	1.58
1853	5.5–8/14	6.75	5.41	1.34
1854	5.5–11.75/15	8.625	6.79	1.84
1855	–	–	7.00	–
1856	7–8.25	7.625	7.83	-0.21
1857	–		7.14	–
1858	7.00	7.00	7.53	−0.53
1859	7–8.5	7.75	5.84	1.91
1860	7.00–9.00	8	7.61	0.39
1861	5.5–9.5	7.5	–	–
1862	7.25–10.00	8.625	8.40	0.23
1863	7.00–10.00	8.5	7.46	1.04
1864	5.00–9.00	7	–	–
1865	5.5–9	7.25	–	–
1866	5.5–8.5	7	10.30	−3.30

Source: For Syros Appendix 3.3. For the Canadian vessels processed data from Sager – Gerald, *Maritime Capital*, 69.

APPENDIX 3.4 *Estimated gross revenue of shipbuilding output of Syros, 1838–1866*

Year	Number of vessels with known shipbuilding cost	Total number of vessels built	Tonnage of vessels with known shipbuilding cost	Estimated tonnage of total number of vessels	Factual cost of vessels with known shipbuilding cost	Estimated gross revenue*
1838	15	54	2700.22	7746.17	393,490	1,108,248.82
1839	41	41	–	8354.74	1,333,403	1,333,403
1840	55	75	10,593.57	13,237.57	1,759,014	2,183,376
1841	39	63	4962.85	8367.19	728,464	1,199,114.01
1842	28	31	2944.34	3044.88	444,504	459,029.01
1843	32	60	4178.09	6743.85	562,360	908,481.02
1844	58	73	7290.89	9397.01	1,039,194	1,340,874.11
1845	77	85	11,301.58	12,073.58	1,785,681	1,907,054.84
1846	86	89	14,174.28	14,488.10	2,466,400	2,522,451.73
1847	71	71	–	19,112.11	4,212,820	4,212,820
1848	68	91	13,911.04	17,928.09	2,918,700	3,742,757.64
1849	84	96	11,744.04	13,800.43	2,343,084	2,722,981.80
1850	100	102	10,378.99	10,479.00	1,848,857	1,865,817.49
1851	72	80	7770.01	8109.79	1,051,608	1,098,663.66
1852	66	73	6168.3	6596.02	1,005,900	1,065,045.13
1853	43	50	8237.07	9416.35	1,278,500	1,467,397.46
1854	33	37	6213.62	6737.07	1,367,000	1,468,036.56
1855	50	63	7384.9	9390.95	1,536,500	1,923,628.13
1856	63	81	10277	11,717.21	2,476,930	2,814,284.09
1857	82	116	9673.77	13,607.78	1,999,345	2,846,022.63
1858	45	74	4397.01	6862.42	952,920	1,480,394.47
1859	10	65	402.9	4537.53	72,655	764,006.22
1860	23	72	1004.7	4600.54	230,615	1,002,138.84
1861	–	–	–	3345.57	–	–
1862	16	27	2926.47	4885.17	612,650	1,090,063.39
1863	48	50	7721.95	7750.65	1,807,725	1,814,426.76
1864	–	–	–	–	–	–
1865	–	–	–	2556.50	–	–
1866	62	63	11,040.34	11,269.35	3,191,000	3,258,729.71

Source: Processed data from Appendices 3.1 and 3.2 and from GSA, Syros, Αρχείο Συμβολαιογράφου Μάξιμου Ταλασλή, Συμβ. Σκαρλάτος Μάξιμος, Κατάστιχα 1–6, 1827–1830, Συμβ.

Ανδρέας Δαβίδ,Κατάστιχα 7–16, 1830–24/1/1835, Λυτά έγγραφα 1835–1862. Συλλογή Ιστορικού Αρχείου Κυκλάδων, Συμβ. Κων. Αγγελίδης, Ευρετήρια, 1–5, 1854–1863, Συμβ. Αντώνιος Αλμπέρτος, Ευρετήρια 1–2, 1853–1864, Συμβ. Μιχ. Ιωάννόπουλος, Ευρ. 1–2, 1843–1845, Συμβ. Χρ. Ιωάννου Ευρ. 1–10, 1846–1860. I/Ναυπηγικά, 1836–1866.
* For the estimation of the yearly gross revenue the following formula was adopted: (Estimated tonnage of total number of vessels—Tonnage of vessels with known shipbuilding cost)* yearly average price/ton+ Factual cost of vessels with known shipbuilding cost).

APPENDIX 3.4.1 *Estimated percentage of the Syros shipbuilding output in the secondary sector and the total GDP, 1838–1866*

Year	Estimated gross revenue	Added value	Conversion in drachmas of Latin Union	Secondary sector in DLU	Percentage of converted added value in the secondary sector	Total GDP	Percentage of converted added value in the total GDP
1838	1,108,248.82	668,828.16	598,601.20	1,253,000	47.77	76,561,464	0.78
1839	1,333,403	804,708.71	720,214.30	1,432,000	50.29	82,158,911	0.88
1840	2,183,376	1,317,667.42	1,179,312.34	1,432,000	82.35	90,511,374	1.30
1841	1,199,114.01	723,665.31	647,680.45	1,778,902	36.41	81,524,303	0.79
1842	459,029.01	277,024.01	247,936.49	1,785,883	13.88	72,050,835	0.34
1843	908,481.02	548,268.30	490,700.13	1,883,438	26.05	70,304,740	0.70
1844	1,340,874.11	809,217.52	724,249.68	1,945,193	37.23	72,286,510	1.00
1845	1,907,054.84	1,150,907.60	1,030,062.30	2,008,022	51.30	72,555,290	1.42
1846	2,522,451.73	1,522,299.62	1,362,458.16	2,605,936	52.28	77,310,985	1.76
1847	4,212,820	2,542,436.87	2,275,481.00	2,676,659	85.01	70,202,232	3.24
1848	3,742,757.64	2,258,754.23	2,021,585.04	2,695,507	75.00	78,740,260	2.57
1849	2,722,981.80	1,643,319.52	1,470,770.97	2,827,663	52.01	81,072,203	1.81
1850	1,865,817.49	1,126,020.86	1,007,788.67	2,971,311	33.92	89,725,822	1.12
1851	1,098,663.66	663,043.52	593,423.95	3,351,775	17.70	93,491,567	0.63
1852	1,065,045.13	642,754.74	575,265.49	4,752,307	12.10	111,072,033	0.52
1853	1,467,397.46	885,574.37	792,589.06	5,516,619	14.37	102,915,915	0.77
1854	1,468,036.56	885,960.06	792,934.26	5,304,772	14.95	118,870,213	0.67
1855	1,923,628.13	1,160,909.57	1,039,014.07	5,810,197	17.88	109,909,135	0.95
1856	2,814,284.09	1,698,420.45	1,520,086.30	6,705,000	22.67	151,598,737	1.00
1857	2,846,022.63	1,717,574.66*	1,537,229.32	6,101,448	25.19	145,799,997	1.05
1858	1,480,394.47	893,418.06	799,609.17	6,807,370	11.75	136,394,946	0.59
1859	764,006.22	461,077.75	412,664.59	7,469,205	5.52	166,176,291	0.25

APPENDIX 3.4.1 *Estimated percentage of the Syros shipbuilding* (cont.)

Year	Estimated gross revenue	Added value	Conversion in drachmas of Latin Union	Secondary sector in DLU	Percentage of converted added value in the secondary sector	Total GDP	Percentage of converted added value in the total GDP
1860	1,002,138.84	604,790.79	541,287.75	7,833,112	6.91	152,205,786	0.36
1861	–	–	–	–	–	–	–
1862	1,090,063.39	657,853.26	588,778.67	10,281,930	5.73	154,490,247	0.38
1863	1,814,426.76	1,095,006.55	980,030.86	11,872,989	8.25	160,133,781	0.61
1864	–	–	–	–	–	–	–
1865	–	–	–	–	–	–	–
1866	3,258,729.71	1,966,643.38	1,760,145.82	12,835,088	13.71	194,257,887	0.91

Source: Appendix 3.4 and Kostelenos et al. *Πηγές οικονομικής ιστορίας*, Table 3-II, 102–03 & Table 6-III, 137–38.
* The estimation of the added value was based on a table of imports in the Island of Syros of 1857 issued in the report of the French consul of Syros and published by Kardasis, *Σύρος*, 86–89. From this estimation was came out the coefficient 0.6035, upon which the calculation of the rest of the yers was made.

APPENDIX 3.5 *Estimated average tonnage of new built vessels in the shipyards of Syros, 1828–1880*

Year	Average tonnage (all types)	Average tonnage of brigs	Year	Average tonnage (all types)	Average tonnage of brigs
1828	181.95	215.23	1855	174.29	202.29
1829	247.54	301.22	1856	166.94	194.26
1830	198.91	242.86	1857	140.95	176.43
1831	124.72	202.07	1858	134.3	166.81
1832	114.17	155.21	1859	128.58	185.83
1833	147.78	162.06	1860	138.27	161.19
1834	120.84	141.79	1861	202.33	194.00
1835	53.06	171.95	1862	247.53	257.83

Year	Average tonnage (all types)	Average tonnage of brigs	Year	Average tonnage (all types)	Average tonnage of brigs
1836	63.53	151.26	1863	234.25	223.30
1837	82.56	162.37	1864	–	–
1838	167.03	191.45	1865	–	–
1839	203.77	199.74	1866	205.98	218.56
1840	193.08	200.73	1867	212.56	–
1841	150.96	181.72	1868	200.40	–
1842	101.53	190.87	1869	223.2	–
1843	150.91	214.22	1870	196.51	–
1844	170.79	200.58	1871	140.35	–
1845	188.21	209.65	1872	89.98	–
1846	194.62	218.25	1873	89.72	–
1847	279.75	291.78	1874	74.4	–
1848	219.29	248.04	1875	119.13	–
1849	155.57	214.25	1876	113.22	–
1850	106.26	189.80	1877	101.3	–
1851	115.36	202.60	1878	135.15	–
1852	102.83	192.93	1879	85.08	–
1853	200.34	254.34	1880	88.11	–
1854	217.3	247.19	–	–	–

Source: For the years 1828–66: processed data from GSA, Syros, Αρχείο Συμβολαιογράφου Μάξιμου Ταλασλή, Συμβ. Σκαρλάτος Μάξιμος, Κατάστιχα 1–6, 1827–1830, Συμβ. Ανδρέας Δαβίδ, Κατάστιχα 7–16, 1830–24/1/1835, Λυτά έγγραφα 1835–1862. Συλλογή Ιστορικού Αρχείου Κυκλάδων, Συμβ. Κων. Αγγελίδης, Ευρετήρια, 1–5, 1854–1863, Συμβ. Αντώνιος Αλμπέρτος, Ευρετήρια 1–2, 1853–1864, Συμβ. Μιχ. Ιωάννόπουλος, Ευρ. 1–2, 1843–1845, Συμβ. Χρ. Ιωάννου Ευρ. 1–10, 1846–1860. I/Ναυπηγικά, 1836–1866.
For the years 1867–70: processed data from: Harlaftis – Vlassopoulos, *Historical Register 'Pontoporeia'.* For the years 1871–1880: Foreign Office/Annual Series, *Diplomatic & Consular Reports on Trade & Finance, Greece, Syros,* 1871–1880.
In italics are referred figures from exiguous sample of one vessel for the years 1859, 1860 and 1861 and three vessels in 1862.

APPENDIX 3.6 *Account of construction costs of the brig* Koletis, *from* Archive du Ministère des Affaires Étrangères, Correspondence Consulaire et Commerciale, *SYRA, 3, 20/4/1849, 267–69*

Compte des Frais de Construction et d'Armement de Navire le Colette, jaugeant 342 Tonneaux, Construit en 1847 à Syra par le Scieur J. Pagidas Constructeur.
[Construction and fitting costs of the vessel *Koletis* 342 tons, built in 1847 by the sawyer I. Pagidas builder.]

Construction de la Coque [Construction of the hull]

—Bois— [Timber]

478 Couples (frames) *à 3 d 20. 1529 Δ. 60 lepta.*
479 « « 3. 90. 1868 10 Drach. lepta.
103 Courbes. (Knees) *401. 70.*
Guirlandes (Breast hooks) and (inner sternpost) *=Σκορπιός 274.40*
Total.....................4073.80

500 bordages=(strakes)*=de Madalie à 5 ½ 2750*
324 « « de Tzanakalesci à 9. 2916 5666
32 bréecintes= (wales)*= « à 14 ½ 464*
15 « « « à 20 300 764
4 pièces de quille= (pieces of keel)*=de Kiobata à 200 800*
5 « « « à 104 ½ 522 25.
5 « « « à 125 625
1 « « de Karagatsi à 100 100
1 mèche de gouvernail.................200 200 2247 25.
[rudder]
5 bois droits, provenant de Xéros.......159
[straight timbers from Xiros of Thrace]
145 « « « « 4488
30 « « « « 1002
17 « « « « ....687 20.
30 « « « « Thassos.......1080 7413 20.
[island of Thasos]
42 Epontilles=(stachions)*..................214*
39 « 351 565
12 tritoires de pameaux= (hatches)*........79 50 79. 50*

Planches et autres bois de petits dimensions. . .348 50. <u>*348 50*</u>
[planks and other small timbers]

Totaux. . . . .<u>*20157. 25*</u>
[Total]

Report 20157
à retrancher pour rente de bois inutiles. 410
Reste, total net du prix du Bois. 20660
[net cost of timber]

—*Main d' oeuvre*— [Labor]

1819 ½ journées de charpentiers=Πελεκάνοι [sic]*: 12466 65.*
[carpenters wages]
456 « *de pesceuter* = Clenchers=*. . . . . .2187* *45.*
84 ½ « *de scieurs de long*= Sawyers=*896 70.*
214 « *de calefats*=Caulkers= *2037 70.* <u>*17588*</u>
Total. . . .2574 journées *dont 712 (. . . . .)*

—*Cloux et Fers*— [Nails and Iron]

7849 *oques de cloux à 66 lepta l' oque. . . . . . . .518034.*
[nails cost 66 lepta per *oka*=1.282 kg]
1123 « « « « *1499 55.*
105 « *de chaînes de haubans*=shrouds= *131.*
326 « *de Galhauban*=backstays *259. 31.*
92 ½ « *de petit chaînes. 100* *7170*
[small chains]
562 « *chevilles en cuivre*=nails *2196 10.*
91 ½ « *de cuivre pour le Gouvernail. 366*
[brass nails for the rudder]
Main d' oeuvre *60* *2622*
[Labor]

—*Goudron Etuppe*— [Pitch, oakum]

1425 oques de Goudron et Résine. 251 27
[Okas of pitch and resin]
200 « *d' Etouppe. 99 94* *351*
[oakum]
8970 *chevilles en bois*=timber nails*. 308*

Salaires du Constructeur. 1200
[builder's wages]

Cadeaux en même.......................351 90
[gift to the builder]
Salaires des matelots surveillantes.......1124 55
[wages of watchmen]
frais de nourriture de même................674 60 *1799*
[Food expenses of watchmen]
Total des frais de Construction de la coque..........52055
[Total cost of the hull]

Agrès et Apparaux
[Rigging and equipment]

59 ½ quintaux de cordages=Ropes from *Trieste....3470 73*
40 ½ « « de Hanott......2577 95 6178 37
2 ½ « de bitord=Spun yarn from *Trieste.......129 69*
2 chaines anglaises pesant 132 quintaux............4203 98
[English chains weighing 132 quintals]
3 ancres « « 34 «............1457 5660 98
[anchors weighing 34 quintals]
2 *Mât, y compris la main d'oeuvre.............1212*
[Masts, labor costs included]
Droits de Douane et Nolis des dits mate.........768 88 1980 88
[Custom duties and freights of the above mentioned masts]
Poulies=Pulleys. *Barces de* (......) *1158*
(*Κορζεταις*)
frais de mâture................706 1844
[masting costs]
15 pièces de toile de Malte par voiles...........1392 92
[cloth pieces from Malta for sails]
9 « « de Bonagousta............1000
4 « « de Hanott.................308 2700 92
façon des voiles..................................263 55
[sails making]
1 guindeau, Μανιβέλον.........................1100
frais de mise en place.......................228 1328
[Placement costs]
4 écubiers=Hawse..................................*178 80 178 80*
7 bariques à eau...506 23
[water barels]
Peintures diverses....................................285 60
[Paintings]

fer blanc pour double les soutes à (.....) 297 83
[tinplates for sheathing the hold...]
fil à voile et cordeaux....................................380 10
[ropes for sails and mooring]
Emménagement du porte et de la chambre.............1009 90
[Division of door and chamber]

Total des frais d'achat d'agrès..........................22615 16
[total costs of rigging]

Dépenses diverses
[Various expenses]

Nolis et portefaix..727 54
[freight and port dues]
1 *habitacle*=binnacle.................................39 20
3 *j'ai d'ancre*=tow................................100
Pavillon...50
[flag]
Couronnement=Πρύμη et figure........................196
[stern and figure head]
4 *guirlandes*=Breast hooks...........................169 70
Droits divers...455 02 1009 92
[various dues]
Dépenses pour le 1er *voyage, vivres,* (...).......................1278 95
[maiden voyage expenses, food supplies (...)]
Total des dépenses diverses..............................3010 39
[total of different expenses]

Récapitulation:
[recapitulation]

Compte de frais pour la coque..............................52058 Δ 59 lepta
[hull costs]
« « *les agrès*.................................22615 15
[« « rigging costs]
« *des dépenses diverses*...................................3010 39
[« other costs]

Total général...77684 14
[general total]

Chapter 4—The Production Process

APPENDIX 4.1 *Ship types 1828–66*

	Brig	Goleta	Schooner	Two-Masted	Polacca	Schooner-Brig	Gabara (Barque)	Karavi	Nava (full rigged ship)
1828	5	–	–	–	–	1	–	1	–
1829	12	1	–	–	–	3	–	–	–
1830	16	–	–	–	–	–	–	–	–
1831	6	–	1	–	–	–	–	1	–
1832	6	4	–	5	–	–	–	1	–
1833	19	4	–	11	–	1	3	1	–
1834	22	4	–	–	–	–	–	–	–
1835	5	11	–	–	1	1	–	–	–
1836	7	10	–	–	–	–	–	–	–
1837	8	8	–	–	–	–	–	–	–
1838	37	3	–	–	–	–	1	–	–
1839	39	1	–	–	–	–	1	–	–
1840	64	2	–	–	–	–	–	–	–
1841	38	6	–	–	–	–	–	–	1
1842	12	8	–	–	–	–	–	–	–
1843	24	8	–	–	–	–	–	1	–
1844	41	5	–	–	–	–	–	–	–
1845	51	8	–	–	–	–	–	1	–
1846	58	7	–	–	–	–	1	–	–
1847	64	–	–	–	–	–	1	–	–
1848	67	5	–	–	–	–	–	–	–
1849	57	15	–	–	–	–	–	–	–
1850	43	16	–	–	–	–	–	–	–
1851	26	25	–	–	–	–	–	–	–
1852	26	14	–	–	–	1	–	–	–
1853	30	9	–	–	–	1	–	–	–
1854	23	2	–	–	–	–	2	–	–
1855	36	11	–	–	–	–	2	–	–

	Brig	Goleta	Schooner	Two-Masted	Polacca	Schooner-Brig	Gabara (Barque)	Karavi	Nava (full rigged ship)
1856	49	16	–	–	–	–	1	–	–
1857	60	28	2	–	–	–	–	–	–
1858	29	10	–	–	–	–	–	–	–
1859	14	7	–	–	–	–	–	–	–
1860	21	9	–	–	–	–	–	–	–
1861	13	3	–	–	–	–	1	–	–
1862	17	–	–	–	–	–	1	–	–
1863	26	4	–	–	–	–	2	–	–
1864	*19*	*9*	*1*	–	–	–	*3*	–	–
1865	*24*	*7*	–	–	–	–	*1*	–	–
1866	40	13	2	–	–	–	3	–	–

Year	Bombarda	Bratsera	Martingana	Tserniki	Fishing Tserniki
1828	–	–	–	–	–
1829	–	–	–	–	–
1830	–	–	1	–	–
1831	–	–	1	1	–
1832	–	–	–	1	–
1833	–	–	1	1	–
1834	1	–	1	–	–
1835	–	1	1	9	–
1836	1	–	1	10	–
1837	–	–	–	10	–
1838	–	–	–	9	–
1839	–	–	–	–	–
1840	–	–	–	2	–
1841	1	–	–	10	–
1842	3	–	–	–	–
1843	6	1	–	7	–
1844	15	–	–	5	–
1845	12	2	–	4	–
1846	11	1	–	2	1
1847	1	–	–	5	–
1848	12	1	–	3	–
1849	8	3	–	1	–
1850	19	11	–	1	1
1851	8	11	–	3	2
1852	–	8	–	5	3
1853	4	1	–	1	–
1854	1	1	–	–	–
1855	4	1	–	2	–
1856	6	2	–	3	–
1857	4	6	–	5	–
1858	10	5	–	4	1
1859	9	10	–	15	–
1860	2	5	–	12	–
1861	2	2	–	3	–
1862	3	–	–	2	–
1863	3	1	–	3	–
1864	*5*	–	–	2	–
1865	*4*	–	–	–	–
1866	1	2	–	–	–

Cutter	Trehandiri	Sacoleva	Sacoleva/Martigos	Sacoleva/Bombarda	Tserniki/Martigos
–	–	–	–	–	–
–	–	–	–	–	–
2	–	–	–	–	–
1	–	–	1	–	–
1	–	–	–	–	1
2	–	–	–	–	–
1	–	–	–	–	–
15	–	12	–	–	–
10	–	2	–	–	–
–	–	1	–	1	–
–	–	2	–	–	–
–	–	–	–	–	–
–	1	1	–	–	–
–	3	1	–	–	–
–	–	5	–	–	–
–	1	1	–	–	–
1	–	2	–	–	–
–	2	1	–	–	–
–	1	1	–	–	–
–	–	–	–	–	–
–	–	1	–	–	–
–	2	–	–	–	–
–	5	1	–	–	–
–	–	1	–	–	–
–	4	–	–	–	–
–	–	–	–	–	–
–	1	–	–	–	–
–	1	–	–	–	–
–	–	–	–	–	–
–	4	1	–	–	–
–	4	1	–	–	–
–	2	2	–	–	–
–	10	–	–	–	–
–	3	1	–	–	–
–	3	–	–	–	–
–	1	–	–	–	–
–	–	–	–	–	–
–	–	–	–	–	–
–	1	1	–	–	–

Year	Lotika	Trabacolo	Mistico	Bellou	Malteza	Trata	Lateener	Feluca	Boat
1828	–	–	–	–	–	–	–	–	–
1829	–	–	–	–	–	–	–	–	–
1830	–	–	–	–	–	–	–	–	–
1831	–	–	–	–	–	–	–	–	–
1832	–	–	–	–	–	–	–	–	–
1833	–	–	–	–	–	–	–	–	–
1834	–	–	–	–	–	–	–	–	–
1835	–	–	–	–	1	–	–	1	–
1836	–	–	2	–	–	–	–	–	–
1837	–	1	–	–	–	–	–	–	–
1838	–	–	–	–	–	1	–	–	–
1839	–	–	–	–	–	–	–	–	–
1840	1	–	–	–	–	1	–	–	3
1841	–	–	1	–	–	1	–	–	–
1842	–	–	–	–	–	–	–	–	–
1843	–	–	–	1	–	3	–	–	5
1844	–	–	–	–	–	–	–	–	2
1845	–	–	–	1	2	–	–	–	1
1846	–	–	–	–	1	1	1	–	2
1847	–	–	–	–	–	–	–	–	–
1848	–	–	–	–	–	–	–	–	1
1849	–	–	–	1	1	1	–	–	4
1850	–	–	–	–	1	–	–	–	3
1851	–	–	–	2	1	–	–	–	–
1852	–	–	–	2	2	1	–	1	4
1853	3	–	–	–	–	–	–	–	–
1854	–	–	–	–	–	–	–	–	1
1855	–	–	–	–	–	1	–	–	3
1856	–	–	–	–	1	–	–	–	1
1857	–	–	–	–	–	–	–	–	2
1858	–	–	–	–	–	–	–	–	3
1859	–	–	–	1	1	–	–	–	2
1860	–	–	–	–	–	1	–	–	8
1861	–	–	–	–	–	2	–	–	2
1862	–	–	–	–	–	–	–	–	1
1863	–	–	–	1	–	–	–	–	–
1864	–	–	–	–	–	–	–	–	–
1865	–	–	–	–	–	–	–	–	2
1866	–	–	–	–	–	–	–	–	–

Year	Tug	Skabavia Boat	Pontoon	Unknown	Steamship	Biga	Slepi	Total
1828	–	–	–	–	–	–	–	7
1829	–	–	–	–	–	–	–	17
1830	–	1	–	–	–	–	–	20
1831	–	–	–	–	–	–	–	12
1832	–	–	–	–	–	–	–	19
1833	–	–	–	–	–	–	–	43
1834	–	–	–	–	–	–	–	29
1835	–	–	–	–	–	–	–	58
1836	–	–	–	–	–	–	–	43
1837	–	–	–	–	–	–	–	29
1838	–	–	–	1	–	–	–	54
1839	–	–	–	–	–	–	–	41
1840	–	–	–	–	–	–	–	75
1841	–	–	–	–	–	–	–	63
1842	–	–	–	–	–	–	–	31
1843	–	–	–	–	–	–	–	60
1844	–	–	–	–	–	–	–	73
1845	–	–	–	–	–	–	–	85
1846	–	–	–	–	–	–	–	89
1847	–	–	–	–	–	–	–	71
1848	–	–	1	–	–	–	–	91
1849	1	–	–	–	–	–	–	96
1850	–	–	–	–	–	–	–	102
1851	–	–	–	–	–	–	–	80
1852	–	1	–	1	–	–	–	73
1853	–	–	–	–	–	–	–	50
1854	1	–	–	–	1	–	–	37
1855	–	–	–	–	–	1	–	63
1856	–	–	–	–	–	–	–	81
1857	4	–	–	–	–	–	–	116
1858	2	–	–	1	–	–	2	74
1859	–	–	–	–	–	–	–	65
1860	–	–	–	2	–	–	–	72
1861	–	–	–	–	–	–	–	35
1862	–	–	–	–	–	–	–	27
1863	2	–	–	–	–	–	2	50
1864	–	–	–	–	–	–	*1*	*40*
1865	–	–	–	–	–	–	–	*39*
1866	–	–	–	–	–	–	–	63

Source: Processed data for the years 1828–66 from GSA, Syros, Αρχείο Συμβολαιογράφου Μάξιμου Ταλασλή, Συμβ. Σκαρλάτος Μάξιμος, Κατάστιχα 1–6, 1827–1830, Συμβ. Ανδρέας Δαβίδ, Κατάστιχα 7–16, 1830–24/1/1835, Λυτά έγγραφα 1835–1862. Συλλογή Ιστορικού Αρχείου Κυκλάδων, Συμβ. Κων. Αγγελίδης, Ευρετήρια, 1–5, 1854–1863, Συμβ. Αντώνιος Αλμπέρτος, Ευρετήρια 1–2, 1853–1864, Συμβ. Μιχ. Ιωάννόπουλος, Ευρ. 1–2, 1843–1845, Συμβ. Χρ. Ιωάννου Ευρ. 1–10, 1846–1860. I/Ναυπηγικά, 1836–1866.
For the years 1864 and 1865: from Vassilis Kardasis *Σύρος*, Table 25, 180–81.

APPENDIX 4.2 *Share of vessels built according their ship type, 1828–66*

Vessel Type	Number of vessels	%	Tonnage	%
Brig	1154	53.11	231,892.8	81.46
Goleta	293	13.48	20,800.66	7.31
Bombarda	156	7.18	7440.97	2.61
Tserniki	141	6.49	2465.89	0.87
Bratsera	75	3.45	2195.29	0.77
Boat	50	2.30	111.87	0.04
Trehandiri	49	2.25	583.93	0.21
Sacoleva	38	1.75	1162.97	0.41
Perama	36	1.66	583.69	0.21
Cutter	33	1.52	1809.37	0.64
Gabara (Barque)	23	1.06	6982.28	2.45
Two-Masted	16	0.74	2634.55	0.93
Trata	13	0.60	95.6	0.03
Malteza	11	0.51	209.61	0.07
Tug	10	0.46	214.3	0.08
Schooner-Brig	9	0.41	958.04	0.34
Bellou	9	0.41	126.86	0.04
Fishing Tserniki	8	0.37	28.99	0.01
Schooner	6	0.28	408.6	0.14
Karavi	6	0.28	1157.46	0.41
Martingana	6	0.28	232.14	0.08
Unknown	5	0.23	–	–
Slepi	5	0.23	806	0.28
Lotika	4	0.18	703.67	0.25
Mistico	3	0.14	38.98	0.01
Feluca	2	0.09	17.48	0.01
Skabavia Boat	2	0.09	9.62	0.003

Vessel Type	Number of vessels	%	Tonnage	%
Polacca	1	0.05	120	0.04
Nava (Full Rigged Ship)	1	0.05	556	0.20
Sacoleva/Martigos	1	0.05	27.79	0.01
Sacoleva/Bombarda	1	0.05	34.18	0.01
Tserniki/Martigos	1	0.05	49	0.02
Trabacolo	1	0.05	87.61	0.03
Lateener	1	0.05	11.29	0.00
Pontoon	1	0.05	82.36	0.03
Steamship	1	0.05	43.97	0.02
Biga	1	0.05		
Total	2173	100.00	284,683.9	100.00

Sources: Processed data from GSA, Syros, Αρχείο Συμβολαιογράφου Μάξιμου Ταλασλή, Συμβ. Σκαρλάτος Μάξιμος, Κατάστιχα 1–6, 1827–1830, Συμβ. Ανδρέας Δαβίδ, Κατάστιχα 7–16, 1830–24/1/1835, Λυτά έγγραφα 1835–1862. Συλλογή Ιστορικού Αρχείου Κυκλάδων, Συμβ. Κων. Αγγελίδης, Ευρετήρια, 1–5, 1854–1863, Συμβ. Αντώνιος Αλμπέρτος, Ευρετήρια 1–2, 1853–1864, Συμβ. Μιχ. Ιωάννόπουλος, Ευρ. 1–2, 1843–1845, Συμβ. Χρ. Ιωάννου Ευρ. 1–10, 1846–1860. I/Ναυπηγικά, 1836–1866.

Chapter 5—Demand: Shipowners and Investors

APPENDIX 5.1 *Investors from Syros – Hermoupolis, 1828–1866*

Place of origin	Number of investors	% General total	% Total of Hermoupolis
Amfissa (Central Greece)	3	0.12	0.29
Anafi (Cyclades)	1	0.04	0.10
Andros (Cyclades)	4	0.17	0.39
Ano Syros (Cyclades)	12	0.50	1.18
Areopoli (Peloponnese)	2	0.08	0.20
Argos (Peloponnese)	1	0.04	0.10
Cephalonia (Ionian Islands)	10	0.42	0.98
Chios (Eastern Aegean)	303	12.59	29.71
Constantinople	3	0.12	0.29
Corfu (Ionian Islands)	1	0.04	0.10

APPENDIX 5.1 *Investors from Syros – Hermoupolis, 1828–1866* (cont.)

Place of origin	Number of investors	% General total	% Total of Hermoupolis
Corsica (France)	1	0.04	0.10
Crete	14	0.58	1.37
Efesos (Turkey)	2	0.08	0.20
Enos (Enez-Turkey)	7	0.29	0.69
Hermoupolis (Cyclades)	201	8.35	19.71
Hydra (sw Aegean)	27	1.12	2.65
Illyria	1	0.04	0.10
Ioannina (Epirus)	2	0.08	0.20
Ionian Islands	1	0.04	0.10
Kalamata (Peloponnese)	1	0.04	0.10
Karystos (Euboea)	1	0.04	0.10
Kasos (Dodecanese)	2	0.08	0.20
Kastellorizo (Dodecanese)	3	0.12	0.29
Kesareia (Kayseri-Turkey)	1	0.04	0.10
Koytali (Sea of Marmara)	1	0.04	0.10
Kranidi (Peloponnese)	1	0.04	0.10
Kydonies (Aivali-Turkey)	6	0.25	0.59
Kynouria (Peloponnese)	1	0.04	0.10
Kythira (Ionian Islands)	2	0.08	0.20
Kythnos (Cyclades)	1	0.04	0.10
Lakonia (Peloponnese)	3	0.12	0.29
Lamia (Central Greece)	2	0.08	0.20
Leonidio (Peloponnese)	1	0.04	0.10
Leros (Dodecanese)	15	0.62	1.47
Lesvos (NE Aegean)	4	0.17	0.39
Limnos (NE Aegean)	10	0.42	0.98
Macedonia	2	0.08	0.20
Megara (Attica)	1	0.04	0.10
Moschonisia (Ayvalik Islands-Turkey)	9	0.37	0.88
Mykonos (Cyclades)	3	0.12	0.29
Nafplio (Peloponnese)	1	0.04	0.10
Naxos (Cyclades)	2	0.08	0.20
Paros (Cyclades)	1	0.04	0.10
Patmos (Dodecanese)	3	0.12	0.29
Peloponnese	1	0.04	0.10

Place of origin	Number of investors	% General total	% Total of Hermoupolis
Psara (Eastern Aegean)	291	12.09	28.53
Rhodes (Dodecanese)	1	0.04	0.10
Samos (SE Aegean)	10	0.42	0.98
Santorini (Cyclades)	1	0.04	0.10
Serres (Macedonia)	1	0.04	0.10
Sifnos (Cyclades)	2	0.08	0.20
Skiathos (Northern Sporades)	2	0.08	0.20
Skyros (Northern Sporades)	1	0.04	0.10
Smyrna (Turkey)	21	0.87	2.06
Sparti (Peloponnese)	1	0.04	0.10
Thessaloniki (Macedonia)	3	0.12	0.29
Tinos (Cyclades)	4	0.17	0.39
Tripoli (Peloponnese)	1	0.04	0.10
Tsesme (Cesme Turkey)	2	0.08	0.20
Zagora (Thessaly)	5	0.21	0.49
Total	1020	42.39	100.00

Sources: processed data from GSA, Syros, Αρχείο Συμβολαιογράφου Μάξιμου Ταλασλή, Συμβ. Σκαρλάτος Μάξιμος, Κατάστιχα 1–6, 1827–1830, Συμβ. Ανδρέας Δαβίδ, Κατάστιχα 7–16, 1830–24/1/1835, Λυτά έγγραφα 1835–1862. Συλλογή Ιστορικού Αρχείου Κυκλάδων, Συμβ. Κων. Αγγελίδης, Ευρετήρια, 1–5, 1854 1863, Συμβ. Αντώνιος Αλμπέρτος, Ευρετήρια 1–2, 1853–1864, Συμβ. Μιχ. Ιωάννόπουλος, Ευρ. 1–2, 1843–1845, Συμβ. Χρ. Ιωάννου Ευρ. 1–10, 1846–1860. Ι/Ναυπηγικά, 1836–1866.

APPENDIX 5.2 *Investors outside Syros – Hermoupolis, 1828–1866*

Place of origin	Number of investors	% General total	% Total of Hermoupolis
Adramyttion (Edremit-Turkey)	1	0.04	0.10
Alexandria (Egypt)	1	0.04	0.10
Amaliapolis/Mitzela (Thessaly)	11	0.46	1.10
Amorgos (Cyclades)	4	0.17	0.40
Anafi (Cyclades)	1	0.04	0.10
Andros (Cyclades)	130	5.40	13.01
Archagelos of Monemvasia (Peloponnese)	1	0.04	0.10
Areopoli (Peloponnese)	2	0.08	0.20

APPENDIX 5.2 *Investors outside Syros – Hermoupolis, 1828–1866* (cont.)

Place of origin	Number of investors	% General total	% Total of Hermoupolis
Athens (Central Greece)	4	0.17	0.40
Athens living, Psara origin	2	0.08	0.20
Ayvali (Turkey)	1	0.04	0.10
Bavaria (Germany)	1	0.04	0.10
Berdiansk (Ukraine)	2	0.08	0.20
Cairo (Egypt)	1	0.04	0.10
Cephalonia (Ionian Islands)	39	1.62	3.90
Chalkida (Euboea)	9	0.37	0.90
Chios (Eastern Aegean)	21	0.87	2.10
Constantinople	26	1.08	2.60
Constantinople living, Chios origin	4	0.17	0.40
Corfu (Ionian Islands)	1	0.04	0.10
Crete	21	0.87	2.10
Cyprus	3	0.12	0.30
Dalmatia (Croatia)	1	0.04	0.10
Egina (Saronic Gulf)	1	0.04	0.10
Egina living, Chios origin	1	0.04	0.10
Erithrea	1	0.04	0.10
Ermioni (Peloponesse)	4	0.17	0.40
Eypatoria (Crimea)	1	0.04	0.10
Fokea (Phocaea-Turkey)	1	0.04	0.10
Folegandros (Cyclades)	1	0.04	0.10
Galatz (Romania)	1	0.04	0.10
Galaxidi (Gulf of Patras)	12	0.50	1.20
Gytheio (Peloponesse)	1	0.04	0.10
Hydra (Argolic Gulf)	121	5.03	12.11
Hydra living, Sifnos origin	1	0.04	0.10
Ikaria (Cyclades)	3	0.12	0.30
Ios (Cyclades)	4	0.17	0.40
Ismaili (Moldova)	1	0.04	0.10
Ithaki (Ionian Islands)	18	0.75	1.80
Kantila Akarnanias (Western Greece)	1	0.04	0.10
Kasos (Dodecanese)	3	0.12	0.30
Kastellorizo (Dodecanese)	2	0.08	0.20
Kastri	1	0.04	0.10

Place of origin	Number of investors	% General total	% Total of Hermoupolis
Kea (Cyclades)	4	0.17	0.40
Kimi (Euboea)	4	0.17	0.40
Kimolos (Cyclades)	12	0.50	1.20
Koroni (Peloponnese)	1	0.04	0.10
Koutali (Sea of Marmara)	2	0.08	0.20
Kranidi (Peloponnese)	14	0.58	1.40
Kydonies (Aivali-Turkey)	3	0.12	0.30
Kythira (Ionian Islands)	16	0.67	1.60
Kythnos (Cyclades)	12	0.50	1.20
Leonidio (Peloponnese)	1	0.04	0.10
Leros (Dodecanese)	6	0.25	0.60
Lesvos (NE Aegean)	5	0.21	0.50
Limni (Euboea)	22	0.91	2.20
Limnos (NE Aegean)	12	0.50	1.20
Livorno (Italy)	1	0.04	0.10
London	1	0.04	0.10
Mahon (Spain)	1	0.04	0.10
Mariupol (Ukraine)	1	0.04	0.10
Massitos	1	0.04	0.10
Messolonghi (Gulf of Patras)	1	0.04	0.10
Milos (Cyclades)	20	0.83	2.00
Milos (Cyclades) living, Crete origin	1	0.04	0.10
Monemvasia (Peloponesse)	1	0.04	0.10
Moshonisia (Ayvalik Islands-Turkey)	3	0.12	0.30
Mount Athos	1	0.04	0.10
Mykonos (Cyclades)	41	1.70	4.10
Mykonos living, Zakynthos origin	1	0.04	0.10
Nafplio (Peloponnese)	7	0.29	0.70
Nafplio living, Chios origin	1	0.04	0.10
Naxos (Cyclades)	10	0.42	1.00
Odessa (Ukraine)	8	0.33	0.80
Ottoman Empire	1	0.04	0.10
Paros (Cyclades)	28	1.16	2.80
Patmos (Dodecanese)	4	0.17	0.40
Patras (Peloponesse)	1	0.04	0.10
Piraeus (Attica)	6	0.25	0.60
Poros (Saronic Gulf)	14	0.58	1.40

APPENDIX 5.2 *Investors outside Syros – Hermoupolis, 1828–1866* (cont.)

Place of origin	Number of investors	% General total	% Total of Hermoupolis
Psara (Eastern Aegean)	16	0.67	1.60
Rensk (Moldova)	1	0.04	0.10
Russia	4	0.17	0.40
Salamina (Saronic Gulf)	1	0.04	0.10
Samos (SE Aegean)	10	0.42	1.00
Santorini (Cyclades)	68	2.83	6.81
Sardegna (Italy) living, Chania (Crete) origin	1	0.04	0.10
Serifos (Cyclades)	2	0.08	0.20
Sifnos (Cyclades)	14	0.58	1.40
Sifnos (Cyclades) living, Crete origin	1	0.04	0.10
Skiathos (Northern Sporades)	1	0.04	0.10
Skopelos (Northern Sporades)	3	0.12	0.30
Skyros (Northern Sporades)	3	0.12	0.30
Smyrna (Turkey)	6	0.25	0.60
Sokia (Söke-Turkey)	1	0.04	0.10
Sparti (Peloponnese)	1	0.04	0.10
Spetses (Argolic Gulf)	42	1.75	4.20
Stylida (Central Greece)	4	0.17	0.40
Taganrog (Russia)	4	0.17	0.40
Tenedos (Turkey)	2	0.08	0.20
Thessaloniki (Macedonia)	4	0.17	0.40
Tinos (Cyclades)	43	1.79	4.30
Trieste (Italy)	6	0.25	0.60
Trikeri (Thessaly)	7	0.29	0.70
Tsesme (Cesme-Turkey)	6	0.25	0.60
Volos (Thessaly)	2	0.08	0.20
Vraila (Braila-Romania)	6	0.25	0.60
Zakynthos (Ionian Islands)	6	0.25	0.60
Total	999	41.52	100.00

Sources: Processed data from GSA, Syros, Αρχείο Συμβολαιογράφου Μάξιμου Ταλασλή, Συμβ. Σκαρλάτος Μάξιμος, Κατάστιχα 1–6, 1827–1830, Συμβ. Ανδρέας Δαβίδ, Κατάστιχα 7–16, 1830–24/1/1835, Λυτά έγγραφα 1835–1862. Συλλογή Ιστορικού Αρχείου Κυκλάδων, Συμβ. Κων. Αγγελίδης, Ευρετήρια, 1–5, 1854–1863, Συμβ. Αντώνιος Αλμπέρτος, Ευρετήρια 1–2, 1853–1864, Συμβ. Μιχ. Ιωάννόπουλος, Ευρ. 1–2, 1843–1845, Συμβ. Χρ. Ιωάννου Ευρ. 1–10, 1846–1860. Ι/Ναυπηγικά, 1836–1866.

APPENDIX 5.3 *Tonnage owned by investors according their place of origin, 1828–1866*

Place of origin	Tonnage owned	% of the Total tonnage
Adramyttion (Edremit-Turkey)	41.5	0.02
Alexandria (Egypt)	15	0.01
Amaliapolis/Mitzela (Thessaly)	1458.80	0.53
Amfissa origin, Hermoupolis living	452.27	0.16
Amorgos (Cyclades)	47.19	0.02
Anafi (Cyclades)	10.00	0.00
Anafi origin, Hermoupolis living	96.00	0.03
Andros (Cyclades)	16,580.87	6.01
Andros origin, Hermoupolis living	991.92	0.36
Ano Syros	2474.62	0.90
Archagelos of Monemvasia (Peloponnese)	12.55	0.00
Areopoli (Peloponnese)	13.42	0.00
Areopoli origin, Hermoupolis living	313.30	0.11
Argos origin, Hermoupolis living	104.50	0.04
Athens (Central Greece)	279.03	0.10
Ayvali (Turkey)	11.27	0.00
Bavaria (Germany)	16.43	0.01
Berdiansk (Ukraine)	445.79	0.16
Cairo (Egypt)	170.82	0.06
Cephalonia (Ionian Islands)	6463.73	2.34
Cephalonia origin, Hermoupolis living	705.11	0.26
Chalkida (Euboea)	557.64	0.20
Chios (Eastern Aegean)	2510.97	0.91
Chios origin, Hermoupolis living	43,748.91	15.86
Constantinople	3386.18	1.23
Constantinople origin, Hermoupolis living	40.29	0.01
Corfu (Ionian Islands)	30.74	0.01
Corfu origin, Hermoupolis living	133.28	0.05
Crete	1343.48	0.49
Crete origin, Hermoupolis living	1983.27	0.72
Crete origin, Milos living	2.88	0.00
Crete origin, Sifnos living	2.88	0.00
Cyprus	145.23	0.05
Dalmatia (Croatia)	29.00	0.01
Efesos origin, Hermoupolis living	58.74	0.02

APPENDIX 5.3 *Tonnage owned by investors* (cont.)

Place of origin	Tonnage owned	% of the Total tonnage
Egina (Saronic Gulf)	19.91	0.01
Enos origin, Hermoupolis living	551.52	0.20
Erithrea	119.61	0.04
Ermioni (Peloponesse)	225.09	0.08
Fokea (Phocaea-Turkey)	131.83	0.05
Folegandros (Cyclades) origin, Hermoupolis living	21	0.01
Galatz (Romania)	210.75	0.08
Galaxidi (Gulf of Patras)	1543.99	0.56
Gytheio (Peloponesse)	4.94	0.00
Hermoupolis	21,360.07	7.75
Hydra (Argolic Gulf)	13,372.52	4.85
Hydra living, Sifnos origin	25	0.01
Hydra origin, Hermoupolis living	2757.14	1.00
Ikaria (Cyclades) Ismaili (Moldova)	34.80	0.01
Illyria	5.58	0.00
Ioannina (Epirus) origin, Hermoupolis living	568.22	0.21
Ionian Islands origin, Hermoupolis living	25	0.01
Ios (Cyclades)	247.83	0.09
Ismaili (Moldova)	191.77	0.07
Ithaki (Ionian Islands)	2972.73	1.08
Kalamata (Peloponnese)	15.9	0.01
Kantila Akarnanias (Western Greece)	168.26	0.06
Karystos (Euboea) origin, Hermoupolis living	48.5	0.02
Kasos (Dodecanese)	435	0.16
Kasos origin, Hermoupolis living	88.39	0.03
Kastellorizo (Dodecanese)	137.72	0.05
Kastellorizo origin, Hermoupolis living	376.17	0.14
Kastri	75.5	0.03
Kea (Cyclades)	100.44	0.04
Kimi (Euboea)	126.64	0.05
Kimolos (Cyclades)	358.17	0.13
Koytali (Sea of Marmara)	290.64	0.11
Koytali origin, Hermoupolis living	240	0.09
Kranidi (Peloponnese)	749.66	0.27

Place of origin	Tonnage owned	% of the Total tonnage
Kranidi origin, Hermoupolis living	122	0.04
Kydonies (Aivali-Turkey)	133.2	0.05
Kydonies origin, Hermoupolis living	320.76	0.12
Kynouria (Peloponnese) origin, Hermoupolis living	400	0.15
Kythira (Ionian Islands)	931.52	0.34
Kythira origin, Hermoupolis living	18.5	0.01
Kythnos (Cyclades)	192.65	0.07
Kythnos origin, Hermoupolis living	8.82	0.00
Lakonia (Peloponnese) origin, Hermoupolis living	71.75	0.03
Lamia origin, Hermoupolis living	30.99	0.01
Leonidio (Peloponnese)	57.5	0.02
Leonidio origin, Hermoupolis living	72.5	0.03
Leros (Dodecanese)	145.5	0.05
Leros origin, Hermoupolis living	1348.24	0.49
Lesvos (NE Aegean)	211.5	0.08
Lesvos origin, Hermoupolis living	288.96	0.10
Limni (Euboea)	1436.03	0.52
Limnos (NE Aegean)	1225.34	0.44
Limnos origin, Hermoupolis living	1046.3	0.38
Livorno (Italy)	105	0.04
London (UK)	107.5	0.04
Macedonia origin, Hermoupolis living	126	0.05
Mahon (Spain)	214.21	0.08
Mariupol (Ukraine)	300	0.11
Massitos	51.67	0.02
Megara (Attica) origin, Hermoupolis living	55.4	0.02
Messolonghi (Gulf of Patras)	295	0.11
Milos (Cyclades)	721.84	0.26
Monemvasia (Peloponesse)	57.5	0.02
Moshonisia (Ayvalik Islands-Turkey)	227.05	0.08
Moshonisia origin, Hermoupolis living	441.76	0.16
Mount Athos	32.83	0.01
Mykonos (Cyclades)	6413.75	2.33
Mykonos living, Hermoupolis origin	635.99	0.23
Mykonos living, Zakynthos origin	194	0.07
Nafplio (Peloponnese)	598.93	0.22

APPENDIX 5.3 *Tonnage owned by investors* (cont.)

Place of origin	Tonnage owned	% of the Total tonnage
Naxos (Cyclades)	293.68	0.11
Naxos living, Hermoupolis origin	46.57	0.02
Odessa (Ukraine)	2215.93	0.80
Ottoman Empire	214.21	0.08
Paros (Cyclades)	569.26	0.21
Paros living, Hermoupolis origin	5.74	0.00
Patmos (Dodecanese)	205.11	0.07
Patmos living, Hermoupolis origin	512.63	0.19
Patras (Peloponesse)	62	0.02
Peloponesse living, Hermoupolis origin	157.44	0.06
Piraeus (Attica)	239.2	0.09
Poros (Saronic Gulf)	404.78	0.15
Psara (Eastern Aegean)	4966.79	1.80
Psara origin, Athens living	331.78	0.12
Psara origin, Hermoupolis living	58,530.08	21.22
Rensk (Moldova)	82	0.03
Rhodes (Hermoupolis)	126	0.05
Russia	1316.25	0.48
Russia origin, Constantinople living	178.93	0.06
Salamina (Saronic Gulf)	51	0.02
Samos (SE Aegean)	620.71	0.23
Samos origin, Braila living	12.11	0.00
Samos origin, Hermoupolis living	1222.58	0.44
Santorini (Cyclades)	9916.85	3.60
Santorini origin, Hermoupolis living	75.50	0.03
Sardegna (Italy), Chania (Crete) origin	237.61	0.09
Serifos (Cyclades)	8	0.00
Serres (Macedonia) origin, Hermoupolis living	181.3	0.07
Sifnos (Cyclades)	838.6	0.30
Sifnos origin, Hermoupolis oiving	75.87	0.03
Skiathos (Northern Sporades)	58.66	0.02
Skiathos origin, Hermoupolis living	34.06	0.01
Skopelos (Northern Sporades)	2.58	0.00
Skyros (Northern Sporades)	38	0.01

Place of origin	Tonnage owned	% of the Total tonnage
Skyros origin, Hermoupolis living	32.01	0.01
Smyrna (Turkey)	1117.35	0.41
Smyrna origin, Hermoupolis living	2418.64	0.88
Sokia (Söke-Turkey)	47.53	0.02
Sparti (Peloponnese)	5.69	0.00
Sparti origin, Hermoupolis living	109.12	0.04
Spetses (Argolic Gulf)	5608.99	2.03
Stylida (Central Greece)	109.87	0.04
Taganrock (Russia)	1270.33	0.46
Tenedos (Turkey)	44	0.02
Thessaloniki (Macedonia)	238.42	0.09
Thessaloniki origin, Hermoupolis living	510.77	0.19
Tinos (Cyclades)	2579.87	0.94
Tinos origin, Hermoupolis living	720.67	0.26
Trieste (Italy)	1110.6	0.40
Trikeri (Thessaly)	633.97	0.23
Tsesme (Cesme-Turkey)	281.86	0.10
Tsesme origin, Hermoupolis living	76.06	0.03
Volos (Thessaly)	94.36	0.03
Vraila (Braila-Romania)	953.03	0.35
Zagora (Thessaly) origin, Hermoupolis living	979.23	0.36
Zakynthos (Ionian Islands)	712.72	0.26
Total	254,405.29	92.25

Sources: Processed data from GSA, Syros, Αρχείο Συμβολαιογράφου Μάξιμου Ταλασλή, Συμβ. Σκαρλάτος Μάξιμος, Κατάστιχα 1–6, 1827–1830, Συμβ. Ανδρέας Δαβίδ, Κατάστιχα 7–16, 1830–24/1/1835, Λυτά έγγραφα 1835–1862. Συλλογή Ιστορικού Αρχείου Κυκλάδων, Συμβ. Κων. Αγγελίδης, Ευρετήρια, 1–5, 1854–1863, Συμβ. Αντώνιος Αλμπέρτος, Ευρετήρια 1–2, 1853–1864, Συμβ. Μιχ. Ιωάννόπουλος, Ευρ. 1–2, 1843–1845, Συμβ. Χρ. Ιωάννου Ευρ. 1–10, 1846–1860. Ι/Ναυπηγικά, 1836–1866.

APPENDIX 5.4 *Value of tonnage owned by investors according their place of origin, 1828–1866*

Place of origin	Value of tonnage (in drachmas)	% total value	Tonnage corresponding to the indicated value	% tonnage
Adramyttion (Edremit-Turkey)	10,292	0.03	41.5	0.02
Alexandria (Egypt)	2437.5	0.01	15	0.01
Amaliapolis/Mitzela (Thessaly)	250,200	0.67	1228.8	0.63
Amfissa origin, Hermoupolis living	960,00	0.26	445.51	0.23
Amorgos (Cyclades)	3110	0.01	40.02	0.02
Anafi (Cyclades)	1400	0.00	10	0.01
Andros (Cyclades)	2,708,707.65	7.30	12,504.86	6.44
Andros origin Hermoupolis living	137,250	0.37	776.68	0.40
Ano Syros	159,221	0.43	865.03	0.45
Archagelos of Monemvasia (Peloponnese)	1200	0.00	12.55	0.01
Areopoli (Peloponnese) origin, Hermoupolis living	494,96	0.13	293.99	0.15
Athens (Central Greece)	70,000	0.19	279.03	0.14
Bavaria (Germany)	4500	0.01	16.43	0.01
Berdiansk (Ukraine)	80,100	0.22	445.79	0.23
Cairo (Egypt)	20,250	0.05	170.82	0.09
Cephalonia (Ionian Islands)	656,379.98	1.77	3431.25	1.77
Cephalonia origin, Hermoupolis living	135,775	0.37	679.43	0.35
Chalkida (Euboea)	78,848.4	0.21	595.69	0.31
Chios (Eastern Aegean)	395,211.4	1.07	2007.78	1.03
Chios origin, Hermoupolis living	7,260,618.16	19.57	35,529.65	18.30
Constantinople	657,150.36	1.77	3344.24	1.72
Corfu (Ionian Islands)	3750	0.01	30.74	0.02

Place of origin	Value of tonnage (in drachmas)	% total value	Tonnage corresponding to the indicated value	% tonnage
Crete	145,264.98	0.39	1233.69	0.64
Crete origin, Hermoupolis living	325,583.33	0.88	1644	0.85
Cyprus	26,000	0.07	145.23	0.07
Dalmatia (Croatia)	5000	0.01	29	0.01
Efesos origin, Hermoupolis living	8166.66	0.02	58.75	0.03
Egina (Saronic Gulf)	4000	0.01	19.91	0.01
Enos origin Hermoupolis living	35,900	0.10	280.78	0.14
Erithrea	14,000	0.04	119.61	0.06
Ermioni (Peloponesse)	40,000	0.11	189	0.10
Fokea (Phocaea-Turkey)	27,000	0.07	131.83	0.07
Folegandros (Cyclades) origin, Hermoupolis living	625	0.00	6	0.00
Galatz (Romania)	38,750	0.10	210.75	0.11
Galaxidi (Gulf of Patras)	284,069.6	0.77	1323.54	0.68
Hermoupolis	3,315,077.87	8.94	18,677.2	9.62
Hydra (Argolic Gulf)	1,560,159.99	4.21	9042.37	4.66
Hydra origin, Hermoupolis living	493,660.66	1.33	2305.52	1.19
Ikaria (Cyclades)	4200	0.01	34.8	0.02
Ioannina (Epirus) origin, Hermoupolis living	57,500	0.16	300.63	0.15
Ionian Islands origin, Hermoupolis living	6250	0.02	50	0.03
Ios (Cyclades)	23,300	0.06	233.48	0.12
Ismaili (Moldova)	24,000	0.06	191.77	0.10
Ithaki (Ionian Islands)	515,800	1.39	2706.97	1.39
Kalamata (Peloponnese) origin, Hermoupolis living	2500	0.01	15.93	0.01
Kasos (Dodecanese)	47,000	0.13	189	0.10

APPENDIX 5.4 *Value of tonnage owned by investors* (cont.)

Place of origin	Value of tonnage (in drachmas)	% total value	Tonnage corresponding to the indicated value	% tonnage
Kasos origin, Hermoupolis living	4000	0.01	20	0.01
Kastellorizo (Dodecanese)	7000	0.02	84.22	0.04
Kastelorizo origin, Hermoupolis living	24,250	0.07	143	0.07
Kea (Cyclades)	7500	0.02	44.92	0.02
Kimi (Euboea)	13,666.66	0.04	83.64	0.04
Kimolos (Cyclades)	26,265	0.07	222.14	0.11
Koytali (Sea of Marmara)	623,33.33	0.17	290.64	0.15
Kranidi (Peloponnese)	93,153.33	0.25	614.65	0.32
Kydonies (Aivali-Turkey)	12,000	0.03	82.17	0.04
Kydonies origin, Hermoupolis living	28,900	0.08	173.35	0.09
Kythira (Ionian Islands)	66,250	0.18	567.06	0.29
Kythira origin, Hermoupolis living	3985	0.01	16	0.01
Kythnos (Cyclades)	15,297.5	0.04	104.1	0.05
Kythnos origin, Hermoupolis living	1200	0.00	8.82	0.00
Lamia origin, Hermoupolis living	1666.66	0.00	8.66	0.00
Leonidio (Peloponnese)	21,000	0.06	130	0.07
Leros (Dodecanese)	17,545	0.05	143.64	0.07
Leros origin, Hermoupolis living	151,901	0.41	892.21	0.46
Lesvos (NE Aegean)	25,500	0.07	125.17	0.06
Lesvos origin, Hermoupolis living	18,325	0.05	126.26	0.07
Limni (Euboea)	195,400	0.53	1534.18	0.79
Limnos (NE Aegean)	201,550	0.54	1225.34	0.63

Place of origin	Value of tonnage (in drachmas)	% total value	Tonnage corresponding to the indicated value	% tonnage
Limnos origin, Hermoupolis living	10,5843.33	0.29	632.77	0.33
Livorno (Italy)	36,500	0.10	105	0.05
London (UK)	67,500	0.18	235	0.12
Macedonia origin, Hermoupolis living	28,000	0.08	126	0.06
Mariupol (Ukraine)	60,000	0.16	300	0.15
Massitos	7000	0.02	51.67	0.03
Megara (Attica) origin, Hermoupolis living	16,000	0.04	55.4	0.03
Messolonghi (Gulf of Patras)	65,000	0.18	295	0.15
Milos (Cyclades)	72,160	0.19	588.62	0.30
Monemvasia (Peloponesse)	11,000	0.03	57.5	0.03
Moshonisia (Ayvalik Islands-Turkey)	56,825	0.15	249.99	0.13
Mykonos(Cyclades)	1,062,705.32	2.86	5904.85	3.04
Mykonos living, Zakynthos origin	50,000	0.13	194	0.10
Mykonos origin, Hermoupolis living	67,300	0.18	410.08	0.21
Mytilini (NE Aegean)	15,000	0.04	53.67	0.03
Nafplio (Peloponnese)	95,490	0.26	654.32	0.34
Naxos (Cyclades)	13,940	0.04	127.84	0.07
Naxos living, Hermoupolis origin	4000	0.01	23.9	0.01
Odessa (Ukraine)	96,870	0.26	985.91	0.51
origin, Hermoupolis living	148,345	0.40	789.59	0.41
Paros (Cyclades)	58,468.33	0.16	424.18	0.22
Paros living, Hermoupolis origin	1000	0.00	5.74	0.00
Patmos (Dodecanese)	27,000	0.07	205.12	0.11

APPENDIX 5.4 *Value of tonnage owned by investors* (cont.)

Place of origin	Value of tonnage (in drachmas)	% total value	Tonnage corresponding to the indicated value	% tonnage
Patmos living, Hermoupolis origin	101,000	0.27	512.63	0.26
Peloponesse living, Hermoupolis origin	21,000	0.06	157.44	0.08
Piraeus (Attica)	32,196	0.09	239.2	0.12
Poros (Saronic Gulf)	58,375	0.16	374.92	0.19
Psara (Eastern Aegean)	477,747.96	1.29	2076.06	1.07
Psara origin, Athens living	71,500	0.19	331.78	0.17
Psara origin, Hermoupolis living	8,4141,78.44	22.68	40,976.55	21.10
Rensk (Moldova)	12,000	0.03	82	0.04
Russia	146,122	0.39	961.19	0.50
Russia origin, Constantinople living	22,194	0.06	178.93	0.09
Salamina (Saronic Gulf)	3500	0.01	51	0.03
Samos (SE Aegean)	97,125	0.26	539.59	0.28
Samos origin, Braila living	2324	0.01	12.11	0.01
Samos origin, Hermoupolis living	190,154.8	0.51	917.69	0.47
Santorini (Cyclades)	1,400,921.42	3.78	7738.21	3.99
Serifos (Cyclades)	600	0.00	6	0.00
Serres (Macedonia)	13,998	0.04	90	0.05
Sifnos (Cyclades)	4237.5	0.01	63.37	0.03
Sifnos origin, Hermoupolis living	10,000	0.03	58.66	0.03
Skiathos (Northern Sporades)	6000	0.02	34.06	0.02
Skiathos origin, Hermoupolis living	500	0.00	2.58	0.00
Skopelos (Northern Sporades)	1765	0.00	10	0.01

Place of origin	Value of tonnage (in drachmas)	% total value	Tonnage corresponding to the indicated value	% tonnage
Smyrna (Turkey)	196,166.66	0.53	1066.52	0.55
Smyrna origin, Hermoupolis living	306,610	0.83	1849.03	0.95
Sokia (Söke-Turkey)	10,000	0.03	47.53	0.02
Sparti origin, Hermoupolis living	18,000	0.05	109.12	0.06
Spetses (Argolic Gulf)	905,850	2.44	5578.33	2.87
Stylida (Central Greece)	15,916.66	0.04	109.4	0.06
Taganrog (Russia)	148,450	0.40	811	0.42
Tenedos (Turkey)	8000	0.02	44	0.02
Thessaloniki (Macedonia)	33,333.33	0.09	238.45	0.12
Thessaloniki origin, Hermoupolis living	96,500	0.26	477	0.25
Tinos (Cyclades)	441,220.89	1.19	2432.69	1.25
Tinos origin, Hermoupolis living	155,500	0.42	631.82	0.33
Trieste (Italy)	211,233.33	0.57	1110.58	0.57
Trikeri (Thessaly)	62,450	0.17	633.98	0.33
Tsesme (Cesme-Turkey)	39,125	0.11	281.86	0.15
Tsesme origin, Hermoupolis living	7500	0.02	51.06	0.03
Volos (Thessaly)	13,300	0.04	94.36	0.05
Vraila (Braila-Romania)	170,000	0.46	953.03	0.49
Zagora (Thessaly) origin, Hermoupolis living	116,300	0.31	959.18	0.49
Zakynthos (Ionian Islands)	103,000	0.28	253.48	0.13
Total	37,096,235.99	194,167.25	100.00	100.00

Sources: processed data from GSA, Syros, Αρχείο Συμβολαιογράφου Μάξιμου Ταλασλή, Συμβ. Σκαρλάτος Μάξιμος, Κατάστιχα 1–6, 1827–1830, Συμβ. Ανδρέας Δαβίδ, Κατάστιχα 7–16, 1830–24/1/1835, Λυτά έγγραφα 1835–1862. Συλλογή Ιστορικού Αρχείου Κυκλάδων, Συμβ. Κων. Αγγελίδης, Ευρετήρια, 1–5, 1854–1863, Συμβ. Αντώνιος Αλμπέρτος, Ευρετήρια 1–2, 1853–1864, Συμβ. Μιχ. Ιωάννόπουλος, Ευρ. 1–2, 1843–1845, Συμβ. Χρ. Ιωάννου Ευρ. 1–10, 1846–1860. I/Ναυπηγικά, 1836–1866.

APPENDIX 5.5 *Maritime profession as investors in Syros – Hermoupolis shipyards, 1828–1866*

Maritime professions	Number of investors	% of total	Tonnage owned	% of total	Value of tonnage owned (tonnage with available data on value)	% of total
Fisherman	14	0.96	190.36	0.10	40,181 (176.33)	0.11
Navy Officer	1	0.07	146,25	0.08	18,750 (146.25)	0.10
Captain in Merchant Ships	30	2.05	5924.61	3.10	1,106,380.66 (5844.61)	3.81
Seafarer	9	0.62	2395.85	1.25	151,003 (1110.54)	0.72
Boatman	8	0.55	67.17	0.04	12,148 (65.17)	0.04
Lighterman	1	0.07	9.19	0.00		0.27
Seaman	8	0.55	885.67	0.46	65,258.33 (415.23)	53.24
Mariner	854	58.41	98,488.62	51.46	15,547,400.57 (81,670.71)	11.70
Captain	154	10.53	25,049.78	13.09	3,280,969.68 (17,954.63)	0.11
Commander of Navy	1	0.07	172.45	0.09	27,000 (172.45)	0.07
Rear Admiral/ Senator	1	0.07	111.66	0.06	26,000 (111.66)	0.11
Total	1081	73.94	133,441.6	69.728	20,275,091.24	69.24

Sources: Processed data from GSA, Syros, Αρχείο Συμβολαιογράφου Μάξιμου Ταλασλή, Συμβ. Σκαρλάτος Μάξιμος, Κατάστιχα 1–6, 1827–1830, Συμβ. Ανδρέας Δαβίδ, Κατάστιχα 7–16, 1830–24/1/1835, Λυτά έγγραφα 1835–1862. Συλλογή Ιστορικού Αρχείου Κυκλάδων, Συμβ. Κων. Αγγελίδης, Ευρετήρια, 1–5, 1854–1863, Συμβ. Αντώνιος Αλμπέρτος, Ευρετήρια 1–2, 1853–1864, Συμβ. Μιχ. Ιωάννόπουλος, Ευρ. 1–2, 1843–1845, Συμβ. Χρ. Ιωάννου Ευρ. 1–10, 1846–1860. I/Ναυπηγικά, 1836–1866.

APPENDIX 5.6 *Mercantile professions as investors in Syros – Hermoupolis shipyards, 1828–1866*

Mercantile professions	Number of investors	% of total	Tonnage owned	% of total	Value of tonnage owned (tonnage with available data on value)	% of total
Coal Burner	1	0.07	7.35	0.004	–	–
Coal Merchant	1	0.07	55.4	0.04	16,000 (55.4)	0,0361
Money Changer	1	0.07	2	0.001	–	–
Milk Seller	2	0.14	46.13	0.01	1687.5 (46.13)	0.03
Commercial Firm	2	0.14	170.65	0.10	29,000 (116.25)	0.08
Secretary in Commercial Firm	1	0.07	4.5	0.003	750 (4.5)	0.003
Clerk in Commercial Firm	1	0.07	121.33	0.11	31,666.66 (121.33)	0.08
Trader and Landowner	1	0.07	159.75	0.10	26,250 (159.75)	0.09
Trade Broker	1	0.07	197.25	0.10	45,000 (187.75)	0.12
Merchant	186	12.72	28,721.82	15.01	4,561,953,93 (23,046.22)	15.02
Fish Seller	7	0.48	56.28	0.03	2050 (15.28)	0.01
Tobacco Seller	3	0.21	210.33	0.11	32,095 (170.5)	0.01
Coffee House Owner	2	0.14	20.75	0.01	2900 (20.75)	0.01
Meat Seller	2	0.14	44.04	0.02	15,000 (44.04)	0.05
Real Estate Broker	1	0.07	10	0.01	1765 (10)	0.01
Vegetables Seller	2	0.14	20.04	0.01	1050 (9.02)	0.004

APPENDIX 5.6 *Mercantile professions as investors* (cont.)

Mercantile professions	Number of investors	% of total	Tonnage owned	% of total	Value of tonnage owned (tonnage with available data on value)	% of total
Broker	1	0.07	15.95	0.01	–	–
Retailer	2	0.14	52.33	0.03	2400 (11.25)	0.01
Timber Merchant	8	0.55	399.96	0.21	16,956.07 (102.91)	0.06
Wine Seller	9	0.62	460.6	0.24	68,325 (450.42)	0.23
Green Grocer	1	0.07	3	0.002		
Sutler	11	0.75	643.24	0.336	115,848.8 (643.24)	0.40
Total	246	16.83	31,367.3	16.39	4,970,697.96	16.98

Sources: Processed data from GSA, Syros, Αρχείο Συμβολαιογράφου Μάξιμου Ταλασλή, Συμβ. Σκαρλάτος Μάξιμος, Κατάστιχα 1–6, 1827–1830, Συμβ. Ανδρέας Δαβίδ, Κατάστιχα 7–16, 1830–24/1/1835, Λυτά έγγραφα 1835–1862. Συλλογή Ιστορικού Αρχείου Κυκλάδων, Συμβ. Κων. Αγγελίδης, Ευρετήρια, 1–5, 1854–1863, Συμβ. Αντώνιος Αλμπέρτος, Ευρετήρια 1–2, 1853–1864, Συμβ. Μιχ. Ιωάννόπουλος, Ευρ. 1–2, 1843–1845, Συμβ. Χρ. Ιωάννου Ευρ. 1–10, 1846–1860. Ι/Ναυπηγικά, 1836–1866.

APPENDIX 5.7 *Primary sector professions as investors in Syros – Hermoupolis shipyards, 1828–1866*

Primary sector professions	Number of investors	% of total	Tonnage owned	% of total	Value of tonnage owned	% of total
Farmer	2	0.14	23.2	0.01	2800 (23.2)	0.01
Landowner	9	0.62	1612.62	0.84	291,208.33 (1175.86)	0.99
Total	11	0.75	1635.82	0.85	294,008.33	1.00

Sources: Processed data from GSA, Syros, Αρχείο Συμβολαιογράφου Μάξιμου Ταλασλή, Συμβ. Σκαρλάτος Μάξιμος, Κατάστιχα 1–6, 1827–1830, Συμβ. Ανδρέας Δαβίδ, Κατάστιχα 7–16, 1830–24/1/1835, Λυτά έγγραφα 1835–1862. Συλλογή Ιστορικού Αρχείου Κυκλάδων, Συμβ. Κων. Αγγελίδης, Ευρετήρια, 1–5, 1854–1863, Συμβ. Αντώνιος Αλμπέρτος, Ευρετήρια 1–2, 1853–1864, Συμβ. Μιχ. Ιωάννόπουλος, Ευρ. 1–2, 1843–1845, Συμβ. Χρ. Ιωάννου Ευρ. 1–10, 1846–1860. I/Ναυπηγικά, 1836–1866.

APPENDIX 5.8 *Secondary sector professions as investors in Syros – Hermoupolis shipyards, 1828–1866*

Secondary sector professions	Number of investors	% of total	Tonnage owned	% of total	Value of tonnage owned (tonnage with available data on value)	% of total
Baker	3	0.21	73.84	0.04	9600 (71)	0.03
Architect	1	0.07	40.12	0.02	8000 (40.12)	0.03
Confectioner	1	0.07	87.5	0.05	1575 (15)	0.01
Laborer	1	0.07	1.41	0.001	100 (1.41)	0.0003
Factory Owner	1	0.07	20.25	0.01	6000 (13.5)	0.02
Caulker	2	0.14	256.85	0.13	–	–
Locksmith	1	0.07	55.8	0.03	11,600 (55.8)	0.04
Joiner	1	0.07	2	0.001	430 (2)	0.001
Hewer	1	0.07	12.5	0.01	2500 (12.5)	0.01
Pulley Maker	1	0.07	123.5	0.06	21,000 (123.5)	0.07
Carpenter	9	0.62	668.2	0.35	86,533.5 (535.83)	0.30
Engineer	1	0.07	43.97	0.02	–	–
Shipwright	25	1.71	15,931.96	8.33	2,645,755.39 (13512.35)	9.04
Bronze Smith	1	0.07	207.5	0.11	37,500 (207.5)	0.13
Sawyer	1	0.07	154.5	0.08	60,000 (154.5)	0.20
Taylor	2	0.14	20.25	0.01	1000 (7.75)	0.00
Sandal Maker	5	0.34	77.35	0.04	34,000 (27.35)	0.12
Blacksmith	3	0.21	127.69	0.07	13,250 (64.59)	0.05
Leather Cutter	1	0.07	126.5	0.07	42,500 (126.5)	0.15
Plasterer	1	0.07	22.33	0.01		
Builder	2	0.14	123.2	0.06	3100 (27.2)	0.01
Weaver	1	0.07	100.8	0.05	7000 (100.8)	0.02

APPENDIX 5.8 *Secondary sector professions as investors* (cont.)

Secondary sector professions	Number of investors	% of total	Tonnage owned	% of total	Value of tonnage owned (tonnage with available data on value)	% of total
Lamp Maker	1	0.07	10.25	0.01		
Farmacist	2	0.14	102.25	0.05	17,500 (102.25)	0.06
Goldsmith	1	0.07	83.8	0.04	20,200 (83.8)	0.07
Total	69	4.72	18,474.32	9.65	3,029,143.89	10.35

Sources: Processed data from GSA, Syros, Αρχείο Συμβολαιογράφου Μάξιμου Ταλασλή, Συμβ. Σκαρλάτος Μάξιμος, Κατάστιχα 1–6, 1827–1830, Συμβ. Ανδρέας Δαβίδ, Κατάστιχα 7–16, 1830–24/1/1835, Λυτά έγγραφα 1835–1862. Συλλογή Ιστορικού Αρχείου Κυκλάδων, Συμβ. Κων. Αγγελίδης, Ευρετήρια, 1–5, 1854–1863, Συμβ. Αντώνιος Αλμπέρτος, Ευρετήρια 1–2, 1853–1864, Συμβ. Μιχ. Ιωάννόπουλος, Ευρ. 1–2, 1843–1845, Συμβ. Χρ. Ιωάννου Ευρ. 1–10, 1846–1860. Ι/Ναυπηγικά, 1836–1866.

APPENDIX 5.9 *Administrative professions as investors in Syros – Hermoupolis shipyards, 1828–1866*

Administrative professions	Number of investors	% of total	Tonnage owned	% of total	Value of Tonnage owned (tonnage with available data on value)	% of total
Officer	1	0.07	309	0.20	60,000 (309)	0.20
Senator	1	0.07	220.12	0.12	45,500 (220.12)	0.16
Port Authority Secretary	1	0.07	81.94	0.04	13,000 (81.94)	0.04
Prefecture of Cyclades Secretary	1	0.07	68.33	0.04	15,000 (68.33)	0.05
Municipal Employee	1	0.07	6	0.003	900 (6)	0.003
Civil Judge	1	0.07	159	0.08	31,000 (159)	0.11

Administrative professions	Number of investors	% of total	Tonnage owned	% of total	Value of Tonnage owned (tonnage with available data on value)	% of total
Priest	1	0.07	475.79	0.25	2000 (16.43)	0.01
Hermoupoli's Harbour Master	1	0.07	84	0.04	14,000 (84)	0.05
Post Office Employee	1	0.07	13	0.01	2000 (13)	0.01
British Consulate Employee	1	0.07	70.35	0.04	–	–
Transit Warehouses Employee	1	0.07	214.24	0.11	35,000 (107.12)	0.12
Total	11	0.75	1701.77	0.93	218.400	0.75

Sources: Processed data from GSA, Syros, Αρχείο Συμβολαιογράφου Μάξιμου Ταλασλή, Συμβ. Σκαρλάτος Μάξιμος, Κατάστιχα 1–6, 1827–1830, Συμβ. Ανδρέας Δαβίδ, Κατάστιχα 7–16, 1830–24/1/1835, Λυτά έγγραφα 1835–1862. Συλλογή Ιστορικού Αρχείου Κυκλάδων, Συμβ. Κων. Αγγελίδης, Ευρετήρια, 1–5, 1854–1863, Συμβ. Αντώνιος Αλμπέρτος, Ευρετήρια 1–2, 1853–1864, Συμβ. Μιχ. Ιωαννόπουλος, Ευρ. 1–2, 1843–1845, Συμβ. Χρ. Ιωάννου Ευρ. 1–10, 1846–1860. Ι/Ναυπηγικά, 1836–1866.

APPENDIX 5.10 *Service professions as investors in Syros – Hermoupolis shipyards, 1828–1866*

Service professions	Number of investors	% of total	Tonnage owned	% of total	Value of tonnage owned (tonnage with available data on value)	% of total
Interpreter	1	0.07	230.20	0.12	17,900 (127.86)	0.06
Medical Doctor	1	0.07	149.25	0.08	–	–
Musician	2	0.14	77.07	0.04	4250 (39.5)	0.01
Clerk	2	0.14	155.14	0.08	500 (2.53)	0.002
Servant	1	0.07	16.11	0.01	–	–
Guardian	1	0.07	33.01	0.02	2625 (33.01)	0.01
Total	8	0.55	660.78	0.35	25,275	0.09

Sources: Processed data from GSA, Syros, Αρχείο Συμβολαιογράφου Μάξιμου Ταλασλή, Συμβ. Σκαρλάτος Μάξιμος, Κατάστιχα 1–6, 1827–1830, Συμβ. Ανδρέας Δαβίδ, Κατάστιχα 7–16, 1830–24/1/1835, Λυτά έγγραφα 1835–1862. Συλλογή Ιστορικού Αρχείου Κυκλάδων, Συμβ. Κων. Αγγελίδης, Ευρετήρια, 1–5, 1854–1863, Συμβ. Αντώνιος Αλμπέρτος, Ευρετήρια 1–2, 1853–1864, Συμβ. Μιχ. Ιωάννόπουλος, Ευρ. 1–2, 1843–1845, Συμβ. Χρ. Ιωάννου Ευρ. 1–10, 1846–1860. I/Ναυπηγικά, 1836–1866.

APPENDIX 5.11 *Women as investors in Syros – Hermoupolis shipyards, 1828–1866*

Women	Number of investors	% of total	Tonnage owned	% of total	Value of Tonnage owned (tonnage with available data on value)	% of total
Female	15	1,03	1549.24	0.81	201,916.65 (890.26)	0.69
Daughter/ Wife	1	0,07	–	–	–	–
Mother	1	0,07	93	0.05	–	–
Wife	16	1,09	1775.21	0.93	217,208.32 (1660.01)	0.74
Widow	3	0,21	771.90	0.40	30,000 (109.5)	0.10
Total	36	2.46	4189.35	2.19	449,124.97	1.53

Sources: Processed data from GSA, Syros, Αρχείο Συμβολαιογράφου Μάξιμου Ταλασλή, Συμβ. Σκαρλάτος Μάξιμος, Κατάστιχα 1–6, 1827–1830, Συμβ. Ανδρέας Δαβίδ, Κατάστιχα 7–16, 1830–24/1/1835, Λυτά έγγραφα 1835–1862. Συλλογή Ιστορικού Αρχείου Κυκλάδων, Συμβ. Κων. Αγγελίδης, Ευρετήρια, 1–5, 1854–1863, Συμβ. Αντώνιος Αλμπέρτος, Ευρετήρια 1–2, 1853–1864, Συμβ. Μιχ. Ιωάννόπουλος, Ευρ. 1–2, 1843–1845, Συμβ. Χρ. Ιωάννου Ευρ. 1–10, 1846–1860. I/Ναυπηγικά, 1836–1866.

APPENDIX 5.12 *Distribution of ownership of ships built in Syros – Hermoupolis, 1828–66*

Number of owners	Number of ships	% of number of ships	Tonnage	% of tonnage	Value of ships	% of value of ships
Single Owner	1304	62.42	169.046,7	59.55	21,128,325	53.37
Two Owners	515	24.65	71.102,31	25.05	11,203,941	28.30
Three Owners	197	9.43	31.561,89	11.12	5,203,336	13.14
Four Owners	54	2.58	8.730,45	3.08	1,433,517	3.62
< 4 Owners	19	0.91	3.441,02	1.21	622,450	1.57
Total	2089	100.00	283,882.40	100.00	39,591,569	100.00

Sources: processed data from GSA, Syros, Αρχείο Συμβολαιογράφου Μάξιμου Ταλασλή, Συμβ. Σκαρλάτος Μάξιμος, Κατάστιχα 1–6, 1827–1830, Συμβ. Ανδρέας Δαβίδ, Κατάστιχα 7–16, 1830–24/1/1835, Λυτά έγγραφα 1835–1862. Συλλογή Ιστορικού Αρχείου Κυκλάδων, Συμβ. Κων. Αγγελίδης, Ευρετήρια, 1–5, 1854–1863, Συμβ. Αντώνιος Αλμπέρτος, Ευρετήρια 1–2, 1853–1864, Συμβ. Μιχ. Ιωάννόπουλος, Ευρ. 1–2, 1843–1845, Συμβ. Χρ. Ιωάννου Ευρ. 1–10, 1846–1860. I/Ναυπηγικά, 1836–1866.

Chapter 6—Factors of Production

APPENDIX 6.1 *Prosopographical data of shipwrights of Hermoupolis*

Shipbuilder	Origin according notarial sources	Origin according municipal rolls	Profession according municipal rolls	Life span*	Active period
Aggelis Christodoulos	Chios	–	–	–	1829–41
Aggelou Georg. Ioannis	Leros	–	Shipcarpenter	1825–	1846–61
Albanezos Dimitrios	Tinos	–	–	–	1845–58
Andreou Grigorios	–	Moschonisia	Mariner	1815–	1847–47
Apostolos Stylianos	–	–	–	–	1838
Babafouris Nikolaos	–	–	–	–	1852
Berdelis Nikolaos	–	–	–	–	1853–54
Betsanis Dimitrios	Skopelos	–	–	–	1853
Bisketzis G. Ioannis	Lesvos	–	–	–	1852–66
Bobiolis Chatzigeorgios	–	–	–	–	1846
Bogiatzoglou Panayotis	–	–	–	–	1858
Boumis A. Petros	–	Hydra	Shipwright	1827-	1866
Bousounakis Michail	–	Kasos	Carpenter	1810-	1842
Chaldaios Dimitrios	–	–	–	–	1851
Christodoulou Georgios	–	Chios	Carpenter	1812–	1851–53

Shipbuilder	Origin according notarial sources	Origin according municipal rolls	Profession according municipal rolls	Life span*	Active period
Christopoulos An. Athanasios	–	–	–	–	1860–62
Chrysakis Geor. Dimitrios	–	Crete	Carpenter	1825-	1852
Chrysinas D. Ioannis	Kranidi	–	–	–	1857–63
Delikonstantis Panagiotis	Chios	–	–	–	1829
Dentas Ioan. Dimitrios	Spetses	–	–	–	1846
Dimitriou Stefanis	Hermoupolis	–	–	–	1851–57
Dramitzas Georgios	Psara	–	–	–	1833–41
Efstratiou Panagiotis			Carpenter	1831–	1859
Eudemon Antonios	–	Thira	Shipwright	1822–	1860
Evagelis (Evagelou) Dimitrios	–	Moschonisia	Carpenter	1814–	1847
Faleros Theodoros	–	–	–	–	1855
Filis K. Nikolaos	–	–	–	–	1849
Flamourakias Chatziioannis	Chios	–	–	–	1833
Floumis Epifanios	Skopelos	–	–	–	1866
Fournarakis Konstantinos	–	Chios	Carpenter	1809–	1846
Fragakis A.	–	–	–	–	1843
Fragos Emmanouil	–	Hydra	Shipwright	1822–1899	1853–61
Georgantas Georgios	–	Chios	Fisherman	–	1849

APPENDIX 6.1 *Prosopographical data of shipwrights of Hermoupolis* (cont.)

Shipbuilder	Origin according notarial sources	Origin according municipal rolls	Profession according municipal rolls	Life span*	Active period
Georgiou Manolis	–	–	–	† 1895	1850
Geragotis Stathis	–	–	–	–	1849
Giannikos Konstaninos	–	–	–	–	1850–51
Ginis Ioannis	–	–	–	–	1850–51
Gionis Ioan. Gionis	–	–	–	–	1842–47
Gionis Ioannis	–	Hydra	Carpenter	1826–	1841–49
Glykas Nikolaos	–	Chios	Sawyer	1805–	1844–45
Glykoyannis (Glykoyannakis) Dimitrios	–	Chios	Carpenter	1785–	1833
Glynos Georgios	–	Hermoupolis	Shipwright	1831–	1858–63
Gourountis Konstantinos	–	Chios	Carpenter	1803 / 1810–1885	1849–61
Ioannou Georgios	Skopelos	–	–	–	1830
Kabosos Emmanouil	Hermoupolis	Patmos	Carpenter	1809–	1857
Kabouris Ath. Panagiotis	Moschonisia	–	Carpenter	–	1844–46
Kabouris P. Athanasios	Moschonisia	–	Carpenter	1814–	1841–52
Kaloudis Ioa. D.	–	–	–	–	1841
Karakonstantis Pan. Stamatios	Chios	–	Carpenter	1822–	1846–55
Karakonstantis Panagiotis	Chios	–	–	–	1832–49
Karalis Dim. Nikolaos	Chios	–	Shipwright	1827–	1850–54

Shipbuilder	Origin according notarial sources	Origin according municipal rolls	Profession according municipal rolls	Life span*	Active period
Karalis Dimitrios	–	–	–	–	1836
Karidis Spyros	Kythira	–	–	–	1834
Kefalas Dimitrios	–	Chios	Carpenter	1812–	1846
Kokkinakis Charalambos	Chios	–	Shipwright	1825–	1850–66
Kokkinakis Georgios	–	Crete	Hewer	1794–	1860
Kokotiris Ioannis	–	–	–	–	1851
Konstantinou Andreas	Chios	–	–	–	1858–59
Koufoudakis Antonios	–	Chios	Joiner	1806–	1835
Koufoudakis Ioan. Stamatios	Chios	–	Joiner	1804/1815/ *1820*–1884	1835–66
Koufoudakis Zannis	Chios	–	Mariner	1815 /1817/ *1818*–1880	1842–66
Koufoudakis I. Dimitrios	Chios	–	Mariner	1820-	1847–48
Koufoudakis Ioannis	Chios	–	Shipwright	1782/ 1794–1852	1831–48
Koumoutzakos Vasileios	–	Gythio	–	–	1861
Koupitoris Dim. Christos	–	–	–	–	1852–57
Koutzinis Petros	Hermoupolis	–	–	–	1828
Krinigas Christodoulos	Chios	–	–	1796–1851	1839–44
Kritikos I. Spyridon	Chios	–	–	–	1858
Krystalis Christofis	Chios	–	Joiner	1813/1815–1888	1845–66

APPENDIX 6.1 *Prosopographical data of shipwrights of Hermoupolis* (cont.)

Shipbuilder	Origin according notarial sources	Origin according municipal rolls	Profession according municipal rolls	Life span*	Active period
Kydis V. Antonios	Chios	Chios	–	1839–1889	1855–63
Labos Konstantinos	Chios	–	Shipwright	1794–	1831–37
Lekas Dimitrios	–	–	–	–	1856
Lekatzas Geor. Panagis	–	–	–	–	1849–52
Leontis Apostolos	Lesvos	–	–	–	1834–35
Lerios St. Ioannis	Hermoupolis	–	–	–	1846
Leriotis Alexandros	Hydra	–	–	–	1840–44
Leriotis St. Dimitrios	Hydra	–	Mariner	1807–	1833–46
Levadaros Kon. Andreas	Chios	–	Shipwright	1835–	1859–66
Linaris Emmanouil	–	–	–	–	1841
Liosis I. Nikolaos	–	–	–	–	1852
Livaros N. Konstantinos	–	–	–	–	1836
Magas Chatziyannis	–	–	–	–	1835–36
Magos Chatzidimitrios	Chios	–	Carpenter	1812–	1850–66
Marakakis Michail	–	–	–	–	1860
Maskas Pantelis	Chios	–	Shipwright	1794–1872	1828–62
Maskas Stamatios	Chios	–	Mariner	1809/1808/*1815*–1879	1833–66

Shipbuilder	Origin according notarial sources	Origin according municipal rolls	Profession according municipal rolls	Life span*	Active period
Mavrothalassitis Io. Dimitrios	–	Tinos	Carpenter	1825–	1850
Michailos Andreas	–	–	–	–	1852
Michelis D. Ioannis	Hermoupolis	–	–	–	1849–62
Moschonisiou Th. Andreas	Mykonos	–	–	–	1836
Nikolaou Ioannis	–	–	–	–	1854
Nikolaou Konstantinos	Santorini	–	–	–	1833
Ntinglozis Anagnostis	–	–	–	–	1850
Ntrivas Emm. Athanasios	–	–	–	–	1841–42
Pagidas Ioannis	Chios	–	Shipwright	**1774**/ 1774–1849	1828–47
Pagidas Nikolaos	Chios	–	Shipwright	*1805*/1809/ 1816–1871	1828–66
Papadakis Theodoros (Kalafatis)	–	Hydra	Caulker	1822–	1852
Papatzios Antonios	Chios	–	Shipwright	1821–	1849–59
Papiolis Chatzigeorgios	–	Crete	Mariner	1780–	1845–46
Paraskevas Nikolaos	–	–	–	–	1852
Peloponisios Emm. Themistoklis	Hermoupolis	–	–	–	1857
Perdikas Dim. Nikolaos	Spetses	–	–	–	1846

APPENDIX 6.1 *Prosopographical data of shipwrights of Hermoupolis* (cont.)

Shipbuilder	Origin according notarial sources	Origin according municipal rolls	Profession according municipal rolls	Life span*	Active period
Perdikis Georgios	Chios	–	Carpenter	1789–	1829–44
Petris Ioannis	–	Rhodes	Joiner	1817–	1850
Petrou Georgios	Skopelos	–	–	–	1830
Petrou Konstantinos	–	–	–	–	1852
Pisanis Aggelos	Malta	–	–	–	1840
Platsoukas Anag. Lazaros	–	–	–	–	1852
Platsoukas Anagnostis	–	–	–	–	1853
Potous Andreas	–	Chios	Mariner	1830/1830–1878	1856–59
Potous Mikes	Chios	–	Architect	**1801**–1867	1829–63
Printezis Ioannis	Syros	–	–	–	1848
Psomas N. Stylianos	–	Hermoupolis	Carpenter	1836–	1866
Rafalias Ioannis	–	–	–	–	1850
Saitos Ioannis	Ano Syros	–	–	–	1850
Samaras Pantelis	–	–	–	–	1845–59
Santorineos Nik. Kostis	–	–	–	–	1836
Sarikakis Christodoulos	–	Cesme	Carpenter	1799–	1839
Sehas Dim. Ioannis	Chios	–	–	–	1845–52
Sehas F. Dimitrios	Chios	–	Shipwright	1830–	1855–59
Sehas I. Fragoulis	Chios	–	Shipwright	1798/1801/*1800*–1868	1829–60

Shipbuilder	Origin according notarial sources	Origin according municipal rolls	Profession according municipal rolls	Life span*	Active period
Sehas Io. Dimitrios	Chios	–	Captain	1795–1864	1833–54
Sfakianos Chatziioannou Dimitrios	–	–	–	–	1849
Sfakianos Chatziioannou Michail	–	–	–	–	1848
Sigidos Ioannis	Chios	–	–	–	1833
Skordoulis Anastasios	Cephalonia	–	–	–	1830–31
Sochos Markos	–	–	–	† 1894	1858
Solomos G. Nikolaos	Lesvos	–	–	–	1833–66
Sotirakis Efstratios	Chios	–	Carpenter	1789–	1830–58
Sousanas Geor. Ilias	–	–	–	–	1848–50
Spyrou Adrianos	–	–	–	–	1845
Stamatiou Ioannis	Spetses	–	–	–	1843–63
Sviros Nikolaos	–	Chios	Shipwright	1795–	1846–48
Theodorou Andreas	Mykonos	–	–	–	1840–48
Tritzas K. Georgios	–	–	–	–	1851
Tsinaris Manolis	–	–	–	–	1838–55
Tsitsinis I. Perialas	–	–	–	–	1857
Tzaknias Aggelos	–	–	–	–	1845
Tzannes Nikolaos	–	–	–	–	1848

APPENDIX 6.1 *Prosopographical data of shipwrights of Hermoupolis* (cont.)

Shipbuilder	**Origin according notarial sources**	**Origin according municipal rolls**	**Profession according municipal rolls**	**Life span***	**Active period**
Tzitzinias I. Emmanouil	–	Hydra	Shipwright	1820–	1847–63
Valsamou Dimosthenis	–	–	–	–	1860
Vasilikos Leonis	Chios	–	–	1801–	1832–48
Vasilikos Nik. Antonios	Chios	Hermoupolis	Carpenter	1834–	1852–59
Vasilikos Nikolaos	Chios	–	Carpenter	1792–	1847–52
Venekos Christos	–	–	–	–	1859–60
Vourgaris Georg. Emmanouil	–	–	–	† 1889	1849–51
Zabelis Theo. Manolis	–	–	–	–	1849–50
Zafirakis Ioan. Charalambos	–	–	–	–	1838
Zafiris Chatziioannis	Chios	–	Carpenter	1784–	1832–36
Zepos Konstantinos	–	–	–	† 1879	1836

Sources: Processed data from GSA, Syros, Αρχείο Συμβολαιογράφου Μάξιμου Ταλασλή, Συμβ. Σκαρλάτος Μάξιμος, Κατάστιχα 1–6, 1827–1830, Συμβ. Ανδρέας Δαβίδ, Κατάστιχα 7–16, 1830–24/1/1835, Λυτά έγγραφα 1835–1862. Συλλογή Ιστορικού Αρχείου Κυκλάδων, Συμβ. Κων. Αγγελίδης, Ευρετήρια, 1–5, 1854–1863, Συμβ. Αντώνιος Αλμπέρτος, Ευρετήρια 1–2, 1853–1864, Συμβ. Μιχ. Ιωάννόπουλος, Ευρ. 1–2, 1843–1845, Συμβ. Χρ. Ιωάννου Ευρ. 1–10, 1846–1860. Ι.Α.Δ.Ε., Ι/Ναυπηγικά, 1836–1866; http://cities.ims.forth.gr/Δ/Ληξιαρχείο (Ε) Θάνατοι. Πρόχειρα βιβλία αποβιώσεων, αρ. 1, 1848–52 και ληξιαρχικά βιβλία αποβιώσεων (διάφορα έτη). Ηλεκτρονικές Βάσεις Δεδομένων, *Δημοτολόγιο Ερμούπολης και Απογραφή Ερμούπολη, 1860, 1870, 1878*; Gavala- Garezou, *Τα γλυπτά μνημεία.*

* E.g. 1800 (Municipal rolls), *1800* (Census), 1800 (Death books), **1800** (Gavala – Garezou, *Τα γλυπτά μνημεία*).

APPENDIX 6.2 *Productive performance of master shipbuilders of Hermoupolis*

Shipbuilder	Estimated value of ships (in drs)	Value of ships according available data	Tonnage built	Tonnage with available data on value	Number of vessels	Average tonnage
Aggelis Christodoulos	350,269.29	20,000.00	2224.21	127	9	247.13
Aggelou Georg. Ioannis	15,641.19	1437	283	26	7	40.43
Albanezos Dimitrios	24,300.00	24,300.00	138.85	138.85	3	46.28
Andreou Grigorios	6540	6540	50.82	50.82	3	16.94
Apostolos Stylianos	–	–	22.33	–	1	22.33
Babafouris Nikolaos	–	–	13	–	1	13
Berdelis Nikolaos	13,500.00	13,500.00	73	73	2	36.5
Betsanis Dimitrios	48,000.00	48,000.00	262.52	262.52	1	262.52
Bisketzis G. Ioannis	127,643.01	91,500.00	793.8	569.03	30	26.46
Bobiolis Chatzigeorgios	1500	1500	11.29	11.29	1	11.29
Bogiatzoglou Panagiotis	2400	2400	13.5	13.5	1	13.5
Boumis A. Petros	640,000.00	640,000.00	1910.91	1910.91	8	238.86
Bousounakis Michail	3000	3000	30.52	30.52	1	30.52
Chaldaios Dimitrios	48,000.00	48,000.00	219	219	1	219
Christodoulou Georgios	90,700.00	90,700.00	473	473	3	157.67
Christopoulos An. Athanasios	1350	450	6	2	2	3
Chrysakis Geor. Dimitrios	10,000.00	10,000.00	79.67	79.67	1	79.67
Chrysinas D. Ioannis	70,538.19	51,100.00	188.7	136.7	13	14.52

APPENDIX 6.2 *Productive performance of master shipbuilders of Hermoupolis* (cont.)

Shipbuilder	Estimated value of ships (in drs)	Value of ships according available data	Tonnage built	Tonnage with available data on value	Number of vessels	Average tonnage
Delikonstantis Panagiotis	–	–	75.78	–	1	75.78
Dentas Ioan. Dimitrios	22,800.00	22,800.00	218.24	218.24	1	218.24
Dimitriou Stefanos	125,805.08	75,000.00	650.06	387.54	4	162.52
Dramitzas Georgios	121,101.29	47,190.00	942.07	367.1	15	62.8
Efstratiou Panagiotis	–	–	13.5	–	1	13.5
Eudemon Antonios	1400	1400	10	10	1	10
Evagelis (Evagelou) Dimitrios	180	180	3.17	3.17	1	3.17
Faleros Theodoros	–	0	2	–	1	2
Filis K. Nikolaos	240	240	2	2	1	2
Flamourakias Chatziioannis	–	0	18.41	–	1	18.41
Floumis Epifanios	265,396.15	203,000.00	974.03	745.03	7	139.15
Fournarakis Konstantinos	2891.19	660	40.17	9.17	3	13.39
Fragakis A.	–	–	2	–	1	2
Fragos Emmanouil	760,088.92	533,750.00	3798.75	2667.56	18	211.04
Georgantas Georgios	1000	1000	5.16	5.16	1	5.16
Georgiou Manolis	5400	5400	38.84	38.84	1	38.84
Geragotis Stathis	138	138	2.87	2.87	1	2.87
Giannikos Konstaninos	6022.83	3500	42.59	24.75	2	21.3

Shipbuilder	Estimated value of ships (in drs)	Value of ships according available data	Tonnage built	Tonnage with available data on value	Number of vessels	Average tonnage
Ginis Ioannis	55,000.00	55,000.00	285	285	2	142.5
Gionis Ioan. Gionis	146,200.00	146,200.00	560.89	560.89	3	186.96
Gionis Ioannis	23,700.00	23,700.00	994	994	4	248.5
Glykas Nikolaos	–	–	4	–	2	2
Glykoyannis (Glykoyannakis) Dimitrios	–	–	360.68	–	5	72.14
Glynos Georgios	51,215.63	40,300.00	325.34	256	9	36.15
Gourountis Konstantinos	350,039.79	274,830.00	2201.38	1728.39	17	129.49
Ioannou Georgios	–	–	22.81	–	1	22.81
Kabosos Emmanouil	–	–	0.22	–	1	0.22
Kabouris Ath. Panayotis	7944.88	3000	92.24	34.83	2	46.12
Kabouris P. Athanasios	478,048.85	391,564.00	3348.31	2742.56	70	47.83
Kaloudis Ioa. D.	–	–	326	–	2	163
Karakonstantis Pan. Stamatios	398,865.36	292,000.00	2606.79	1908.37	15	173.79
Karakonstantis Panagiotis	148,280.51	127,075.00	957	820.14	6	159.5
Karalis Dim. Nikolaos	108,643.80	46,500.00	866.3	370.78	7	123.76
Karalis Dimitrios	–	–	6	–	1	6
Karidis Spyros	–	–	200.54	–	2	100.27
Kefalas Dimitrios	46,000.00	46,000.00	218	218	1	218
Kokkinakis Charalambos	828,281.84	395,270.00	4075.15	1944.73	45	90.56
Kokkinakis Georgios	360	360	2	2	1	2
Kokotiris Ioannis	–	–	6	–	1	6
Konstantinou Andreas	34,359.97	20,500.00	310.48	185.24	4	77.62

APPENDIX 6.2 *Productive performance of master shipbuilders of Hermoupolis* (cont.)

Shipbuilder	Estimated value of ships (in drs)	Value of ships according available data	Tonnage built	Tonnage with available data on value	Number of vessels	Average tonnage
Koufoudakis Antonios	–	–	49.7	–	2	24.85
Koufoudakis Ioan. Stamatios	2,996,016.39	2,260,950.00	12,047.30	9091.52	82	146.92
Koufoudakis Zannis	5,585,577.69	5,163,030.00	26,368.75	24,373.96	145	181.85
Koufoudakis I. Dimitrios	275,355.68	234,050.00	1653.44	1405.41	8	206.68
Koufoudakis Ioannis	2,459,280.85	1,697,836.00	13,271.26	9162.2	81	163.84
Koumoutzakos Vasileios	–	–	17.85	–	1	17.85
Koupitoris Dim. Christos	92,100.00	92,100.00	607.13	607.13	7	86.73
Koutzinis Petros	–	–	117.46	–	1	117.46
Krinigas Christodoulos	235,665.63	202,290.00	1332.13	1143.47	10	133.21
Kritikos I. Spyridon	–	–	13	–	1	13
Krystalis Christofis	3,280,722.55	2,754,200.00	13,815.02	11,597.85	66	209.32
Kydis V. Antonios	40,367.39	7215	392.54	70.16	35	11.22
Labos Konstantinos	24,798.17	1000	919.02	37.06	24	38.29
Lekas Dimitrios	–	–	196.33	–	1	196.33
Lekatzas Geor. Panagis	49,800.00	49,800.00	323.3	323.3	3	107.77
Leontis Apostolos	–	–	227.21	–	4	56.8
Lerios St. Ioannis	1228	1228	10.37	10.37	2	5.19
Leriotis Alexandros	–	–	564.21	–	3	188.07
Leriotis St. Dimitrios	234,404.90	202,000.00	1656.5	1427.5	9	184.06

Shipbuilder	Estimated value of ships (in drs)	Value of ships according available data	Tonnage built	Tonnage with available data on value	Number of vessels	Average tonnage
Levadaros Kon. Andreas	1,441,379.22	949,675.00	7141.64	4705.38	51	140.03
Linaris Emmanouil	–	–	31	–	1	31
Liosis I. Nikolaos	–	–	13	–	1	13
Livaros N. Konstantinos	–	–	64	–	1	64
Magas Chatziyannis	–	–	34.31	–	2	17.16
Magos Chatzidimitrios	592,892.70	493,000.00	3129.8	2602.48	20	156.49
Marakakis Michail	–	–	28.7	–	2	14.35
Maskas Pantelis	4,557,976.88	3,171,000.00	27,263.40	18,967.24	152	179.36
Maskas Stamatios	1,985,918.75	1,542,030.00	10,497.54	8151.15	58	180.99
Mavrothalassitis Io. Dimitrios	60	60	1.61	1.61	1	1.61
Michailos Andreas	175	175	3.36	3.36	1	3.36
Michelis D. Ioannis	9200	9200	18.16	18.16	2	9.08
Moschonisiou Th. Andreas	–	–	33.06	–	1	33.06
Nikolaou Ioannis	–	–	13	–	1	13
Nikolaou Konstantinos	–	–	32.01	–	1	32.01
Ntinglozis Anagnostis	3900	3900	18	18	1	18
Ntrivas Emm. Athanasios	79,300.00	79,300.00	554.54	554.54	4	138.64
Pagidas Ioannis	1,337,859.29	414,000.00	11,387.38	3523.82	55	207.04
Pagidas Nikolaos	9,934,885.65	7,913,217.00	50,770.23	40,438.90	275	184.62
Papadakis Theodoros (Kalafatis)	200	200	3	3	1	3

APPENDIX 6.2 *Productive performance of master shipbuilders of Hermoupolis* (cont.)

Shipbuilder	Estimated value of ships (in drs)	Value of ships according available data	Tonnage built	Tonnage with available data on value	Number of vessels	Average tonnage
Papatzios Antonios	498,568.18	426,220.00	3308.55	2828.44	54	61.27
Papiolis Chatzigeorgios	4950	4950	40.47	40.47	3	13.49
Paraskevas Nikolaos	420.58	420	3.42	3.42	1	3.42
Peloponisios Emm. Themistoklis	5500	5500	21.46	21.46	1	21.46
Perdikas Dim. Nikolaos	168,000.00	168,000.00	1307.87	1307.87	8	163.48
Perdikis Georgios	44,692.05	430	207.87	2	2	103.94
Petris Ioannis	3000.33	3000	28.28	28.28	1	28.28
Petrou Georgios	–	–	–	–	1	
Petrou Konstantinos	–	–	79.67	–	1	79.67
Pisanis Aggelos	22,000.00	22,000.00	91	91	1	91
Platsoukas Anag. Lazaros	15,000.00	15,000.00	120.56	120.56	1	120.56
Platsoukas Anagnostis	17,000.00	17,000.00	262.52	262.52	1	262.52
Potous Andreas	423,223.00	271,600.00	1782.71	1144.04	15	118.85
Potous Mikes	2,183,108.56	1,508,496.00	13,258.95	9161.74	82	161.69
Printezis Ioannis	24,000.00	24,000.00	140	140	1	140
Psomas N. Stylianos	95,000.00	95,000.00	413.24	413.24	4	103.31
Rafalias Ioannis	–	–	75	–	1	75
Saitos Ioannis	372	372	2	2	1	2
Samaras Pantelis	2,926.06	1,670.00	69.91	39.9	5	13.98
Santorineos Nik. Kostis	–	–	58	–	1	58
Sarikakis Christodoulos	19,980.00	19,980.00	183.74	183.74	1	183.74

Shipbuilder	Estimated value of ships (in drs)	Value of ships according available data	Tonnage built	Tonnage with available data on value	Number of vessels	Average tonnage
Sehas Dim. Ioannis	494,179.88	452,000.00	2436.93	2228.93	11	221.54
Sehas F. Dimitrios	308,433.50	277,000.00	1305.03	1172.03	5	261.01
Sehas I. Fragoulis	4,054,838.32	2,798,583.00	22,507.59	15,534.37	123	182.99
Sehas Io. Dimitrios	349,128.05	293,100.00	1788.51	1501.49	9	198.72
Sfakianos Chatziioannou Dimitrios	9600	9600	45	45	1	45
Sfakianos Chatziioannou Michail	57,278.90	46,500.00	376.23	305.43	3	125.41
Sigidos Ioannis	–	–	198	–	1	198
Skordoulis Anastasios	–	–	715.15	–	4	178.79
Sochos Markos	1891.01	280	23.3	3.45	3	7.77
Solomos G. Nikolaos	972,301.72	749,471.00	6037.17	4653.58	113	53.43
Sotirakis Efstratios	97,639.91	42,326.00	787.56	341.4	30	26.25
Sousanas Geor. Ilias	63,482.90	20,110.00	363.03	115	4	90.76
Spyrou Adrianos	200	200	13	13	1	13
Stamatiou Ioannis	390,323.64	177,580.00	2009.47	914.22	27	74.42
Sviros Nikolaos	367,600.00	367,600.00	1746.51	1746.51	8	218.31
Theodorou Andreas	13,300.00	13,300.00	105.38	105.38	3	35.13
Tritzas K. Georgios	1700	1700	22.55	22.55	1	22.55
Tsinaris Manolis	3360.83	500	40.33	6	4	10.08
Tsitsinis I. Perialas	22,000.00	22,000.00	172.32	172.32	1	172.32
Tzaknias Aggelos	200	200	13	13	1	13

APPENDIX 6.2 *Productive performance of master shipbuilders of Hermoupolis* (cont.)

Shipbuilder	Estimated value of ships (in drs)	Value of ships according available data	Tonnage built	Tonnage with available data on value	Number of vessels	Average tonnage
Tzannes Nikolaos	8000	8000	56.8	56.8	1	56.8
Tzitzinias I. Emmanouil	552,569.96	368,000.00	3172.13	2112.57	18	176.23
Valsamou Dimosthenis	–	–	72.5	–	1	72.5
Vasilikos Leonis	133,020.30	84,568.00	1028.01	653.56	32	32.13
Vasilikos Nik. Antonios	3876.64	1260	21.26	6.91	3	7.09
Vasilikos Nikolaos	15,314.86	15,008.00	164.7	161.4	5	32.94
Venekos Christos			26		2	13
Vourgaris Georg. Emmanouil	15,530.00	15,530.00	115.1	115.1	3	38.37
Zabelis Theo. Manolis	11,025.00	11,025.00	94.4	94.4	3	31.47
Zafirakis Ioan. Charalambos	–	–	22.33	–	1	22.33
Zafiris Chatziioannis	–	–	285.5	–	5	57.1
Zepos Konstantinos	–	–	66	–	1	66

Sources: Processed data from GSA, Syros, Αρχείο Συμβολαιογράφου Μάξιμου Ταλασλή, Συμβ. Σκαρλάτος Μάξιμος, Κατάστιχα 1–6, 1827–1830, Συμβ. Ανδρέας Δαβίδ, Κατάστιχα 7–16, 1830–24/1/1835, Λυτά έγγραφα 1835–1862. Συλλογή Ιστορικού Αρχείου Κυκλάδων, Συμβ. Κων. Αγγελίδης, Ευρετήρια, 1–5, 1854–1863, Συμβ. Αντώνιος Αλμπέρτος, Ευρετήρια 1–2, 1853–1864, Συμβ. Μιχ. Ιωάννόπουλος, Ευρ. 1–2, 1843–1845, Συμβ. Χρ. Ιωάννου Ευρ. 1–10, 1846–1860. Ι/Ναυπηγικά, 1836–1866.

Sources and Bibliography

Sources

Archival Sources

Γ.Α.Κ./Αρχείο Νομού Κυκλάδων, Σύρος. [*General State Archives, Archive of District of Cyclades, Syros.*]
Αρχείο Συμβολαιογράφου Μάξιμου Ταλασλή.[Archive of Notary Maximos Talaslis]

A. Κώδικες του Δημόσιου Μνήμονα Σύρου Σκαρλάτου Μάξιμου [Books of Notary Skarlatos Maximos]

1. Α. Τίτλος. Πωλητήρια καραβίων καὶ ἄλλων πλοίων καὶ ναυλοσυμφωνητικὰ καὶ ἄλλα θαλασσινὰ τοῦ Δημοσίου Ὑπογραφέως τῆς νήσου Σύρας βιβλίον 1827, Τόμος α. Ὁ δημόσιος ὑπογραφεὺς τῆς νήσου Σύρας Σκαρλάτος Μάξιμος. Ἀρ.1.
2. Α. Τίτλος. Πωλητήρια καραβίων καὶ ἄλλων πλοίων καὶ ναυλοσυμφωνητικὰ τοῦ Δημοσίου Μνήμωνος τῆς νήσου Σύρας, Βιβλίον 1829, Τόμος Β, ἀρ. 2.
3. Δ. Τίτλος. Συμφωνητικὰ Ἑταιριῶν, ἐνοικίων, μισθῶν καὶ τῶν τοιούτων τοῦ Δημοσίου Μνήμωνος τῆς νήσου Σύρας βιβλίον 1827, Τόμος Α΄. Ἐξακολούθησις ἄλλου βιβλίου τοῦ α΄τόμου, τὴν ὁποίαν ἐκάμομεν πρὸς ἀποφυγὴν τῶν συχνῶν τόμων. Ἐξακολουθεῖ δὲ τὸ παρὸν βιβλίον τὴν τοῦ πρὸ αὐτοῦ σελίδα 164, ὥστε τὰ δύο αὐτὰ βιβλία ἐννοοῦνται ὁμοῦ διὰ εἷς καὶ ὁ αὐτὸς τόμος. Ἀρ. 8.
4. Β. Τίτλος. Πωλητήρια τόπων, οἴκων, ἀγρῶν καὶ τῶν τοιούτων τοῦ Δημοσίου Μνήμωνος τῆς νήσου Σύρας. Βιβλίον τόμος Α. Ἐξακολούθησις ἄλλου βιβλίου τοῦ α΄τόμου, τὴν ὁποίαν ἐκάμαμεν πρὸς ἀποφυγὴν τῶν συχνῶν τόμων. Ἐξακολουθεῖ δὲ τὸ παρὸν βιβλίον τὴν τοῦ πρὸ αὐτοῦ σελίδα 378, ὥστε τὰ δύο αὐτὰ βιβλία ἐννοοῦνται ὁμοῦ διὰ εἷς καὶ ὁ αὐτὸς τόμος. Ἀρ. 4.
   Γ. Τίτλος. Προικοσύμφωνα, καί Διαθῆκαι τοῦ Δημοσίου Ὑπογραφέως τῆς Νήσου Σύρας, Τόμος α΄, 1827. Ὁ Δημόσιος Ὑπογραφεύς τῆς Νήσου Σύρας Σκαρλάτος Μάξιμος.
5. Β. Τίτλος. Πωλητήρια τόπων, οἴκων, ἀγρῶν, καὶ τῶν τοιούτων τοῦ Δημοσίου Μνήμονος τῆς νήσου Σύρας. Βιβλίον 1830 Δεκεμβρίου α΄. Τόμος Β.
6. Τῶν μνημονιακῶν πράξεων τοῦ Δημοσίου Μνήμονος τῆς νήσου Σύρας βιβλίον Α΄. Ἄρχεται ἀπὸ τὴν α[ην] τοῦ ἔτους 1831. Ὁ Δημόσιος Μνήμων τῆς Ν. Σύρας Σκαρλάτος Μάξιμος.

B. Κώδικες του Δημόσιου Μνήμονα Σύρου Ανδρέα Δαυΐδ [Books of Notary Andreas David]

7. Βιβλίον εἰσερχομένων.
8. Βιβλίον μνημονικῶν πράξεων ὑπὸ στοιχεῖον Β΄.

9. Βιβλίον μνημονικῶν πράξεων ὑπὸ στοιχεῖον Γ'. Ἡμερομ.: 9 Δεκ. 1831–26 Ἰουλ. 1832, ἀρ. 838–1656, σσ. 365.
10. Βιβλίον μνημονικῶν πράξεων ὑπὸ στοιχεῖον Δ'. Ἡμερομ.: 27 Ἰουλ.–14 Νοεμ. 1832, ἀρ. 1657–2054, σσ. 191.
11. Βιβλίον μνημονικῶν πράξεων ὑπὸ στοιχεῖον Ε'. Χρον.: 15 Νοεμ.–31 Δεκ. 1832, ἀρ. 2055–2212 καὶ 2 Ἰαν.–21 Ἰουλ. 1833, ἀρ. 1–836, σσ. 384.
12. Βιβλίον Μνημονικὸν ὑπὸ στοιχεῖον Ζ'. Ἡμερομ.: 2 Ἰουλ.–31 Δεκ. 1833, ἀρ. 837–1722 καὶ 2 Ἰαν.–18 Ἰαν. 1834, ἀρ. 1–62, σσ. 352.
13. Βιβλίον Μνημονικὸν ὑπὸ στοιχεῖον Η'. Ἡμερομ.: 18 Ἰαν.–15 Μαΐου 1834, ἀρ. 3–820, σσ. 309.
14. Βιβλίον Μνημονικὸν ὑπὸ στοιχεῖον Θ'. Ἡμερομ.: 15 Μαΐου 1834–20 Σεπτ. 1834 ἀρ. 821–1830, σσ. 389.
15. Βιβλίον Ι'. Ἡμερομ.: 20 Σεπτ. 1834–21 Ἰαν 1835, ἀρ. 1831–2582, σσ. 306.
16. Βιβλίον Κ'. Ἡμερομ.: 21 Ἰαν.–24 Ἰαν. 1835, ἀρ. 2583–2609, σσ. 11.

Γ. Συμβολαιογραφικές πράξεις (Λυτά έγγραφα) συμβολαιογράφου Ερμουπόλεως Σύρου Ανδρέα Δαυΐδ [Unbound notarial acts of Andreas David]
Αρ. 1–32569, έτη 1835–1865.

Δ. Συμβολαιογραφικές πράξεις (Λυτά έγγραφα) συμβολαιογράφου Ερμουπόλεως Σύρου Α. Λέτσου:
Αρ. 1–5859, έτη 1863–1872. [Unbound notarial acts of A. Letsos]

Παλαιοί Συμβολαιογράφοι Ερμουπόλεως-Σύρου. [Old notaries of Hermoupolis-Syros]

I. Συλλογή Ιστορικού Αρχείου Κυκλάδων.
Συμβολαιογράφος Κων/νος Αγγελίδης.
Ευρετήρια:

1. 7/5/1854–10/5/1855, αρ. 6976–8354.
2. 28/8/1859–29/7/1860, αρ. 15993–18012.
3. 29/7/1860–6/5/1861, αρ. 18013–19712.
4. 6/5/1861–25/6/1862, αρ. 19013–21225.
5. 7/2/1863–26/11/1863, αρ. 22992–24448.

Συμβολαιογράφος Αντώνιος Αλμπέρτος.
Ευρετήρια:

1. 4/3/1853–26/9/1861, αρ. 1–3245.
2. 29/9/1861–9/7/1864, αρ. 3246–3800.

Συμβολαιογράφος Μιχ. Ιωαννόπουλος.
Ευρετήρια:
1. 20/10/1843–30/3/1845, αρ. 74–1774.
2. 2/4/1845–9/6/1845 και 13/6/1845–15/2/1846, αρ. 1–844.

Συμβολαιογράφος Χριστόδουλος Ιωάννου.
Ευρετήρια:
1. 15/2/1846–25/10/1846, αρ. 845–1759.
2. 27/10/1846–13/9/1847, αρ. 1760–2956.
3. 13/9/1847–5/7/1848, αρ. 2957–4091.
4. 5/7/1848–4/5/1849, αρ. 4092–5237.
5. 5/5/1849–18/8/1850, αρ. 5238–6399.
6. 18/8/1850–29/4/1852, αρ. 6400–7866.
7. 30/4/1852–22/2/1854, αρ. 7867–9284.
8. 22/2/1854/1/9/1855, αρ. 9285–10740.
9. 1/9/1855–12/11/1857, αρ. 10741–12563.
10. 14/11/1857–9/2/1860, αρ. 12564–13424.

Δημοτικό Αρχείο Ερμουπόλεως. [Municipal Archive of Hermoupolis]

II. Δήμος Ερμουπόλεως, Α΄. Έγγραφα.
Διοικητική Υπηρεσία (Δ)
Δ/Γραμματεία (Α)

Δ/Α/Δικαστικά, φάκελοι:
24. υποφ. 2.
25. υποφ. 4.
Ιδιαίτερα (Ι).

Ναυπηγικά, φάκελοι:
1. 1836–1845.
2. 1846–1849.
3. 1850–1855.
4. 1856–1859.
5. 1860–1866.
6. 1861–1877.
7. 1867–1874.
Τεχνική Υπηρεσία (Τ).

Δημοτικά Έργα, φάκελοι:

6. 1848–1879.

77. 1871–1883.

80. 1855–1875.

230. 1848–1880.

II. Δήμος Ερμουπόλεως, Β'. Κατάστιχα.
Διοικητική Υπηρεσία (Δ).

Ληξιαρχείο (Ε):
Θάνατοι.
Δ/Ε/Πρόχειρα βιβλία αποβιώσεων.

1. 1848–1852.

Δ/Ε/Ληξιαρχικά βιβλία αποβιώσεων.
Διάφορα έτη.

Γ.Α.Κ./Κεντρική Υπηρεσία, Αθήνα. [*General State Archives, Athens*].
Συλλογή Βλαχογιάννη, Κατάστιχα πρωτόκολλα Αγώνα/Καποδίστρια, φ. 16.
Συλλογή Βλαχογιάννη, Δ', Μικραί 'Ιδιωτικαί Συλλογαί, κυτίο 118.
Συλλογή Βλαχογιάννη, Ε' Μικραί 'Ιδιωτικαί Συλλογαί, Αρχείον Παλαμήδη, 'Υλη Ιστορική.
Οθωνικό Αρχείο, Υπουργείο Ναυτικών, φ. 41–43.
Αυτοτελή Αρχεία, Αρχείο Σχεδίων Πόλεων, φ. 51.

Archive du Ministère des Affaires Étrangères (AMAE).
Serie: Correspondance Consulaire et Commerciale.
Syra, vol. 1–5, 1834–1858.

Ιδιωτικό αρχείο. Συλλογή εγγράφων οικογένειας Μικέ Ποτού. [*Private Archive of Potous Family*]

Published Sources

Ιστορικό Αρχείο Εθνικής Τραπέζης Ελλάδος (Ε.Τ.Ε.), *Αθήνα.* [*Historical Archive of National Bank of Greece, Athens*]
Foreign Office, Annual Series, *Diplomatic and Consular Reports on Trade and Finance.*
Syra, *Report by Consul Ruby on the Trade and Commerce of the Cyclades during the Year 1871, 1872, 1873.*
Syra, *Report by Consul Binney on the Trade and Commerce of the Cyclades during the Year 1874–1880.*
Leghorn, *Report by Consul Inglis on the trade and commerce for the year 1883.*

Electronic Sources

Institute for Mediterranean Studies/Foundation of Research Technology Hellas

Christos Loukos (ed.), Database, Hermoupolis Municipal Rolls, Project: The City in Modern Times, (http://cities.ims.forth.gr/search_population).

Christos Loukos (ed.), Database, Hermoupolis Censuses, 1860, 1870 and 1878. Project: The City in Modern Times, (http://cities.ims.forth.gr/search_census).

Department of History/Ionian University

Database "Amphitrete", in 'Pythagoras' I, Research Programme, 2004–07, financed from the European Union and the Greek Ministry of Education, Department of History, Ionian University, *The Maritime History of the Greeks, 1700–1821.*

Newspapers and Periodicals

Ἑρμῆς, [Hermes] Hermoupolis, 1840–1856.
Αἴολος, [Eolos] Hermoupolis, 1844–1855.
Ἀστὴρ τῶν Κυκλάδων,[Star of Cyclades] Hermoupolis 1858–1868.
Ἑρμούπολις, [Hermoupolis] Hermoupolis, 1864–1865.
Ἥλιος, [Sun] Hermoupolis, 1903–1904.
Θάρρος,[Courage] Hermoupolis, 1925.
Ἑλλάς, [Hellas] Hermoupolis, 1839.
Ἕνωσις, [Union] Hermoupolis, 1851–1857.
Τηλέγραφος τῶν Κυκλάδων, [Cyclades Telegraph] Hermoupolis, 1856–1857.
Ἐφημερὶς τῆς Κυβερνήσεως, [Government Gazette] Athens, 1833.
Πανδώρα, [Pandora] Athens, 1852–1857.

Bibliography

Agriantoni, Christina. "Η θέση της Ερμούπολης στην Ελληνική Οικονομία τον 19ο αιώνα. Οι παγίδες των πηγών" ["The position of Hermoupolis in Greek Economy in the nineteenth century. The deception of sources."]. *Τα Ιστορικά-Historica*, 1, (1983): 193–99.

———. *Οι Απαρχές της Εκβιομηχάνισης στην Ελλάδα τον 19° αιώνα*, [*The Beginnings of Industrialization in Greece in the 19th century*]. Athens: Historical Archive of the Commercial Bank of Greece, 1986.

———. "Η ελληνική οικονομία', ['Greek Economy']. In *Ιστορία του Νέου Ελληνισμού, 1770–2000* [*History of Modern Hellenism, 1770–2000*] vol. 5, edited by Vassilis Panayotopoulos, 55–70. Athens: Ellinika Grammata, 2003.

———. "Προσαρμογές του επιχειρηματικού κόσμου της Ερμούπολης" ["Adaptations of the entrepreneurs of Hermoupolis"]. In *Σύρος και Ερμούπολη. Συμβολές στην ιστορία του νησιού, 15ος–20ος αι.* [*Syros and Hermoupolis. Contributions to the history of the island, 15th–20th cent.*], edited by Christina Agriantoni and Dimitris Dimitropoulos, 143–153. Athens: IHR/NHRF, 2008.

Agriantoni, Christina and Aggeliki Fenerli. *Hermoupolis-Syros. A historical tour*. Athens: Olkos Publishers, 2000.

Ambelas, Timoleon. *Ιστορία της νήσου Σύρου από των αρχαιοτάτων χρόνων μέχρι των καθ'ημάς*. [*History of the island of Syros from Ancient Times to the present day*]. Hermoupolis: 1874.

Amin, Ash. "Industrial Districts". In *A Companion to Economic Geography*, edited by Eric Sheppard and Trevor J. Barnes, 149–68. Malden-Oxford-Victoria: Blackwell Publishing, 2003.

Anagnostaki, Katerina. "Δημιουργία, ανάπτυξη ακμή και παρακμή της Ερμούπολης μέσα από την επεξεργασία των επαγγελμάτων των δημοτολογίων". [Creation, growth and decline of Hermoupolis through the professions registered in Municipality Rolls]. MA essay, University of Crete, 2007.

Anselmi, Sergio. "Tipologia navale italiana in eta moderna (secoli XVIII–XIX)". In *La penisola italiana e il mare. Costruzioni navali, trasporti e commerci tra XV e XX secolo*, edited by Tommaso Fanfani, 233–48. Naples: Edizione Scientifica Italiana, 1993.

Argenti, Philip. *The Occupation of Chios by the Genoese and their administration of the island 1346–1566*. Cambridge: Cambridge University Press, 1958.

Asheim, Bjorn T. "Industrial Districts". In *The Oxford Handbook of Economic Geography*, edited by Gordon Clark, Maryann Feldman and Meric Gerlter, 413–31. Oxford: Oxford University Press, 2003.

Babudieri, Fulvio. "Maritime Commerce of the Hapsburg Empire: The Port of Trieste, 1789–1913". In *Southeast European maritime commerce and naval policies from the mid-eighteenth century to 1914*, edited by Apostolos Vakalopoulos, Konstantinos Svolopoulos, and Béla Király, 221–44. Thessaloniki: Columbia University Press, 1988.

Basch, Lucien. "Ancient wrecks and the archaeology of the ships", *International Journal of Nautical Archaeology and Underwater Exploration*, 1, (1972): 1–58.

Berrino, Annunziata. "I sorrentini e il mare". In *A Vela e a Vapore. Economie, culture e istituzioni del mare nell' Italia dell' Ottocento*, edited by Paolo Frascani, 29–53. Rome: Donzelli Editore, 2001.

Bjelovučić, Harriet. *The Ragusan Republic: victim of Napoleon and its own conservatism*. Leiden: E.J. Brill, 1970.

Boukas, Miltiadis. *Οδηγός Εμπορικός, Γεωγραφικός & Ιστορικός του έτους 1875*, [*Commercial, Geographic and Historical Guide of the year* 1875]. Athens: 1875.

Bourdieu, Pierre. "The forms of Capital". In *The sociology of economic life*, edited by Mark Granovetter and Richard Swedberg, 96–111. Colorado-Oxford: Westview Press, 2001.

Boyce, Gordon. "Network structures, processes and dynamics: Inter-firm cooperative frameworks in the shipping industry". In *International merchant shipping in the 19th and 20th centuries. The comparative dimension*, Research in Maritime History, 37, edited by Lewis R. Fischer and Even Lange, 165–78. St John's-Newfoundland: International Economic History Association, 2008.

———. *Cooperative structures in global business. Communicating, transferring knowledge and learning across the corporate frontier*. London-New York: Routledge, 2001.

Boyce, Gordon and Simon Ville. *The Development of Modern Business*. New York: Palgrave Macmillan, 2002.

Braudel, Fernand. *The Mediterranean and the Mediterranean World in the Age of Philip II*. Volume I. Berkeley-Los Angeles: University of California Press, 1995.

Campodonico, Pierangelo "Genoese shipbuilding in the 19th century". In *Shipbuilding and Ships in the eastern Mediterranean during the 18th and 19th century*, edited by Kostas Damianidis, 163–76. Chios: Homerion Cultural Center of Chios Municipality, 1999.

Carlos, Ann and Nicholas Stephen, "Managing the Manager: An Application of the Principal Agent Model to the Hudson's Bay Company". *Oxford Economic Papers*, New Series, 45, 2, (April 1993): 243–56.

Carosio, Giovanni. "La costruzione navale ligure nell' Ottocento: solo tradizione?". In *Dal Mediterraneo all' Adriatico. La marineria ligure nei mari del mondo*, edited by Pierangelo Campodonico, 303–20. Genoa: Tormena, 1993.

Casson, Mark. "Entrepreneurial networks in international business". *Business and economic history* 26, 2 (Winter 1997): 811–23.

———. "The economics of the family firm". *Scandinavian Economic History Review*, 47, (1999): 10–23.

Casson, Mark and Godley Andrew, "Entrepreneurship and historical explanation". In *Entrepreneurship in Theory and History*, edited by Youssef Cassis and Ioanna Pepelasis Minoglou, 25–60. New York: Palgrave Macmillan, 2005.

Casson, Mark et al., "Introduction". In *The Oxford Handbook of Entrepreneurship*, edited by Anuradha Basu, Mark Casson, Nigel Wadeson, and Bernard Yeung, 1–30. New York: Oxford University Press, 2006.

Caty, Roland and Eliane Richard. *Armateurs Marseillais au XIXe siècle*. Marseille: Chambre de Commerce et d'Industrie de Marseille, 1986.

Chandler, Alfred D., Jr. *Scale and Scope. The Dynamics of Industrial* Capitalism. London: Harvard University Press, 1990.

Chatziioannou, Maria Christina. "Greek Merchant Networks in the Age of Empires (1770–1870)". In *Diaspora Entrepreneurial Network. Four centuries of History* edited by Ina Banghdiatz Mc Cabe, Gelina Harlaftis, and Ioanna Pepelasi-Minoglou, 371–82. Oxford-New York: Berg, 2005.

———. *Οικογενειακή στρατηγική και εμπορικός ανταγωνισμός. Ο οίκος Γερούση τον 19ο αιώνα.* [*Family Strategy and Commercial Competition. The Firm of Gerousi in the 19th Century*]. Athens: Cultural Foundation of National Bank of Greece, 2003.

———. "Οι εμποροκαπετάνιοι μετά την Επανάσταση. Μερικές παρατηρήσεις" ['The merchant captains after the Revolution. Some observations"]. In *Η Επανάσταση του 1821. Μελέτες στη μνήμη της Δέσποινας Θεμελή-Κατηφόρη*, [*The 1821 Revolution. Studies in the memory of Despoina-Themeli Katifori*], collective volume, 157–72. Athens: EMNE, 1994.

Cipolla, Carlo. *Before the Industrial Revolution. European Society and Economy, 1000–1700*. London: Routledge, 1993.

Clark, Arthur H. *The Clipper Ship Era: An Epitome of Famous American and British Clipper Ships, their Owners, Builders, Commanders and Crews, 1843–1869*. New York and London: G.P. Putnam's sons, 1911.

Coe Neil M., Philip F. Kelly and Henry W. Yeung C. *Economic Geography. A Contemporary Introduction*. Malden-Oxford-Victoria: Blackwell Publishing, 2007.

Colli, Andrea. "Family Business". In *The Oxford handbook of Business History*, edited by Geoffrey Jones and Jonathan Zeitlin, 194–218. Oxford-New York: Oxford University Press, 2007.

———. *The history of family business, 1850–2000*. Cambridge: Cambridge University Press, 2003.

Colli, Andrea and Mary Rose. "Families and Firms: The Culture and Evolution of Family Firms in Britain and Italy in the Nineteenth and Twentieth Centuries". *Scandinavian Economic History Review*, 47, (1997): 24–47.

Crossick, Geoffrey and Heinz-Gerhard Haupt. *The petit bourgeoisie in Europe, 1780–1914. Enterprise, family and independence*. London-New York: Routledge, 1995.

Crowther, Simeon J. "The Shipbuilding Output of the Delaware Valley, 1722–1776". *Proceedings of the American Philosophical Society*, 117, 2, (April 1973): 90–104.

Damianidis, Kostas. *Ελληνική Παραδοσιακή Ναυπηγική* [*Greek Vernacular Boatbuilding*]. Athens: Hellenic Bank of Industrial Development, 1998.

Davis, Robert. C. *Shipbuilders of the Venetian Arsenal. Workers and Workplace in the Pre-industrial City*. Baltimore: The John Hopkins University Press, 1991.

De Negri, Carlo. *Vele italiane del XIX secolo*. Milano: Mursia, 1974.

De Voogd, Cees "Shipbuilding, Commercial". In *The Oxford Encyclopaedia of Maritime History*, vol. 3, edited by John B. Hattenford, 572–75. Oxford-New York: Oxford University Press, 2007.

Deane, Phyllis. "The Industrial Revolution in Great Britain". In *The Fontana Economic History of Europe*, vol. 1, edited by Carlo Cipolla, 161–227. London: Collins/Fontana Books, 1976.

Delis, Apostolos. "Mediterranean Wooden Shipbuilding in the nineteenth century: Production, Productivity and Ship Types in Comparative Perspective". *Cahiers de la Méditerranée*, 84, (2012): 349–66.

———. "From Lateen to Square-Rig: The evolution of the Greek-owned merchant fleet and its ships in the eighteenth and nineteenth centuries". *Mariner's Mirror*, 100, 1, (2014): 44–58.

———. "Rodokanakis family", *Encyclopaedia of the Hellenic World, Black Sea* http://blacksea.ehw.gr/forms/fLemma.aspx?lemmaId=11590, 2007.

———. "Lykiardopoulos family", *Encyclopaedia of the Hellenic World, Black Sea*, http://blacksea.ehw.gr/forms/fLemma.aspx?lemmaId=11583, 2007.

———."Ερμούπολη (Σύρος): το ναυπηγικό κέντρο της ιστιοφόρου ναυτιλίας, 1830–1880" ["Hermoupolis (Island of Syros): the shipbuilding centre of the sailing merchant marine, 1830–1880"], (PhD diss., Ionian University), 2010.

Denham, H.M. "Aegean Caiques, 1915–1980". *Mariner's Mirror*, 72, 3, (1986): 277–93.

Dervenis, Dimitris K. "Τα παραδοσιακά εργαλεία του ξυλοναυπηγού", ['The traditional tools of the shipwright"]. In *Shipbuilding and ships in the eastern Mediterranean in the 18th & 19th centuries*, edited by Kostas Damianidis, 289–98. Chios: Homerion Cultural Center of Chios Municipality, 1999.

Doria, Marco. "La marina mercantile a vela in Liguria dalla metà dell'Ottocento alla prima guerra mondiale". In *A Vela e a Vapore. Economie, culture e istituzioni del mare nell' Italia dell' Ottocento*, edited by Paolo Frascani, 83–107. Rome: Donzelli Editore, 2001.

Dotson, John. "Economics and logistics of Galley warfare". In *The Age of the Galley. Mediterranean oared vessels since pre-classical times. Conway's History of the Ship*, edited by Robert Gardiner, 217–23. London: Conway Maritime Press, 1995.

Drakakis, Andreas. *Ιστορία του οικισμού της Ερμουπόλεως (Σύρας),1821–1825*. [*History of the settlement of Hermoupolis (Syros),1821–1825*] vol. A΄. Athens: 1979.

———. *Ιστορία του οικισμού της Ερμουπόλεως (Σύρας), 1827–28* [*History of the settlement of Hermoupolis (Syros), 1827–1828,*] vol. B΄. Athens: 1983.

———. "Πρωτότυποι νομικοί θεσμοί εις την οικιζόμενην Ερμούπολιν (1821–1830)" ["Original legal institutions in Hermoupolis (1821–1830)"]. *Επετηρίς του Κέντρου Ιστορίας του Ελληνικού Δικαίου της Ακαδημίας Αθηνών* [*Yearbook of the Center for the History of Greek Law in the Academy of Athens*], 18, (1971): 169–220.

———. "Η πειρατεία εις τάς Κυκλάδας κατά την Επανάστασιν του 1821", ["Piracy in Cyclades during the Greek War of Independence"]. *Μνημοσύνη* [*Mnemosyni*], 5, (1974–75): 325–65.

Drikos, Thomas., *Η πορνεία στην Ερμούπολη το 19ο αιώνα (1820–1900)*, [*The prostitution in Hermoupolis in the 19th century (1820–1900)*]. Athens: Ellinika Grammata, 2002.

Exadaktylou-Bekiaroglou, Aikaterini. "Μετακινήσεις τεχνιτών από τη Χίο στο ναυπηγείο της Κωνσταντινούπολης", ['Transfers of craftsmen from Chios to the Constantinople shipyards"]. In *Shipbuilding and ships in the eastern Mediterranean in the 18th & 19th centuries*, edited by Kostas Damianidis, 39–46. Chios: Homerion Cultural Center of Chios Municipality, 1999.

Fairburn, William Armstrong. *Merchant Sail*. Maine: Center Lovell, 1945–55.

Fanfani, Tommaso. "Lo scenario generale". In *La penisola italiana e il mare. Costruzioni navali, trasporti e commerci tra XV e XX secolo*, edited by Tommaso Fanfani, 3–22. Naples: Edizione Scientifica Italiana, 1993.

Faucher, Albert. "The Decline of Shipbuilding at Quebec in the Nineteenth Century". *The Canadian Journal of Economics and Political Science/Revue canadienne d'Economique et de Science politique*, 23, 2, (May, 1957): 195–215.

Fenerli, Aggeliki. "Les premiers constructeurs de navires à Hermoupolis (île de Syra), 1823–1835". In *The evolution of wooden shipbuilding in the Eastern Mediterranean during the 18th and 19th centuries. First International Workshop*, edited by Kostas Damianidis, 25–31. Athens: INR/NHRF, 1993.

———. "Η υποδοχή του ατμού στην Ερμούπολη από τους παραδοσιακούς ναυπηγούς τον ΙΘ'αιώνα" ['The reception of steam by the traditional shipbuilders in Hermoupolis in the nineteenth century"]. In *Shipbuilding and ships in the eastern Mediterranean in the 18th & 19th centuries*, edited by Kostas Damianidis, 121–28. Chios: Homerion Cultural Center of Chios Municipality, 1999.

———. "Ο καλλωπισμός της πόλης. Ένας πρωτότυπος συμμετοχικός τρόπος χρηματοδότησης δημοσίων κτιρίων στην Ερμούπολη (19ος αι.)" ['The embellishment of the town. An original participatory method to finance public buildings in Hermoupolis (19th cent.)". In *Η πόλη στους νεότερους χρόνους. Μεσογειακές και Βαλκανικές όψεις (19ος–20ος αι.)* [*The city in modern times. Mediterranean and Balkan aspects (19th -20th cent.)*]. Proceedings of the second international congress, 173–82. Athens: EMNE, 2000.

———. "Σχέδια της Ερμούπολης και η έναρξη του σχεδίου πόλης" ["Plans of Hermoupolis and the beginning of the final city's plan"]. Paper presented in the 21st *Hermoupolis Seminars*, Hermoupolis, June 28–July 10 2005.

———. 'Τα πρώτα βήματα οικοδόμησης της Ερμούπολης." ["The first steps in the building of Hermoupolis"]. Paper presented in the 22th *Hermoupolis Seminars*, Hermoupolis, July 5–15, 2006.

———. 'Το πρόβλημα του νερού στην Ερμούπολη (1823–1923)" ['The problem of water supply in Hermoupolis (1823–1923)"]. Paper presented in the 24th *Hermoupolis Seminars*, Hermoupolis, July 3–15, 2008.

Fischer, Lewis R. "The Port of Prince Edward Island, 1840–1889: a preliminary analysis". In *Ships and Shipbuilding in the North Atlantic Region*, edited by Keith Matthews and Gerald Panting, 41–70. Newfoundland: Memorial University, 1978.

Fischer, Lewis R. and Helge W., Nordvik. "Θαλάσσιες μεταφορές και ενοποίηση της οικονομίας του βόρειου Ατλαντικού, 1850–1914", ["Maritime transport and the unification of the North-Atlantic economy, 1850–1914"]. In *Ιστορία και Ναυτιλία, 16ος–20ος αιώνας*, [*History and Shipping, 16th–20th cent.*], edited by Gelina Harlaftis 271–306. Athens: Stachi Publishers, 2001.

Forni Mario and Sergio Paba. "Spillovers and the Growth of Local Industries". *The Journal of Industrial Economics*, 50, 2, (June, 2002): 151–71.

Frangakis-Syrett, Elena. *The commerce of Smyrna in the 18th century (1700–1820)*. Athens: Centre for Asia Minor Studies, 1992.

Frangidis, Andreas. *Ιστορία της νήσου Σύρου. [History of the island of Syros]*. Athens: Association of the Syriots of Athens and Piraeus, 1975.

French, Christopher J. "Productivity in the Atlantic Shipping Industry: A Quantitative Study". *Journal of Interdisciplinary History*, 17, 3, (Winter 1987); 613–38.

———. "Mechant Shipping of the British Empire". In *The Heyday of Sail. The Merchant Sailing Ship, 1650–1830. Conway's History of the Ship*, edited by Robert Gardiner, 10–33. London: Conway Maritime Press, 1995.

Friel, Ian. "The Carrack: The Advent of the Full Rigged Ship". In *Cogs, Caravels & Galleons. The history of sailing ship, 1000–1650. Conway's History of the Ship*, edited by Robert Gardiner, 77–90. London: Conway Maritime Press, 1994.

Fujita Masahisa and Jaques- Francois Thisse. *Economics of Agglomeration, Cities, Industrial Location and Regional Growth*. Cambridge: Cambridge University Press, 2002.

Gallant, Thomas. *Modern Greece*. London: Bloomsbury Academic, 2001.

Gavala, Pepi and Eleni Garezou. *Τα γλυπτά μνημεία του κοιμητήριου του Αγίου Γεωργίου. Ερμούπολη Σύρου (19ος–20ος αιώνας), [The sculptures of the St George Cemetery. Ermoupolis, Syros. (19th–20th centuries)]*. Athens: Ministry of Aegean,-Municipality of Ermoupolis, Gnosis Editions, 1994.

Gatti, Luciana. *"Un raggio di convenienza". Navi mercantili, costruttori proprietari in Liguria nella prima metà dell' Ottocento*. Genoa: Società Ligure di Storia Patria, 2008.

Gerasimidis K., and E. Monoyios. *Το πανόραμα της Σύρου [The panorama of Syros]*. Syros: 1933.

Glaeser Edward L. "Urban and Regional Growth". In *The Oxford Handbook of Economic Geography*, edited by Gordon Clark, Maryann Feldman and Meric Gerlter 83–98. Oxford: Oxford University Press, 2003.

Gourgouris, Efthimios. *Το Γαλαξείδι στον καιρό των Καραβιών, [Galaxidi in the age of sailing ships]*. Athens: 1983.

Graham Gerald S., "The Ascendancy of the Sailing Ship 1 850–85", *The Economic History Review*, New Series, vol. 9, No. 1, 1956, p. 87 -88.

Granovetter, Mark. "Economic action and social structure: The problem of Embeddedness". In *The sociology of economic life*, edited by Mark Granovetter and Richard Swedberg 53–81. Boulder-San Francisco-Oxford: Westview Press 1992.

Greenhill, Basil. "Introduction". In *Sail's Last Century. The Merchant Sailing Ship, 1830–1930. Conway's History of the Ship*, edited by Robert Gardiner 7–19. London: Conway Maritime Press, 1995.

Hadjianargyros, A.A. *Τα Σπετσιωτικά*, [*The Spetses affaires*], vol. 1 Athens: 1861 and vol. 2 Piraeus: 1925.

Hadjiiossif, Christos. "Crise conjoncturelle et problèmes structurels dans la marine marchande grecque au XIXe siècle: Les réactions de l'état et des intérêts privés". In *Actes du IIe Colloque International d'Histoire. Economies Méditerranéennes. Equilibres et Intercommunications. XIIIe–XIXe siècles*, Tome II, edited by M.C. Chatziioannou and A. Tabaki, 377–394. Athens: INR/NHRF, 1986.

Harris, Robin. *Dubrovnik: a history*. London: SAQI, 2006.

Harlaftis, Gelina. "From Diaspora Traders to Shipping Tycoons: The Vagliano Bros". *Business History Review*, 81, (2007): 237–68.

———. *Ιστορία της Ελληνόκτητης Ναυτιλίας* [*History of the Greek-owned shipping*]. Athens: Nefeli, 2001.

———. A *History of Greek-Owned Shipping: The Making of an International Tramp Fleet, 1830 to the Present Day*. London and New York: Routledge, 1996.

———. "Mapping the Greek Maritime Diaspora". In *Diaspora Entrepreneurial Network. Four centuries of History* edited by Ina Banghdiatz Mc Cabe, Gelina Harlaftis, and Ioanna Pepelasi-Minoglou, 147–72. Oxford-New York: Berg, 2005.

———. "The fleet 'dei Greci'. Ottoman and Venetian Greeks in the Mediterranean sea-trade, eighteenth century". In *Making the Waves in the Mediterranean*, edited by Michela d'Angelo, Gelina Harlaftis and Carmell Vassalo, 383–416. Messina: Istituto di Studi Storici Gaetano Salvemini, 2010.

Harlaftis, Gelina and Sofia Laiou. "Ottoman state policy in Mediterranean Trade and Shipping, c. 1780–c. 1820: The Rise of the Greek-Owned Ottoman Merchant Fleet". In *Networks of power in modern Greece: Essays in honour of John Cambell*, edited by Mark Mazower, 1–34. New York: Columbia University Press, 2008.

Harlaftis, Gelina and Nikos Vlassopoulos. *Historical Register 'Pontoporeia'. Sailing Ships and Steamships, 1830–1939*. Athens: Hellenic Literary and Historical Archive, 2002.

Harlaftis, Gelina, Helen Beneki and Manos Haritatos. *Ploto, Greek shipowners from the late 18th century to the eve of WWII*. Athens: ELIA/Niarchos Foundation, 2003.

Harlaftis, Gelina and George Kostelenos. "International shipping and national economic growth: shipping earnings and the Greek economy in the nineteenth century". *Economic History Review*, 65, 4, (2012): 1403–27.

———. "Services and economic growth: estimating shipping income in the 19th century Greek economy", *Greek Economic History Society* working paper (http://hdoisto.gr/gr/library/seminar-proceedings), 13–11–2006.

Harley, C. Knick. "Ocean Freight Rates and Productivity, 1740–1913: The Primacy of Mechanical Invention Reaffirmed", *The Journal of Economic History*. 48, 4, (Dec., 1988): 851–76.

———. "Aspects of the Economics of Shipping, 1850–1913". In *Change and Adaptation in Maritime History. The North Atlantic Fleets in the 19th century*, edited by Lewis R.

Fischer and Gerald E. Panting, 167–86. St John's: Memorial University of Newfoundland, 1985.

Harvey, Mose Lofley. "The Development of Russian Commerce on the Black Sea and its Significance". PhD diss., University of California, 1938.

Hearder, Harry. *Europe in the 19th century, 1830–1880*. London: Longman, 1988.

Heers, Jacques. *Gênes au xve siècle. Activité économique et problèmes sociaux*. Paris: SEVPEN, 1961.

Hengst, Sjoerd and Alan A. Lemmers. "Shipyards". In *The Oxford Encyclopaedia of Maritime History*, vol. 3, edited by John B. Hattenford 703–06. Oxford-New York: Oxford University Press, 2007.

Herlihly, Patricia. *Odessa: a history, 1794–1914*. Cambridge Mass.: Harvard Ukrainian Research Institute, 1986.

Hobsbawm, Eric. *The age of revolutions (1789–1848)*. New York: Vintage Books, 1962, reprint 1996.

———. *The Age of Capital, 1848–1875*, (Greek translation). Athens: Cultural Foundation of the National Bank, 2003.

Hocker, Frederick, M. "Shipbuilding: philosophy, practice and research". In *The Philosophy of Shipbuilding. Conceptual approaches to the study of wooden ship*, edited by Frederick, M. Hocker and Cheryl A. Ward, 1–11. College Station, Texas: Texas A&M University Press, 2004.

Hohenberg, Paul M. – Hollen Lees Lynn. *The making of urban Europe, 1000–1994*. Cambridge, Massachusetts and London: Harvard University Press, 1995.

Howorth, Carole, Mary Rose and Eleanor Hamilton. "Definitions, diversity and development: key debates in family business research". In *The Oxford Handbook of Entrepreneurship*, edited by Anuradha Basu, Mark Casson, Nigel Wadeson, and Bernard Yeung, 225–43. Oxford: Oxford University Press, 2006.

Hutchins, John G.B. "The Declining American Maritime Industries: An Unsolved Problem, 1860–1940". *The Journal of Economic History*, 6, Supplement: The Tasks of Economic History, (May 1946): 103–22.

———. *The American Maritime Industries and Public Policy, 1789–1914*. New York: Russell and Russell, 1941.

Jones, Geoffrey. *Merchants to Multinationals: British Trading Companies in the Nineteenth and Twentieth Centuries*. New York: Oxford University Press, 2000.

Kahane Henry and Renée and Andrea Tietze. *The Lingua Franca in the Levant. Turkish nautical terms of Italian and Greek origin*. Istanbul: ABC Kitabevi, 1988.

Kardasis, Vasilis. *Σύρος. Σταυροδρόμι της ανατολικής Μεσογείου (1832–1857)*. [Syros. *A crossroad of the Eastern Mediterranean (1832–1857)*]. Athens: Cultural Foundation of National Bank of Greece, 1987.

———. *Έλληνες ομογενείς στη Νότια Ρωσία, 1775–1861*[*Greeks in Southern Russia, 1775–1861*]. Athens: Alexandria Publishers, 1998.

Kaukiainen, Yrjö. "Aspects of competition between steam and sail". In *Sail and Steam: selected maritime writings of Yrjö Kaukiainen*, Research in Maritime History, 27, edited by Lars U. Scholl and Merja-Liisa Hinkkanen, 113–28. St John's, Newfoundland: International Economic History Association 2004.

———. "Growth, diversification and globalization: Main trends in International Shipping since 1850". In *International Merchant Shipping in the 19th and 20th centuries. The comparative dimension*, Research in Maritime History, 37, edited by Lewis R. Fischer and Even Lange, 1–56. St John's, Newfoundland: International Economic History Association 2008.

———. *A History of Finnish Shipping*. New York-London: Routledge, 1993.

Kolodny, Emile. "Hermoupolis-Syra: naissance et évolution d'une ville insulaire grecque". *Méditerranée*, 10e année, 2, (1969): 189–220.

Komis, Kostas. "Μετακινήσεις πληθυσμών. Πολεμικές καταστροφές και νέες εγκαταστάσεις." ["Population transportation. War disasters and new settlements. "]. In *Ιστορία του Νέου Ελληνισμού, 1770–2000* [*History of Modern Hellenism, 1770–2000,*], vol. 2, edited by Vassilis Panayotopoulos, 235–44. Athens: Ellinika Grammata, 2003.

Konstantinidis, Tryfonas. *Καράβια, Καπεταναίοι και Συντροφοναύται 1800–1830*, [*Ships, Captains and Fellow seamen, 1800–1830*]. Athens: 1954.

Kostelenos, George, Sokratis Petmezas, Dimitrios Vasileiou, Emmanouil Kounaris, and Michail Sfakianakis. *Πηγές οικονομικής ιστορίας της Νεότερης Ελλάδας. Ποσοτικά στοιχεία και στατιστικές σειρές. Ακαθάριστο Εγχώριο Προϊόν, 1830–1939*, [*Sources of economic history of Modern Greece. Quantitative data and statistical series. Gross Domestic Product, 1830–1939*] Athens: Historical Archive of National Bank of Greece -Center of Programming and Economic Research, 2007.

Kougeas, Nikolas. *Η τιμή του συναλλάγματος και η νομισματική πολιτική στην Ελλάδα (1843–1879)*, [*The exchange rates and the monetary policy in Greece (1843–79)*]. Athens: Cultural Foundation of National Bank of Greece, 1992.

Kremmydas, Vassilis. "Quelques aspects de la navigation et des liaisons commerciales en Méditerranée, au XVIIIe au début du XIXe siècle". In *Actes du IIe Colloque International d'Histoire. Economies Méditerranéennes. Equilibres et Intercommunications. XIIIe–XIXe siècles*, Tome I, edited by M.C. Chatziioannou and A. Tabaki, 143–62. Athens: INR/NHRF, 1986.

———. *Ελληνική Ναυτιλία, 1776–1835.Οι Μηχανισμοί*, [*Greek Shipping, 1776–1835. The mechanisms*], vol. B′. Athens: Historical Archive of the Commercial Bank of Greece, 1986.

———. *Αρχείο Χατζηπαναγιώτη. Χατζηπαναγιώτης-Πολίτης* [*Hadjipanayotis Archive. Hadjipanayotis-Politis*]. Athens: 1973.

Kriedte, Peter, Jurgen Schlumbohm and Hans Medick. *Industrialization before Industrialization. Rural Industry in the Genesis of Capitalism*. Cambridge: Cambridge University Press, 1981.

Kotsovillis, Georgios I. *Περί εξαρτισμού των πλοίων*. Syros: 1919, (reprint), Athens: 1995.

L.G.C.- L. "The origins of the Schooner Rig". *Mariner's Mirror*, 1, 1, (1911): 28.

Landes, David S. "French entrepreneurship and industrial growth in the 19th century". In *Family Business*, edited by Mary Rose, 45–61. Aldershot: Edward Elgar 1996.

Lane, Frederick. *Venice: a maritime republic*. Baltimore: The John Hopkins University Press, 1973.

Leon (Leontaritis), Georgios "Ελληνική Εμπορική Ναυτιλία". In *Ελληνική Εμπορική Ναυτιλία, 1453–1821*, [*Greek Merchant Marine, 1453–1821*], edited by S. Papadopoulos 32–43. Athens: National Bank of Greece, 1972.

Leontidis, Tassos. "Longitudinal fastenings in traditional Greek wooden boats". In *Shipbuilding and Ships in the eastern Mediterranean during the 18th and 19th century*, edited by Kostas Damianidis, 283–88. Chios: Homerion Cultural Center of Chios Municipality, 1999.

Liata, Eftichia. *Φλωριά δεκατέσσερα στένουν γρόσια σαράντα. Η κυκλοφορία των νομισμάτων στον ελληνικό χώρο, 15ος–19ος αι.*, [*"Fourteen florins make forty gurus". The circulation of currencies in the Hellenic areas, 15th to 19th centuries*]. Athens: Department of Neohellenic Research Editions, 1996.

Licht, Amir N. and Jordan Siegel. "The social dimension of entrepreneurship". In *The Oxford Handbook of Entrepreneurship*, edited by Anuradha Basu, Mark Casson, Nigel Wadeson, and Bernard Yeung, 511–39. New York: Oxford University Press, 2006.

Lougheed, Alan. "Industry and technical change". In *The European Economy 1750–1914: A Thematic Approach*, edited by Derek H. Aldcroft and Simon P. Ville, 158–63. Manchester-New York: Manchester University Press, 1994.

Loukos, Christos. "Ερμούπολη. Μία ελληνική πόλη σε παρακμή στο β΄μισό του 19ου αιώνα", ['Hermoupolis, a city in decline in the second half of the nineteenth century']. *Νεοελληνική πόλη. Οθωμανικές κληρονομιές και ελληνικό κράτος. Πρακτικά του Διεθνούς Συμποσίου Ιστορίας*, [*Neohellenic polis. Ottoman legacies and Greek State.,*]. Proccedings of International Symposium of History, 591–601. Athens: EMNE 1985.

———. "Επιδημία και κοινωνία. Η χολέρα στην Ερμούπολη (1854)" ["Disease and Society. The Cholera in Hermoupolis (1854)"]. *Μνήμων* [*Mnimon*], 14, (1992): 49–61.

———. *Πεθαίνοντας στη Σύρο τον 19° αιώνα*, [*Dying in Syros in the nineteenth century*]. Iraklion: Crete University Press, 2000.

Loukos, Christos and Demetra Samiou. "Οικονομική συμπεριφορά, ψυχολογία και βιοτικό επίπεδο ενός συριανού τοκιστή: Στέφανος Δ. Ρήγας" [Economic behaviour, psychology and standards of living of a money lender from Syros: Stefanos D. Rigas]. *Θεωρία και μελέτες ιστορίας* [*Theory and historical studies*], n. 11. Athens: EMNE-Mnimon, 1991.

Lyman, John. "Pole-masted Rigs". *Mariner's Mirror*, 56, 2, (1970): 161–67.

———. "The Martingana". *Mariner's Mirror*, 58, 2, (1972): 203–04.

Malikoutis, Matina. *Η εξέλιξη του αστικού Πειραιά, 1834–1922*, [*The development of Urban Piraeus, 1834–1922*]. Athens: Efesos, 2000.

Maresca, Massimo. "Cantieri navali in penisola sorrentina nell' Ottocento. Il costruttore Aniello Castellano". *Estratto da Navis*, 3, (2006): 21–30.

Matthews, Keith. "The shipping industry of Atlantic Canada: Themes and Problems". In *Ships and Shipbuilding in the North Atlantic Region*, edited by Keith Matthews and Gerald Panting, 1–18. Newfoundland: Memorial University, 1978.

McCann, Philip. "Regional Development: Clusters and Districts". In *The Oxford Handbook of Entrepreneurship*, edited by Anuradha Basu, Mark Casson, Nigel Wadeson, and Bernard Yeung, 651–70. New York: Oxford University Press, 2006.

McCulloch, J.R. *Dictionary, practical, theoretical and historical of Commerce & Commercial Navigation*. London: 1859.

Mc Gregor, David. "The Wooden Sailing Ship Over 300 Tons". In *Sail's Last Century. The Merchant Sailing Ship, 1830–1930. Conway's History of the Ship*, edited by Robert Gardiner 20–41. London: Conway Maritime Press, 1995.

———. "The Wooden Sailing Ship: Under 300 Tons". In *Sail's Last Century. The Merchant Sailing Ship, 1830–1930. Conway's History of the Ship*, edited by Robert Gardiner 42–51. London: Conway Maritime Press, 1995.

———. *Merchant Sailing Ship, 1815–1850, The Supremacy of Sail*. London: Conway Maritime Press, 1984.

———. *Merchant Sailing Ship, 1850–1875, The Heyday of Sail*. London: Conway Maritime Press, 1984.

Mendels, Franklin F. "Proto-Industrialization: The First Phase of the Industrialization Process". *The Journal of Economic History*, 32, 1, The Tasks of Economic History. (March, 1972): 241–61:

Metaxas, Basil. *The Economics of Tramp Shipping*. London: Athlone Press, 1971.

Moore, Alan. "Sails and Rigging. Rig in Northern Europe". *Mariner's Mirror*, 42, 1 (1956): 6–37.

Nance, R.M. "Spritsails". *Mariner's Mirror*, 3, 2 (1913): 155–57.

Nikodimos, Konstantinos. *Υπόμνημα της Νήσου Ψαρών*, [*History of the Island of Psara*]. Athens: 1862.

Nikolaou, Despina. "Αναζητώντας τους εργάτες στη Σύρο του 19ου αιώνα" ["Searching the workers at Syros in 19th century"]. MA diss., University of Crete, 2004.

North, Douglass. "Conference Summary". In *Merchant shipping and economic development in Atlantic Canada*, edited by Lewis R. Fischer and Eric Sager E., 229–33. St John's, Newfoundland: Maritime History Group, Memorial University of Newfoundland, 1982.

———. "Ocean Freight Rates and Economic Development 1750–1913". *The Journal of Economic History*, 18, 4 (December 1958): 537–55.

———. "Transaction costs, Institutions, and Economic Performance". *Occasional Papers*, ICEGP 30, San Francisco, 1992, 1–11.

———. *Structure and Change in Economic History*. New York: Norton, 1981.

———. *Institutions, Institutional Change and Economic Performance*. Cambridge: Cambridge University Press, 1990.

Ogilvie, C. Sheilagh and Markus Cerman. "The Theories of Proto-Industrialization". In *European proto-industrialization*, edited by Sheilagh C. Ogilvie and Markus Cerman 1–11. Cambridge: Cambridge University Press, 1996.

Ojala, Jari. "Productivity and technological change in 18th and 19th century sea transport: a case study of sailing ship efficiency in Kokkola, Finland, 1721–1913". *International Journal of Maritime History*, IX, 1, (1997): 98–114.

Palmer, Sarah. "The British Shipping Industry, 1850–1914". In *Change and Adaptation in Maritime History. The North Atlantic Fleets in the 19th century*, edited by Lewis R. Fischer and Gerald E. Panting, 87–114. St John's: Memorial University of Newfoundland, 1985.

———. *Politics, Shipping, and the repeal of the Navigation Laws*. Manchester and New York: Manchester University Press, 1990.

Panzac, Daniel. "L'escale de Chio: un observatoire privilégié de l'activité maritime en mer Egée au XVIIIe siècle". *Histoire, économie et société*, 4e année, 4, (1985): 541–61.

Papathanassopoulos, Konstantinos. *Ελληνική εμπορική ναυτιλία (1833–1856). Εξέλιξη και αναπροσαρμογή*. [*Greek Merchant Marine, (1833–1856). Development & Readjustment*]. Athens: Cultural Foundation of National Bank, 1983.

Parker, Lewis W.J. "The Schooner in America". In *Sail's Last Century. The Merchant Sailing Ship, 1830–1930. Conway's History of the Ship*, edited by Robert Gardiner 118–31. London: Conway Maritime Press, 1995.

Pavlidis, Laurent. "La production des bâtiments de mer en bois dans les chantiers privés provençaux au XIXe siècle". *Provence historique*, LIX, 237, (2009): 329–54.

Peterson, William N. *"Mystic Built". Ships and shipyards of the Mystic River, Connecticut, 1789–1914*.Mystic, Connecticut: Mystic Seaport Museum, 1989.

Pfister-Langanay, Christian. *Constructeur, charpentier et navires à Dunkerque du XVIIe au XXe siècle*. Dunkirk: Société Dunkerquoise d'Histoire et d'Archéologie, 2005.

Pigné, Hélène "Εξωτερικό και διανησιωτικό εμπόριο στη Χίο τον ιη' αιώνα", ["Overseas and inter-island trade in Chios in the eighteenth century"]. *Τα Ιστορικά,-Historica*, 8, (1988): 115–22.

Pinol, Jean-Luc. *Ο κόσμος των πόλεων τον 19ο αιώνα* [*The world of the cities in the 19th century*]. Athens: Plethron Publishers, 2000.

Polemis, Demetrios I. "Shipbuilding on Andros during the period 1830–1850". In *The evolution of wooden shipbuilding in the Eastern Mediterranean during the 18th and 19th centuries. First International Workshop*, edited by Kostas Damianidis, 45–53. Athens: INR/NHRF, 1993.

———. *Τα ιστιοφόρα της Άνδρου,* [*The Andros sailing ships*]. Andros: Agra Publishers, 1991.

Porter, Michael E. "Locations, Clusters, and Company Strategy". In *The Oxford Handbook of Economic Geography*, edited by Gordon Clark, Maryann Feldman and Meric Gerlter, 253–73. Oxford: Oxford University Press, 2003.

Portes, Alejandro and Julia Sensenbrenner. "Embeddedness and Immigration: Notes on the Social Determinants of Economic Action". In *The sociology of economic life*, edited by Mark Granovetter and Richard Swedberg, 112–138. Colorado-Oxford: Westview Press, 2001.

Prins, A.H.S. "Mediterranean Ships and Shipping, 1650–1850." In *The Heyday of Sail. The Merchant Sailing Ship, 1650–1830. Conway's History of the Ship*, edited by Robert Gardiner, 77–104. London: Conway Maritime Press, 1995.

Pryor, John. "The Mediterranean round ship". In *Cogs, Caravels & Galleons. The history of sailing ship, 1000–1650. Conway's History of the Ship*, edited by Robert Gardiner, 59–76. London: Conway Maritime Press, 1994.

Quataert, Donald. "The Age of Reforms, 1812–1914". In *An Economic and Social History of the Ottoman Empire, 1300–1914*, edited by Halil Inacik and Donald Quataert 759–933. Cambridge: Cambridge University Press, 1994.

Rallis, G.A. *Ερμηνεία του Ελληνικού Εμπορικού Δικαίου*, [*Interpretation of the Greek Commercial Law*] vol. B΄. Athens: 1865.

Rao, P.K. *The Economics of Transaction Costs. Theory, Methods and Application, The Economics of Transaction Costs. Theory, Methods and Application*. New York: Palgrave Macmillan, 2003.

Raptis, Kostas. "Αστικές τάξεις και αστικότητα στην Ευρώπη, 1789–1914" ["Bourgeois class and bourgeoisie in Europe 1789–1914"]. *Μνήμων* [*Mnimon*], 20, (1998): 211–43.

Roidis, Emmanuel. *Ψυχολογία Συριανού Συζύγου* [*Psychology of a husband from Syros*]. Thessaloniki: Ianos Publishers (written in 1894), 2005.

Rose Mary, *Firms, networks and business values. The British and American cotton industry since 1750*, New York, Cambridge University Press, 2000.

Rostow, W.W. "The Beginnings of Modern Growth in Europe: An Essay in Synthesis". *The Journal of Economic History*, 33, 3 (Sept, 1973): 547–80.

Rynyan, Timothy J. "The Cog as a warship". In *Cogs, Caravels & Galleons. The history of sailing ship, 1000–1650. Conway's History of the Ship*, edited by Robert Gardiner, 47–58. London: Conway Maritime Press, 1994.

Safford, Jeffrey J. "The Decline of the American Merchant Marine 1850–1914: A Historiographical Appraisal". In *Change and Adaptation in Maritime History. The North Atlantic Fleets in the 19th century*, edited by Lewis R. Fischer and Gerald E. Panting, 51–86. St John's: Memorial University of Newfoundland, 1985.

Sager, Eric. "The Port of St. John's, Newfoundland, 1840–1889; A Preliminary Analysis". In *Ships and Shipbuilding in the North Atlantic Region*, edited by Keith Matthews and Gerald Panting, 19–40. Newfoundland: Memorial University, 1978.

———. *Seafaring Labour: The Merchant Marine of Atlantic Canada, 1820–1914*. Montreal, Kingston and London: McGill-Queen's University Press, 1989.

Sager, Eric W. and Gerald E. Panting. "Staple Economies and the Rise and Decline of the Shipping Industry in Atlantic Canada, 1820–1914". In *Change and Adaptation in Maritime History. The North Atlantic Fleets in the 19th century*, edited by Lewis R. Fischer and Gerald E. Panting, 1–46. St John's: Memorial University of Newfoundland, 1985.

———. *Maritime Capital. The shipping industry in Atlantic Canada, 1820–1914*. Montreal and Kingston: McGill-Queen's University Press, 1990.

Sakelaropoulos, Theodoros. *Οι κρίσεις στην Ελλάδα. Οικονομικές, πολιτικές και κοινωνικές όψεις. (1830–1857)* [*The crises in Greece, Financial, social and political aspects, (1830–1857)*], 2 vols. Athens: Kritiki Publishers, 1994.

Sheppard, Eric. "Competition in Space and Between Places". In *A Companion to Economic Geography*, edited by Eric Sheppard and Trevor J. Barnes, 168–86. Malden-Oxford-Victoria: Blackwell Publishing, 2003.

Sifneos, Evridiki. "Οι αλλαγές στο ρωσικό σιτεμπόριο και η προσαρμοστικότητα των ελληνικών εμπορικών οίκων" ['The changes in Russian grain trade and the adaptability of the Greek merchant houses"]. *Τα Ιστορικά- Historica*, 40, (June 2004): 53–96.

Spiliotopoulou, Maria. "Η Σαντορίνη στην Τουρκοκρατία. Κοινωνικές και οικονομικές πρακτικές στο πλαίσιο της οικογένειας" ["Santorini during the Ottoman Period. Social and economic practices within the family context"]. PhD diss., University of Crete, 2005.

Starkey, David J. "The Shipbuilding Industry of Southwest England, 1790–1913". In *Shipbuilding in the United Kingdom in the 19th Century: a Regional Approach*, Research in Maritime History, 4, edited by Simon Ville, 75–110. St John's, Newfoundland: International Economic History Association, 1993.

———. "Schooner Development in Britain". In *Sail's Last Century. The Merchant Sailing Ship, 1830–1930. Conway's History of the Ship*, edited by Robert Gardiner, 131–46. London: Conway Maritime Press, 1995.

Stoianovich, Traian. "L'espace maritime segmentaire de l'empire ottoman". In *Actes du IIe Colloque International d'Histoire. Economies Méditerranéennes. Equilibres et Intercommunications. XIIIe–XIXe siècles*, Tome I, edited by M.C. Chatziioannou and A. Tabaki, 213–18. Athens: INR/NHRF, 1986.

Stopford, Martin. "Shipping market cycles". In *The handbook of maritime economics and business*, edited by Costas Th. Grammenos, 203–24. London-Hong Kong: LLP, 2002.

———. *Maritime Economics*. London-New York: Routledge, 1997.

Strandenes, Siri Pettersen. "Economics of the market for ships". In *The handbook of maritime economics and business*, edited by Costas Th. Grammenos, 186–202. London-Hong Kong: LLP, 2002.

Strong, F. *Greece as a Kingdom. A statistical description of that country from the arrival of King Otho, in 1833 down to the present time*. London: 1842.

Summers, Lewis S. "The Prediction of Shipyard Costs". *Marine Technology*, 10, 1, (January 1973): 8–15.

Sunley, Peter. "Urban and Regional Growth". In *A Companion to Economic Geography*, edited by Eric Sheppard and Trevor J. Barnes, 187–202. Malden-Oxford-Victoria: Blackwell Publishing, 2003.

Swedberg, Richard. "Markets in Society". In *The Handbook of Economic Sociology*, edited by Neil J. Smelser and Richard Swedberg, 233–53. Princeton and Oxford: Princeton University Press, 2005.

Syngros, Andreas. *Απομνημονεύματα*, [*Memoirs*], 2 vols. Athens: first published 1908, republished by Estia Publishers, 1998.

Theotokas, Ioannis and Gelina Harlaftis. *Leadership in World Shipping: Greek Family Firms in International Business*. New York- London: Palgrave/Macmillan, 2009.

Thiesen, William H. *Industrializing American Shipbuilding. The transformation of ship design and construction, 1820–1920*. Gainesville: University Press of Florida, 2006.

Travlos, Ioannis and Aggeliki Kokkou. *Ερμούπολη. Η δημιουργία μίας νέας πόλης στη Σύρο στις αρχές του 19ου αιώνα* [*Hermoupolis. The creation of a new town in Syros in the beginning of the 19th century*]. Athens: Commercial Bank of Greece, 1980.

Tsokopoulos, Vasias. *Πειραιάς 1835 1870. Εισαγωγή στην ιστορία του ελληνικού Μάντσεστερ*, [*Piraeus 1835–70. Introduction to the history of Greek Manchester*]. Athens: Kastaniotis, 1984.

Ucbasaran, Deniz, Paul Westhead and Mike Wright. "Habitual Entrepreneurs". In *The Oxford Handbook of Entrepreneurship*, edited by Anuradha Basu, Mark Casson, Nigel Wadeson, and Bernard Yeung, 461–83. New York: Oxford University Press, 2006.

Underhill, Harold A. *Deep-Water Sail*. Glasgow: Brown Son & Ferguson, 1952.

Unger, Richard W. "Introduction". In *Cogs, Caravels & Galleons. The history of sailing ship, 1000–1650. Conway's History of the Ship*, edited by Robert Gardiner, 7–10. London: Conway Maritime Press, 1994.

———. "Technology & industrial organization: Dutch Shipbuilding to 1800". *Business History*, XVII, 1, (1975): 56–72.

———. *The Ship in the Medieval Economy, 600–1600*. Montreal and London: McGill-Queen's University Press, 1980.

Unknown. *A Shipbuilding History, 1750–1932. Alexander Stephen & Sons Ltd.* London-Cheltenham: 1932.

Van Doorninck, Frederick H. "Serçe Limani". In *Encyclopedia of Underwater and Maritime Archaeology*, edited by James P. Delgado, 367–70. New Haven-London: Yale University Press, 1997.

Vickers, Daniel with Vince Walsh. *Young Men and the Sea. Yankee Seafarers in the Age of Sail*. New Haven: Yale University Press, 2005.

Vikelas, Dimitrios. *Λουκής Λάρας*, [*Loukis Laras*]. Athens: Estia Publishers, 2000.

Ville, Simon. "The Transition to Iron and Steel Construction". In *Sail's Last Century. The Merchant Sailing Ship, 1830–1930. Conway's History of the Ship*, edited by Robert Gardiner 52–73. London: Conway Maritime Press, 1995.

———. *English Shipowning during the industrial revolution. Michael Henley and son, London shipowners, 1770–1830*. Manchester: Manchester University Press, 1987.

———. "Shipbuilding in the Northeast of England in the 19th Century". In *Shipbuilding in the United Kingdom in the 19th Century: a Regional Approach*, Research in Maritime History, 4, edited by Simon Ville, 1–43. St John's, Newfoundland: International Economic History Association, 1993.

Vlahogiannis, Ioannis. *Χιακό Αρχείο* [*Archive of Chios*], vol. E. Athens: 1910.

Vlami, Despina. *Το φιορίνι, το σιτάρι και η οδός του Κήπου. Έλληνες έμποροι στο Λιβόρνο 1750–1868*. [*The Florin, the Grain and the Garden Street. Greek Merchant in Livorno, 1750–1868*]. Athens: Themelio, 2000.

Vlastos, Alexandros. *Χιακά ἤτοι Ἱστορία τῆς νήσου Χίου*, [*History of the Island of Chios*]. Hermoupolis: 1840.

Walton, Gary M. "Sources of Productivity Change in American Colonial Shipping, 1675–1775". *The Economic History Review*, New Series, 20, 1 (April 1967): 67–78.

Welch, Richard F. *An Island's Trade. Nineteenth century shipbuilding on Long Island.* Mystic, Connecticut: Mystic Seaport Museum, 1993.

Woodwell, William H. "The Woodwell Shipyard, 1759–1852". *Bulletin of the Business Historical Society*, 21, 3 (June, 1947): 58–74.

Yannakopoulou, Helene. "L'architecture navale en Grece de l'Ouest". In *Shipbuilding and Ships in the eastern Mediterranean during the 18th and 19th century*, edited by Kostas Damianidis, 47–67. Chios: Homerion Cultural Center of Chios Municipality, 1999.

Yannitsiotis, Yannis. *Η κοινωνική ιστορία του Πειραιά. Η συγκρότηση της αστικής τάξης, 1860–1910*, [*Social History of Piraeus. The making of the bourgeois class, 1860–1910*]. Athens: Nefeli, 2006.

Zei, Eleftheria. "La proposition du voyageur Ch. Sonnini sur l'organisation du commerce français dans l'Archipel grec (Voyage en Grèce et en Turquie, Paris 1801): une première théorie d'insularité économique". *Proceedings of 4th International Congress of Maritime History*, Corfu, 2004. (in CD-Rom).

Zolotas, Georgios. *Ιστορία της Χίου*, [*History of Chios*], vol. A1. Athens: 1921.

Index

www.ingramcontent.com/pod-product-compliance
Lightning Source LLC
La Vergne TN
LVHW010542300926
849162LV00002B/215